AF479010

Eye on a Century

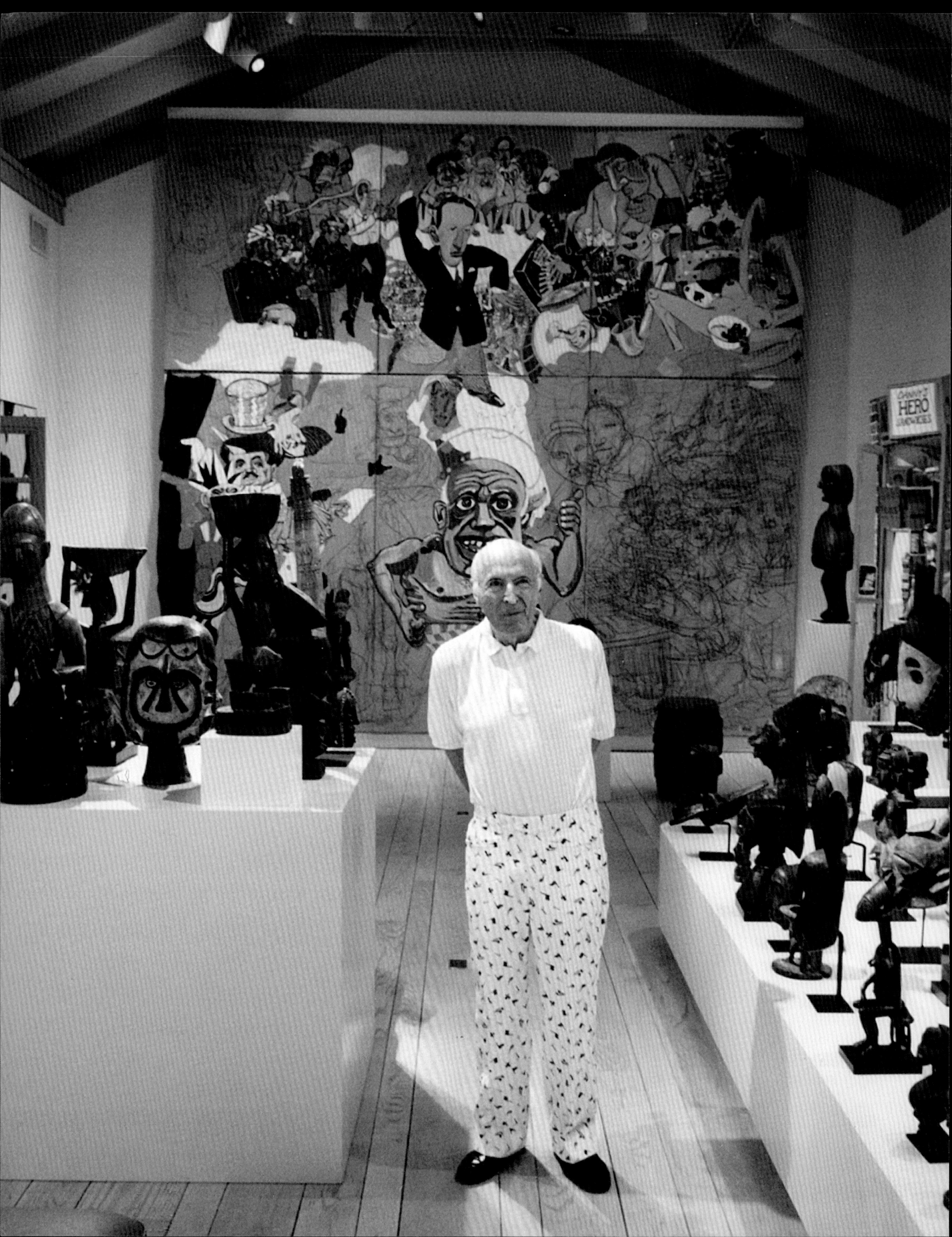

Modern and
Contemporary Art
from the
Charles B. Benenson
Collection
at the
Yale University
Art Gallery

Eye on a Century

Cathleen Chaffee

with contributions by
Katherine D. Alcauskas
Amy Canonico
Robin Jaffee Frank
Jennifer R. Gross
Jennifer Josten
Megan R. Luke
Keely Orgeman
Emily M. Orr
Sarah K. Rich
Maria Taroutina
Elisabeth Thomas
Diane C. Wright

Yale University Art Gallery
New Haven

Distributed by Yale University Press
New Haven and London

Publication made possible by an endowment created
with a challenge grant from the National Endowment
for the Arts. Additional support provided by Laurie and
Bruce W. Benenson, Frederick Benenson, and Lawrence B.
Benenson in memory of Charles B. Benenson, B.A. 1933.

First published in 2012 by the
Yale University Art Gallery
P.O. Box 208271
New Haven, CT 06520-8271
www.artgallery.yale.edu

and distributed by
Yale University Press
P.O. Box 209040
New Haven, CT 06520-9040
www.yalebooks.com/art

Tiffany Sprague, Director of Publications and
Editorial Services
Molly Balikov, Associate Editor
Christopher Sleboda, Director of Graphic Design

Copyeditor: Petra Dreiser
Proofreader: Lori Harris

Set in Graphik (Christian Schwartz, 2007) and Greta Text
(Peter Bil'ak, 2007)
Printed by GHP in West Haven, Connecticut

Cover design by Christopher Sleboda

Library of Congress Cataloging-in-Publication Data
Yale University. Art Gallery.
  Eye on a century : modern and contemporary art from
the Charles B. Benenson collection at the Yale University
Art Gallery / Cathleen Chaffee; with contributions by
Katherine D. Alcauskas, Amy Canonico, Robin Jaffee
Frank, Jennifer R. Gross, Jennifer Josten, Megan R. Luke,
Keely Orgeman, Emily M. Orr, Sarah K. Rich, Maria
Taroutina, Elisabeth Thomas, Diane C. Wright.
     pages cm
  Includes bibliographical references and index.
  ISBN 978-0-300-18494-5 (alk. paper)
1. Art, Modern—20th century—Catalogs. 2. Benenson,
Charles B., 1913-2004—Art collections—Catalogs.
3. Art—Private collections—Connecticut—New Haven—
Catalogs. 4. Yale University. Art Gallery—Catalogs.
I. Chaffee, Cathleen. II. Title.
  N6487.N34Y344 2012
  709.040074'7468—dc23
                    2012010850

10 9 8 7 6 5 4 3 2 1

Cover illustration: Saul Steinberg, *Evolution* (detail,
cat. 48), 1967, drawing for the *New Yorker* cover,
November 11, 1967
Frontispiece: Charles B. Benenson, 1997
Page 12: Charles B. Benenson, ca. 1993, with David
Smith's *Bec-Dida Day* (cat. 34)

Contents

Director's Foreword

The collection of modern and contemporary art at the Yale University Art Gallery has been enriched since its inception through extraordinary gifts and bequests from legendary collections, including those of Stephen Carlton Clark, B.A. 1903; Katharine Ordway; Mr. and Mrs. Paul Mellon, B.A. 1929; and John Hay Whitney. Art from 1920 to 1950 is richly represented in the Société Anonyme Collection, a gift of the artists of the Société Anonyme, which was overseen by Katherine S. Dreier and Marcel Duchamp. Along with the exceptional collections of Richard Brown Baker, B.A. 1935, and Thurston Twigg-Smith, B.E. 1942, the gift of Charles B. Benenson's collection of modern and contemporary art has fundamentally transformed the Gallery's ability to provide students with the opportunity to experience firsthand the diversity and brilliance of international postwar art.

I met Charles B. Benenson, "Charlie," shortly after becoming director in 1998. From the moment of our first encounter, his quiet generosity never ceased to surprise and humble me. Charlie was a graduate of Yale University, Class of 1933, and throughout his life he remained a supporter of his alma mater and especially of the Yale University Art Gallery, on whose governing board he actively served from 1991 to his death in 2004. His crucial support enabled the opening of new and expanded galleries for modern and contemporary art at Yale in 2012. Fittingly, generations of art lovers will discover the Gallery's masterpieces of modern art and cutting-edge contemporary art—among them many works from Charlie's own collection—in the Charles B. Benenson Galleries of Modern and Contemporary Art.

Charlie first began collecting modern painting and sculpture in the 1950s. It was a hobby that soon became a passionate avocation. He enjoyed purchasing extraordinary works at auction, such as Stuart Davis's *Combination Concrete #2* (cat. 19), and also seeking out overlooked gems in art dealers' back rooms and warehouses. After beginning to collect African art in the 1970s, he immersed himself in that endeavor as well, and it took only a few decades for him to assemble one of the most respected private collections of African art in the United States, which he also gifted to the Gallery, along with funds to endow its first curatorship of African art. This African collection is studied in the companion volume to the present publication, *Accumulating Histories: African Art from the Charles B. Benenson Collection at the Yale University Art Gallery*. In entrusting the vast majority of both of these collections to the Gallery, Charlie has inestimably enriched its teaching potential.

When considering the impact these collections have already had on the way the history of art is presented and taught at Yale, I am reminded of Saul Steinberg's observation from 1965: "[E]volution doesn't lead to perfection but to the invention or discovery of new regions." * Like Charlie's, all great collections evolve from the zeal of individuals who find common ground with artists in their mutual search for invention and discovery. When such private collections merge with a larger public collection, they evolve from one form to another, much like a stream joining a river, increasing the river's force and changing its path forever.

One of the opportunities that has emerged as a result of Charlie's gift is the chance for the careful examination and scholarly contextualization of the individual works in his collection. The present volume is the result of this research. In all, 75 artists of 13 nationalities are represented among the 119 exemplary works of modern and contemporary art. The works range in scale from the dynamic welded-steel sculptures of Richard Stankiewicz to the single sheets of Jean Dubuffet's pen-and-ink drawings, packed with frenetic energy. The collection is vibrant and full of intelligence and wit, much like the man who assembled it.

Gratitude for this publication is due first and foremost to Charlie's generosity, but also to his beloved wife, Jane, and his sons, Bruce William, Frederick, and Lawrence, as well as Bruce William's wife, Laurie, who have helped at every step of the way in the preparation of this catalogue.

The catalogue entries and essays represent the scholarship of thirteen researchers, including Gallery curators and fellows, and current and former Yale students. The publication would not have been possible without the research and guidance of Cathleen Chaffee, the Horace W. Goldsmith Assistant Curator of Modern and Contemporary Art, working in collaboration with the entire Department of Modern and Contemporary Art. Notably, Jennifer R. Gross, the Seymour H. Knox, Jr., Curator of Modern and Contemporary Art, and Amy Canonico, Museum Assistant, both contributed to all aspects of the publication and authored numerous catalogue entries. Susan Greenberg Fisher, Executive Director of the Renee and Chaim Gross Foundation and former Horace W. Goldsmith Associate Curator of Modern and Contemporary Art at the Gallery, was crucial to the early conceptualization of this publication. Special thanks are owed to Maria Taroutina, a Ph.D. candidate in the History of Art at Yale, who contributed substantial research as a graduate research assistant and authored many of the book's catalogue entries.

Eye on a Century: Modern and Contemporary Art from the Charles B. Benenson Collection at the Yale University Art Gallery is only the first effort to communicate the depth of Charlie's contribution to the collections of modern and contemporary art at Yale. Much like his collection, this publication will undoubtedly provide a springboard for the research of future generations of scholars and students, both at Yale and throughout the world.

Jock Reynolds
The Henry J. Heinz II Director
Yale University Art Gallery

*Saul Steinberg, "Straight from the Hand and Mouth of Steinberg," Life, December 10, 1965, 59.

Acknowledgments

This publication is dedicated to Charles B. Benenson, whose quick eye and generosity have immeasurably deepened the collections of the Yale University Art Gallery. We hope that Benenson's family, including his wife, Jane, and his sons, Bruce William, Frederick, and Lawrence, as well as Bruce William's wife, Laurie—along with his friends, colleagues, and fellow Governing Board members at the Gallery—will see the research presented here as a fitting tribute to his passionate commitment to the art of his time.

Jock Reynolds, the Henry J. Heinz II Director, champions the innovative presentation and contextualization of works of art in the Gallery's collection. Without his enthusiasm for this project and his support of new research on works gifted to Yale by Benenson, this publication could not have been realized. Susan B. Matheson, the former chief curator and the Molly and Walter Bareiss Curator of Ancient Art, was an invaluable source of guidance throughout the publication's preparation. Beginning in 2006, L.Lynne Addison, Registrar; Jennifer Bossman, Registrar; Carol DeNatale, Deputy Director for Operations and Planning; Burrus Harlow, Director of Collections; Charlene Senical, Assistant Business Manager; and Jill Westgard, Deputy Director for Museum Resources and Stewardship, oversaw the first stages of this publication with the smooth transfer of Benenson's gift of modern and contemporary art to the Gallery.

The texts here were guided through the editing process with great care and attention by Molly Balikov, Associate Editor, under the skilled advisement of Tiffany Sprague, Director of Publications and Editorial Services. The striking book design by Christopher Sleboda, Director of Graphic Design, allowed this diverse collection to come to life in printed form. In the Department of Prints, Drawings, and Photographs, Suzanne Greenawalt, Museum Assistant, and Diana Brownell, Senior Museum Technician/Preparator, offered important assistance in preparing the many works on paper for study and photography. John ffrench, Director of Visual Resources, and Anthony De Camillo, Senior Photographer, spent innumerable hours arranging for the beautiful photographs of every work in this collection. Patricia Sherwin Garland, Senior Conservator of Paintings, Carol E. Snow, Deputy Chief Conservator, and Theresa Fairbanks-Harris, Chief Conservator of Paper at the Yale Center for British Art, all provided skilled object care and shared their expertise with the catalogue's authors. Jessica Labbé, Deputy Director of Finance and Administration, and Charlene Senical, Assistant Business Manager, attended to the many pragmatic details required to make this publication a reality.

Many outside scholars contributed their time and knowledge to answer research questions related to artists and works in Benenson's collection. I particularly thank Peter Brooke, Nicolas Descharnes, Véronique Gautherin, Elliott King, Sergiusz Michalski, Rosemarie Napolitano, Iris Schmeisser, and Sheila Schwartz. The insights of Gabrielle Giattino, Andrea Merkx, and Saul Ostrow are also appreciated. Lawrence B. Benenson's close reading of the publication's manuscript, and the information he provided, were of great assistance. Warm thanks are owed to all the artists and representatives of the artists' estates who took the time to attend to our research queries, especially Red Grooms, whose interview on his memories of Benenson as a collector proved most helpful.

It seems fitting that a publication on part of the Gallery's permanent collection should benefit from the scholarship of so many current and former students, fellows, and staff. It was a distinct pleasure to work with the contributors to this project: Katherine D. Alcauskas, Collection Specialist in the Department of Prints and Illustrated Books at the Museum of Modern Art in New York and former Florence B. Selden Fellow in the Department of Prints, Drawings, and Photographs at the Gallery; Amy Canonico, Museum Assistant in the Department of Modern and Contemporary Art; Robin Jaffee Frank, Chief Curator and Krieble Curator of American Painting and Sculpture at the Wadsworth Atheneum, in Hartford, Connecticut, and former Alice and Allan Kaplan Senior Associate Curator of American Paintings and Sculpture at the Gallery; Jennifer R. Gross, the Seymour H. Knox, Jr., Curator of Modern and Contemporary Art; Jennifer Josten, Assistant Professor of Art History at the University of Pittsburgh; Megan R. Luke, Assistant Professor of Art History at the University of Southern California; Keely Orgeman, Acting Assistant Curator of American Paintings and Sculpture; Emily M. Orr, former Marcia Brady Tucker Senior Fellow in the Department of American Decorative Arts; Sarah K. Rich, Associate Professor of Art History at the Pennsylvania State University; Maria Taroutina, Ph.D. candidate in the History of Art at Yale University and former graduate research assistant in the Department of Modern and Contemporary Art; Elisabeth Thomas, Dedalus Fellow in the Museum of Modern Art Archives in New York and former bursary student in the Department of Modern and Contemporary Art at the Gallery; and Diane C. Wright, Adjunct Professor at Parsons The New School for Design and the Rhode Island School of Design and former Marcia Brady Tucker Senior Fellow in the Department of American Decorative Arts at the Gallery. Special thanks are owed to Susan Greenberg Fisher, Executive Director of the Renee and Chaim Gross Foundation. As the former Horace W. Goldsmith Associate Curator of Modern and Contemporary Art, Susan developed the initial structure of this publication, and her excellent planning proved central to its success. Amy Canonico, in addition to her role as a contributing author, managed images for the publication and oversaw the accurate cataloguing of each work in the Charles B. Benenson Collection with good humor and exceptional attention to detail. In addition to working with Benenson's collection since it was first given to Yale, Jennifer R. Gross provided important input on all the scholarship in this volume. Each facet of this publication bears the mark of her critical eye and careful study.

The efforts of students working in the Department of Modern and Contemporary Art were central to the realization of this publication. Sarah Horowitz assisted with the early stages of catalogue research, while Elisabeth Thomas, Bahij Chancey, and Allegra Krasznekewicz refined many details here. Interns Megan Conroy and Helen Goldenberg were most helpful in the publication's organization. Particular thanks are owed to Maria Taroutina, who, in her role as a graduate research assistant, conducted research on all the works in the Charles B. Benenson Collection. I thank her and all of the contributors.

Cathleen Chaffee
The Horace W. Goldsmith Assistant Curator of Modern and Contemporary Art
Yale University Art Gallery

Preface

My father's art collection was awesome! This volume, *Eye on A Century*, attempts to divulge the depth and breadth of Charles B. Benenson's singular vision.

Charlie loved searching for and finding the greatest artworks. His favorite find was Kurt Schwitters's *Merzbild mit Regenbogen* (Merz Picture with Rainbow; cat. 13). While visiting a gallery in New York one afternoon, my father asked to go into the storage area to see what was there. He encountered Schwitters's masterpiece, was told the price was $10,000, and bought it. Ten minutes later William Rubin, curator at the Museum of Modern Art (MoMA), wandered into the back room and declared that the museum wanted the object. "I'm sorry," he was told, "Mr. Benenson just bought it." My father loved this acquisition experience for many reasons, not least of which was that it proved when gallery owners say, "A museum is interested in this piece," it is sometimes true! The year before my father died, John Elderfield of MoMA was in my father's office asking for the Schwitters painting as a gift to the museum. But Dad wanted Yale to have it and the other remarkable works catalogued in this book.

What's great about this book is that its short essays on specific works of art place the works in context. They attempt to instill the reader with an understanding of the artists' thought processes and their desires for their creations. Charlie was an intellectual. However, he was neither involved with nor consumed by art theory and criticism. He liked the pictures.

When my father had bought and paid for a painting, he wanted to live with it as soon as possible. One August he was in London and bought *View of the Thames from the Vicker's Building, Millbank*, by Oskar Kokoschka (cat. 32). Now it was October, and the painting was not yet in his house. He called the gallery and the owner was incredulous. "There's about to be a nuclear war and you're calling about a painting?" My father said, "There's not going to be any war. Just send my painting to me." The year was 1962 and the Cuban Missile Crisis was soon resolved.

My father loved each object he owned, and he missed them when they were on loan. In order to display all the art he bought, he built three additions to his house. Less than 2 percent of his art was stored. He treasured roaming around his galleries, looking up and around in wonder at the art environment he had created. To him, it was just his home.

Many of the artworks Dad bought were outlandish. As you looked at the latest off-the-wall piece in gape-mouthed surprise, he always said, "You don't have to like it. I like it." He understood each painting and sculpture on its own terms and did not bother with artists' statements. The art explained the artist. When Richard Lindner encountered my father at a cocktail party one evening, the artist was surprised. Knowing Charlie had recently purchased his painting *The Scream* (cat. 21), Lindner said, "You don't look like the type of man who'd buy such a wild and crazy painting." My father replied, "You don't look like the kind of guy who would paint it."

In 1969 my father attended the opening of a Fernando Botero gallery show. He met the Colombian artist there and arranged to visit his studio, where he bought the large charcoal drawing *Niña Sentada* (1969, Collection of Frederick Benenson, formerly in the collection of Charles B. Benenson, B.A. 1933). Since Botero told him that he painted from his imagination, my father was amused that women universally hated the picture. In the late 1950s, my father purchased one of his favorite paintings, *Hot Horizon*, by Adolph Gottlieb (cat. 20). The fact that Gottlieb later proposed trading with my father his choice of any painting in his studio to get *Hot Horizon* back thrilled Charlie.

Despite these interactions, he had no desire to befriend the artists whose creations he pursued with extreme determination. The only artists with whom my father had real relationships were Saul Steinberg and Red Grooms. He loved Steinberg's drawings and vociferously campaigned for the Whitney Museum of American Art to put on a show of his work. Eventually the museum complied. I remember Dad bringing me a poster of the famous *New Yorker* magazine cover *View of the World from Ninth Avenue* (1976), signed by Steinberg. That was really cool! I also remember visiting Steinberg with my father in the artist's apartment. Charlie collected *seventeen* drawings by him (see cats. 45–51).

The relationship with Red Grooms was even closer and was actually a friendship. My father visited Grooms in his studio and the artist was a frequent visitor to our house in Connecticut. My father first laid eyes on Grooms's *Picasso Goes to Heaven* (cat. 52) at the studio. He inquired about it and Grooms said, "Oh, that's not finished yet." My father replied, "Yes, it is," and bought it. That painting was only the third largest Grooms painting he bought. The others were *Studio at the Rue des Grands-Augustins* (cat. 53), which depicts Pablo Picasso painting *Guernica* (1937, Museo Reina Sofía, Madrid), and *Cedar Bar* (cat. 54). Charlie subsequently went to Grooms's wedding and received a painted Christmas card every year. They had a gracious relationship. Red was enthralled with and revered my father. He said, "Charlie could have been like Frank Sinatra playing a 'western gunslinger.'"

Going through Dad's library after he passed away, I saw a Joseph Beuys monograph. I was intrigued. I opened the book and read, "To Charles Benenson. Great meeting you. Joseph Beuys." But, my father neither had Joseph Beuys's art nor did he collect conceptual art. He attended no art classes. The art itself, not the backstory, was what mattered to him. Visual art needs to stand on its own. Explanations can enhance enjoyment, but the immediate thrill felt standing in front of an artwork was what Charlie Benenson cared about.

Charles B. Benenson was a revered, admired, and beloved businessman and philanthropist. His eye for real estate was matched only by his eye for art. His democratic enjoyment of each of his objects was indefatigable and fascinating to behold. While you read this book and marvel at the visual vitality of the artworks, you may begin to comprehend the sheer pleasure my father experienced owning this art.

Lawrence B. Benenson

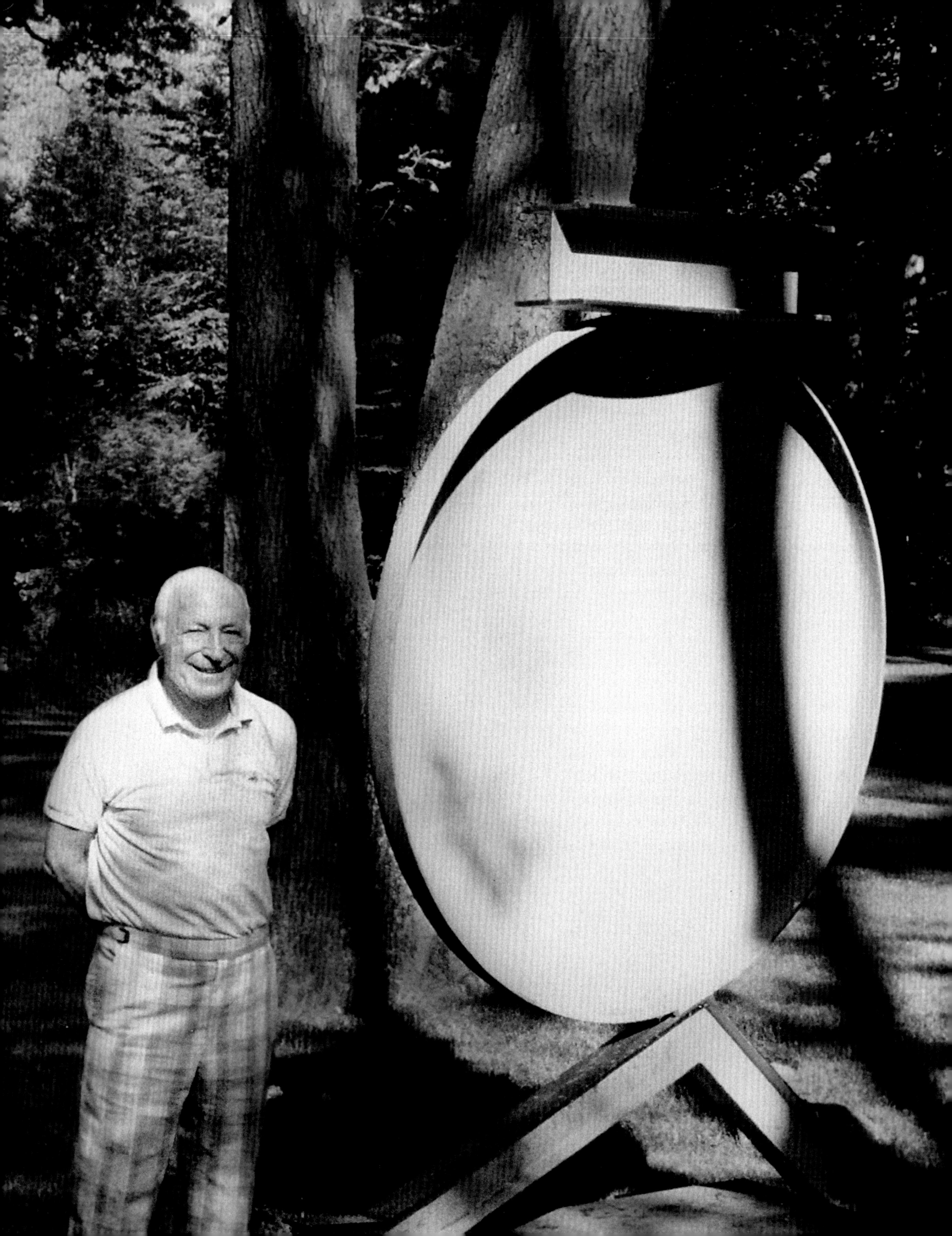

Cathleen Chaffee

A Legacy of Looking

On a trip to Europe in the early 1950s, Charles B. Benenson realized that although he was becoming increasingly interested in modern art, he was more familiar with the collections in foreign museums than with those in his native New York; his work as a real estate developer kept him too busy to enjoy the art in his own backyard. Thereafter, Benenson began carving time out of his working days and weekends to visit galleries, speak with collectors, and attend auctions. In this way, he learned about developments in Modernism for several years before purchasing the first work that he would deem "important," after seeing a Joan Miró exhibition at the Pierre Matisse Gallery in New York in 1958.[1] The impressive show of Miró's *Peintures sauvages* was already sold out, but Benenson appealed to the former curator of modern art at the Art Institute of Chicago, Katharine Kuh, who was then working as an art consultant. She found him an available painting in which the Spanish artist captured some of the anger he felt over the tragic civil war in his native country (fig. 1). Benenson would treasure this vibrantly colored, anguished figure under an acidic sky for the rest of his life. Subsequently, however, he seldom worked with consultants in modern art, preferring to continue a self-directed art education.

In an age of specialization the term *amateur* has become a pejorative, evoking dilettantism rather than the freshness and fervor of a nonprofessional devotee. But it is in this original sense of the word that Benenson's collection of modern and contemporary art can be called an exceptional example of an enlightened amateur's efforts. It represents, not the results of an organized strategy for collecting, but rather decades of ambling walks through the museums and galleries of New York, Chicago, London, and Paris, as well as more than forty years of inspired one-on-one encounters with artworks and artists.[2]

Drawn to bold shapes, bright colors, and exaggerated figuration, Benenson took pride in appreciating works that others might deem eccentric, often heading straight to gallery storage to see what artworks were not on display. While bypassing Russian Constructivism, or Minimalism, he sought out lesser-known artists from the first half of the twentieth century such as the German satirist Karl Hubbuch, and he championed the contemporary artists Red Grooms and Saul Steinberg before their caricatural figuration became fashionable. He did not focus on particular groups of artists or on genres. Instead, his acquisitions were almost exclusively the result of encountering, sometimes by happenstance, artworks that appealed either to his sense of humor or to his belief that the individual work possessed a communicative greatness. As a result, he frequently bought works that were a few degrees to the left or right of what was fashionable at the time, judgments that often proved prescient. Benenson's highly personal, eclectic taste meant that his take on the twentieth century was also surprisingly broad and nondogmatic. He was the exceptionally rare collector who delighted in both Émile Antoine Bourdelle and Jean-Michel Basquiat, Jean Arp and Jack Beal.

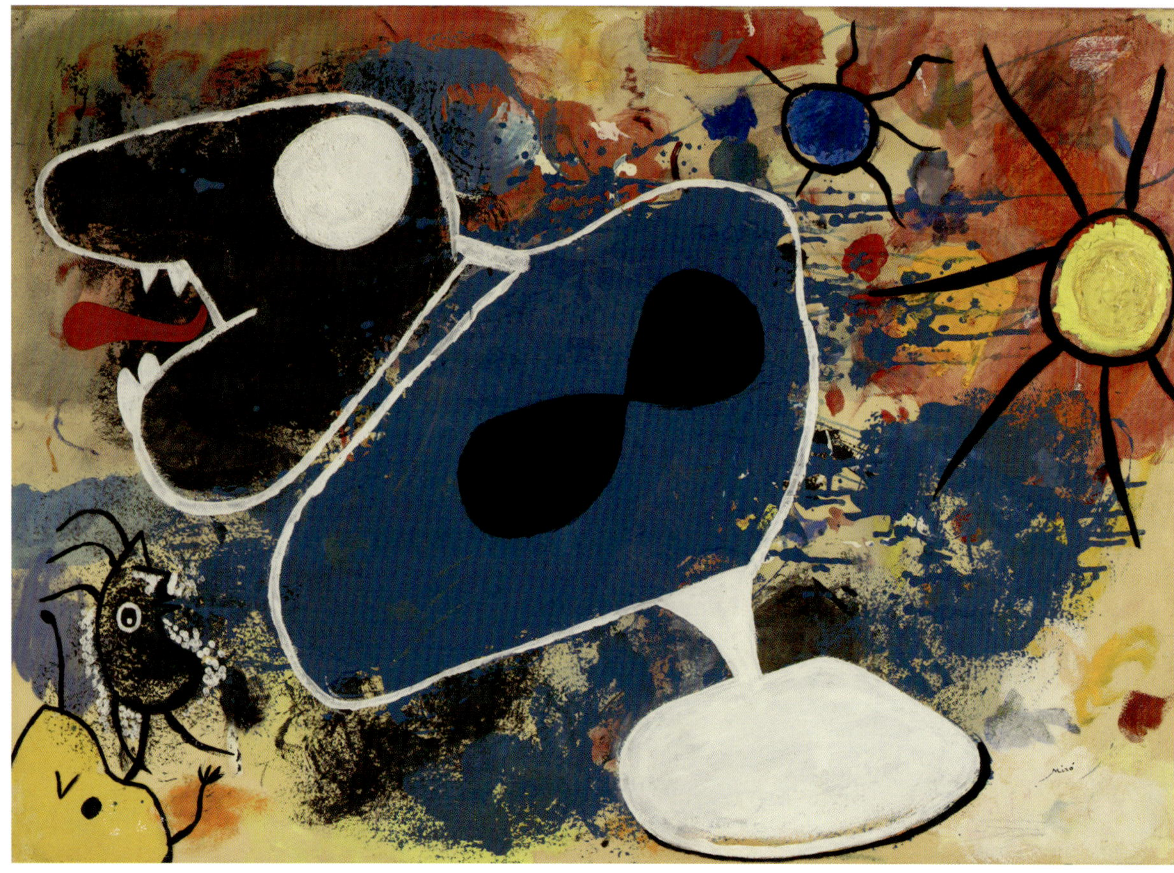

Fig. 1.
Joan Miró, *Le vol de l'oiseau* (The Flight of the Bird), 1938. Oil and gouache on paper, 22 1/16 × 30 5/16 in. (56 × 77 cm). Collection of Frederick Benenson, formerly in the collection of Charles B. Benenson, B.A. 1933

Benenson started building his collection during watershed years for the art market. Leo Castelli opened his first New York gallery in 1957 and began showing European Surrealism. Despite a marked downturn in the Parisian market, Pablo Picasso's foremost dealer, Daniel-Henry Kahnweiler, opened a new gallery in that city, and a number of high-grossing auctions established nineteenth-century artists such as Vincent van Gogh, Paul Gauguin, and Claude Monet as gold standards. The record-breaking sales suggested that more recent artists could be profitable investments, as painters who had been dead less than a century became valuable "Old Masters" almost overnight. Yet at the end of the 1950s, there were still fewer than a dozen galleries for contemporary art in New York.[3] The scene was navigable, and relatively congenial. It was a good time to become a collector.

If works by the recently deceased Jackson Pollock were among the most sought-after in the United States in the late 1950s, Benenson looked backward in terms of Expressionism, purchasing a vibrantly colored 1919 landscape by the German Expressionist Max Pechstein (fig. 2), a late riverscape by Oskar Kokoschka (cat. 32),

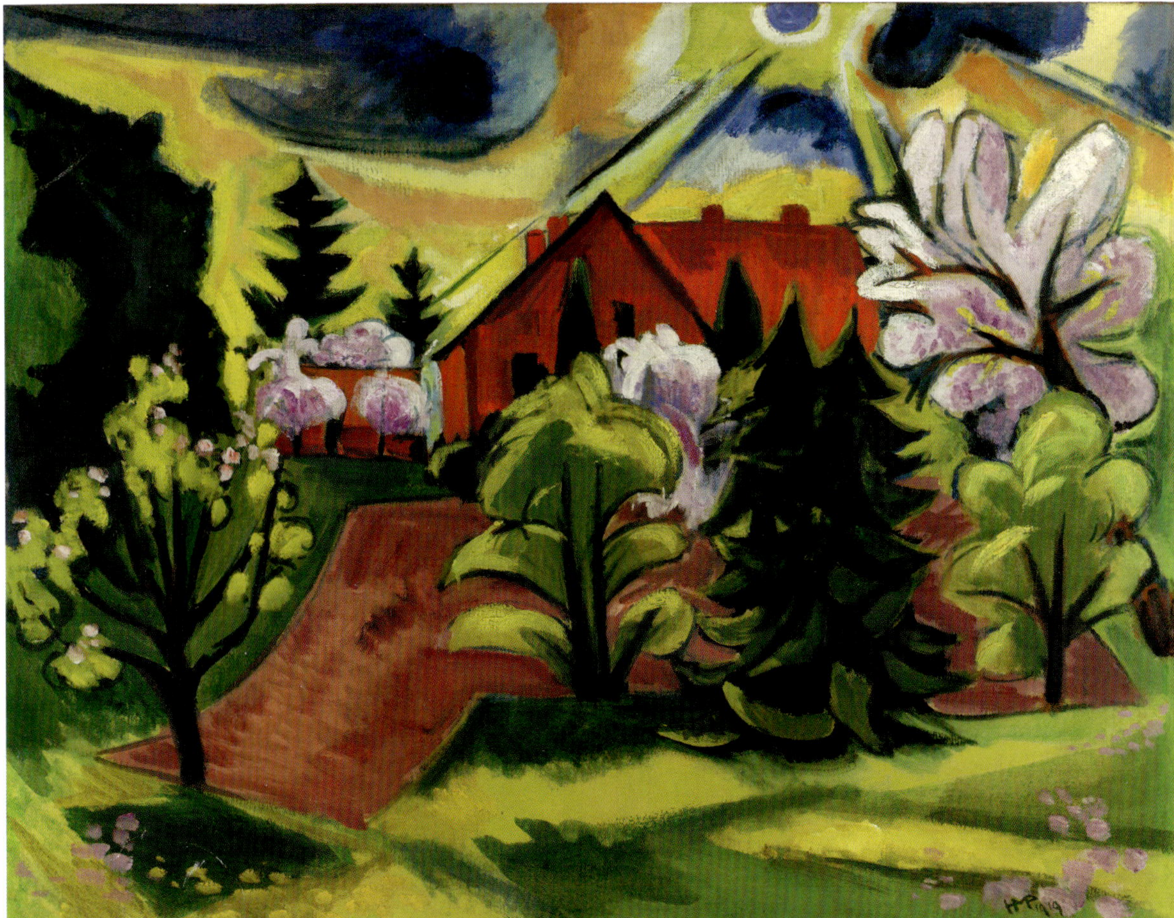

and attenuated sculptures by Alberto Giacometti. Throughout the years, Benenson acquired important works by David Smith, as well as mature paintings, sculptures, and drawings by other artists associated with Abstract Expressionism, such as Franz Kline, John Chamberlain, Richard Stankiewicz, and Arshile Gorky. Frequently drawn to earlier abstractions that were more anchored in figuration, he sought out Cubist works by Albert Gleizes, Jean Metzinger, Louis Marcoussis, Roger de La Fresnaye, Jacques Lipchitz, and Fernand Léger, including a mechanomorphic painting from 1924 (cat. 7), one of the most celebrated moments in Léger's career. Perhaps unsurprising for a collector attracted to caricature, Benenson's interest in Pop art came early. He purchased an important 1962 painting by one of the fathers of Pop, Larry Rivers (cat. 33). The expressionistic portrait of Napoléon was based on the leader's iconic appearance on the French one-hundred-franc note. Although Benenson acquired works by other Pop artists sparingly, he chose prints by Claes Oldenburg, a sculpture comprised of cartoonish three-dimensional wooden portrait heads by Marisol (cat. 31), and an enigmatic reinterpretation of Edvard Munch's *The Scream* by Richard Lindner (cat. 21). Another treasured work was the second great painting he purchased by Stuart Davis, an artist who merged references to advertising and popular culture with abstraction and thus came to be seen as proto-Pop (fig. 3).

Davis's *Combination Concrete #2* (cat. 19) had been one of several dozen paintings and sculptures on view at the Cold War–era United States National Exhibition at the 1959 World's Fair in Moscow. It served as the illustration for a *New York Times* article in which the curator Edith Halpert remarked, "Several [Russians] have inquired with special interest how American artists can 'see their homeland as differently as Hopper with his *Lighthouse* and Davis with his *Combination Concrete, Number Two*.'" [4] The celebrity of this group of works increased when selections,

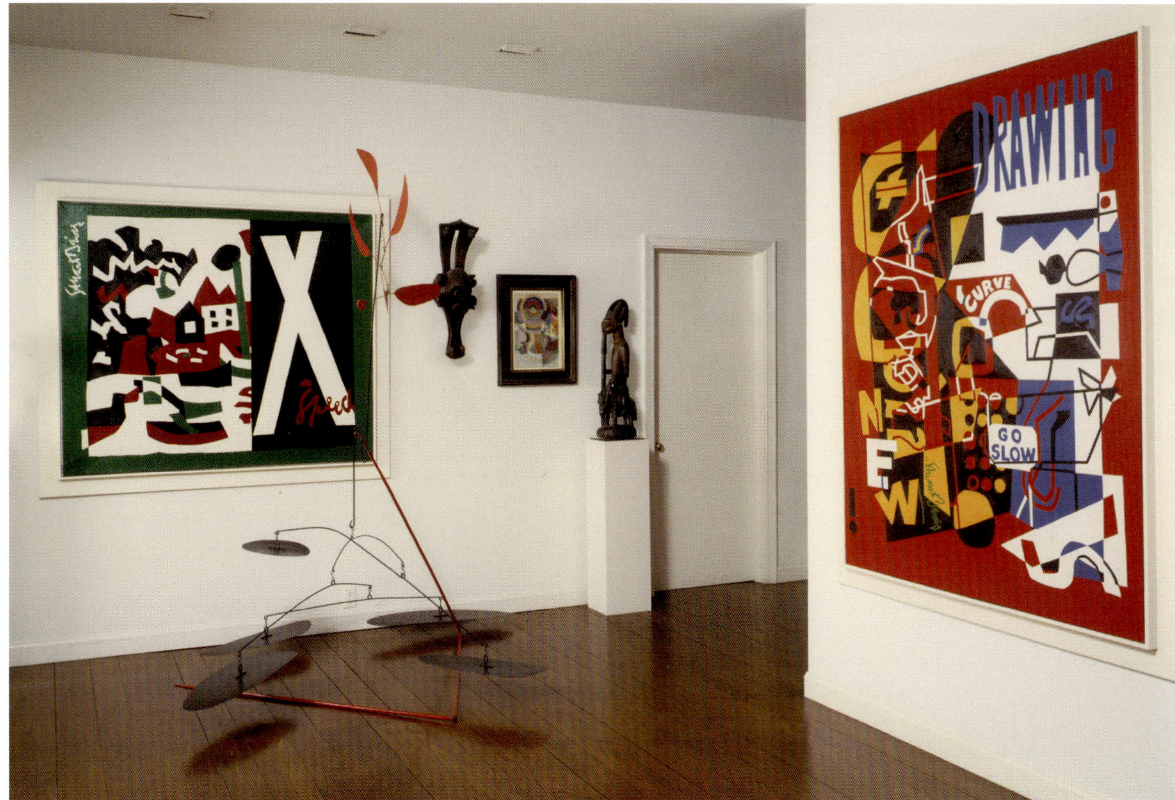

Fig. 3.
Stuart Davis, *Lesson One* (cat. 18) and *Combination Concrete #2* (cat. 19), installed in Charles B. Benenson's home. Also pictured: Alexander Calder, *Cinq noirs* (Five Blacks), 1966, metal with paint, 95 × 70 × 57 in. (241.3 × 177.8 × 144.8 cm), Collection of Bruce W. Benenson, formerly in the collection of Charles B. Benenson, B.A. 1933; and Sonia Delaunay, *Zig Zag*, 1914, gouache on paper, 17 × 11½ in. (43.2 × 29.2 cm), Collection of Frederick Benenson, formerly in the collection of Charles B. Benenson, B.A. 1933

including the Davis work, were exhibited at the Whitney Museum of American Art in fall 1959.[5] Less than two years later, Benenson bought the painting at auction, outbidding Halpert, who was also Davis's dealer. He relished owning a work that had become an international symbol of American art's diversity.

Perhaps the most important of Benenson's acquisitions during this period came by happenstance. While looking for a David Smith sculpture in the Marlborough Gallery warehouse, Benenson caught sight of the large Kurt Schwitters assemblage *Merzbild mit Regenbogen* (Merz Picture with Rainbow; cat. 13), and he purchased it immediately. Previously, Benenson had not aggressively pursued works by Dada artists. While Surrealists in exile had helped make a version of that movement a familiar reference point for the Abstract Expressionists, Dada began in the United States as a noncanonical rumor or a footnote. The movement became the subject of increasing interest, however, following the publication in 1951 of an anthology titled *The Dada Painters and Poets,* by the Abstract Expressionist Robert Motherwell, and a 1953 Dada exhibition at the Sidney Janis Gallery.[6]

From about 1958 until the early 1960s, the term *Neo-Dada* was commonly used to describe a group of contemporary artists including Robert Rauschenberg, Allan Kaprow, Jasper Johns, and Jim Dine. Often used derisively in its early years, *Neo-Dada* began as something of a placeholder term for artists who came after Abstract Expressionism and before Pop. Those associated with Neo-Dada affronted formal conventions by juxtaposing everyday materials, such as house paint and newspapers, with objects from daily life in an attempt, like their Dada predecessors, to bridge the gap between art and life. Unlike the Dada artists of the early twentieth century, however, whose anti-art stance centered on upsetting societal and political complacency and on upending bourgeois notions of art itself, those referred to as Neo-Dada made reference to art and history more than they took political positions or critiqued popular culture. Despite these differences, Dada was an appealing reference for contemporary critics, as it placed the new artists within a historical avant-garde narrative and distinguished them from their Surrealist-influenced predecessors.

Schwitters was a pivotal but anomalous participant in the Dada circle whose poetic and lyrical approach to collage was not politically stringent enough for many artists in the movement. However, along with Marcel Duchamp, another atypical Dadaist who moved around the edges of the group, Schwitters became one of the best-known faces of Dada in the United States as a result, at least partially, of solo exhibitions at the Sidney Janis Gallery. (Sidney Janis held exhibitions of Duchamp in 1952, 1953, 1956, and 1959 and of Schwitters in 1952, 1953, and 1956.) With its three-dimensional found objects, rainbow spectrum, and painted shadows, Schwitters's *Merzbild mit Regenbogen* (1920–39) could serve as a textbook illustration of why Johns and Rauschenberg were associated with the earlier avant-garde movement as it was understood in the United States at the time. Early works by Johns and Rauschenberg could more accurately have been called "neo-Duchamp" or "neo-Schwitters." While collectors and museums fought over works by such Neo-Dadaists, Benenson's purchase of the Schwitters was brilliant; at the time of its acquisition, the painting was arguably the most contemporarily relevant historic painting on the market.[7] Today it remains an anchor of the Benenson Collection.

Into the early 1970s Benenson dabbled in contemporary art, but he largely sought out Modernist masters. As works from the first half of the twentieth century became less accessible, however, their market grew increasingly competitive. Perhaps as a result of this shift in availability, Benenson pursued more contemporary art, but he focused at first on recent works by artists such as Alexander Calder, Mark di Suvero, Miró, and Dine, whose reputations had already been established in previous decades. At the same time, he began building what became one of the best private collections of African art in the world, a collection discussed in detail in the companion volume to this publication, *Accumulating Histories: African Art from the Charles B. Benenson Collection at the Yale University Art Gallery*. The first African sculpture he bought came from J. J. Klejman's diminutive eight-by-two-foot Madison Avenue display window. Perhaps the smallest art space in New York, Klejman's was known for jewel-like thematic exhibitions of museum-quality works from all periods and cultures that could include, for example, an archaic Greek horse, a medieval ivory, and African sculptures of gazelles.[8] Benenson's knowledge that many artists in his collection were motivated by an appraisal of African art may have helped catalyze his desire to begin collecting in this new direction.

More than a decade before the acrimonious debate about whether the Museum of Modern Art's 1984 exhibition *"Primitivism" in Twentieth-Century Art: Affinity of the Tribal and the Modern* had, instead of studying African art on its own terms, instrumentalized its role for modern artists, Benenson began installing his collections in dialogue (figs. 4–5, 7). His juxtapositions were not didactic ones staged to illustrate that the bold figuration of African sculpture merited interest because it provided inspiration for a Picasso portrait.[9] Instead Benenson created expansive, overlapping installations that were designed to amplify his visitors' appreciation of the vigor and force in both Modernist and African artworks.

As the 1970s waned, Benenson began purchasing contemporary works by artists whose reputations were somewhat less sure, and whose prices were therefore often lower. Consequently, in addition to a large number of acquisitions of African art, the volume of his contemporary acquisitions accelerated, mirroring a swift, worldwide art-market boom that took hold around 1980. Newly flush collectors, fueled by a red-hot Japanese economy and a period of dizzying economic growth in the United States and in Western Europe, turned away from what had come to

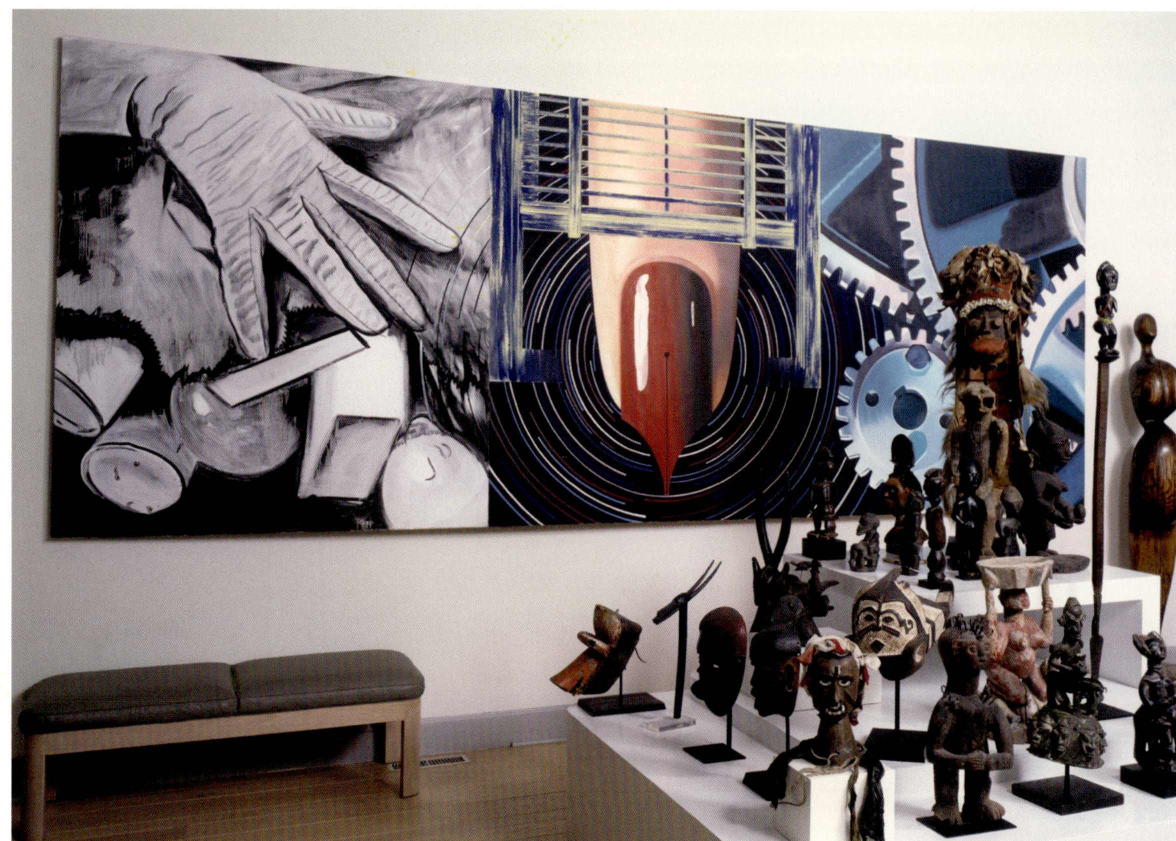

characterize the art of the previous decade. Many of the innovative artists from the late 1960s through the 1970s had expanded the definition of a work of art to include photographic documentation of performance actions, data, video, installation, and sound. It was a period of great pluralism in the art world, an eclectic pursuit of a broad range of media and subject matter. In some quarters it was marked by aesthetic austerity and intellectualism, with Conceptual artists such as Douglas Huebler and Robert Barry attempting to broaden and problematize art's distribution strategies with documentary artworks and invisible sculptures, while artists from Lee Lozano to Hans Haacke openly critiqued the ethics of the art market itself.

Very early in the 1980s, as the market took off, it became clear that the pluralism of subject matter and address that had characterized the 1970s would remain, but that the earlier decade's relative austerity would be thrown out the window. Benenson seems to have responded enthusiastically to the almost reactionary push away from 1970s aesthetic sobriety, which he would continue to sidestep in his collection. Figuration, oversized, bold painting, and artists whose technique or subject matter riffed on art history became major trends. The critic Richard Cork wrote in a 1983 survey of new art at the Tate Gallery, "Ten years ago [art was] an affair of the brain rather than the heart. But the early 1980s is witnessing a widespread reassertion of anxiety, vehemence, wit, theatricality and decorative excess. Rigorous intellectualism has given way to unashamed flamboyance, often explosive in character." [10] When Haacke in the 1960s and 1970s stripped bare the economics of power and prestige embedded in the real estate market, or the politics of art provenance, he presented his sometimes shocking findings in dry, factual language or in tabulated balance sheets: this was data as critique. In the 1980s such data dominated the art and popular press, but in the form of incredulous reports of astronomical auction results for modern and contemporary art. [11] As mainstream journalists began following along, it became a popular diversion to track the value of artworks in a collection like components of a stock-investment portfolio.

Expressionist painting, relatively dormant since the end of the 1950s, returned with a vengeance, most markedly among German artists such as A. R. Penck, Georg Baselitz, and Anselm Kiefer. The appropriation of photography and the language of advertising became significant tools in the practice of American artists belonging to the Pictures Group, including Sherrie Levine, Barbara Kruger, Robert Longo, and Richard Prince.[12] The blending of historical painting styles and referents characterized the work of the Europeans R. B. Kitaj (fig. 5), Sandro Chia, and Francesco Clemente. On the West Coast, Mike Kelley, Raymond Pettibon, and Lari Pittman made provocative and sometimes openly sexual work that would not find a truly receptive audience in New York until the 1990s. The New Image artists—an umbrella term for those combining representational images and painterly rendering—included three very different, but wildly successful painters: Eric Fischl, David Salle, and Julian Schnabel. Schnabel, in fact, was described as "probably the most exhibited, financially successful and aggressively self-promoting American artist of his generation."[13]

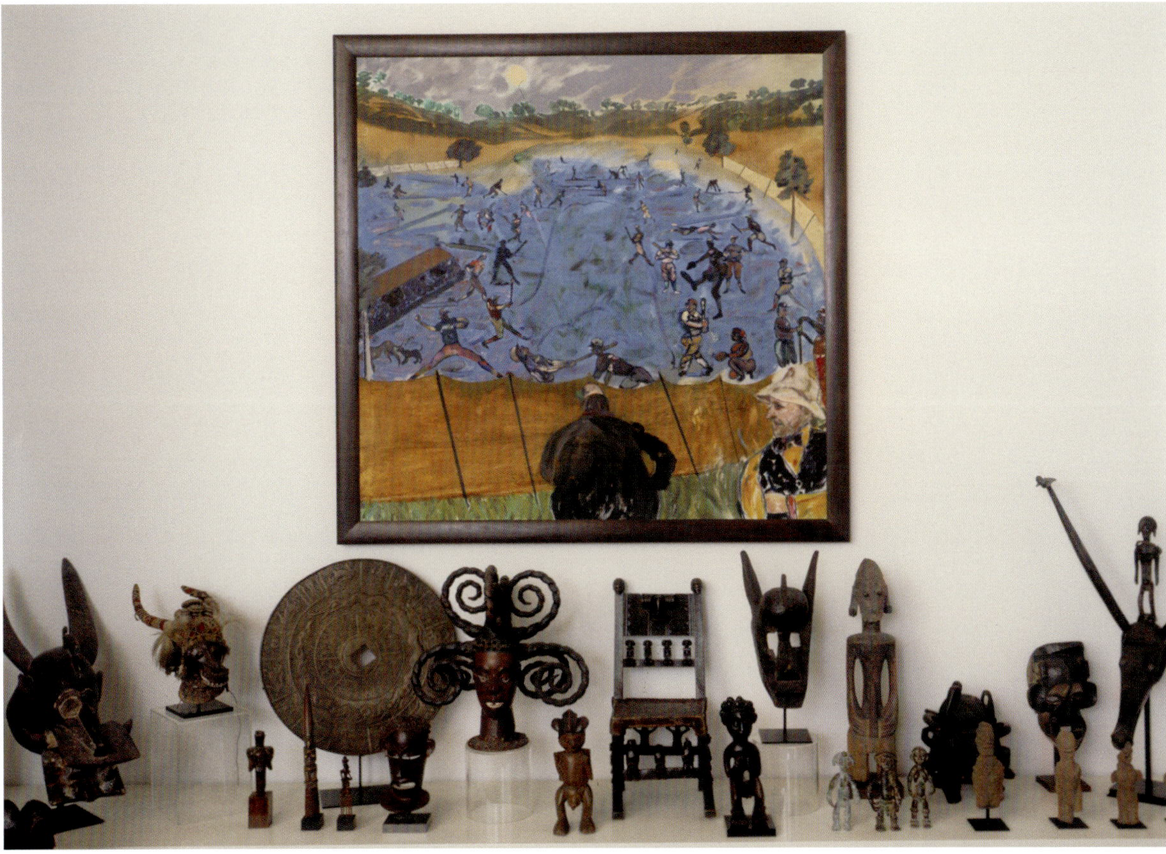

The East Village's scene was the most diverse in 1980s New York, merging the truly talented and the merely spectacular in fashion design, music, performance, sculpture, video, photography, and painting. Graffiti and other forms of art that manifested outside the gallery and the museum were quickly embraced by the official art world, with Basquiat and David Wojnarowicz perhaps the most renowned artists to bring their art to the East Village music scene and streets—before taking it to SoHo galleries. International with Monument gallery exhibited artists as diverse as Jeff Koons and Peter Halley. Koons and Haim Steinbach re-presented everyday commodities such as vacuum cleaners and lava lamps in galleries, combining an appraisal of Duchamp's Readymades with interrogations of marketing and display. Galleries such as Nature Morte, Civilian Warfare, and Gracie Mansion were known for huge openings and for collaborating with artists to create theme nights (an idea first popularized in the concurrent club scene), such as "the Wild West," "Too Young for Vietnam," and "Romance and Catastrophe."[14]

Although Benenson was not immersed in the East Village art scene, its vivid colors and boldly naive approach to form resonated with the numerous satiric works already in his collection by artists such as George Grosz, Grooms, and Steinberg (fig. 6). We can suspect that Benenson's appreciation for these earlier artists' energetic and sometimes politically acerbic caricatures prepared him to recognize the importance of works he acquired by progenitors of the downtown scene: Basquiat, Wojnarowicz, and Martin Wong. By the time the scene achieved celebrity outside New York in the second half of the 1980s, some of the best artists had been lost to drugs, including Basquiat in 1988. Many artists began dedicating their energies to activism as the East Village became an epicenter of the AIDS crisis in the United States. The disease eventually took the lives of Wong, Wojnarowicz, and thousands more in New York's arts community.

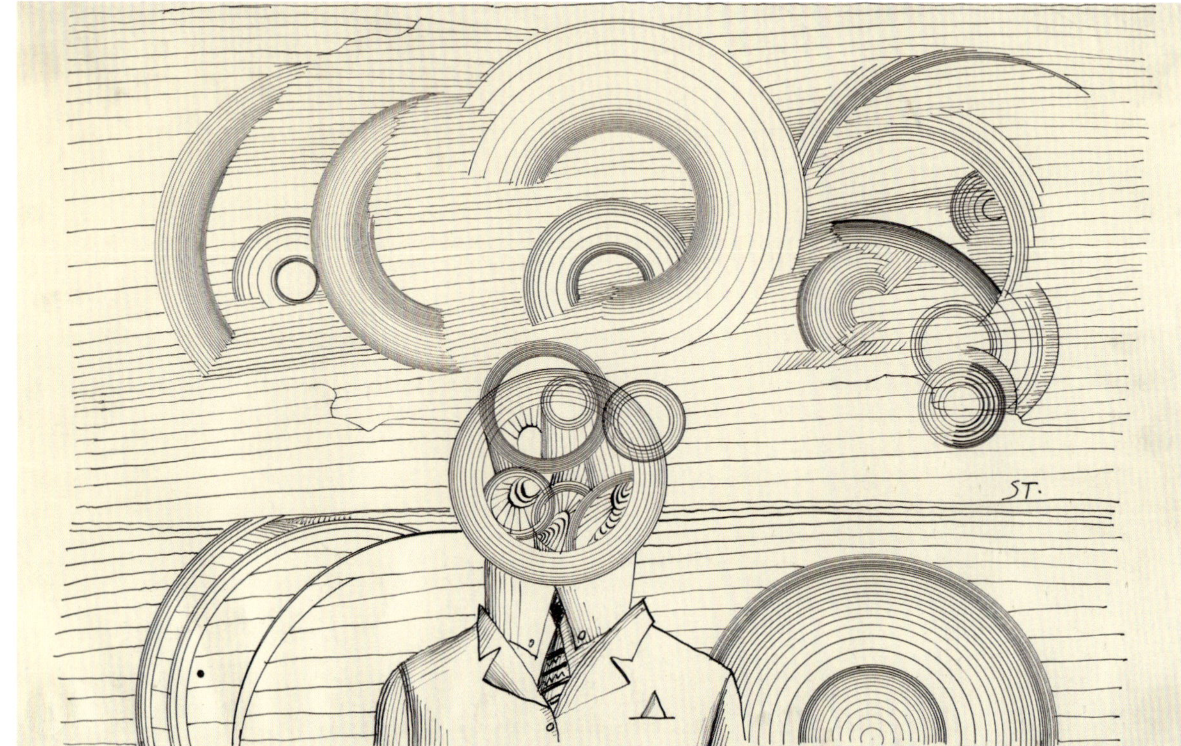

Fig. 6.
Saul Steinberg, Untitled, 1965. Pen and black ink, 14 ½ × 24 ¼ in. (36.8 × 61.5 cm). Yale University Art Gallery, Charles B. Benenson, B.A. 1933, Collection, 2006.52.110

This panoply of widely divergent trends and the ever-accelerating cycle of publicity that characterized art and its high-stakes markets in the 1980s could have made choosing what to follow a difficult task for a collector with tastes as diverse as Benenson's.[15] In reality, however, his attraction to bright geometries had anticipated a dominant 1980s aesthetic: the intense colors of the Italian design collaborative the Memphis group and a reprise of the International Style movement in art and design. The eclecticism that had characterized Benenson's collecting since the 1950s became the order of the day. In this way, he remained consistent in the 1980s—when many art lovers followed trends to the detriment of their overall collections—by continuing to build on his collection's strengths: vibrantly colored abstraction, bold symbolism, off-kilter and exaggerated figuration, and wit. As he had rarely collected photography, it is not surprising that Benenson bypassed Pictures Group artists such as Cindy Sherman and Sherrie Levine, whose relatively cerebral works are now central to how 1980s art is taught in art and art history programs. The works by splashier 1980s artists that Benenson did choose were frequently not the easiest to digest or exhibit. For example, he acquired works by the

monumental sculptor Reuben Nakian and a fourteen-foot, bright blue male nude
by the hugely popular Jonathan Borofsky (cat. 73), which formed a representational
keystone in the artist's otherwise symbol-filled 1988 solo show at the Paula Cooper
Gallery.[16] Benenson avoided superstars with inflated prices like Schnabel and Salle.
Instead, he acquired a dramatically skewed painting by the Chicago funk artist
Ed Paschke (cat. 67), as well as paintings by Kitaj that were based on art historical
referents, and new photographs by Gilbert & George in which the British artists
moved from the arch humor that characterized their 1970s work and toward ribald
and boldly imagist compositions (cat. 63).

In his attraction to humor and outsized figuration throughout the 1970s,
Benenson was at the forefront of an important trend. After the influence of car-
toons on Pop artists of the 1950s and 1960s, the late 1970s and 1980s saw a growing appreciation of caricature, what the art historian Ernst Gombrich called "the
illusion of life which can do without any illusion of reality."[17] Drawings by the carica-
turists Ranan Raymond Lurie and David Levine were collected as works of fine art,
and Steinberg, whose work Benenson had supported for decades and collected in
great depth, was the subject of a traveling retrospective at the Whitney Museum
of American Art.[18] In 1979 Benenson bought Red Grooms's *Picasso Goes to Heaven*
(cat. 52), the first of many significant works purchased from the artist's studio.
Within a week, the *New York Times* reviewer Hilton Kramer called the fifteen-by-
sixteen-foot art historical pastiche "one of the worst things of its kind ever exhibited in a serious [New York] gallery."[19] Grooms later recalled his gratitude to
Benenson for supporting his career, and for purchasing a work whose large scale
limited its appeal to collectors: "I loved him for that. He was my hero, to vindicate
me so politically after getting lambasted."[20] It was only a short time later that the
blue-chip Marlborough Gallery began representing Grooms, whose absurdist
humor and multimedia constructions exemplified many aspects of 1980s taste in
general, and of Benenson's in particular (fig. 7).

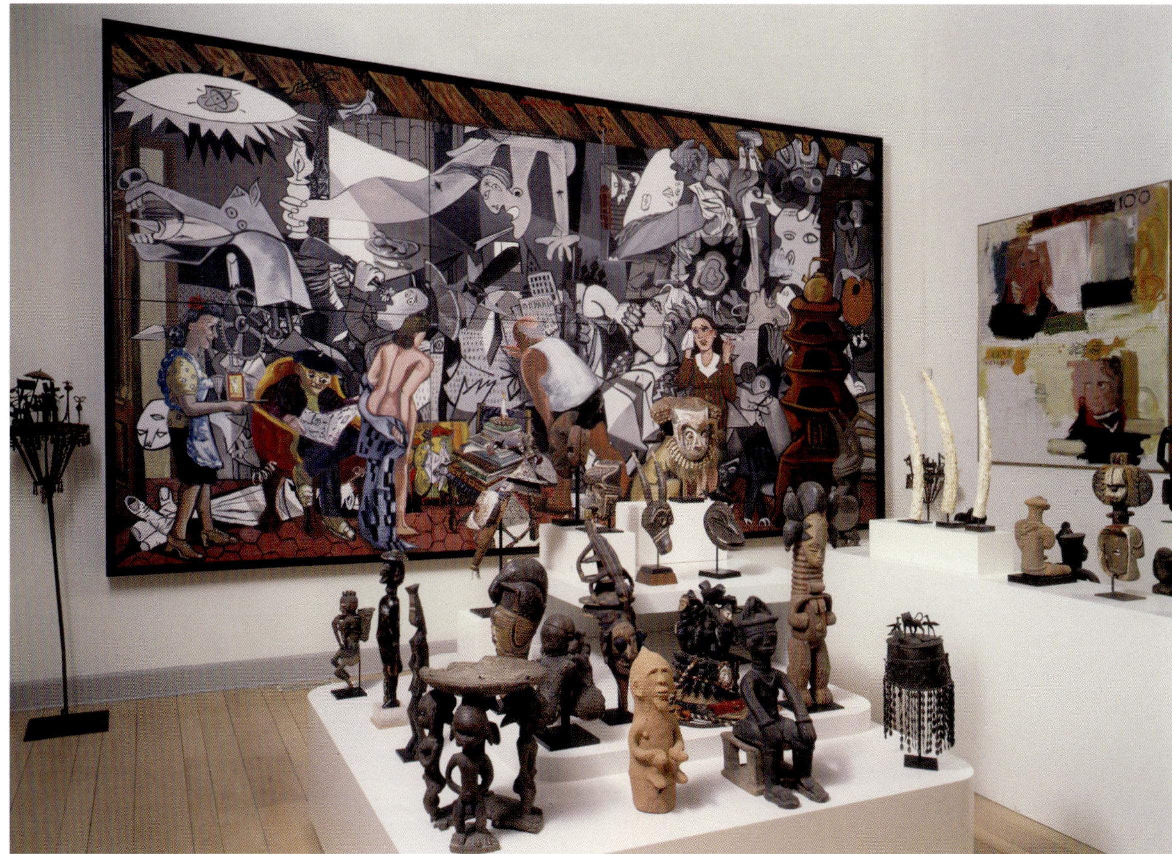

Fig. 7.
Red Grooms, *Studio at the Rue des Grands-Augustins* (cat. 53), and Larry Rivers, *Double French Money* (cat. 33), installed in Charles B. Benenson's home

At the end of the 1950s, there had been just a handful of contemporary galleries in New York. By 1971 there were nearly one hundred.[21] At the end of the 1980s the number had quadrupled to four hundred, with the galleries no longer concentrated on Madison Avenue but peppered throughout SoHo and the East Village.[22] Auction prices for Impressionist paintings rose 974 percent from the beginning of the 1980s to the end of the decade, by which time, as the analyst Peter Watson noted, the collecting of contemporary art had become twice as popular as collecting modern art, "three times as popular as collecting Impressionists and four times as popular as collecting Old Masters."[23] Sotheby's estimated that by the end of the 1980s, there were about four hundred thousand serious collectors worldwide who spent $10,000 or more per year on art.[24]

Within a few years of the 1987 stock market crash, the art market experienced a dramatic crisis. Between 1990 and 1992, for example, the price of individual works at auction decreased, on average, by 44 percent.[25] Many art dealers declined to repudiate the motivation of high-stakes buyers and sellers who had driven the market during that heady decade, suggesting instead that the great collectors had simply downshifted. In 1991 the dealer Mary Boone said, "Real collectors never stop buying. They buy more carefully and ask for bigger discounts these days. People used to give you a decision within twenty-four hours; now they want to think about it."[26] The pace of collecting for Benenson also slowed in the 1990s, although it was generally because he began focusing on large-scale sculpture—works that were harder to site, such as Ursula von Rydingsvard's *Three Bowls* (cat. 77), carved from rough-hewn cedar. Benenson, who only resold a handful of objects during his decades of collecting, took advantage of the market downturn to acquire works that had made an impact in the 1980s. Among them were James Rosenquist's epic *While the Earth Revolves at Night* (see fig. 4 and cat. 64), which he purchased at auction in the early 1990s, and Louise Bourgeois's enormous *Shredder* (cat. 66), which had been included in her presentation at the Whitney Biennial in 1983.

Benenson explained his growing interest in outdoor sculpture during the later years of his life as a matter of practicality: the magnificent spaces for African, modern, and contemporary art in his home had become too full. As Benenson turned his focus outdoors (fig. 8), he also began considering the life of his collection in the world after his death, planning for it to come to the Yale University Art Gallery. As a free-of-charge museum open to the public and the university community, the Gallery was designed to share with its local audiences a privilege often only enjoyed by private collectors such as Benenson: the opportunity to live in proximity to freely accessible great works of art. At Yale, Benenson's collection of modern and contemporary art might never be installed in the same elaborate, diachronic dialogue with African art that he staged in his home. The informed, poetic juxtapositions he created will, however, be restaged even more imaginatively when Yale's students embark on research or reverie, and as works in this wonderful collection populate seminar presentations, term papers, and student-curated exhibitions. The world in which Benenson's collection was first assembled, and then first displayed, will continue to have a life as these works are studied and treasured in a new environment by successive generations of students and the public.

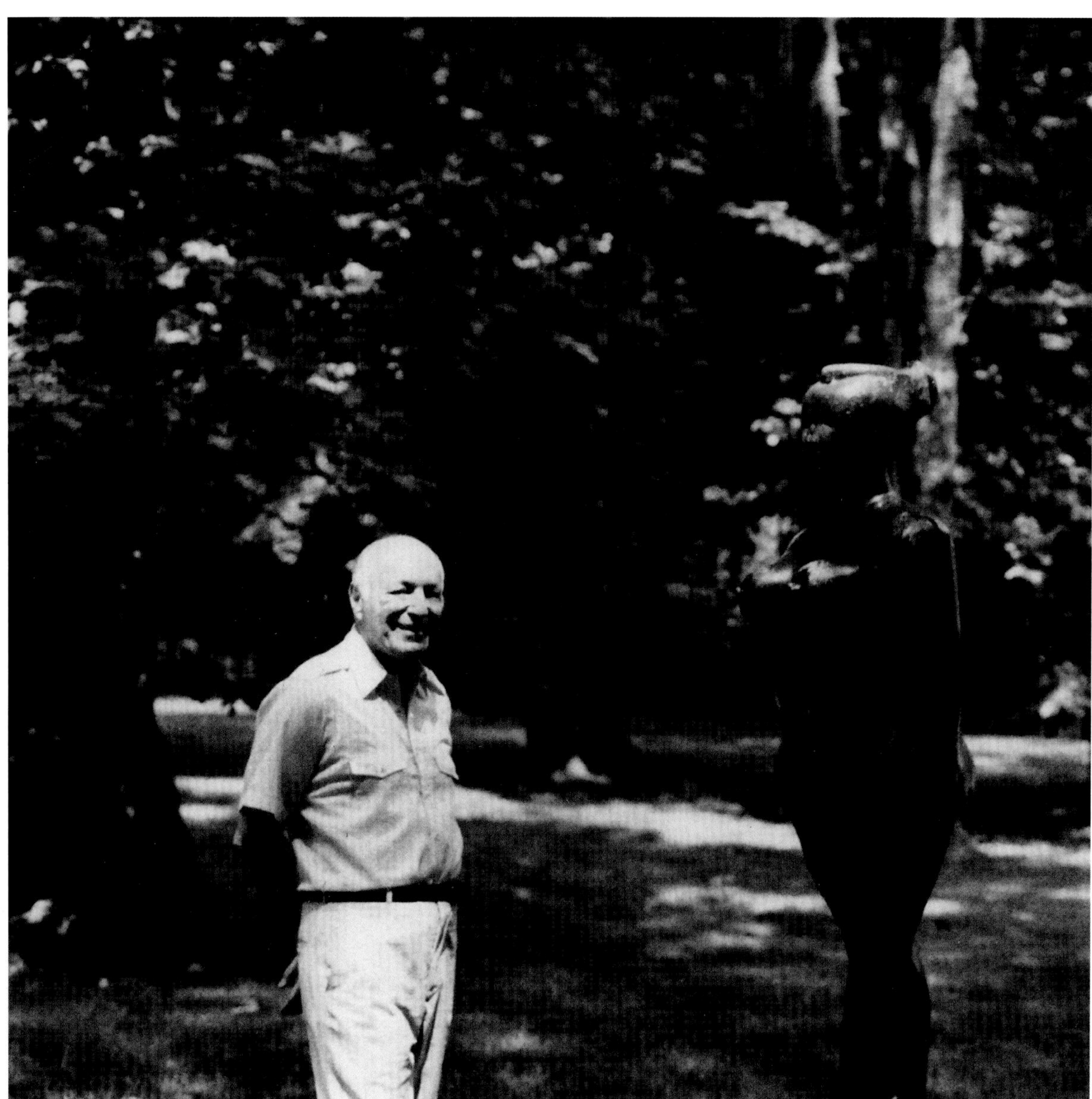

Fig. 8.
Charles B. Benenson in his sculpture garden.
On right: Jean Ipoustéguy, *La Terre* (Earth), 1962. Bronze, 74 ¹³⁄₁₆ × 27 ⅝ × 19 ¹¹⁄₁₆ in. (190 × 70.1 × 50 cm). Collection of Lawrence B. Benenson, formerly in the Collection of Charles B. Benenson, B.A. 1933

Notes

1. The exhibition was held from November 4 to 29. James Fitzsimmons, Miró, *"Peintures sauvages," 1934 to 1953*, exh. cat. (New York: Pierre Matisse Gallery, 1958).

2. Many dates of acquisition and details of provenance were not available for this study, as Benenson did not keep detailed diaries of the exhibitions he saw or the works he purchased. It has therefore been necessary to take clues to Benenson's acquisition strategies from the exhibition histories of the works themselves.

3. Calvin Tomkins, *Off the Wall: Robert Rauschenberg and the Art World of Our Time* (Garden City, N.Y.: Doubleday, 1980), 279.

4. Edith G. Halpert, "Moscow Greeting," *New York Times*, August 2, 1959, X15. Elsewhere at the fair the infamous Kitchen Debates between then Vice President Richard Nixon and Soviet Premier Nikita Khrushchev were under way.

5. See John Canaday, "Art: What Moscow Saw," *New York Times*, October 28, 1959, 33.

6. *Dada, 1916–1923* was held at the Sidney Janis Gallery, in New York, from April 15 to May 9, 1953.

7. In a story Benenson often recounted, this fact was underlined for him when William Rubin, then a curator at the Museum of Modern Art, offered to buy the work only minutes after Benenson had purchased it.

8. John Canaday, "Art: A Museum Only Eight Feet Wide and Two Feet Deep," *New York Times*, December 16, 1967, 46.

9. William Rubin, *"Primitivism" in Twentieth-Century Art: Affinity of the Tribal and the Modern*, exh. cat. (New York: Museum of Modern Art, 1984). On the debate following the 1984 exhibition, see Thomas McEvilley, "Doctor Lawyer Indian Chief," *Artforum*, November 1984, 54–61. This article prompted letters from exhibition curators William Rubin and Kirk Varnedoe, along with a rejoinder by McEvilley, all published in *Artforum*, February 1985, 42–51. See also Jack D. Flam, ed., *Primitivism and Twentieth-Century Art: A Documentary History* (Berkeley: University of California Press, 2003).

10. Richard Cork, "New Art at the Tate" (September 15, 1983); reprinted in Cork, *New Spirit, New Sculpture, New Money: Art in the 1980s* (New Haven, Conn.: Yale University Press, 2003), 42.

11. Richard Cork described how "auction reports played a more and more prominent part in newspaper coverage of the arts, while the tabloid press only deigned to discuss painting or sculpture when the latest saleroom sensation was given yet another exclamatory headline." Ibid., 16.

12. The Pictures Group was codified in the exhibition *Pictures*, organized by Douglas Crimp in September 1977 at Artists Space, in New York.

13. Derrick R. Cartwright, "Schnabel, Julian," *Grove Art Online*, Oxford Art Online, http://www.oxfordartonline.com/subscriber/article/grove/art/T076681 (accessed January 5, 2011).

14. As artist Keiko Bonk recalled in an interview with Sylvère Lotringer published in *David Wojnarowicz: A Definitive History of Five or Six Years on the Lower East Side*, ed. Giancarlo Ambrosino (New York: Semiotext(e), 2007), 35.

15. For a discussion of the different "camps" in 1980s art, see the March and April 2003 issues of *Artforum* and David Salle and Richard Phillips, *Your History Is Not Our History*, exh. cat. (New York: Haunch of Venison, 2010).

16. *Jonathan Borofsky*, Paula Cooper Gallery, New York, April 2–30, 1988.

17. Ernst Gombrich, *Art and Illusion* (Princeton, N.J.: Princeton University Press, 1961), 336.

18. Over the years, Benenson attempted to convince, among others, curators William Lieberman at the Museum of Modern Art, New York, and Philippe de Montebello at the Metropolitan Museum of Art to organize a Saul Steinberg retrospective. He was thrilled when the Whitney Museum of American Art eventually decided to pursue such an exhibition. See the transcript of a recorded conversation between Lawrence Benenson and Charles B. Benenson, Greenwich, Conn., March 28 and April 2, 1998. A copy is on file with the Gallery's Department of Modern and Contemporary Art.

19. Hilton Kramer, "Two Streams of American Art at the Whitney and Six-Gallery Show," *New York Times*, September 14, 1979, C1.

20. Transcript of an unpublished interview with Red Grooms conducted by Amanda Maples, Yale University Art Gallery, October 6, 2009. A copy is on file with the Gallery's Department of Modern and Contemporary Art.

21. Tomkins, *Off the Wall*, 349.

22. As Peter Watson noted: "According to *Art & Auction*, in the 1950s there were barely a dozen art galleries on [Fifty-seventh Street], but 'today there are almost sixty . . . stacked in four blocks between Park and Seventh Avenues.'" When SoHo and Madison Avenue were taken into account, the figure topped one hundred (and was four hundred by 1987). See Peter Watson, *From Manet to Manhattan: The Rise of the Modern Art Market* (New York: Random House, 1992), 365.

23. Ibid., 419. For the statistics on the rise of auction prices, see Cork, "New Art at the Tate," 15.

24. Watson, *From Manet to Manhattan*, 429.

25. Olav Velthuis, "Accounting for Taste: The Economics of Art," *Artforum*, April 2008, 304–9.

26. Mary Boone, quoted in Peter Plagens, "Cents and Sensibility: Collecting the '80s," *Artforum*, April 2003, 255.

Catalogue

The following entries are arranged chronologically based on the first work discussed in each entry, then alphabetically by artist name. The catalogued works are numbered according to their order of appearance in the text.

For all objects, principal medium is given first, followed by other media in order of importance. For two dimensional objects, height precedes width; for sculpture, height precedes width precedes depth. Dimensions for works on paper are of the sheet, unless otherwise noted.

Jules Pascin

American, born Bulgaria, 1885–1930

1
Café Scene, **1906–7**
Black ink and graphite, 8 ³⁄₁₆ × 12 ¼ in.
(20.8 × 31.1 cm)
2006.52.36

Although it later became an umbrella term for artists working in the Parisian neighborhoods of Montparnasse and Montmartre before World War II, the descriptive *École de Paris* (School of Paris) was originally used to distinguish French-born artists from the growing number of foreign artists—many of whom were Jewish, including Jules Pascin, Chaim Soutine, and Amedeo Modigliani—who were drawn to bohemian Paris in the early years of the twentieth century and in the interwar years. Born in Bulgaria, educated in Vienna and Munich, and naturalized as an American citizen, Pascin spent most of his life in the French capital, where he was as famous for constantly sketching as he was for his studio parties, generosity with poorer artist friends, and patronage of the city's cafés, nightclubs, and brothels. Although he most frequently depicted nude and seminude women, Pascin began his career as a satirical caricaturist for the highly influential German magazine *Simplicissimus,* a job he continued until 1914.

The present drawing was created during Pascin's first stay in Paris from 1905 to 1914, one of many he made in popular Parisian cafés and nightclubs in the years immediately before World War I. Although the drawing calls to mind the vivid representations of Parisian nightlife by Édouard Manet, or Henri de Toulouse-Lautrec, Pascin's energetic dinner scene is more of a quick caricature than a finished work by one of those artists. Here, no less than three diners openly pick their teeth while still savoring a meal that seems to have recently ended. In the foreground a bearded man rests his hands contentedly on his belly, and his companion stands while finishing her drink. Another patron smokes a cigarette and leans back, his vest unbuttoned and shirt swelling open. His rotundity is echoed in the balloon-shaped diner at the far left who accompanies a woman wielding a knife. On the right, a server waits attentively, seemingly poised to answer the call of a diner in the upper left who stands and snaps his fingers for assistance.

The fluid quality of Pascin's drawing is one of its most defining characteristics. His pen's sharp line resembles that of the stylus used to make etchings, creating a sense of immediacy and depth with little modeling or shading. Pascin was friends with George Grosz, and like such German artists associated with Expressionism and New Objectivity, he resisted the trend toward abstraction in the early years of the twentieth century. Here, the diners' facial features and corpulence are exaggerated, but, in general, Pascin's satire is less biting than Grosz's. What we see is a humorous pantomime of the most common of Parisian rituals: dinner in a café.

The banality of Pascin's subject resonates with the chapter Ernest Hemingway penned on the artist in his memoir *A Moveable Feast.* In it, Pascin arrives at the Café du Dôme with two models on his arm and invites the American writer to drink and discuss work. The conversation quickly turns to sex. In Hemingway's telling, Pascin's invitation was not an exceptional occurrence, but an enjoyable one that affirmed his own place in the cultural life of Paris at that moment.[1] Like Pascin, Hemingway chose the café to illustrate the basic pleasures and humor in the social theater of everyday life.

—Cathleen Chaffee

---

1. See Ernest Hemingway, "With Pascin at the Dôme," in *A Moveable Feast: The Restored Edition* (New York: Charles Scribner's Sons, 2009), 81–86. *A Moveable Feast* was originally published in 1964, after Hemingway's death.

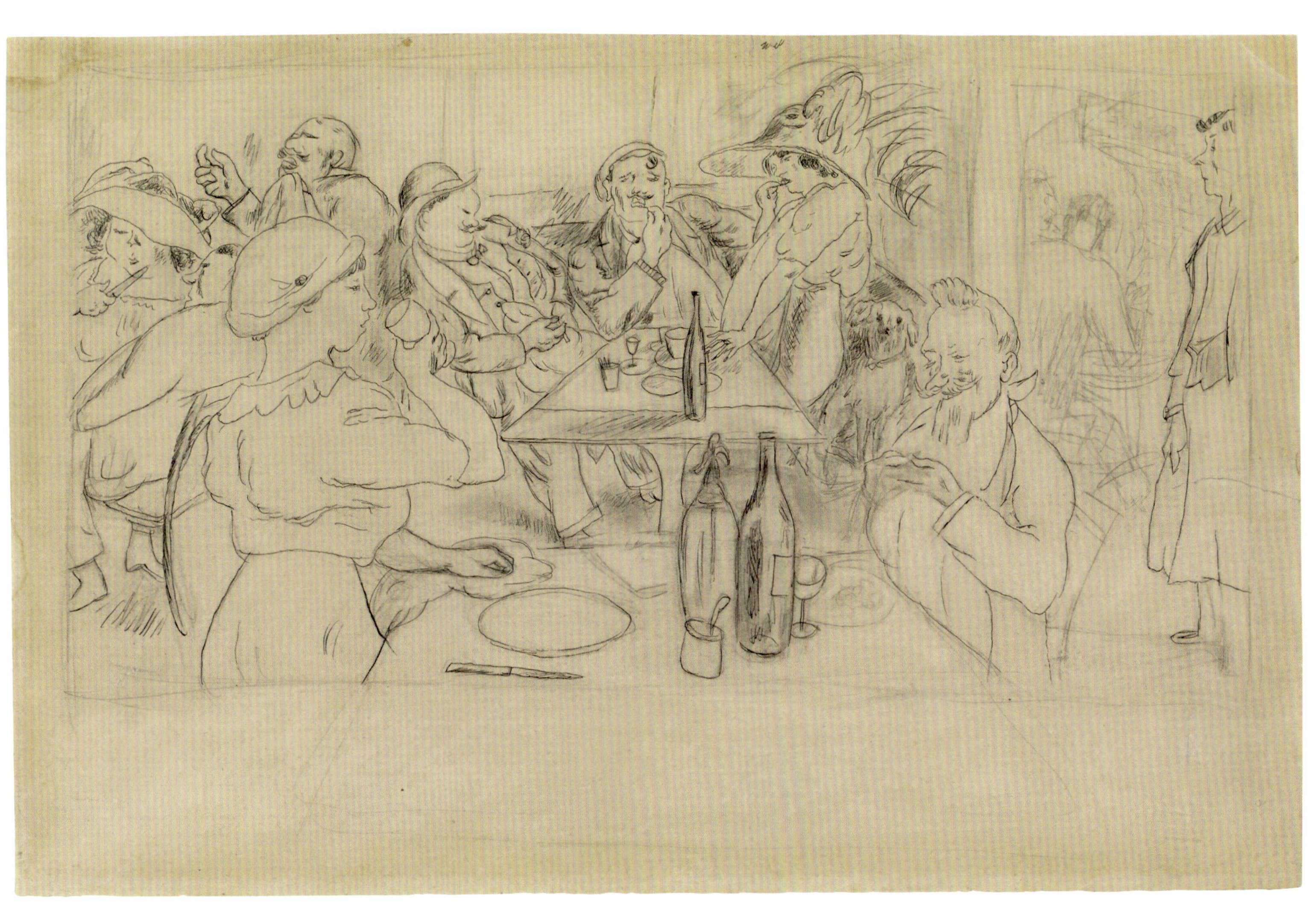

1

Roger de La Fresnaye

French, 1885–1925

2
***Deux fantassins casqués* (Two Helmeted Infantrymen), 1917**
Pen and black ink with wash,
12 ⅛ × 7 ⅝ in. (30.8 × 19.4 cm)
2006.52.7

In this drawing of French soldiers, Roger de La Fresnaye recorded everyday military routine while injecting it with a sense of vitality and even humor, underscoring camaraderie rather than aggression. In 1908 La Fresnaye studied with Maurice Denis and Paul Sérusier at the Académie Ranson, where he trained in the tradition of Paul Gauguin and Paul Cézanne.[1] By the time La Fresnaye first exhibited at the Salon d'Automne in 1910, his work had already begun to incorporate simultaneous multiple perspectives and a reduction of forms, displaying the influence of the incipient Cubist movement. Although engaged by the Cubism practiced by Georges Braque and Pablo Picasso, La Fresnaye shed the austerity of their compositions, in part by incorporating bright colors. His work tended toward Synthetic Cubism, in which geometric shapes are incorporated into a composition to depict a unified, rather than a fractured, representational subject. In this regard, he shared a visual and ideological approach with artists who gravitated toward Marcel Duchamp and Raymond Duchamp-Villon, including Jean Metzinger, Albert Gleizes, Robert Delaunay, Fernand Léger, František Kupka, and Guillaume Apollinaire.[2]

La Fresnaye entered the French army in 1914, creating a limited body of watercolors and drawings during World War I. *Deux fantassins casqués* (Two Helmeted Infantrymen) dates from this period. The 1917 drawing foregrounds two soldiers, the foremost of whom is defined by a prominent mustache. Although it lacks the coloration representative of La Fresnaye's work, *Deux fantassins casqués* reflects the artist's interest in creating a sense of volume and varied tonality through the use of a dry ink wash to model the figures' helmets, cheeks, and the foremost figure's collar. In addition, La Fresnaye's contours function as textural elements and resemble his paintings' *tache*, or brushstroke, for he applied ink in a series of abbreviated strokes rather than in flowing lines. This element challenges the graphic quality of the drawing established by solid planes contrasted with large, evenly distributed swatches of untouched paper. Vertical elements, all slightly atilt, are juxtaposed with the arcs of the soldiers' helmets and the fanciful, almost baroque curves of the background figures' whiskers and the foremost figure's mustache, ear, and helmet insignia.

In the upper corners, the chins and whiskers of two other figures, one of whom smokes a pipe, are evident. The pipe is a motif that appears again in La Fresnaye's drawing of 1919, *Soldat fumant* (Soldier Smoking), suggesting that the artist derived his war compositions from mundane and oft-repeated moments of military life, rather than from those of action and engagement (fig. 1). Indeed, the only militaristic emblems portrayed in *Deux fantassins casqués* are the two helmets at the center of the composition, sites for the artist's wide arcs and textured modeling—elements that temper the severity of the surrounding planes.

—**Katherine D. Alcauskas**

---

1. La Fresnaye also attended the Académie Julian (1903-4) and the École des Beaux-Arts (1904-8).
2. La Fresnaye exhibited with the group in 1912 at the Salon de la Section d'Or.

Fig. 1.
Roger de La Fresnaye, *Soldat fumant* (Soldier Smoking), 1919. Watercolor, 10¼ × 7 ⅞ in. (26 × 20 cm). Donation Geneviève et Jean Masurel (Paris) in 1979 LaM, Lille Métropole Musée d'Art Moderne, d'Art Contemporain et d'Art Brut

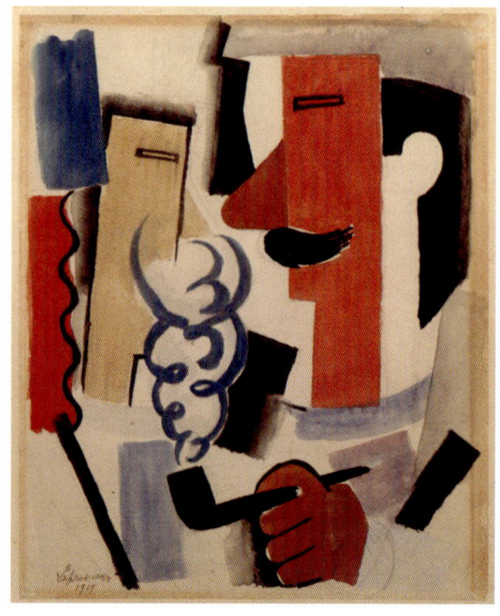

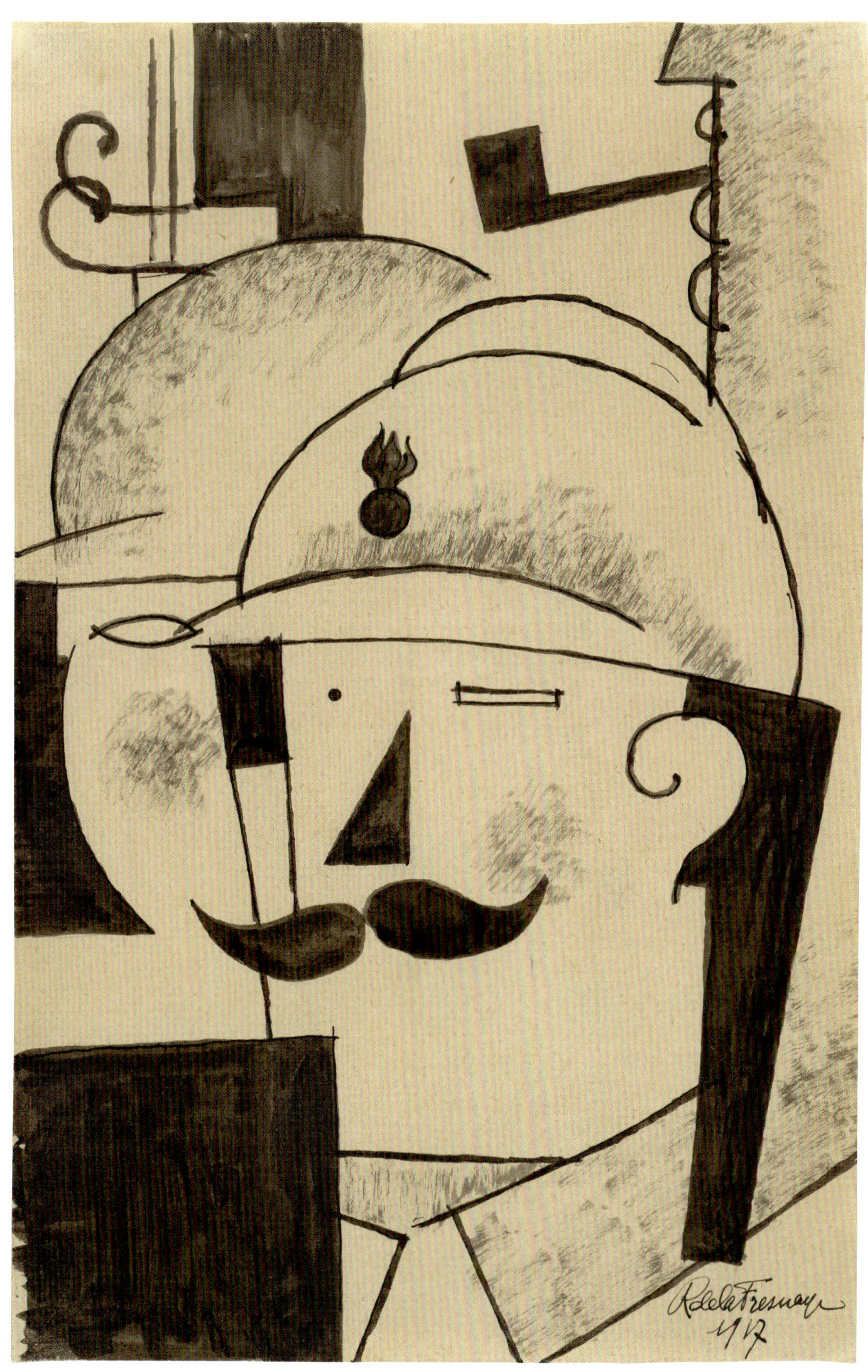

2

Jean Metzinger

French, 1883–1956

3
***Nature morte* (Still Life), 1918**
Oil on canvas, 31 ¾ × 25 ¾ in.
(80.6 × 65.4 cm)
2006.52.19

Although he has often been considered a relatively minor Cubist artist, Jean Metzinger was in fact a pivotal figure in the inception and development of the movement. From 1909 onward, Metzinger was a frequent visitor to Le Bateau-Lavoir, the building containing Parisian artists' studios including Pablo Picasso's, and he was intimately familiar with the formal innovations of Picasso and Georges Braque as they developed Cubism. Metzinger was likewise a member of the so-called Puteaux Group of Cubists, which included Marcel Duchamp, Raymond Duchamp-Villon, Jacques Villon, Robert Delaunay, Henri Le Fauconnier, Albert Gleizes, Juan Gris, and Fernand Léger. It was these artists—rather than Braque and Picasso—who were first labeled "Cubists" by critics at the 1911 Salon des Indépendants.

In 1912, together with Gleizes, Metzinger wrote the first treatise on Cubism, *Du Cubisme*. In it he formally outlined a theory of Cubism as a modern pictorial language, one that "condemns all systems . . . [eliminating] everything that does not exactly correspond to the conditions of the plastic material."[1] Cubism, as Metzinger conceived it, involved breaking down three-dimensional objects into two-dimensional planes. In looking at a Cubist painting, the viewer could "reconstruct the original volumes mentally and . . . imagine within the space the object I had looked at."[2] A mathematics enthusiast from an early age, Metzinger explored the pictorial possibilities of non-Euclidean geometry, claiming that "all *lasting* art is never anything more than a mathematical expression of the relations that exist between . . . the self and the world."[3] For Metzinger, art was primarily an intellectual, idea-driven endeavor.

In his 1918 *Nature morte* (Still Life), Metzinger translated the complex spatial relationships between three-dimensional objects into a flat, two-dimensional pictorial grid. The work depicts two chessboards, a kettle, a variegated glass decanter, a creased tablecloth, and a number of bottles on a tabletop. The surfaces of the chessboards and the table are represented vertically, as if viewed from above, while the remaining objects are shown head-on, parallel to the picture plane. Rather than using a gradated diminution of receding objects, Metzinger indicates spatial recession through the overlapping of forms. He entirely abandons traditional chiaroscuro effects and the modeling of objects in favor of a new system of visual signs that respects the two-dimensionality of the painting's flat support. The eye is confronted with a layering of geometric shapes, patterns, and tones.

In contrast to the almost monochromatic Cubist works produced by Picasso and Braque during the early 1900s, Metzinger's works display a varied palette. His pre–World War I works in particular were saturated with bright hues. Only after his experiences as a stretcher-bearer in the war did Metzinger's colors take on the more restrained tonalities of the present work. Instead of the landscapes and portraits of the prewar period, Metzinger increasingly gravitated toward the still life after the war, as he continued to methodically and systematically advance his own mode of Cubist abstraction. Ultimately, Metzinger remained Cubism's first true theorist, one who claimed that "[t]he End . . . isn't the subject, nor the object, nor even the picture—the End, it is the idea."[4]

—**Maria Taroutina**

1. Jean Metzinger and Albert Gleizes, *Du Cubisme* (Paris: Figuière, 1912); reprinted and translated by Robert L. Herbert in *Modern Artists on Art: Ten Unabridged Essays* (Englewood Cliffs, N.J.: Prentice-Hall, 1964), 18.
2. Jean Metzinger, *Le Cubisme, 1911–1918* (Paris: Galerie de France, 1945); quoted in Joann Moser, *Jean Metzinger in Retrospect*, exh. cat. (Seattle: University of Washington Press, 1985), 43.
3. Jean Metzinger, letter to Albert Gleizes, July 4, 1916; quoted in Moser, *Jean Metzinger in Retrospect*, 21.
4. Jean Metzinger, letter to Albert Gleizes, July 26, 1916; quoted in Moser, *Jean Metzinger in Retrospect*, 21.

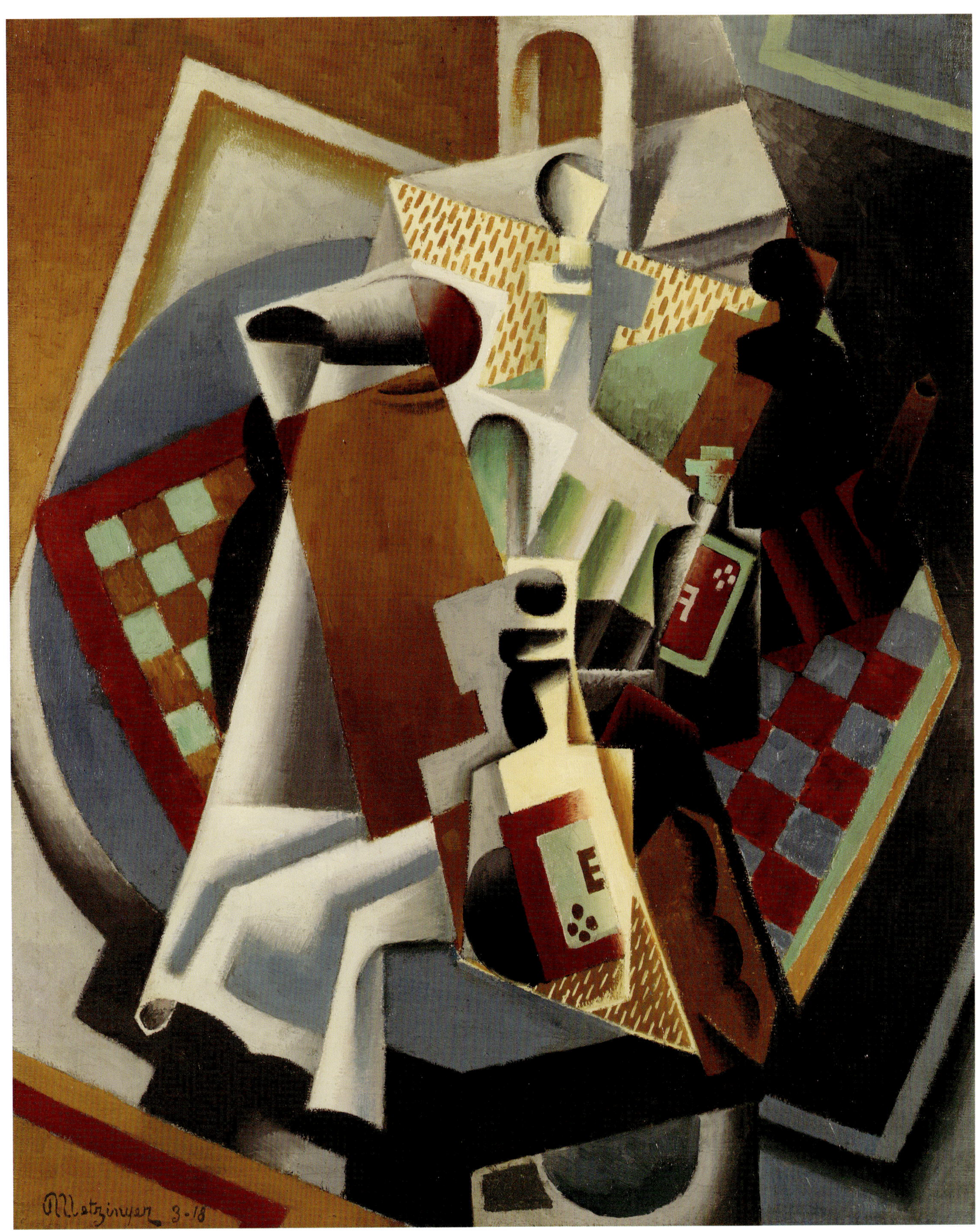

Metzinger 3-18

Wyndham Lewis

British, born Canada, 1882–1957

4
Seated Man, 1920
Black crayon, 20⁵⁄₁₆ × 14 ¹⁵⁄₁₆ in.
(51.5 × 37.9 cm)
2006.52.17

Wyndham Lewis was an artist and writer and, on both fronts, a staunch champion of the English avant-garde. Although he began his artistic career as a caricaturist and satirist, when first exhibited publicly in 1912, his work displayed the influence of European abstraction. In 1913, Lewis precipitated a rift in the English art world by severing ties with the prominent art critic Roger Fry and his conservative Omega Workshop. In its place, he helped establish the Rebel Art Centre, whose followers' geometric, abstracted style became known as Vorticism. Considered "England's only truly avant-garde movement," Vorticism responded to an amalgam of styles emerging throughout Europe and attempted to adapt Cubism, Futurism, and Expressionism to a northern tradition.[1]

Like many artists, Lewis redefined his style following World War I. In the place of abstraction he took up figuration with new zeal, creating numerous nude figure studies and portraits. This drawing of Edward Wadsworth (1889–1949), an English Vorticist artist, is similar in its minimal nature to other figure studies created in 1920. Lewis made a series of portraits of Wadsworth in the early 1920s, perhaps commissions from the sitter himself, who at the time provided Lewis with financial assistance (fig. 1). The drawing employs the same smooth arcs and assured lines as Lewis's Vorticist works, subtly melding figural and abstract traditions. Lewis portrays Wadsworth seated on a chair with his right knee drawn up toward his chest. His back and shoulders are rounded, and his body condensed in a way that was typical of the artist's figure studies. The composition directs the viewer's eye toward the point where Wadsworth grabs his shin, his hands appearing to project forward in space.

In this drawing, Lewis emphasizes contour over mass and employs minimal shading, selectively drawing out subsidiary elements. The simplified, almost caricatural depiction of Wadsworth's face contrasts with the realism of contemporary portraits by Lewis and harks back to the artist's early satirical drawings. He would more fully explore their themes the following year with his "tyros," sardonic, grinning figures that anticipated the characters of his biting 1930 book, *The Apes of God*. In the novel, Lewis, who had trouble accepting the patronage of artists whom he saw as his inferiors, publicly lampooned Wadsworth and others he had once considered friends.

—**Katherine D. Alcauskas**

---

1. Paul Edwards, *Wyndham Lewis: Painter and Writer* (New Haven, Conn.: Yale University Press for Paul Mellon Centre for Studies in British Art, 2000), 100.

Fig. 1.
Wyndham Lewis, *Portrait of Edward Wadsworth*, 1920. Black chalk and wash, 12 × 11¹⁄₁₆ in. (30.5 × 28 cm). The Pembroke College Oxford Junior Common Room Art Collection Fund

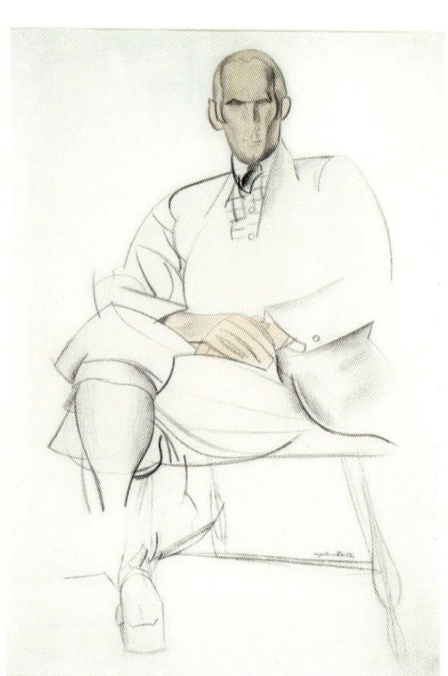

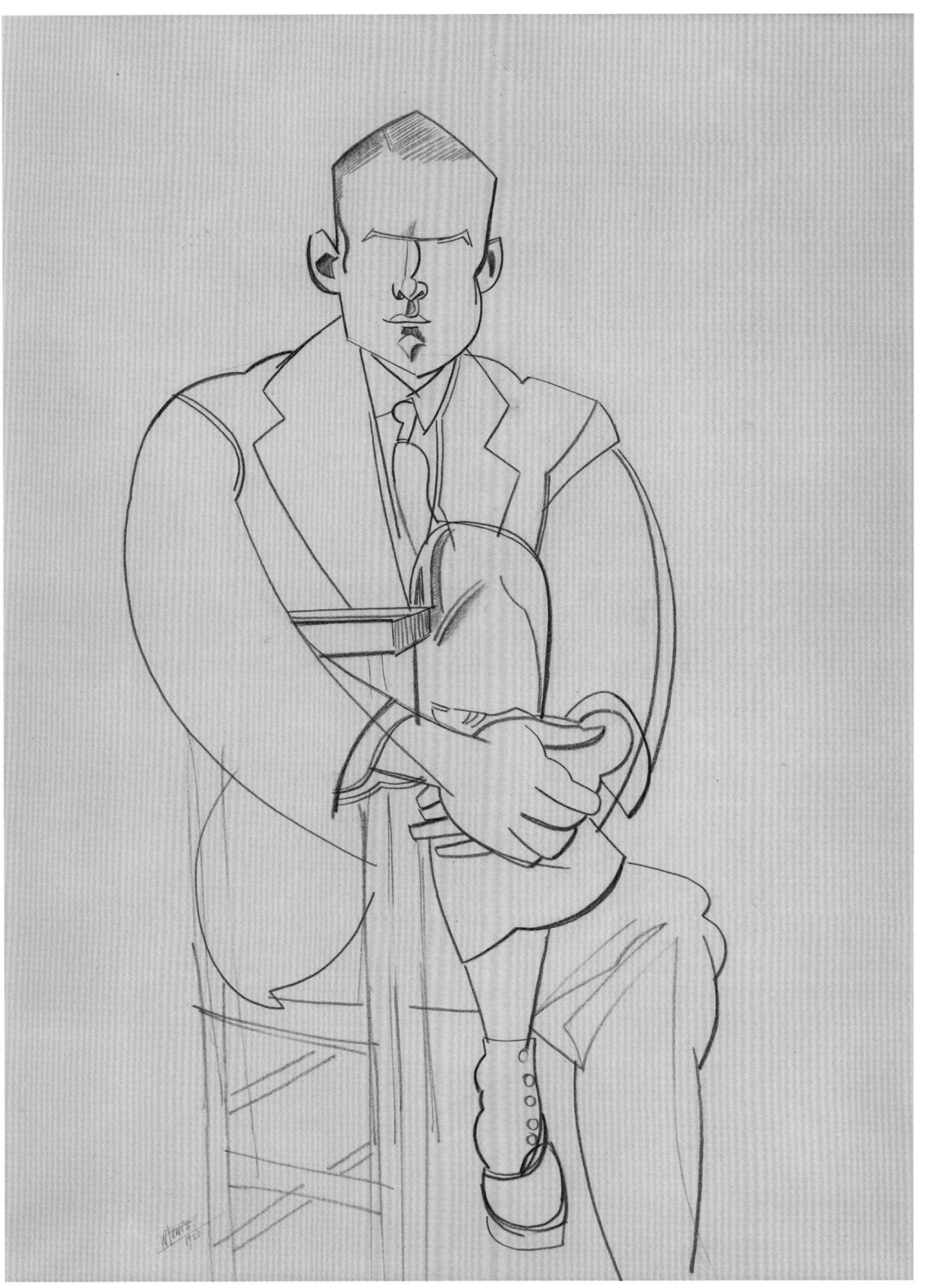

George Grosz

American, born Germany, 1893–1959

5
Haifische **(Sharks), 1920–21**
Transfer lithograph, 14 ⅞ × 20 in.
(37.8 × 50.8 cm)
2006.52.75

6
Chemist, **ca. 1925**
Black ink, 25 ½ × 19 ¾ in.
(64.8 × 50.2 cm)
2006.52.34

An exponent of the Berlin Dada movement, the artist George Grosz advocated an engaged, polemical art that critiqued the politics and culture of the post–World War I Weimar Republic. Disillusioned and embittered by his experiences as a German soldier, Grosz lampooned the cigar-smoking, bourgeois ruling classes, whom he blamed for Germany's increasing economic and political instability. According to the artist, it was the capitalist excesses and corrupt politics of the 1920s that led to the rise of Nazism in the 1930s. Consequently, images of conspicuous consumption, erotic violence, and big-city crime prevail in Grosz's artwork.

Haifische (Sharks; cat. 5) is one such image, depicting three seated figures around a table: two clothed men and a naked woman. The fine suits worn by the men and the woman's fur stole, hat, and jewelry identify all three as members of the bourgeoisie, amusing themselves in a fashionable bar or café. It is unclear if the woman's nudity is imagined by her male companions or whether it is a visual metaphor for her own lasciviousness and immorality. The title underscores this ambiguity. Are the men intending to procure the woman, or is it she who hopes to use her charms to exploit them?

Haifische repeats the composition and motifs of the 1919 watercolor *Schönheit, Dich will ich preisen!* (Beauty, I Wish to Praise Thee!; fig. 1). In particular, the fat, bald man at the center seems to have been directly lifted from the earlier work, which was included in Grosz's 1923 anthology, *Ecce Homo*. The allegedly pornographic content of this notorious cycle resulted in the artist being tried and fined. Grosz often juxtaposed naked women with clothed men in his art, suggesting the transactional and debased nature of their interactions. Such works extended beyond the depiction of individual erotic encounters to signify the moral collapse of Weimar society as a whole.

Chemist (cat. 6), produced around the same time, continued the themes of corruption and exploitation explored in *Haifische*. Here, however, Grosz targeted German academics—the intellectual class whose supposedly enlightened research was meant to move society forward. But the rotund figure, with his double chin and lit cigarette, seems interested in his own profit, rather than in scientific advancement. The brick factory tower, visible in the upper right corner, is echoed in the raised test tube the man holds in his left hand. Instead of aiding humanity, the science practiced here fuels industry and capitalism.

Both *Haifische* and *Chemist* demonstrate Grosz's virtuosic use of line. With just a few basic contours the artist captures the different physiognomies, and even personalities, of his characters. For example, the placid face of the woman in *Haifische* contrasts sharply with the tense, gaunt expression of the man on the left and the smug, well-fed complacency of the central figure. Unlike Grosz's more angular, fragmented, and geometric drawings from the period of 1915 to 1920, the present works manifest a fluid, curvilinear technique that speaks to a more mature, confident hand. In *Chemist,* in particular, the artist demonstrates a rich variety of line-making that ranges from the minute, energetic strokes in the man's garments to the flowing, sinuous contours of the winding staircase.

In their comical, almost grotesque quality these images approach low rather than high art. Grosz officially joined the Dada movement in 1918 and participated in the notorious *First International Dada Fair* in the summer of 1920, whose slogan "Dilettantes, Revolt against Art!" rallied the public to reject traditional "bourgeois" art. Rather than an exercise in aesthetics, Dada served as a critical conduit of ideas. Cultural theorist Walter Benjamin described the movement as "an instrument of ballistics," which "hit the spectator like a bullet."[1]

Although Grosz also produced oil paintings and watercolors, it is his graphic work that most closely adhered to Dada philosophy. Many of his ink drawings were specifically intended for lithographic reproduction as parts of larger pictorial cycles to be disseminated in magazines and journals—self-consciously borrowing the structures of modern communication and exchange. Grosz's graphic oeuvre thus exemplified Dada's assault on the expression of individual subjectivity and on the notion of the unique artistic masterpiece. *Haifische* and *Chemist* can be understood as pointed attacks on bourgeois discursive formations both in terms of their appearance and in terms of subject matter. In their uncompromising and acerbic critique, these two images pierce the viewer: a powerful, polemical art.

—**Maria Taroutina**

1. Walter Benjamin, "The Work of Art in the Age of Mechanical Reproduction" (1939), *Illuminations: Essays and Reflections*, ed. Hannah Arendt, trans. Harry Zohn (New York: Harcourt, Brace, and World, 1968), 231.

Fig. 1.
George Grosz, *Schönheit, Dich will ich preisen!* (Beauty, I Wish to Praise Thee!), 1919. Watercolor, pen, and ink, 16 ⁹⁄₁₆ × 11⅞ in. (42 × 30.2 cm). Karsch/Nierendorf collection, Berlin

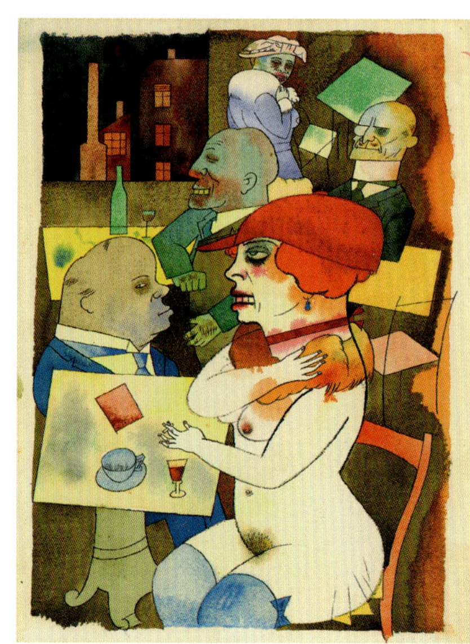

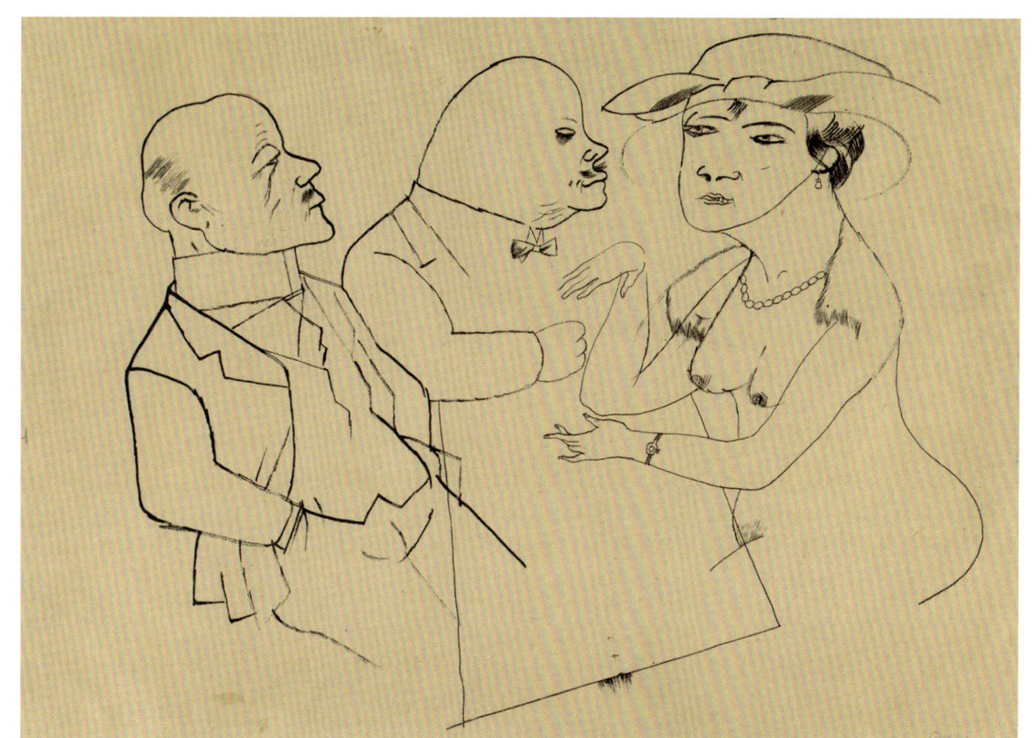

5

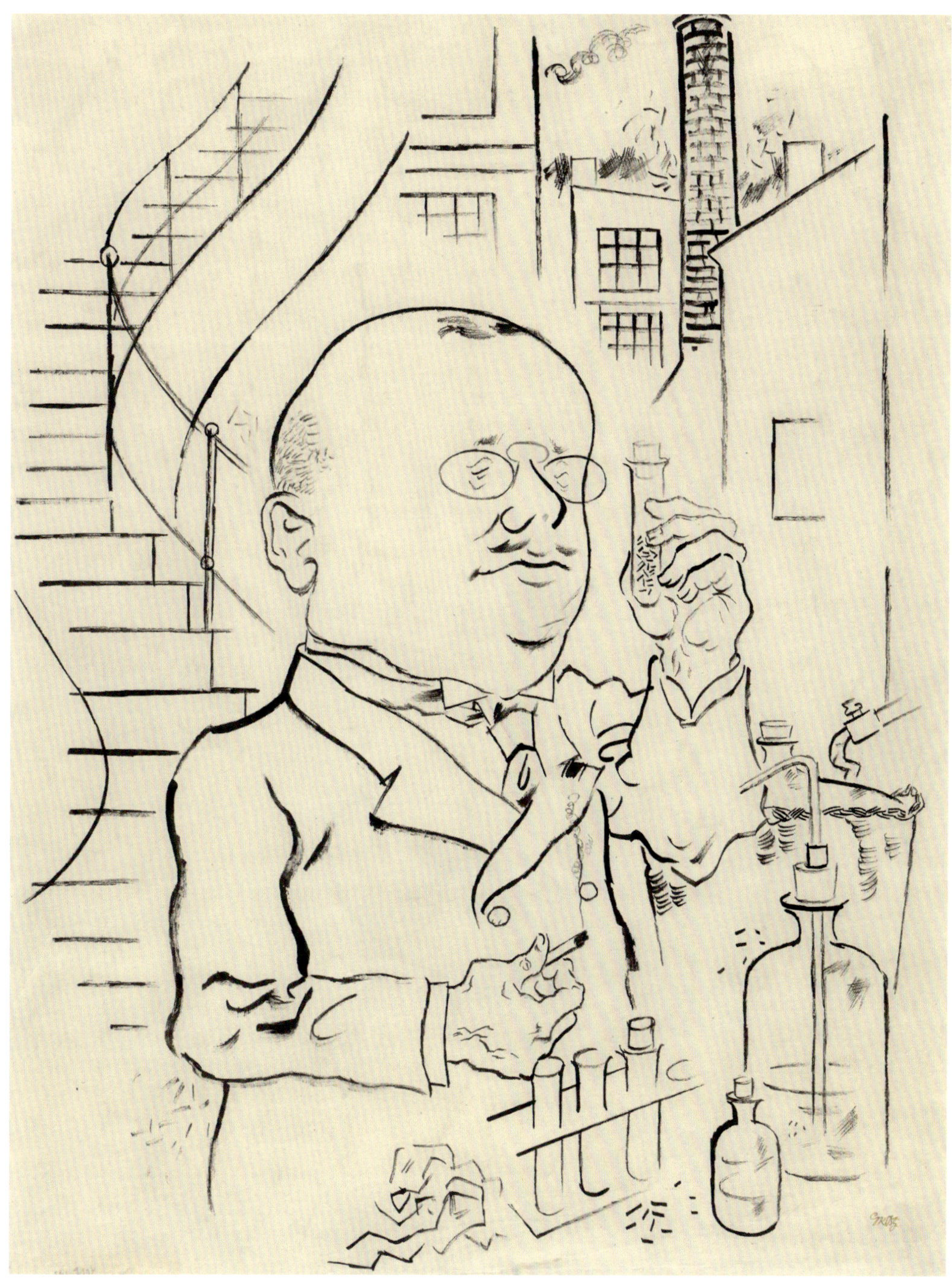

6

Fernand Léger

French, 1881–1955

7
Éléments mécaniques
(Mechanical Elements), 1924
Oil on canvas, 36 × 26 in.
(91.4 × 66 cm)
2006.52.16

8
Masque nègre **(Negro Mask), 1942**
Oil on canvas, 29 × 36½ in. (73.7 × 92.7 cm)
2006.52.25

I have made use of the machine as others have used the nude body or the still life.

—**Fernand Léger, "Propos d'artistes" (1925)**

As a soldier in the French army during World War I, Fernand Léger came into contact with large-scale military equipment. Its might and mechanistic grandeur made such a profound impression on the artist that on returning to the easel, Léger fervently advocated the rejection of conventional subject matter in favor of industrial and mechanical objects, which were equally capable of expressing a "lyric and plastic power."[1]

Éléments mécaniques (Mechanical Elements; cat. 7) is one of several oil-on-canvas variations of a 1923 pencil drawing and depicts a densely configured, vertical arrangement of glistening metallic forms, colored shapes, and patterned planes against a pale gray background. At the time of its production, Léger was working on the fourteen-minute silent film *Ballet mécanique* (1924), which contains a rapid succession of images of body parts, pots, pans, abstract shapes, spinning cylinders, and turbines. The film brings to life inanimate objects in a rhythmic modern dance, and its echoes appear in *Éléments mécaniques*. The centripetal composition, manifold layering of planes, and energetic projection of forms in all directions generate a kinetic dynamism—the forms appear to be frozen mid-dance, held together by an invisible magnetic force.

Éléments mécaniques emphatically departs from the flattened grids of Léger's earlier, more impressionistic Cubist-inspired works, both in its pronounced graphic character and in its distinctive three-dimensionality. The arch in the center of the composition, as well as the tubular forms around it, has a weighty, physical presence, and it protrudes into the viewer's space in an almost tangible fashion. Similarly, the hard contours, flat, unmodulated color planes, and tightly grouped shapes suggest a disciplined, structural approach to art-making, more akin to design than to expressive, painterly spontaneity.

In 1924 the architect Le Corbusier invited Léger to contribute a number of mural paintings to L'Esprit Nouveau, his pavilion at the Exposition of Modern Decorative and Industrial Arts in Paris, in 1925. The works that Léger produced for this project closely resembled *Éléments mécaniques* in their architectonic quality, color scheme, and machine references. Trained as an architect himself, Léger shared Le Corbusier's ideas on the interrelationship of architecture, painting, and industrial design, and much of his work from 1923 to 1925 engages these concepts.

Léger's continued fascination with the spectacle of modern architecture and modern living came to a head during his stay in New York from 1940 to 1946. Forced to flee Nazi-occupied Paris, Léger spent these years teaching and also producing more than one hundred paintings. *Masque nègre* (Negro Mask; cat. 8), also known as *The Great Mask*, was painted at this time and thematizes the dynamism of modern life that Léger associated with New York. Impressed by the vertical rush of Manhattan's skyscrapers, the artist described the city as "the greatest spectacle in the world"[2] and as a confrontation "with a power in movement, with a force in reserve without end. An unbelievable vitality . . . . One has the impression that there is too much of everything."[3]

This impression is faithfully captured in *Masque nègre*, where a small, open-mouthed figure stares up at a whirling, riotous mass of color and form that dominates the canvas and evokes the visual cacophony of Times Square. A distorted face looms large in the center of the work, while the right side of the canvas is occupied by stylized upside-down figures from Léger's earlier paintings known as the *Diving* series. These visually disconnected and thematically unrelated images imitate a motley modern landscape of illuminated signs, food stands, kiosks, and advertising billboards. In particular, Léger attributed his novel experimentation with color in the 1940s to his memorable encounter with the bright neon signs on Broadway, "which swept the street": "This color, the color of the spotlight projector, is free; it exists in space. I wanted to do the same thing in my paintings."[4] Consequently, in *Masque nègre* Léger uses broad swathes of primary color outside the confines of form and line, a technique that radically departs from his earlier, more controlled works such as *Éléments mécaniques*. In *Masque nègre* color is used evocatively rather than descriptively; together with the dramatic undulating lines and loose brushwork it generates an expressionistic celebration of modernity.

—**Maria Taroutina**

1. Fernand Léger, "A New Realism: The Object (Its Plastic and Cinematographic Value)," trans. Rosamond Gilder, *Little Review* (New York), Winter 1926, 7.
2. Fernand Léger, quoted in Carolyn Lanchner, *Fernand Léger*, exh. cat. (New York: Museum of Modern Art, 1998), 36.
3. Fernand Léger, quoted in André Warnod, "America Isn't a Country—It's a World," *Architectural Forum*, April 1946, 54.
4. Fernand Léger, quoted in Dora Vallier, "La vie fait l'oeuvre de Fernand Léger," *Cahiers d'arts*, no. 2 (1954): 154. Author's translation.

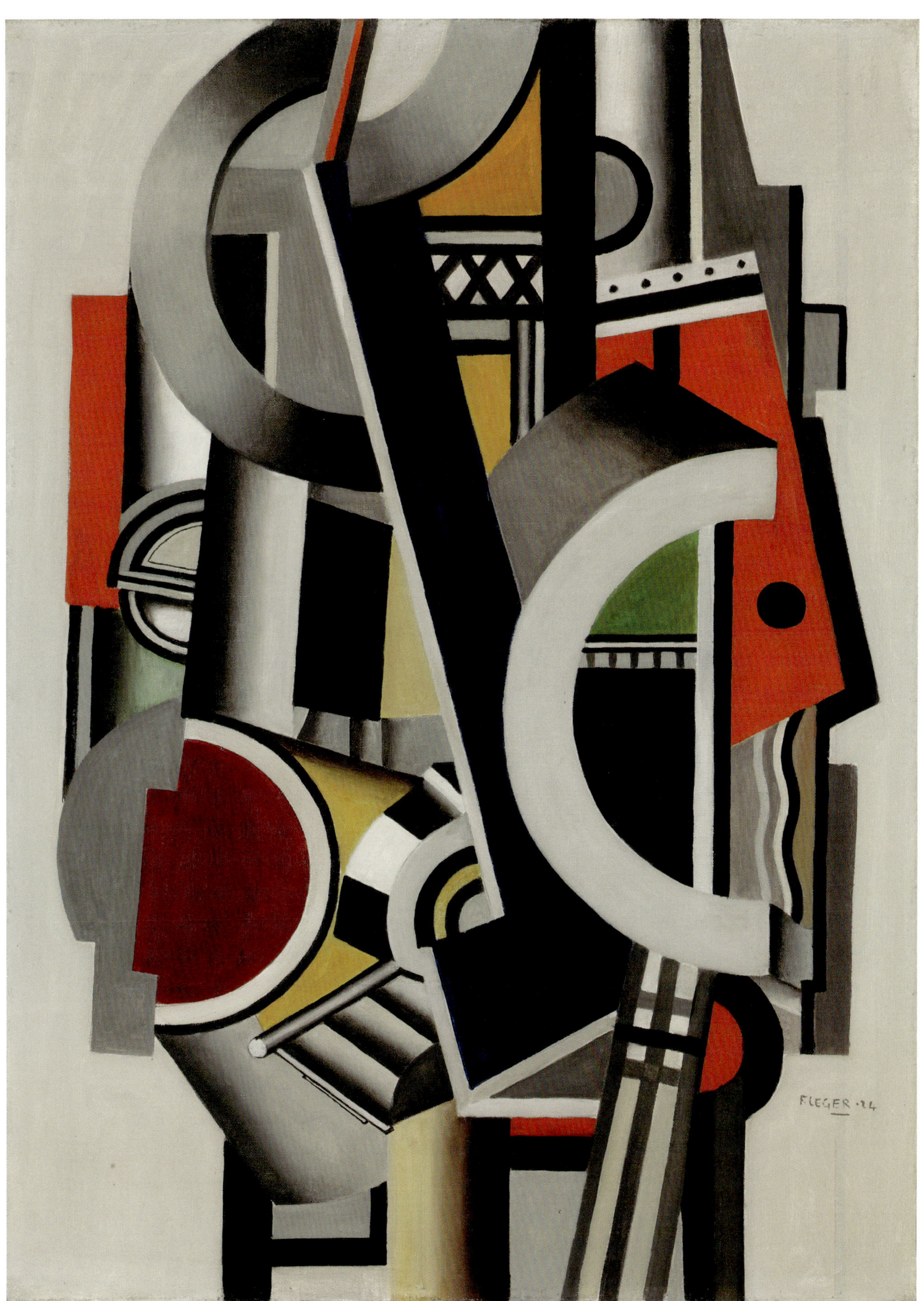

F.LEGER ·24

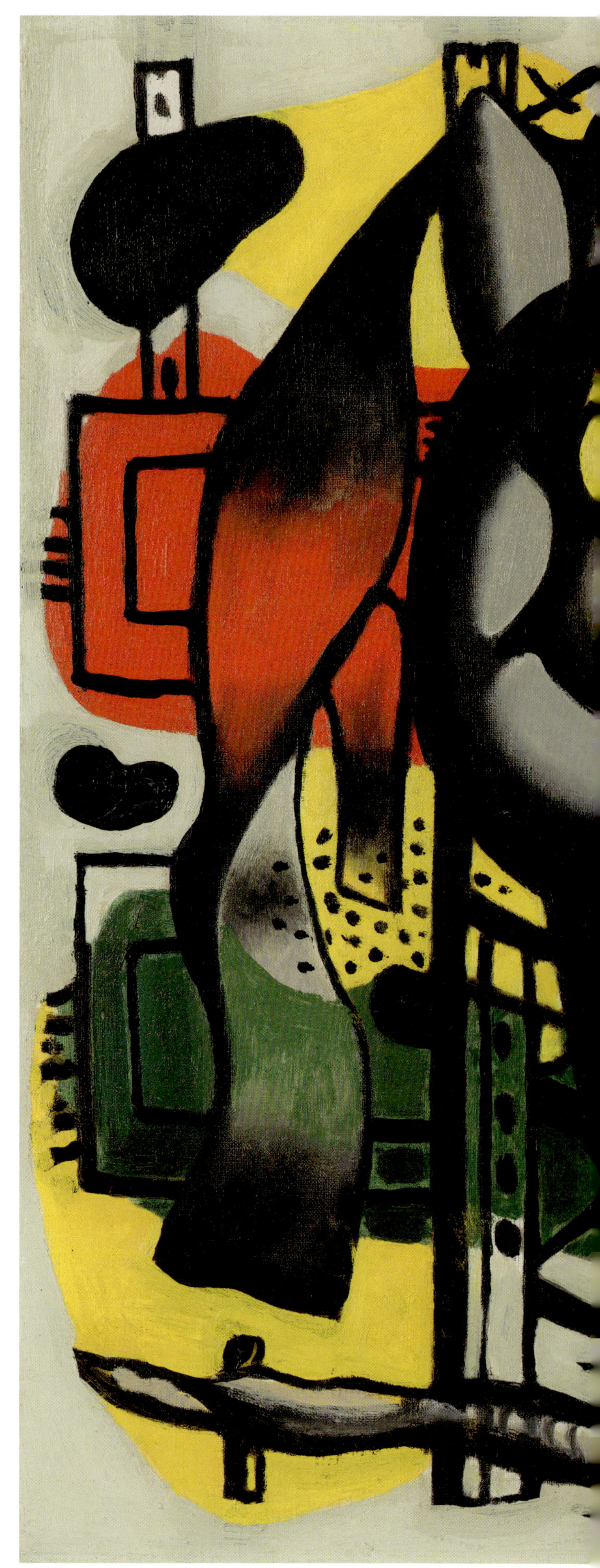

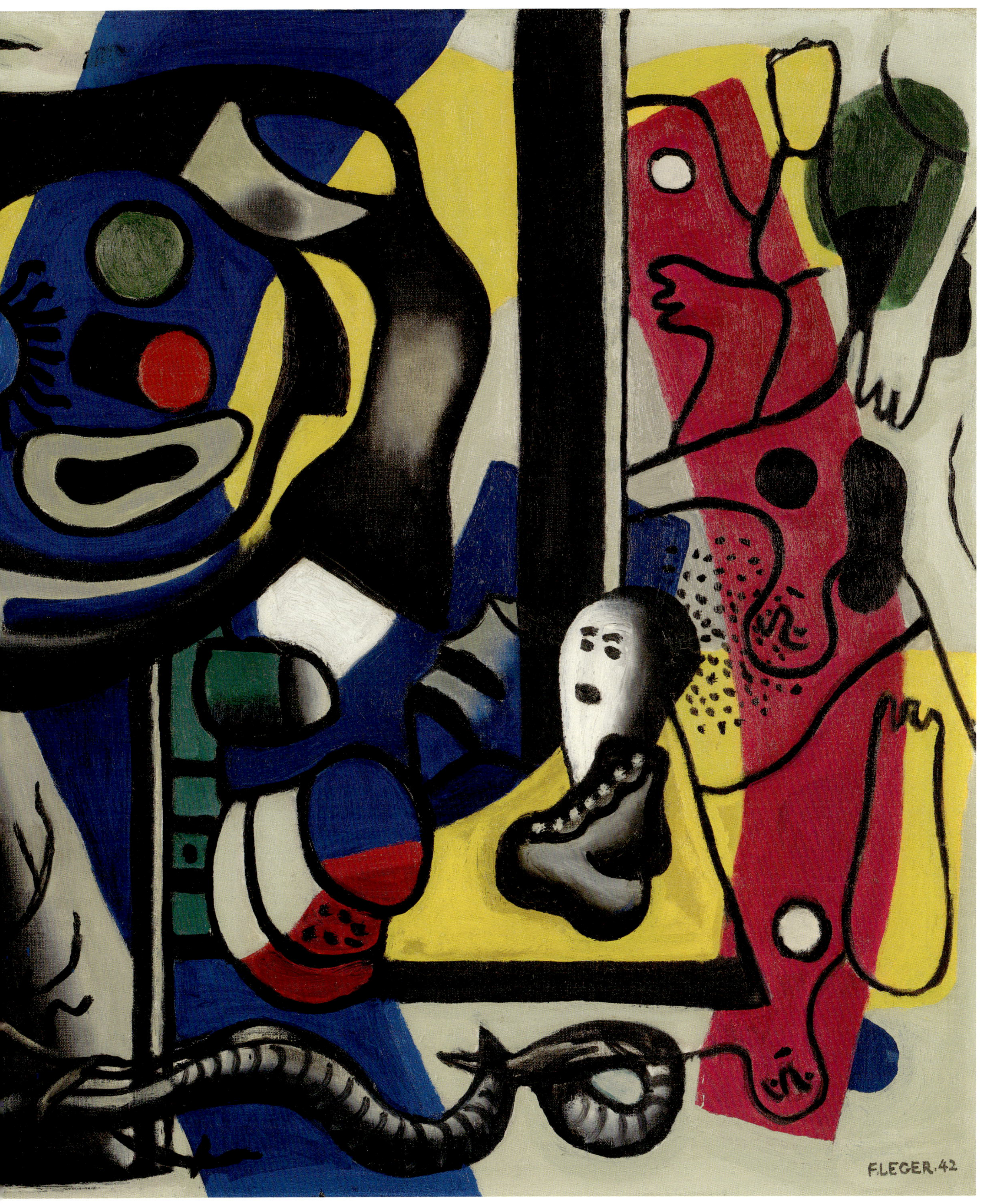

Louis Marcoussis

French, born Poland, 1878–1941

9
Anvers (Antwerp), 1928
Oil on canvas, 58 × 39 in. (147.3 × 99.1 cm)
2006.52.93

Polish-born Louis Marcoussis lived and worked in Paris for most of his life. *Anvers* (Antwerp), painted in 1928, marks a pivotal moment in the artist's career, when Marcoussis increasingly began to synthesize Surrealist aesthetics with his own Cubist style.

Marcoussis met Georges Braque and Pablo Picasso between 1910 and 1912, the crucial years in which they were developing their signature Cubist vocabulary. Marcoussis quickly evolved his own brand of Synthetic Cubism, which combined simplified shapes, patterns, and color planes to represent still-life groupings. He likewise populated his canvases from 1911 to 1919 with elements from Cubism's thematic repertoire such as guitars, pipes, bottles, glasses, and playing cards.

By 1926, however, the mood of Marcoussis's paintings began to change as he increasingly adopted Surrealist motifs such as partly opened doors and windows, as well as looming, ominous shadows. His palette and brushwork also changed from the bright colors and pronounced textures of Synthetic Cubism to Surrealism's more subdued tones and smoother, polished surfaces. At this time Marcoussis was associating with prominent Surrealist writers and thinkers such as André Breton, Tristan Tzara, and Paul Éluard. In the year that he painted *Anvers*, Marcoussis illustrated a volume of Tzara's poems, *Indicateur des chemins de cœur*. This direct engagement with Surrealist theory and practice affected the present painting both in style and subject matter.

In March 1928, Marcoussis traveled to Brussels for his one-man show at the Centaure Gallery. While in Belgium, he visited Antwerp, where he painted *Anvers*, using the French name for that city. A dense configuration of objects, *Anvers* pays homage to the Dutch still-life painting tradition, particularly in its inclusion of a dead hare, which hangs on a nail by its back leg. The composition is dominated by a table covered with a bowl of fruit, a loaf of bread, a knife, and a bustlike sculptural form that casts a black shadow. In his depiction of the horizontal tabletop as a vertical surface, Marcoussis adopted a representational strategy frequently used by Cubist artists, with the result that the objects on top of the table appear parallel to the picture plane. He also used overlapping shapes, colors, and textures in place of those that traditional still-life painters would have employed to create the illusion of reality, such as rational chiaroscuro effects or perspectival recession.

Such Cubist tactics are simultaneously interrupted, however, by other elements in the painting that suggest pictorial illusionism. In fact, Marcoussis's prominent use of shadows—such as those cast by the hare, the bust, the door, and the table—is characteristic of Surrealist artists, for whom shadows could allude to the subconscious realm of dreams and nightmares. The table is placed incongruously in an open doorway, and a staircase leads into a mysterious, dimly lit realm. The Surrealists often cultivated psychological disquietude in their viewers, both by depicting animate figures as frozen or static and by representing inanimate objects as if they were unexpectedly animate, such as the dead hare and the sculptural bust. By combining the divergent visual vocabularies of Surrealism and Cubism, Marcoussis created an innovative and haunting image that challenged clear-cut taxonomies.

—Maria Taroutina

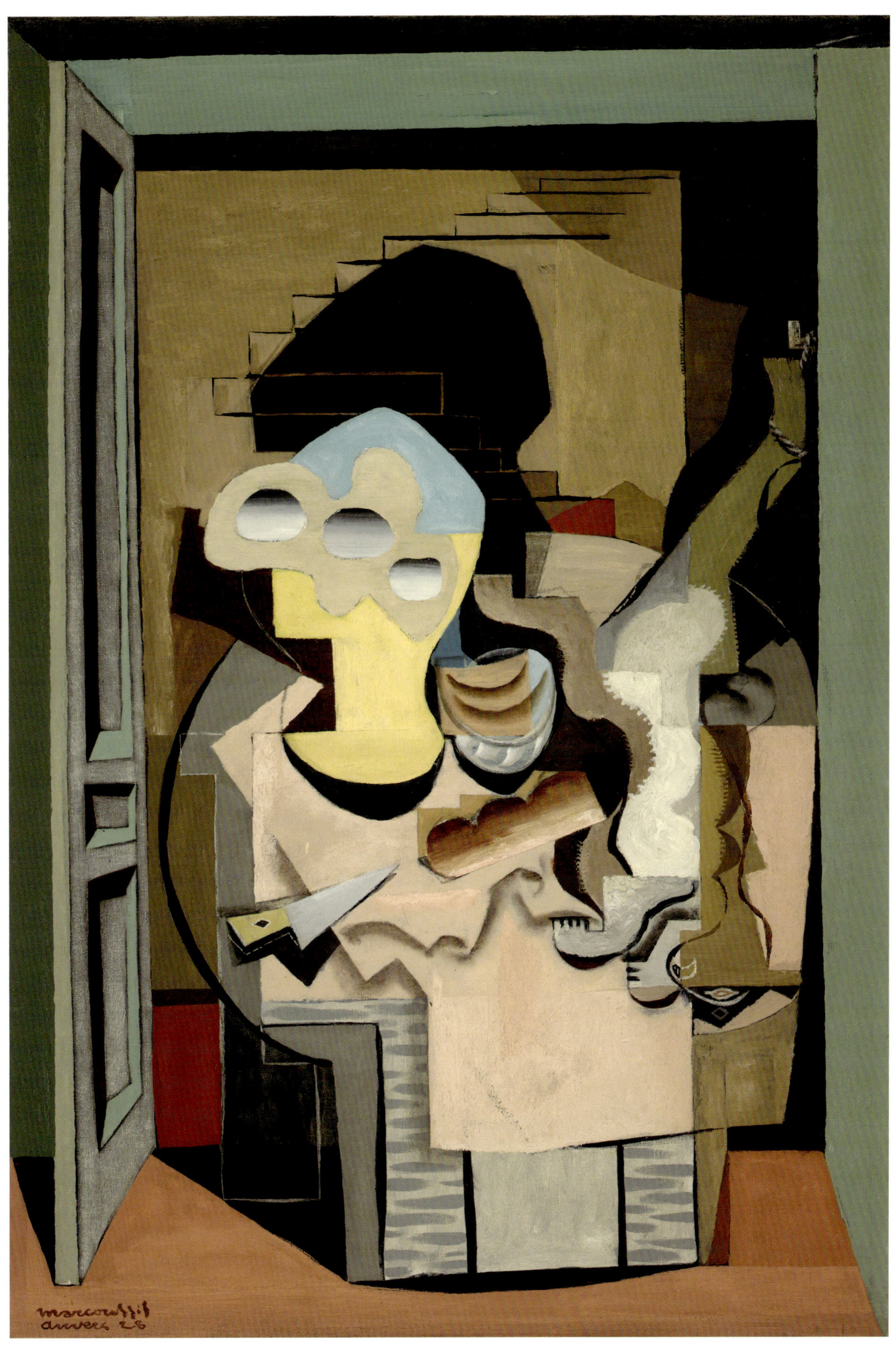

Theodore Roszak

American, 1907–1981

10
Untitled, 1934
Black ink and red colored pencil on lined paper, 10½ × 7¹⁵⁄₁₆ in. (26.6 × 20.1 cm)
2006.52.37.1

11
Untitled, 1934
Black ink on lined paper,
10½ × 7¹⁵⁄₁₆ in. (26.6 × 20.1 cm)
2006.52.37.2

Theodore Roszak's protean artistic accomplishments include painting, sculpture, photography, and lithography. Like many artists of his era, however, Roszak regarded drawing as essential to his practice. After a formative sojourn in Europe (1929–31), which exposed him to the avant-garde movements of Surrealism and Constructivism, Roszak returned to the Depression-stricken United States eager to further the Constructivist principle that a unification of art, architecture, and industrial design would result in utopian order. He attended design and tool-making classes and established a shop in his New York City studio for the fabrication of sculptures from such materials as copper, aluminum, stainless steel, and Plexiglas. Beginning with an exploratory drawing process, Roszak would then execute schematic drawings for those items he wished to translate into three dimensions, noting his desired color, media, and construction technique.[1] Such works, however, occupied a relatively brief period in Roszak's artistic career. In the wake of World War II, he became disillusioned with technology and machines for the roles they had played in tearing society apart, rather than in building it up. Roszak's subsequent works investigated nature in an apocalyptic tone. These expressionistic artworks registered his protest over the lost promises of the 1930s.[2]

Despite this shift, drawing remained central to Roszak's practice, whether as studies for sculpture, complete works in their own right, or simply reflections of his simmering ideas.[3] The two ink and pencil drawings in the Charles B. Benenson Collection may fall into the latter category; unlike Roszak's precise, diagrammatic renderings on graph paper, the drawings on these pages are organic. Roszak referred to the drawing process as innate and automatic, subtly linking himself to the Surrealists who had such a clear influence on his work.[4] For example, a composition at the bottom of the second page (cat. 11), featuring starbursts and expressive organisms, recalls the work of Joan Miró. Free association led Roszak to simultaneously explore various forms and ideas on a single page, a practice that also tapped into his diverse interests including philosophy, astronomy, and mechanics, among others.[5] A stylized ear at the lower right of the first drawing (cat. 10) and a harplike form in the center of the second hint at Roszak's lifelong passion for music.[6]

In his work in all media, Roszak sought to achieve equilibrium in oppositions. These drawings reveal his interest in maintaining such balance between male and female, the logical and the irrational, the organic and the mechanical.[7] The forms in the Miró-influenced sketch at once evoke a nebula and a petri dish. Isolating a single amoebic shape from this sketch, Roszak explores its possibilities up the length of the first sheet of drawings and repositions its dotted lines as vectors in space. Roszak similarly transforms the harp across the middle of the page and develops it into more abstract variations, some pierced with straight and arced antennae that suggest the potential for sound transmission. Constantly in flux, the drawings themselves reflect the organic and mechanical systems that captured Roszak's imagination.

—**Amy Canonico**

---

1. Douglas Dreishpoon, *Theodore Roszak: Constructivist Works, 1931–1947*, exh. cat. (New York: Hirschl and Adler Galleries, 1992), 12; and Joan M. Marter, "Theodore Roszak's Early Constructions: The Machine as Creator of Fantastic and Ideal Forms," *Arts Magazine*, November 1979, 110–13.
2. Dreishpoon, *Theodore Roszak: Constructivist Works*, 16.
3. Joan M. Marter, "Mythic Visions: The Drawings of Theodore Roszak," in *Theodore Roszak: The Drawings*, exh. cat. (New York: Drawing Society, 1992), 10.
4. Theodore Roszak, quoted in Dreishpoon, *Theodore Roszak: Constructivist Works*, 8.
5. Ibid., 11.
6. Douglas Dreishpoon, "Theodore Roszak: Painting into Sculpture," in *Theodore Roszak: Paintings and Drawings from the Thirties*, exh. cat. (New York: Hirschl and Adler Galleries, 1989), 20–23.
7. Dreishpoon, *Theodore Roszak: Constructivist Works*, 14.

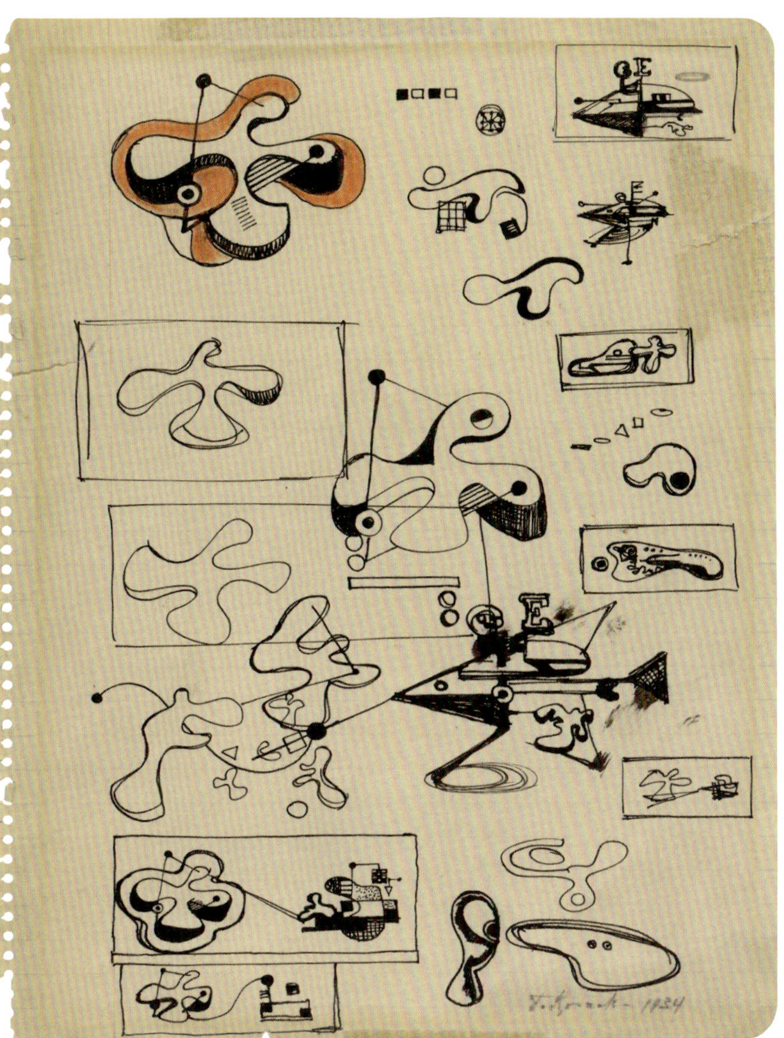

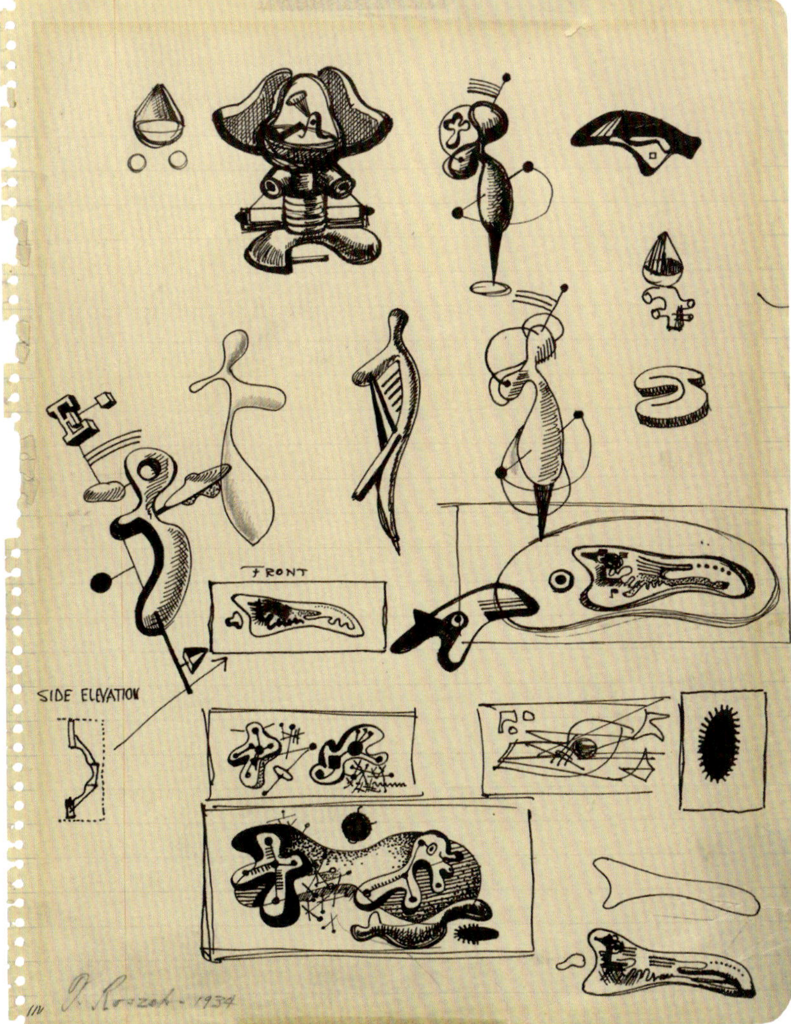
FRONT
SIDE ELEVATION

Kurt Schwitters

German, 1887–1948

12
Untitled (Der Wunsch des Künstlers)
(The Artist's Wish), 1934
Collage on paper, 12¾ × 10¼ in.
(32.4 × 26 cm)
2006.52.5

13
Merzbild mit Regenbogen
(Merz Picture with Rainbow), 1920–39
Mixed media on plywood,
61⅝ × 47¾ × 10½ in. (156.5 × 121.3 × 26.7 cm)
2006.52.4

On January 2, 1937, Kurt Schwitters boarded a ferry from Hamburg to Oslo, never to return to Germany again. Mere weeks after the Nazi party had assumed control of the government, his artistic activities were curtailed and publicly denigrated. Authorities quickly confiscated his work in public collections, including the now lost assemblage *Das Merzbild* (1919), the very work that gave his particular collage aesthetic its name, *Merz*. Shortly after his arrival in Oslo, Schwitters received a final blow: the Gestapo was seeking to implicate him in the resistance activities of friends and relatives who had already been incarcerated. This news left no doubt that he would live in exile as long as the Nazis remained in power.

This narrative of persecution and transience indelibly marks both artworks by Schwitters in the Charles B. Benenson Collection, which dramatically enrich the Yale University Art Gallery's strong commitment to his work in exile.[1] In terms of its material and formal composition, *Untitled (Der Wunsch des Künstlers)* (The Artist's Wish) (1934; cat. 12) is characteristic of many of his *Merz* collages: within a centrifugally organized gridlike structure, we see commercial wrappers, newspaper clippings, and a ticket to the cinema, which tempt us to read the image as a diaristic record of the artist's life in a world governed by consumption and waste. Schwitters's collages from the 1920s deliberately resisted such interpretation, for his ambition had been to transfigure the debris of everyday life into pure color, line, and plane. As he prepared for exile, however,

he no longer attempted to subsume his autobiography under the goal of disinterested abstraction. Rather, references to the artist's self in the early years of the Third Reich explicitly comment on the vulnerability of his carefully cultivated network of international collaborators, which had been so vital to his practice and efforts to emigrate. A large mailing label declaring the artist's name is sutured together with another, one rotated by 180 degrees and addressed in Schwitters's own hand to Hans Freudenthal, a friend whose help he sought that year as he contemplated fleeing Germany for the Netherlands.[2] This pair, in turn, overlays fragments from a printed sheet whose black spots have been misaligned. Schwitters often excerpted such printer's errors for his *i-Drawings*, a series of works that presented the (unintentional) compositions of others as readymade images; indeed, this same sheet was the source for one of these "drawings" from 1928. As one of only seven known collages from 1934, this work demonstrates how Schwitters abandoned a Romantic conception of creative mastery in favor of a subjectivity that is less secure and more contingent.[3] Whereas with his early work in collage Schwitters attempted a virtuosic display of the artist's exclusive command over material, here we are poignantly reminded that the constitution of the work and the security of his selfhood are only "the artist's wish," and subject to the generosity of others for fulfillment.

Merzbild mit Regenbogen (Merz Picture with Rainbow) (1920–39; cat. 13) is far more ambitious in its interrogation of readymade material and self-citation, and as such, it not only counts among Schwitters's most monumental assemblages but also stands as a defining work for his late period. In 1938, he wrote to the artist Sophie Taeuber-Arp, responding to a rare request for reproductions of his work for a new journal she had founded in Paris: "My most important Merz works since 1919 arrived here 8 days ago, rescued. I am working through them all and will let [my son] Ernst photograph them. I will send you a selection of prints of them later for *Plastique*."[4] *Merzbild mit Regenbogen* was among this cache of early work

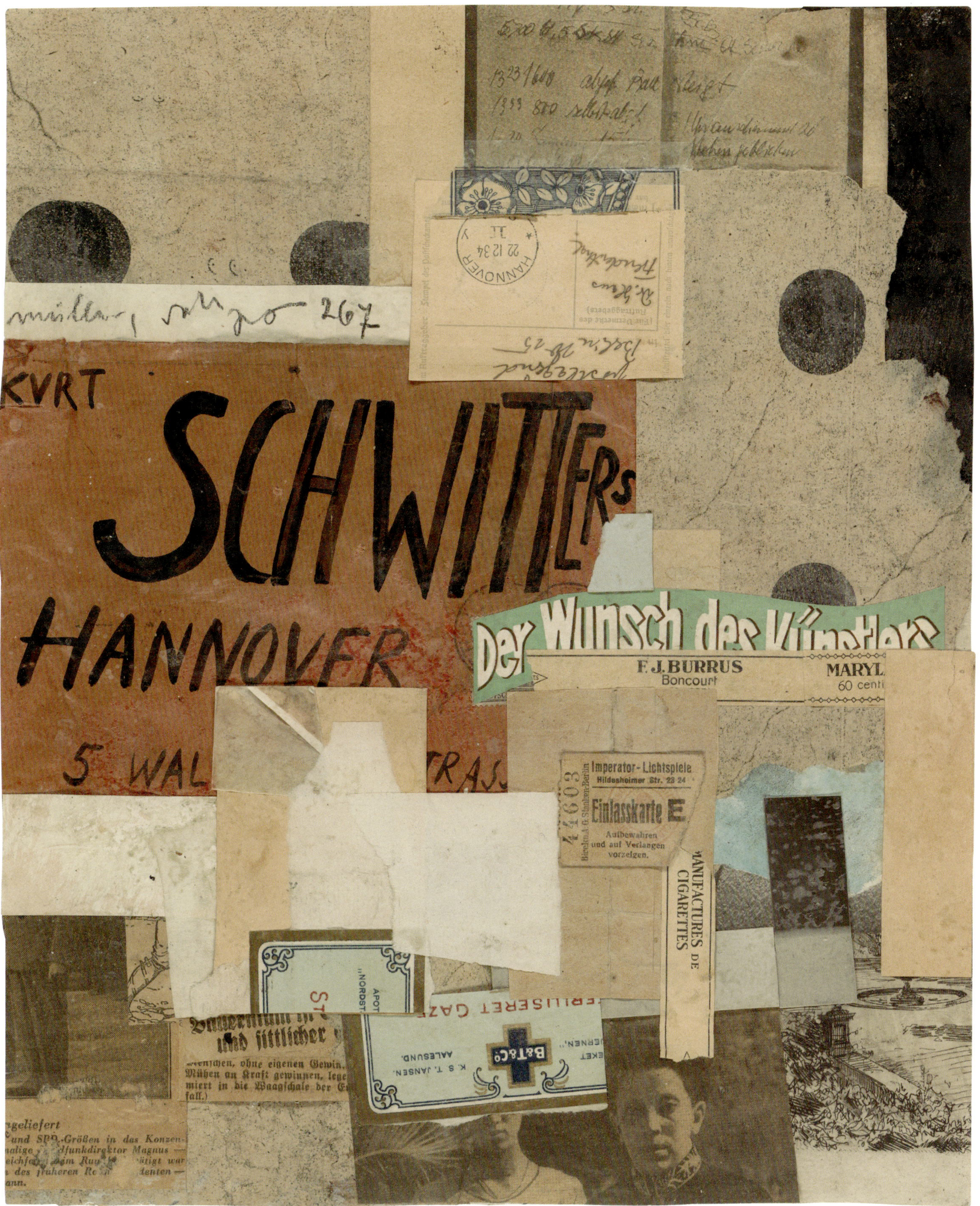

that his wife shipped to him in exile, and that initiated an unusual campaign of revising past works from the perspective of his current isolation and rootlessness.[5]

With this assemblage, Schwitters courts a deliberate confusion between real and painted shadows, causing our attention to oscillate restlessly between the illusion of space created by the arrangement of painted forms and the real world.[6] This play between physical contour and painted edge, between real and depicted depth, unites disparate elements into a composition just as it simultaneously alienates them from one another, suggesting the fundamental insecurity of such a unified composition. Similarly, the artificiality of the painted rainbow color spectrum removes it from the cloudy and muted tones of the background and instead unites it with the fragment of a wooden crate that it buttresses, despite the obvious disparity between the applied and the "found" color of these two elements. Raw, unpainted chips of wood might masquerade as patches of color, but they can never be identical to them. In some areas they appear to float over the painted forms and, elsewhere, to stack against them, depending on whether Schwitters wished to reinforce or violate the internal edges of the composition. Here, too, cast and painted shadows interrupt and overlay one another, in a meditation on the representational connection and spatial disparity between two- and three-dimensional forms.

As he reworked this assemblage, Schwitters was busy reconstructing his ambitious *Merzbau*, a sculptural installation in his Hanover studio that had dominated his practice in the 1930s, thereby duplicating from scratch in Norway what had taken several years to develop in Germany. A hallmark of his response to exile, therefore, was a retrospective meditation on his early career, treating it as if it were the work of another and critically engaging with it as he once had with the efforts of his peers or the anonymous producers of mass culture. Moreover, in the face of his tenuous situation in Norway, *Merzbild mit Regenbogen* extends his research into our perception of space.

This meant rejecting the centered compositions of his first great assemblages of 1919 and 1920 in favor of an artistic practice that privileges dispersal over formal stability and hierarchy.

—**Megan R. Luke**

---

1. The Gallery's collection of work by Schwitters was established by Katherine S. Dreier, the artist's most important patron. For more on Schwitters's relationship to Dreier, see Gwendolen Webster, "Kurt Schwitters and Katherine Dreier," *German Life and Letters* 52, no. 4 (1999): 443–56. While the three assemblages and sculptures by Schwitters that Dreier entrusted to the Gallery date from the 1920s and his involvement with De Stijl abstraction, of the twelve collages she gave, five originate from the artist's years in exile. The Benenson gifts join these works and a collage donated by Richard Brown Baker to establish the most important collection in the United States of Schwitters's art from this period.
2. See letters from Schwitters to Freudenthal and his wife, October 4 and 21, 1934, reprinted in *Kurt Schwitters Almanach* 9 (1990): 19, 21.
3. When Schwitters produced this collage, his priority was no longer autonomous pictorial composition but rather his *Merzbau*, transforming his studio into an immersive and participatory sculptural environment. In 1934, he began to extend this project into other rooms of his home.
4. Letter to Sophie Taeuber-Arp, May 10, 1938, reprinted in Kurt Schwitters, *Wir spielen, bis uns der Tod abholt: Briefe aus fünf Jahrzehnten*, ed. Ernst Nündel (Frankfurt am Main: Ullstein, 1974), 145.
5. The only other European artist known to respond to exile by critically reworking earlier paintings in this way was Piet Mondrian. See Harry Cooper, "Looking into the Transatlantic Paintings," in *Mondrian: The Transatlantic Paintings*, ed. Cooper and Ron Spronk (New Haven, Conn.: Yale University Press, 2001), 28–32, 45, and 65n.71.
6. This dynamic brings this work uncannily close to another major painting in the collection of the Yale University Art Gallery, *Tu m'* (1918) by Marcel Duchamp, from the Société Anonyme Collection. Despite both men's close ties to Katherine Dreier and Schwitters's work for the Société Anonyme in Germany, it is unclear if the two artists ever met, though evidence does suggest that Duchamp accompanied Dreier on a visit to Schwitters's studio in 1929. See a letter to Schwitters from Ella Bergmann-Michel, October 27, 1947, reprinted in *Kurt Schwitters Almanach* 7 (1988): 68.

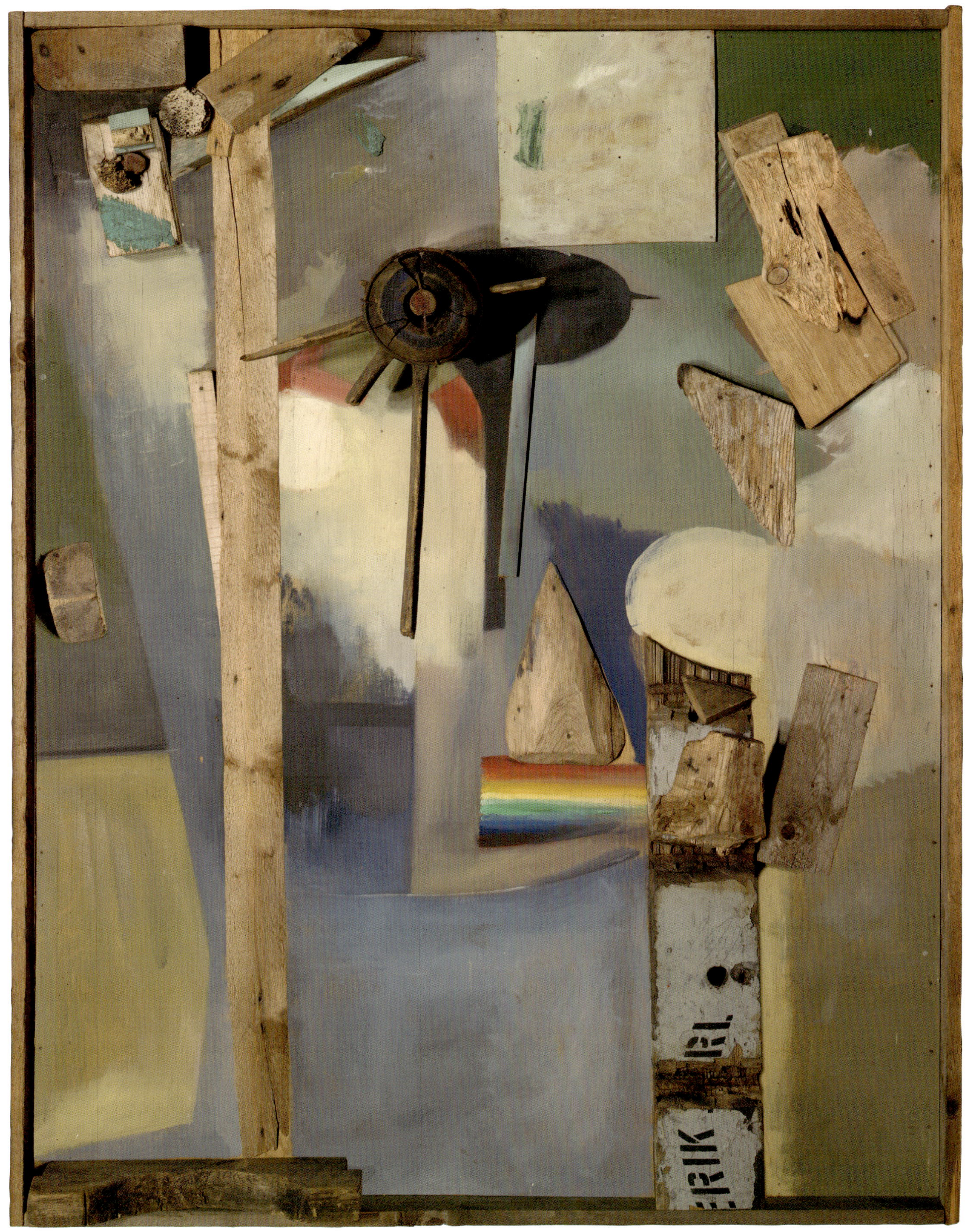

ERIK

Paul Delvaux

Belgian, 1897–1994

14
The Forest, 1935
Oil on canvas, 59 × 79 in. (149.9 × 200.7 cm)
2006.52.12

Typical of Paul Delvaux's 1930s work, *The Forest* depicts four partially dressed women in a dark wood. Although two of the women are nearly life-size, they remain strangely distant, inhabiting a surreal, dreamlike space. For Delvaux, "woman" was a rhetorical figure, symbolizing the carnal and irrational, in opposition to the masculine world of reason. This latter world was increasingly witnessing a systematic breakdown as Europe gradually fell prey to the inexorable rise of Fascism and Nazism. Consequently, whether standing or reclining, in natural or urban landscapes, alone or in the company of men, Delvaux's haunting, inanimate women heralded an impending catastrophe.

In *The Forest* the figures wear long, conservative dresses, but these are stripped down to the waist to reveal bare shoulders and round, heavy breasts. This erotic unveiling undermines their static monumentality, producing an uncanny division between the concealed, rigid lower bodies and the naked, gesturing upper torsos. Although their wide eyes stare out at the viewer, they are empty and expressionless. Resembling somnambulists or automatons more than flesh-and-blood beings, the women stand outside of time and lived reality.

Despite the illusionistic rendition of *The Forest*, the woodland setting likewise remains peculiarly otherworldly. The stylized, uniform trees and lurid green lighting generate an elusive, claustrophobic atmosphere. Although it portrays an outdoor scene, *The Forest* invokes an interior or psychic space.

Delvaux attributed his interest in automatons, the uncanny, and the irrational to two formative experiences: his encounters in Brussels with Pierre Spitzner's Grand Musée Anatomique et Ethnologique in 1932 and with Surrealism in 1934. Exhibited at fairgrounds throughout Europe, Spitzner's collection contained a disturbing mixture of real and invented objects such as human and animal skeletons, medical curiosities, and wax anatomical models. In particular, Delvaux cited the figure of a "sleeping Venus" as something that had "completely changed [his] conception of painting" with its eerie, mechanized simulation of human life.[1]

Delvaux found himself similarly affected by the Surrealist works of Giorgio de Chirico, Max Ernst, Salvador Dalí, René Magritte, and Joan Miró at the *Minotaure* exhibition held in Brussels's Palais des Beaux-Arts in 1934. A dark, forbidding woodland interior was often evoked by the Surrealists as an allegory of the human unconscious; to them, both the woods and the unconscious mind could be obscure and unchartable spaces. Painted only a year after Delvaux's first encounter with Surrealism, *The Forest* clearly manifests a debt to the movement.

Yet despite his participation in the *International Exhibition of Surrealism* in Paris in 1938 and Mexico in 1940, Delvaux never formally joined the movement or accepted its political tenets. It was the visual poetics rather than the ideological positions of the Surrealists that proved central to Delvaux's artistic practice. These poetics were effectively captured in Paul Éluard's 1936 Surrealist poem, "Exile," which the author dedicated to Delvaux. Indeed, one passage describes enigmatic women like those in *The Forest*:

> *Diminishing the sky*
> *Tall women motionless . . .*
> *Neither empty they are nor sterile*
> *But lacking boldness*
> *And their breasts bathing their mirror*
> *Naked eye in the glade of expectation*[2]

—Maria Taroutina

1. "Interview de Renilde Hammacher avec Paul Delvaux," in *Paul Delvaux*, by Renilde Hammacher-Van den Brande and Liesbeth Brande-Corstius, exh. cat. (Rotterdam: Museum Boijmans Van Beuningen, 1973), 13–14. *The Sleeping Venus* was a life-size wax figure of a sleeping woman whose chest was made to heave by means of an unseen motor in an imitation of breathing. Delvaux produced a number of paintings inspired by the Spitzner display, including *Sleeping Venus* (Tate Collection, 1944).
2. Both the original French and this English translation of Paul Éluard's "Exile" can be found in *Paul Delvaux*, conceived by Jean Saucet, text by Antoine Terrasse, trans. Eleanor Levieux (Chicago: J. P. O'Hara, 1973), 17.

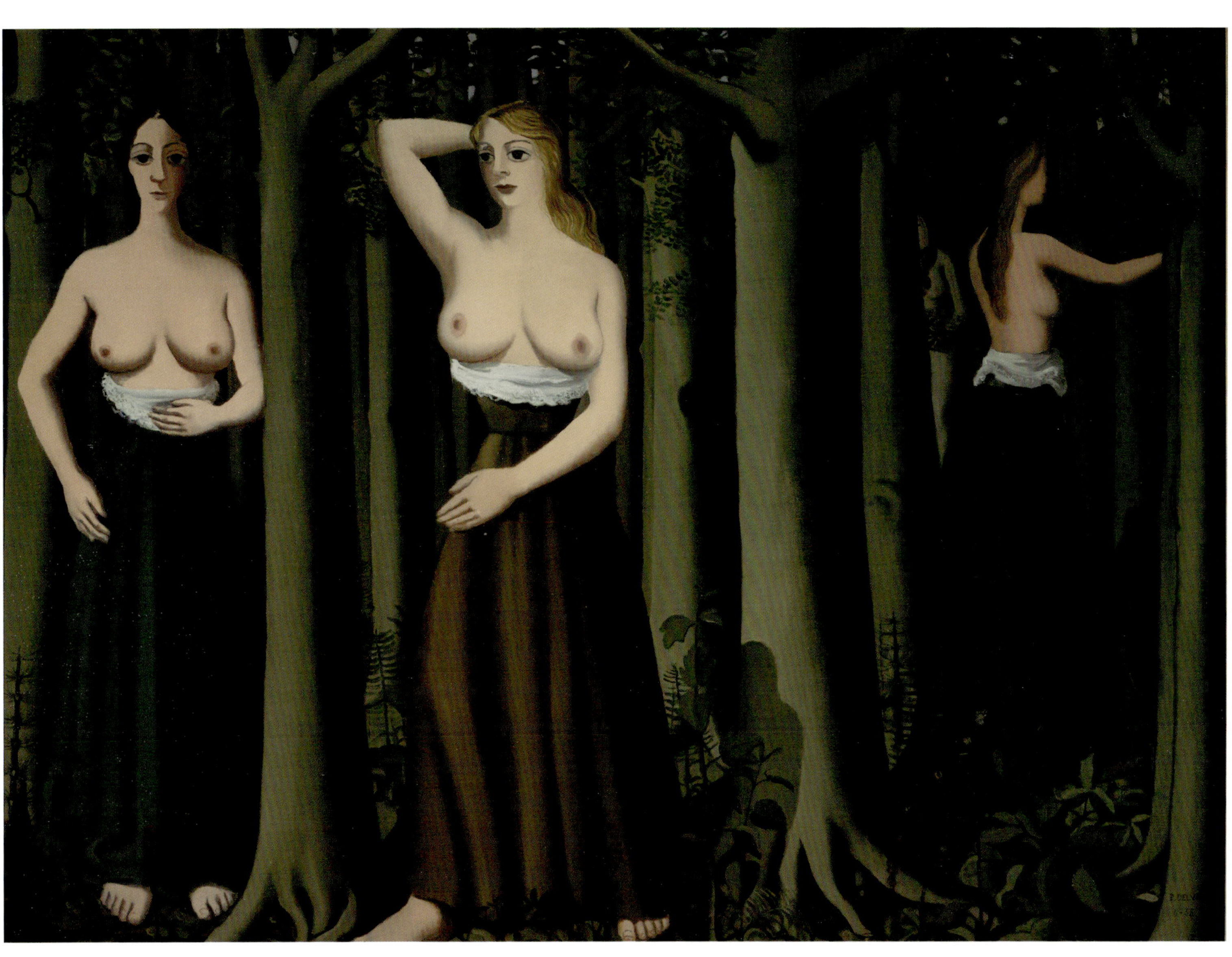

Pablo Picasso

Spanish, active in France, 1881–1973

15
***Femme assise* (Seated Woman), 1936**
Oil on canvas, 28¾ × 23½ in. (73 × 59.7 cm)
2006.52.22

Femme assise (Seated Woman) combines Picasso's two chief obsessions in the mid-1930s: his re-engagement with the art of his lifelong rival, Henri Matisse, and his passionate love affair with Marie-Thérèse Walter. The painting depicts a woman in a floral hat seated next to a sunlit window. The facial features are unmistakably Walter's, whose distinctive chin, large, almond-shaped eyes, Roman nose, and shoulder-length hair appear repeatedly in Picasso's paintings from the 1930s. The cleft face, simultaneously representing a frontal and a profile view, was a motif that Picasso had first developed in the mid-1920s and that came to characterize his portraits of Walter. Unlike Picasso's other images of his young mistress, the present work approaches the caricatural and grotesque, rather than the lyrical and romantic. The garish colors, bulbous body, disjointed eyes, and splitting head topped by a flowered hat register as a mockery.

It is unlikely that Picasso intended to deride the mother of his newborn child, whom he had so lovingly depicted in preceding weeks. Rather, the painting belongs to a series of works that directly attempt to work through formal strategies employed by Matisse. In the summer of 1931, Picasso visited the largest Matisse retrospective to date at the Galeries Georges Petit in Paris. The show brought together three decades of Matisse's work, positioning the artist as a monumental figure in twentieth-century art. Picasso was deeply impressed and unsettled by the exhibition and immediately canceled his own long-awaited American retrospective at the Museum of Modern Art, New York, originally projected for fall 1931. The explanation to the museum's director, Alfred H. Barr, Jr., was that he first needed to bring his current work to "its culmination."[1] Works from the ensuing five years strongly exhibit the influence of Matisse. *Femme assise* in particular recalls Matisse's 1905 Fauvist painting *Femme au chapeau* (Woman with a Hat; fig. 1). Picasso's heightened hues, especially the acidic green of Walter's face and hand, replicate those of Matisse's work. The awkward floral hat, the positioning of the arm across the chest, and even the minute detail of a green outline around the nose are all reproduced in Picasso's painting. In *Portrait of Madame Matisse: The Green Line*, Matisse had also separated his wife's face into two symmetrical halves with a prominent yellow-green line that ran vertically from her forehead to her chin (fig. 2). Although in the 1930s Picasso increasingly employed Matisse's artistic idioms such as bright colors, intense patterning, and sweeping arabesques, the qualities borrowed from Matisse in *Femme assise* remain superficial and seem to satirically comment on the other artist's work. In the end Picasso refers to Matisse's subject matter and palette only to reassert his own formal devices in a painting that could never be mistaken for the work of his French contemporary.

—**Maria Taroutina**

---

1. Pablo Picasso, quoted in Michael C. FitzGerald, *Making Modernism: Picasso and the Creation of the Market for Twentieth-Century Art* (New York: Farrar, Straus, and Giroux, 1995), 213.

Fig. 1.
Henri Matisse, *Femme au chapeau* (Woman with a Hat), 1905. Oil on canvas, 31¾ × 23½ in. (80.7 cm × 59.7 cm). San Francisco Museum of Modern Art, Bequest of Elise S. Haas

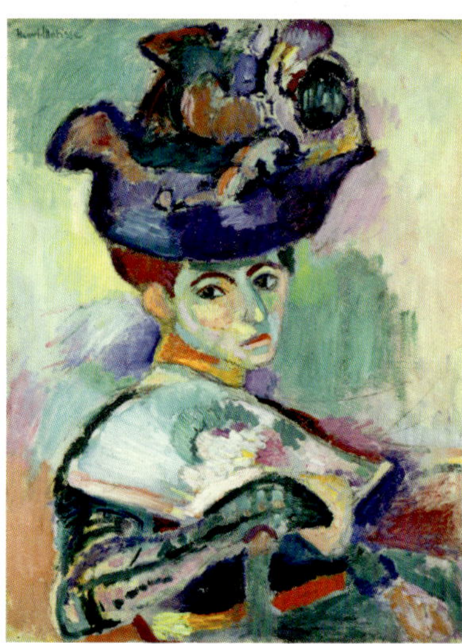

Fig. 2.
Henri Matisse, *Portrait of Madame Matisse: The Green Line*, 1905. Oil on canvas, 15¹⁵⁄₁₆ × 12¹³⁄₁₆ in. (40.5 × 32.5 cm). National Gallery of Denmark, Copenhagen

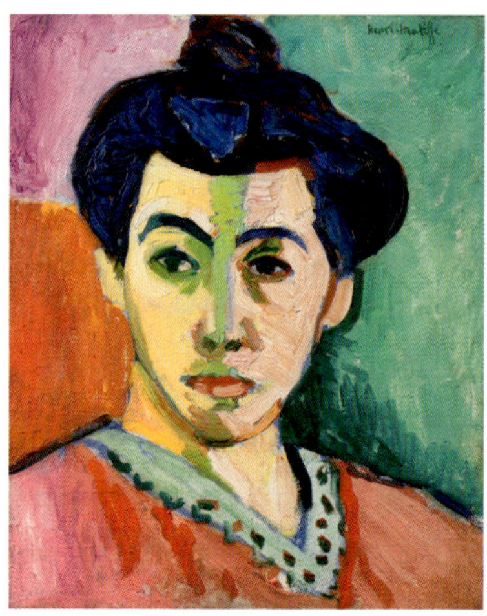

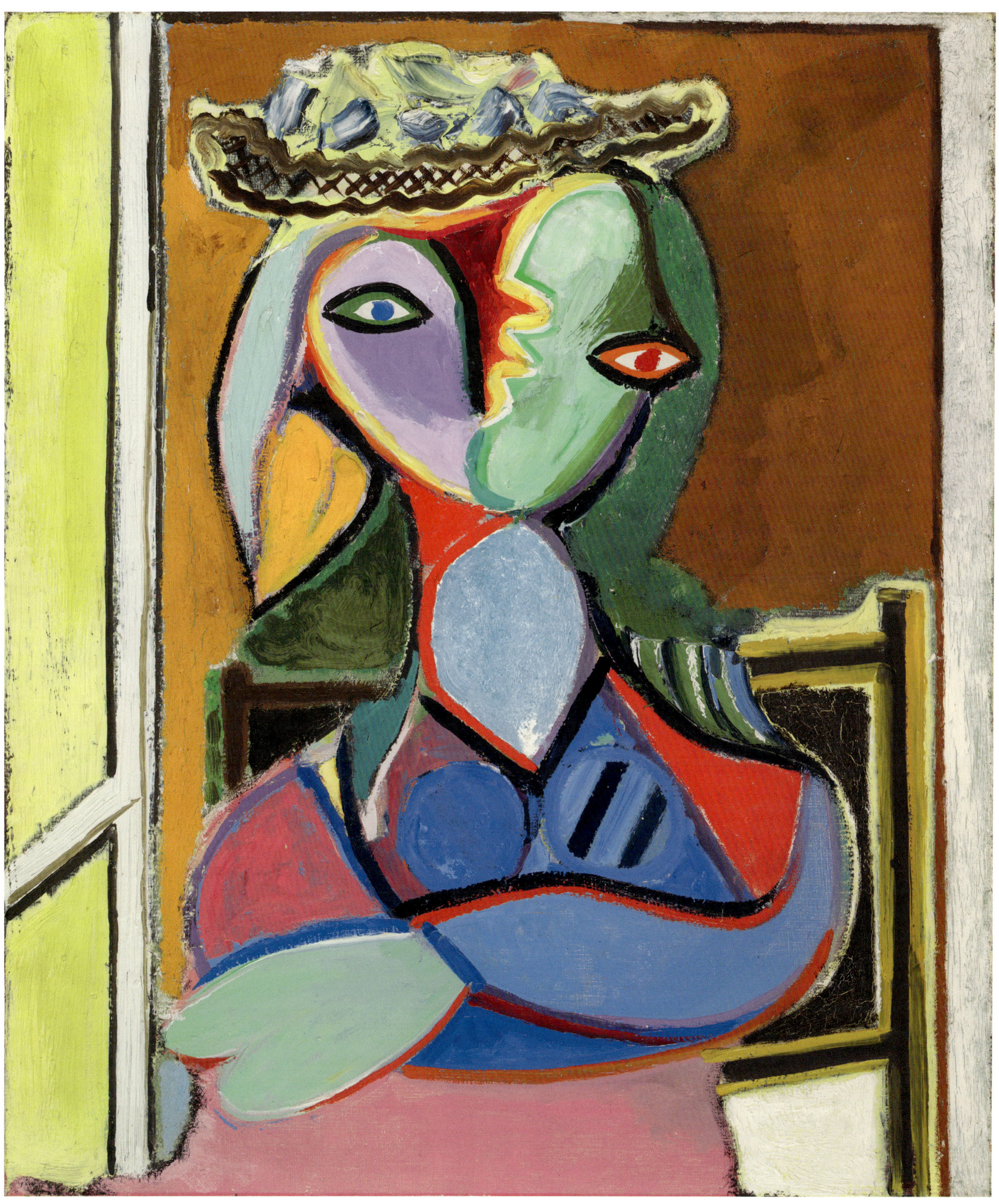

15

Pablo Picasso

Spanish, active in France, 1881–1973

16
***Chevalier, page et moine* (Horseman, Page, and Monk), 1951**
Gesso and oil on panel, 17 × 21¾ in. (43.2 × 55.2 cm)
2006.52.21

17
***Le peintre dans son atelier* (The Painter in His Studio), 1963**
Oil on canvas, 23⅜ × 35⅞ in. (59.4 × 91.1 cm)
2006.52.23

Chevalier, page et moine (Horseman, Page, and Monk) and *Le peintre dans son atelier* (The Painter in His Studio) exemplify a central concern in Picasso's 1950s and 1960s work: his increasing engagement with the past and with the history of art. Unlike the more somber works of the 1930s and 1940s, these paintings remain light in mood despite treating serious themes. Their tongue-in-cheek playfulness speaks to the relative stability of Picasso's personal and professional life after a long period of turmoil and uncertainty.

Chevalier, page et moine (cat. 16) is one of numerous 1951 works on the subject of medieval jousting. Prompted by the outbreak of the Korean War in the summer of 1950, Picasso ridiculed the pageantry of combat. In 1959 Picasso told a group of friends how he saw war, describing it as "medieval children playing nasty, medieval games."[1] In contrast to his 1937 tragic masterpiece, *Guernica* (Museo Reina Sofía, Madrid), the present painting is a satire, not an outraged critique. It depicts an armored knight marching toward the arena, attended by a monk and a page boy. Unlike Picasso's robust cavaliers of preceding months, the knight in *Chevalier, page et moine* has a dainty wasp waist and a tiny head that make him look vain and impotent, rather than virile and heroic. Picasso's juxtaposition of the horse's exaggerated, cartoonish grin with the serious expressions of the two attendants further amplifies the humor. Bravura and machismo are comically inverted to parody the historical parade of masculinity. Produced the same day as the larger oil painting *Jeux de pages* (Game of Page Boys) (Musée Picasso, Paris), the present work

was likely a preparatory study. In the bigger version, Picasso added a second page boy and made the knight's armor even more theatrical. The artist repeated the same iconography and formal arrangement in at least five other works, in media ranging from lithography to ceramics. It is therefore not surprising that *Chevalier, page et moine* formally recalls a lithograph both in its treatment of line and in its black-and-white palette. Here, as in much of his work from this period, Picasso blurred the boundaries between different media.

The artist's fascination with the art and cultures of the past was just a part of Picasso's growing preoccupation with his own place in art history. His 1963 studio paintings actively thematize these concerns. In just three months, Picasso executed thirty drawings and fifty paintings that took "the artist" as their subject. In most of these the painter, seated on the left, paints a reclining model or a plaster cast placed opposite him, on the right. In *Le peintre dans son atelier* (The Painter in His Studio; cat 17), however, the model is entirely eliminated, producing a direct confrontation between the artist and his art, emphasized by the energetic eruption of marks at the point where his brush touches the canvas. While in other versions the artist is bearded, bespectacled, and sporting a head of curly hair, here he is shown clean-shaven, balding, and with Picasso's characteristic profile, suggesting that this work is less about the general condition of artistic creation and more about Picasso's personal legacy. Picasso produced two nearly identical versions of *Le peintre dans son atelier*, both rendered in the expressive, gestural strokes and vivid colors typical of his late style. Two minor variations differentiate them: here a lamp hanging above the artist is transformed into a window, and an indistinct mass of red paint in the background is changed into a giant hand, resembling a boxer's glove. The hand is a central component in the painting's complex triangulation between the artist, the easel, and the outside world. Almost larger than the artist's head, the hand is depicted as the real locus of artistic production, symbolizing the instinctual and innate, rather than

intellectual, source of creativity. The oversized hand implies that one must be born a genius like Picasso; it is impossible to become one through training.

—**Maria Taroutina**

1. As recounted by Picasso's biographer John Richardson in "How Political Was Picasso?," *New York Review of Books*, November 25, 2010, 27-30.

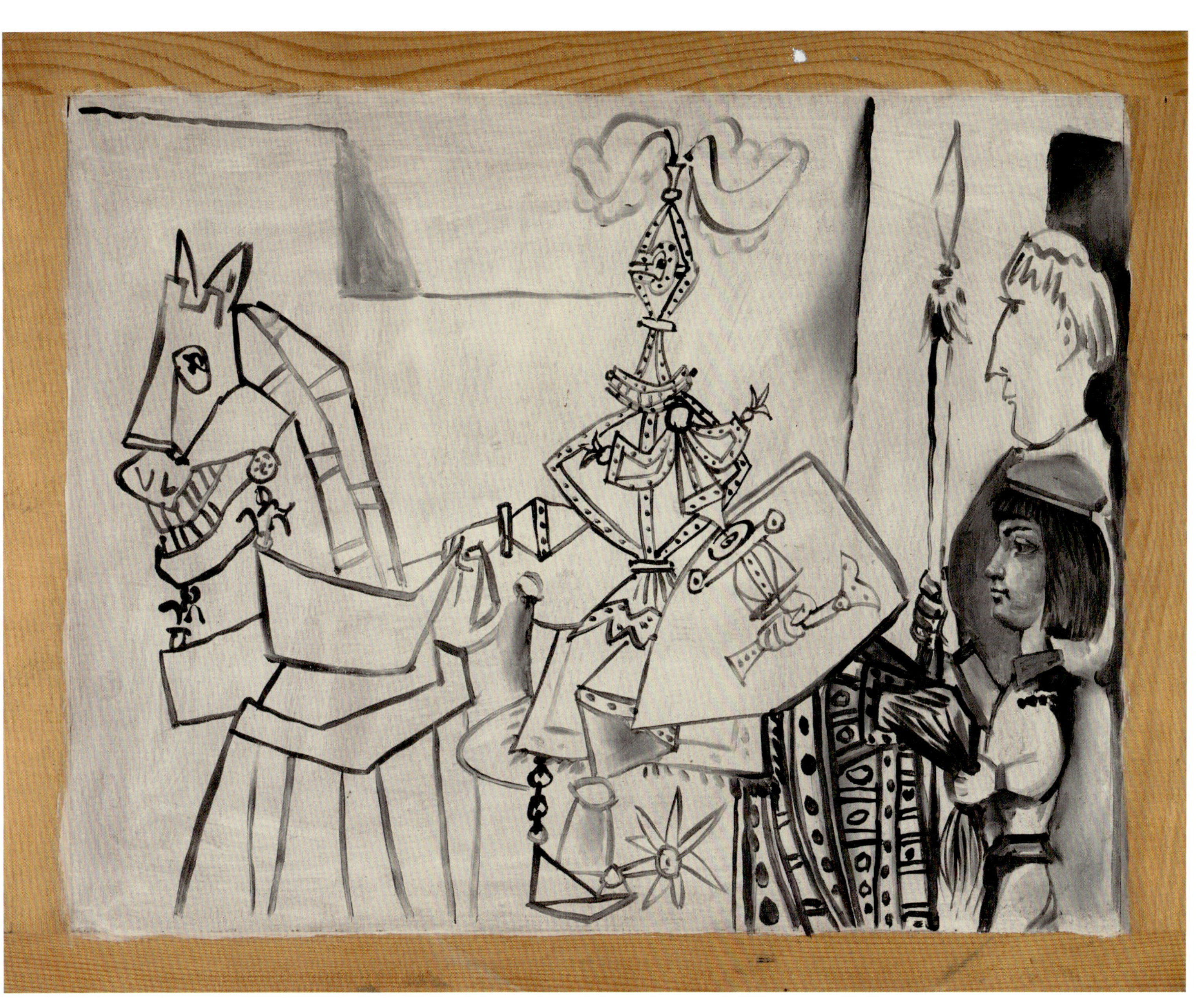

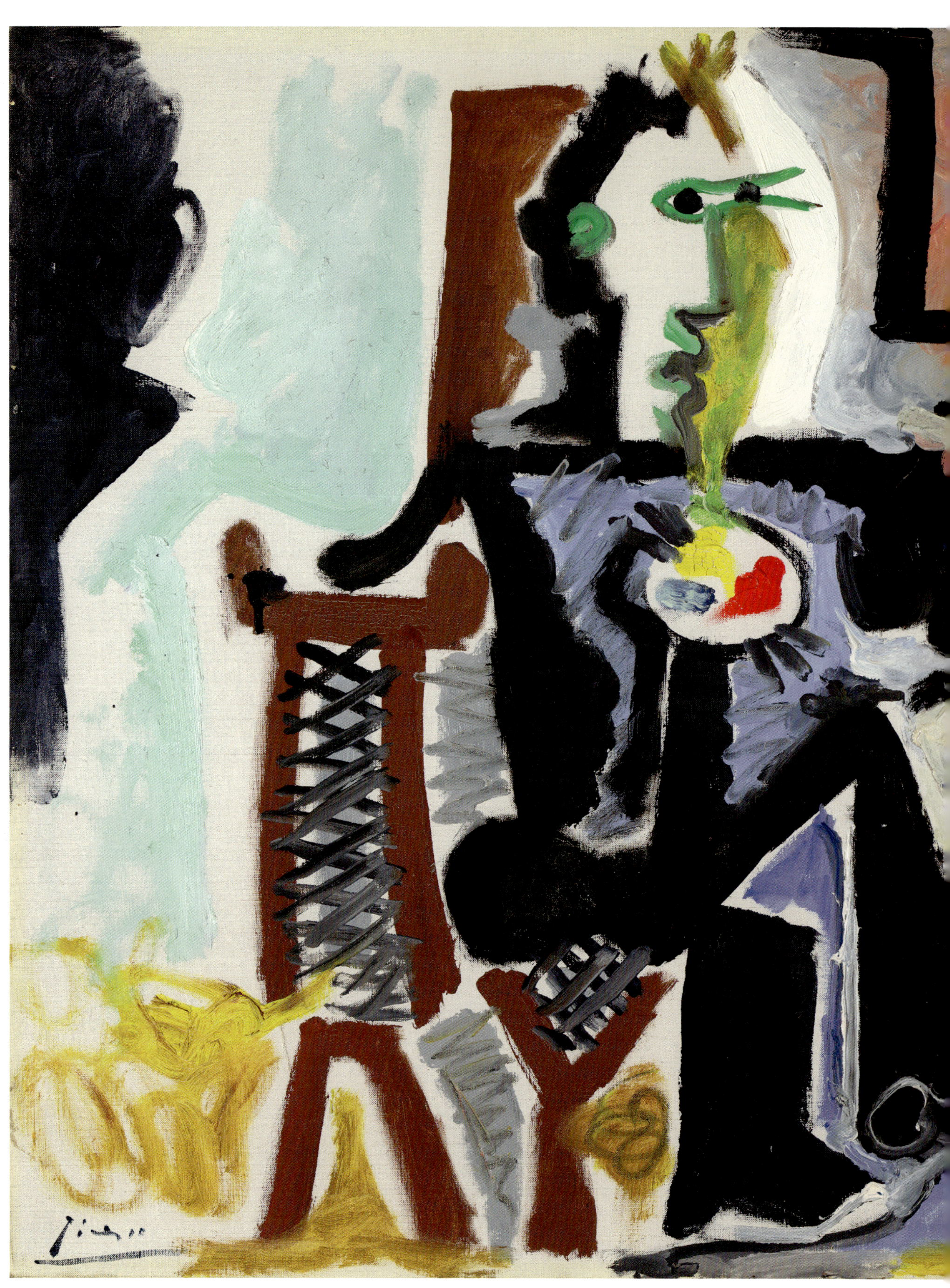

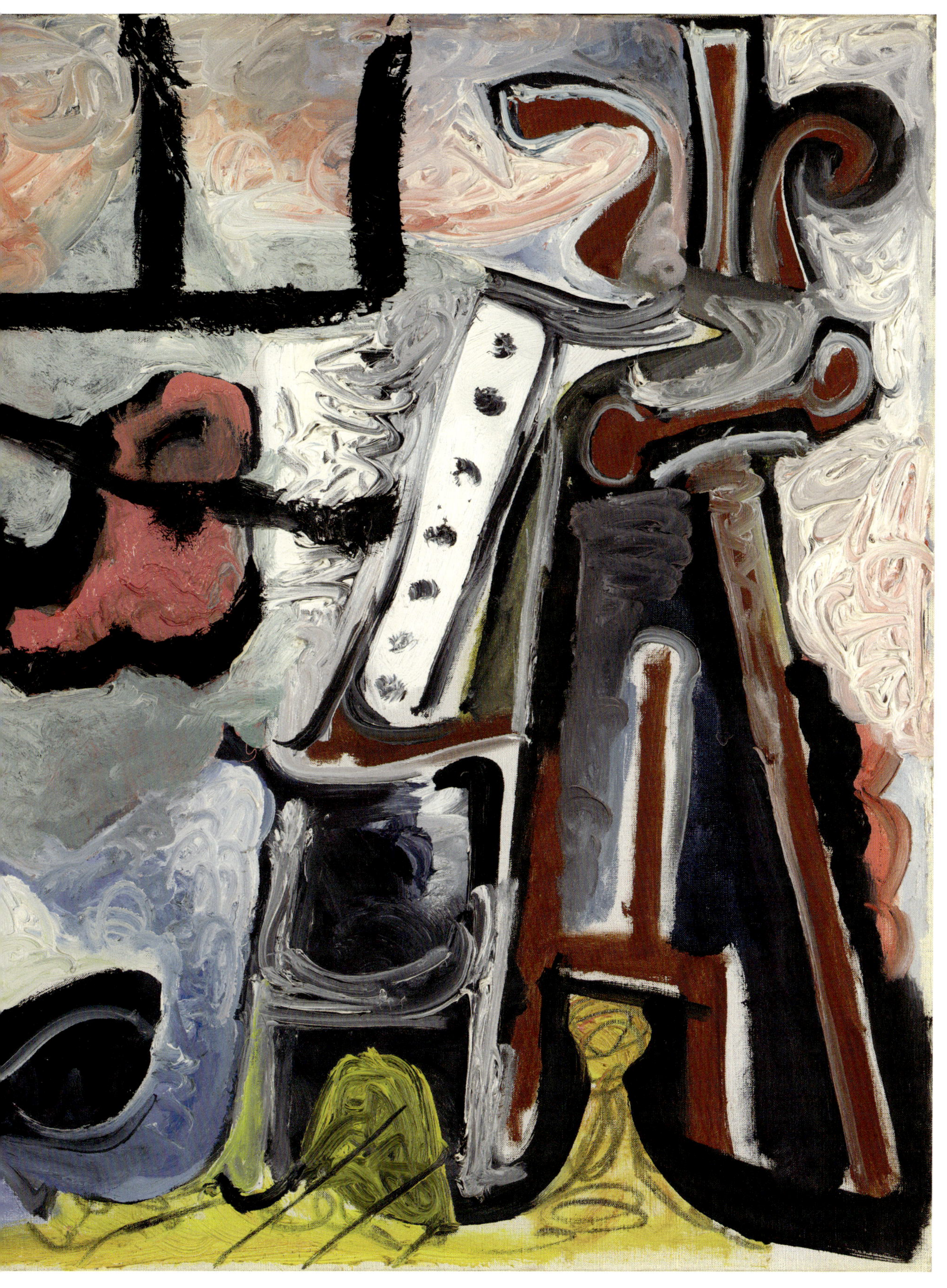

Stuart Davis

American, 1892–1964

18
Lesson One, 1956
Oil on canvas, 52 × 60⅛ in. (132.1 × 152.7 cm)
2006.52.2

Stuart Davis believed that artists must begin with reality—what he called "the dynamic American scene"—and the sensory experiences of urban contemporary culture played an essential role in his development as an artist. His list of the "things which have made me want to paint" included "fast travel by train, auto, and aeroplane which brought new and multiple perspectives; electric signs; . . . movies and radio; Earl Hines hot piano and Negro jazz music in general." More surprising, "the landscape and boats of Gloucester," Massachusetts, also made his list.[1] The New York–based Davis spent nineteen summers in Gloucester, and the crisp angles of the coastal town's topography, architecture, and schooners struck him as inherently abstract. On the left side of *Lesson One*, flat areas of red, green, black, and white allude to trees, buildings, anchored boats, a mast, water, and sky. These landscape elements first appeared in an undated line drawing that Davis translated into colored shapes in a 1955 gouache that he then projected onto this canvas in early March 1956.[2] By late October he had obliterated the right side of his earlier composition.[3] Only the tip of a cloud above the vertical slice of a building and the bow of a boat suggest what lies behind a black rectangle marked with a monumental white *X*, and overlaid with "Speed" in red script.[4]

The *X* looms like the eye-catching lettering on a commercial sign that suddenly blocks our view of the Gloucester scenery, as though it were glimpsed through the window of a racing car. The inscription of "Speed" asserts that a painting in the fast-moving United States must respond to new ways of seeing by creating the instantaneous impact of a billboard. *Lesson One*'s binary design also finds echoes in the bipartite structure of jazz, notably in pianist Earl Hines's legendary left-hand technique, used to break up stride rhythms without ever losing the beat. For

Davis, Hines represented "the achievement of an abstract art of real order."[5]

Davis incorporated enigmatic letters and words into his art to experiment with spatial relationships and to achieve graphic impact, but he also used them to amplify his theoretical ideas. An *X* appears frequently in his notebooks as a shorthand reference to the "external relations" that inspired him, in contrast to the intensely personal "subjective feelings" that motivated the younger Abstract Expressionists who then dominated the New York art scene.[6] While working on *Lesson One*, Davis had made a sketch of the composition with the rectangle on the right filled not with an *X* but rather with diagonal ovals evoking the drips characteristic of action painting. He reasoned: "The acceptance of 'Speed' as a proper category of contemporary Subject must not be naively interpreted in a Naturalistic way as 'Drip' or identified as an equation Speed of Brush equals Idea of Speed."[7] In *Lesson One*, it was not the artist's brush that moved swiftly across the canvas during the creative process, but rather the viewer's eye that jumped rhythmically across the cadenced shapes. Davis's painstaking manipulation of flattened space, hard-edged line, clean color, charged words, and idiosyncratic symbols offered a persuasive alternative to the spontaneity of action painting.

—**Robin Jaffee Frank**

1. Stuart Davis, "The Cube Root," *Art News*, February 1943, 33–34.
2. Ani Boyajian and Mark Rutkoski, *Stuart Davis: A Catalogue Raisonné*, 3 vols. (New Haven, Conn.: Yale University Art Gallery and Yale University Press, 2007). Cat. nos. 722, *Study for "Natural Scene"* (private collection); 1299, *Natural Scene* (unlocated); and 1693, *Lesson One*.
3. Stuart Davis's calendar entries, October 26 and 28, 1956, Estate of Stuart Davis Archives, collection of Earl Davis.
4. The word has been plausibly interpreted as "Speech"; yet Davis identifies it as "Speed" in calendar entries on June 17, October 10, and October 28, 1956. See Lewis Kachur, "Stuart Davis's Word-Pictures," in *Stuart Davis: American Painter*, ed. Lowery Stokes Sims, exh. cat. (New York: Metropolitan Museum of Art, 1991), 107.
5. Letter from Stuart Davis to John Hammond, March 12, 1940, Estate of Stuart Davis Archives, collection of Earl Davis.
6. On external relations, see Kachur, "Stuart Davis's Word-Pictures," 106–107; and Sims, catalogue entries in *Stuart Davis: American Painter*, 246, 284. The quote on "subjective feelings" is taken from Stuart Davis, "The Place of Painting in Contemporary Culture: The Easel Is a Cool Spot at an Arena of Hot Events," *Art News*, Summer 1957, 30.
7. Stuart Davis, art theory text dated June 14, 1956, 3, Estate of Stuart Davis Archives, collection of Earl Davis.

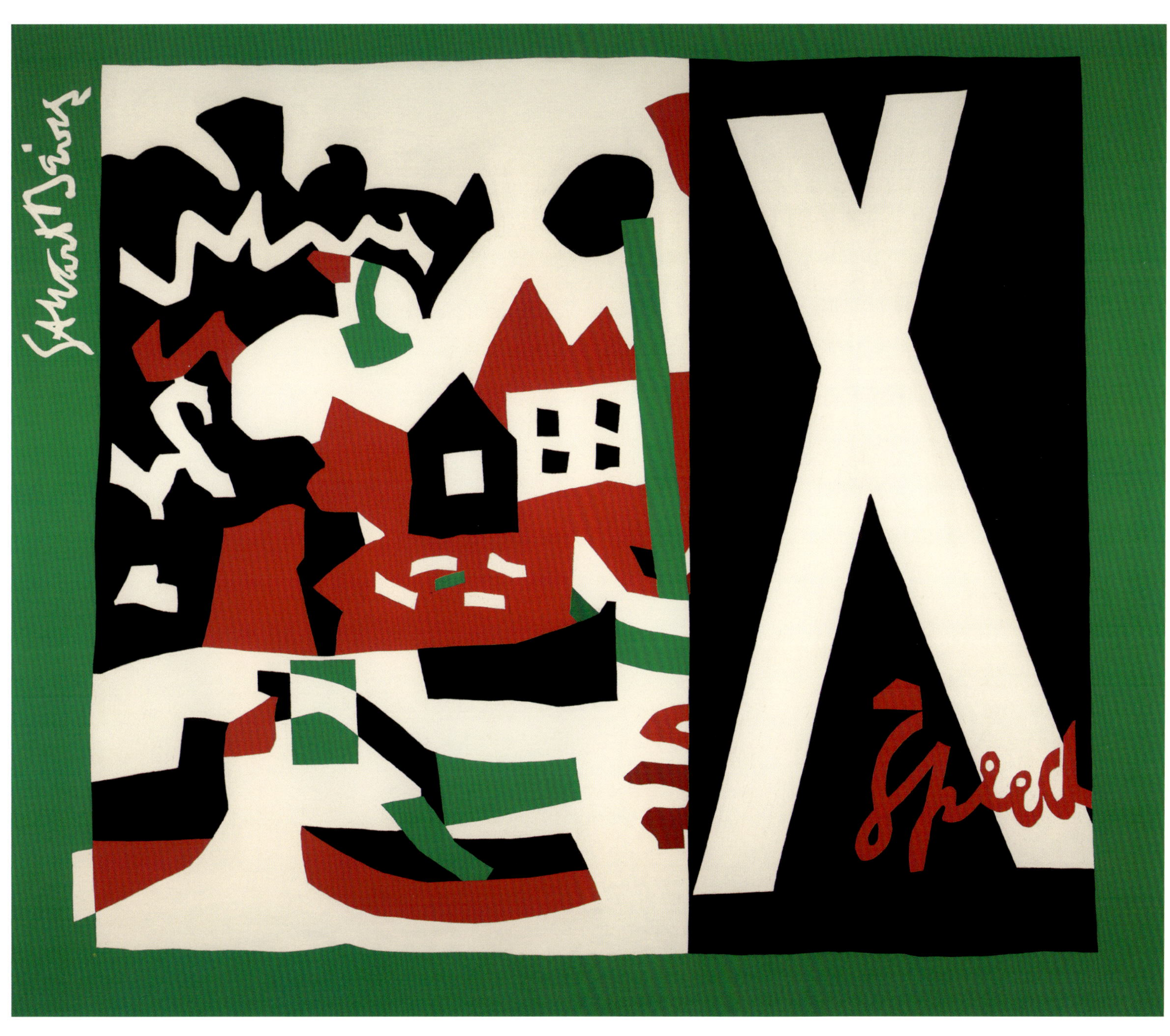
Speed

Stuart Davis

American, 1892–1964

19
Combination Concrete #2, 1956–58
Oil on canvas, 71 × 53 in. (180.3 × 134.6 cm)
2006.52.1

Throughout the 1950s, Stuart Davis appropriated his own past art to make formally innovative new art, paralleling the way jazz musicians turned old songs into improvisational variations that embodied the ebullience of the era. Davis's *Combination Concrete #2* riffs on a landscape that he painted more than thirty years earlier in Gloucester, Massachusetts.[1] *Curve Go Slow* (fig. 1) incorporates cautionary road signs, "CURVE" and "GO SLOW." By mixing words and images, Davis embraced the exchanges between poetry and painting in the Parisian avant-garde. He proclaimed, "As [Guillaume] Apollinaire's poetry encroaches on painting, let painting encroach on poetry. . . . The hint of 'JOURNAL' in cubism should be carried on."[2] But Davis's art also wedded the experimentation of European Modernism to the vernacular American scene; "[E]verywhere you look," he explained, "you see words."[3] In *Curve Go Slow,* he melded his personal interpretation of Cubism with his experience of navigating Gloucester's rocky terrain and his memories of mapping topography as an army cartographer during World War I: white dashes on blue indicate waterways; yellow stippling on green suggests land; and a Y-shape in the upper left represents a tree.

Thirty-four years later, Davis translated the landscape into a larger black-and-white design (fig. 2). He repeated "CURVE" and "GO SLOW" and overlaid this armature with lines forming shapes, squiggles, letters, and numbers. At left, "1922" acknowledges the date of his landscape source, while the words "NEW" and "DRAWING" affirm this drawing's status as an autonomous work of art and its linear structure—on which he would continue to build—to be his true subject. On the same day that he drew the "elegant word DRAWING" on this canvas, he declared his belief that "[t]he new is a Recovery not a discovery,"[4] similar to the musical themes and improvisations of jazz.

On November 15, 1956, Davis "projected" this scaffold onto a bigger canvas and then translated the lines into the edges of colored shapes.[5] He used a hot palette of orange, red, blue, black, and white that interacts in unexpected ways with the armature. The recurring colors penetrate the planes and vibrate spatially, creating a syncopated rhythm that makes the sounds of jazz visible. This brilliant variation on his earlier compositions voices a new relationship between color and line, surface and depth. Satisfied with *Combination Concrete #2,* Davis converted a rectangle that appears in the lower left of the black-and-white version into an exclamation mark, and eventually completed the work on October 12, 1958.

This lively interaction of letters, words, punctuation, spaces, and shapes on a canvas finds echoes in the visual manipulation of text on a page in avant-garde poetry, including the radical writings of Davis's close friend Bob Brown.[6] In 1956, while Davis was formulating his dynamic composition, an international exhibition of concrete poetry was held in São Paulo, where Brown had moved sixteen years earlier. Significantly for Davis's title choice of *Combination Concrete,* the essence of a concrete poem lies in its appearance, for the typographical arrangement of words and letters, and sometimes that of symbols and images, form an abstract structure akin to painting.

—**Robin Jaffee Frank**

1. On this large family of works, see Lowery Stokes Sims, *Stuart Davis: American Painter,* exh. cat. (New York: Metropolitan Museum of Art, 1991), 157, 159, 297–300; Diane Kelder, *Stuart Davis: Art and Theory,* exh. cat. (New York: Pierpont Morgan Library, 2002), 20–21; and Ani Boyajian and Mark Rutkoski, *Stuart Davis: A Catalogue Raisonné,* 3 vols. (New Haven, Conn.: Yale University Art Gallery and Yale University Press, 2007); cat. nos. 1309–10, 1476, 1698, 1700–1704, and 1721.
2. Stuart Davis's journal entry, March 12, 1921; quoted in John R. Lane, *Stuart Davis: Art and Art Theory* (New York: Brooklyn Museum, 1978), 96.
3. "The All-American," *Time,* March 15, 1954, 84.
4. Stuart Davis, calendar entry, June 30, 1956, Estate of Stuart Davis Archives, collection of Earl Davis. Stuart Davis, notebook entry, June 30, 1956, Stuart Davis Papers, Fogg Art Museum, Harvard University Art Museums, Cambridge, Mass.
5. Stuart Davis, calendar entry, November 15, 1956, Estate of Stuart Davis Archives, collection of Earl Davis.
6. On the profound impact of their friendship, see Lewis Kachur, "Stuart Davis and Bob Brown: *The Masses* to *The Paris Bit,*" *Arts Magazine,* October 1982, 70–73.

Fig. 1.
Stuart Davis, *Curve Go Slow,* 1922. Oil on artist's board, 15¼ × 11½ in. (38.7 × 29.2 cm). Yale University Art Gallery, Gift of Mr. and Mrs. Gifford Phillips, UGRD 1942, by exchange, 2004.115.1

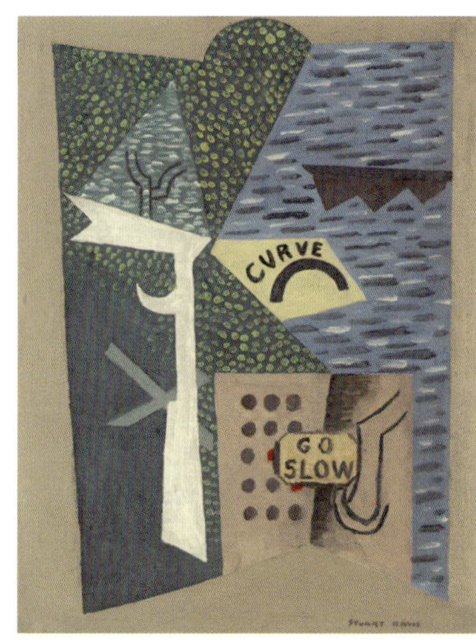

Fig. 2.
Stuart Davis, *Combination Concrete # 2* (*Black and White Version*), 1956. Casein on canvas, 60 × 45 in. (152.4 × 114.3 cm). Yale University Art Gallery, Gift of Mr. and Mrs. Gifford Phillips, UGRD 1942, by exchange, 2004.115.2

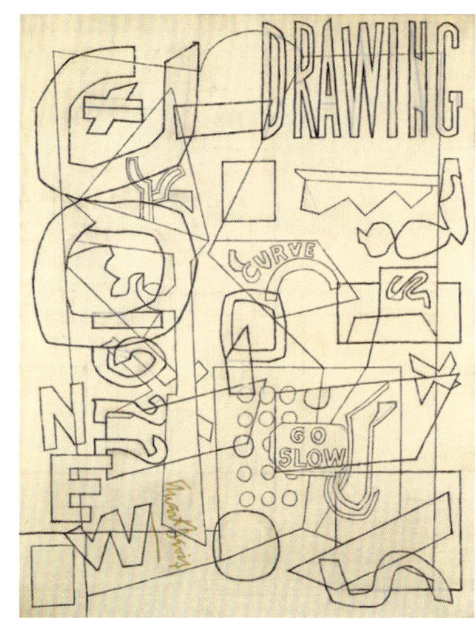

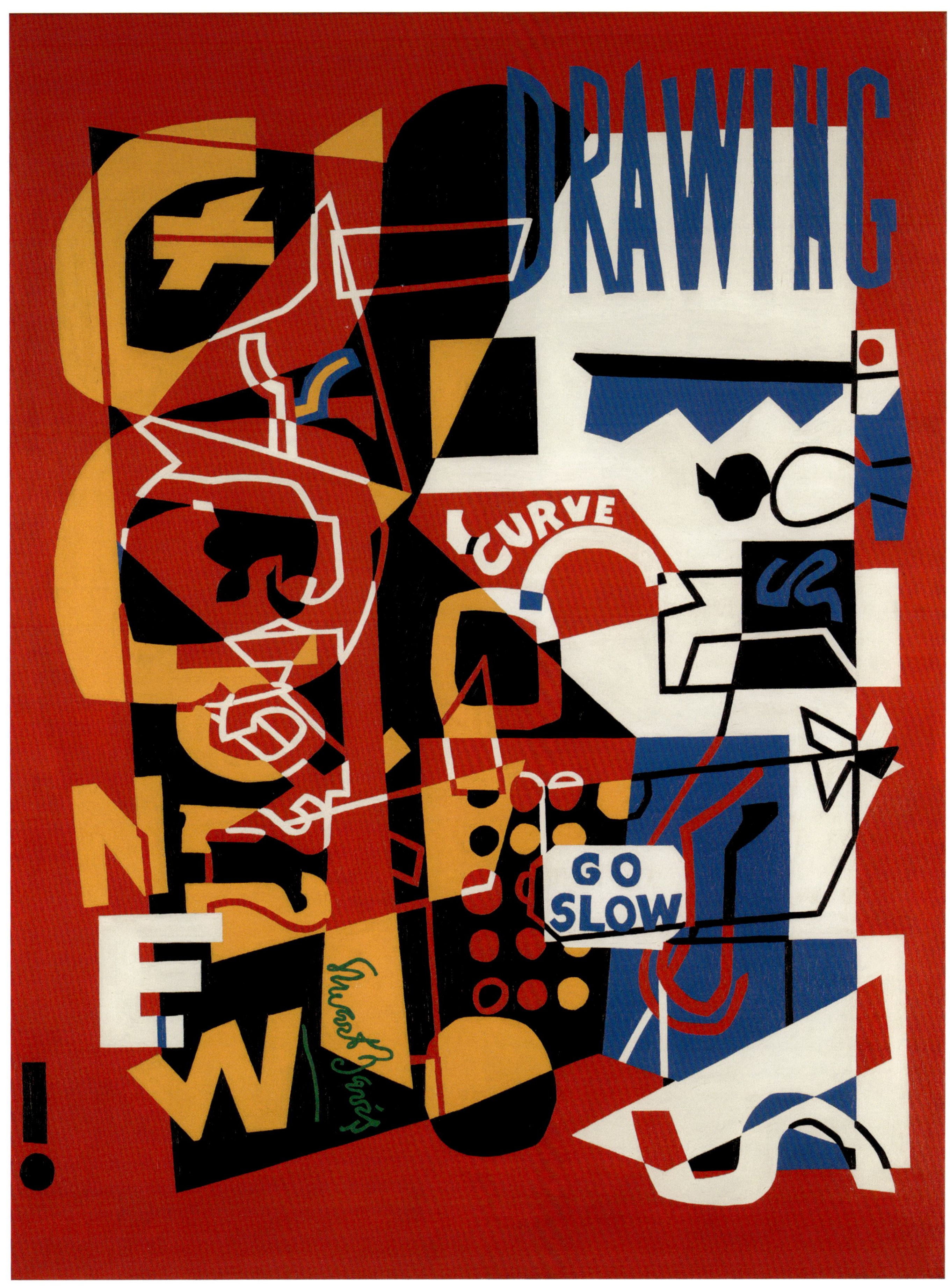

DRAWING
CURVE
GO
SLOW

Adolph Gottlieb

American, 1903–1974

20
Hot Horizon, 1956
Oil on canvas, 49¾ × 71⅞ in.
(126.4 × 182.6 cm)
2006.52.6

Part of the *Imaginary Landscape* series, *Hot Horizon* illustrates a critical formal and conceptual shift in Adolph Gottlieb's work. By the time it was painted, Gottlieb was already well known for his 1940s *Pictograph* series, which consisted of crudely painted totemic images, rendered in subdued tones within a vertical grid format. Inspired by Carl Jung's psychoanalytical theories on the existence of a premodern universal language of signs, Gottlieb's *Pictographs* aimed to reaffirm a positive view of humanity in the onslaught of World War II.

By contrast, *Hot Horizon* signaled a stylistic change. Painted along a horizontal axis with thick impasto and a vibrant palette, it is divided into two distinct areas existing in tense equilibrium. A red band overlaid with black shapes occupies the top part, while the bottom is turned over to an expansive area of turbulent marks. By 1950, Gottlieb considered the "all-over" compositions of artists such as Jackson Pollock—as well as his own *Pictographs*—to have become Abstract Expressionist clichés. Consequently, the reintroduction of a centered composition in *Hot Horizon* marked a formal breakthrough for the artist.

Hot Horizon likewise indicated an important conceptual shift. While the *Pictographs* remained figurative and relatively specific, the gestural markings in *Hot Horizon* occupy an ambiguous space between signification and decoration. Gottlieb spent the summer of 1956 vacationing by the sea in Cape Cod, and several *Imaginary Landscapes* from that year, such as *Waves* (Collection of the Adolph and Esther Gottlieb Foundation, New York) or *Sea and Tide* (Metropolitan Museum of Art, New York), clearly allude to seascapes. The turbulent marks and blue patches in *Hot Horizon* likewise intimate water. However, the word *hot* in the work's title also hints at a desert setting, recalling Gottlieb's 1937 to 1938 stay in Arizona, where he was deeply impressed by the landscape, comparing it to the sea: "I think the emotional feeling I had in the desert was that it was like being at sea."[1] It is notable that Gottlieb stressed the feeling produced by the landscape rather than the actual site. Gottlieb was committed to art as a vehicle of personal expression and regarded meaning as open-ended and evocative, rather than fixed and determined.

Consequently, *Hot Horizon* should not be read as a literal landscape, but as a general division between static and chaotic forces operating within the artist, as expressed by Gottlieb: "I have an urge towards serenity and calmness. . . . I'm also inclined to be nervous and energetic . . . if I were to paint in a way which was completely aggressive and in which everything was jagged I'd be false to myself because I have an opposite tendency too."[2]

In visual terms, the polarity first achieved in the *Imaginary Landscapes* became subsequently refined in the *Burst* paintings (1957-74), often considered the zenith of Gottlieb's career. There, the division was further distilled into a controlled circular form in the top half of the canvas and unrestrained markmaking in the bottom. *Hot Horizon* thus marks an important transitional phase between the *Pictographs* and *Bursts*—a pictorial crossroads.

—Maria Taroutina

1. Adolph Gottlieb, interview with Martin Friedman, New York, August 1962, unpublished typescript, tape 1B, p. 14; quoted in Mary Davis MacNaughton, "Adolph Gottlieb: His Life and Art," in *Adolph Gottlieb: A Retrospective*, by MacNaughton, Sanford Hirsch, and Lawrence Alloway, exh. cat. (New York: Arts Publisher, in association with the Adolph and Esther Gottlieb Foundation, 1981), 21.
2. Erin Bundis Coe, *Adolph Gottlieb: 1956*, exh. cat. (Glens Falls, N.Y.: Hyde Collection, 2005), 13.

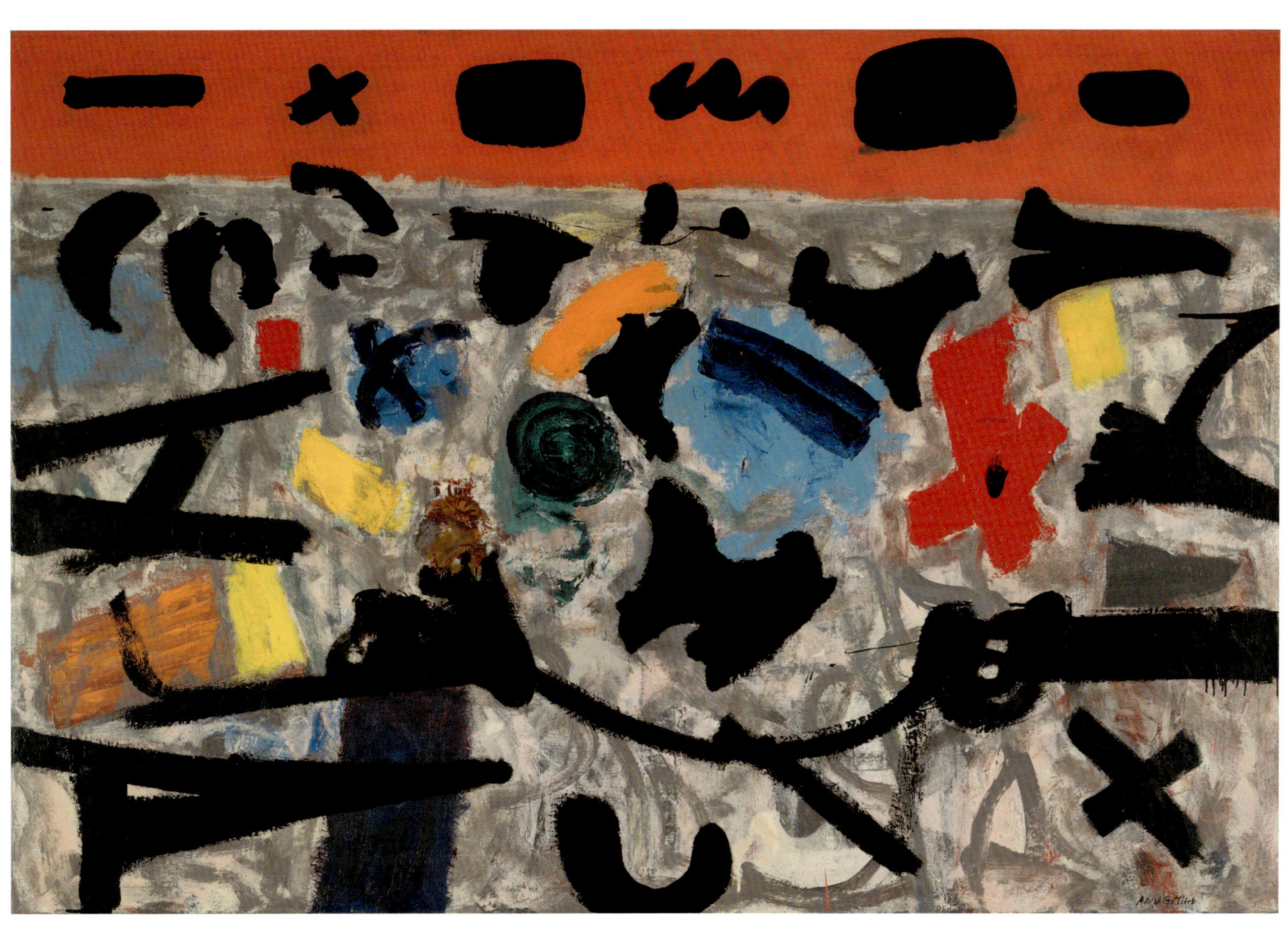

20

Richard Lindner

American, born Germany, 1901–1978

21
The Scream, **1958**
Oil on canvas, 60 × 40 in. (152.4 × 101.6 cm)
2006.52.9

Fleeing from his native Germany to escape the Nazi regime, Lindner first moved to Paris in 1933 and then to New York in 1941. Although the artist maintained that the United States provided inspiration for his art, he remained a quintessentially European artist in exile, outside the mainstream of postwar American artistic movements.[1]

The Scream, produced in 1958, deliberately invokes its celebrated nineteenth-century predecessor of the same name (fig. 1), painted by the Norwegian Symbolist artist Edvard Munch. That Lindner had Munch's masterpiece in mind is evident from his preparatory pencil sketch (fig. 2), in which the outline of a figure in the immediate foreground, positioned in front of a rush of perspectival lines, resembles Munch's composition. What attracted Lindner to Munch's painting was its unsettling, ominous quality. In 1925, while still in Germany, Lindner saw art made by the mentally ill patients of the psychiatric clinic at the University of Heidelberg, which he claimed had a powerful and lasting effect on his subsequent artistic production.

Unlike Munch's *The Scream,* which employs painterly, nervous, undulating lines, Lindner's version is characterized by a hard-edged abstraction. Although entirely painted in oil, the work has a pieced-together quality reminiscent of collage. The space is disjunctive and fragmented, and the colors are intentionally discordant. Flat, geometric planes are overlapped by a strange amorphous form in the foreground, composed of a mélange of different shapes and colors and dominated by an uncannily sentient, black-and-white target eye. A far cry from Lindner's legible pencil sketch, this form no longer registers as a coherent whole, although it still retains a disturbing animate quality.

Directly above it, circumscribed in a red semicircle, is a large, illusionistically rendered head of a roaring tiger, which closely resembles a commercial photograph. Is the "scream" of the painting produced by the tiger or by the ambiguous form in the foreground, potentially pursued by the feline predator? This narrative uncertainty generates an uncomfortable psychological tension, even a sense of panic: *The Scream* is clearly a scene of violence, but who or what is being violated remains unclear.

The Scream constitutes an outlier in Lindner's mostly figurative oeuvre. The artist was chiefly known for his voyeuristic, garish depictions of New York's inhabitants in the 1960s and 1970s, which thematize the malaise and absurdity of the modern urban environment. Lindner himself described his work as "a reflection of Germany of the 1920s."[2] Indeed, his depiction of social degeneration recalls the polemical art of the Weimar Republic, which critiqued Germany's post–World War I culture of excess. Although *The Scream* does not literally portray a vulgar street scene or a dubious urban type as do many of Lindner's other works, its jagged geometries and abrasive colors speak to the dislocation of the modern human psyche in a large, fast-paced metropolis. In many ways Lindner's *The Scream* projects the tormented cry of Munch's painting into 1950s New York.

—**Maria Taroutina**

---

1. Richard Lindner, interview with John Gruen (April 1978), *ARTnews,* Summer 1978, 77.
2. Ibid.

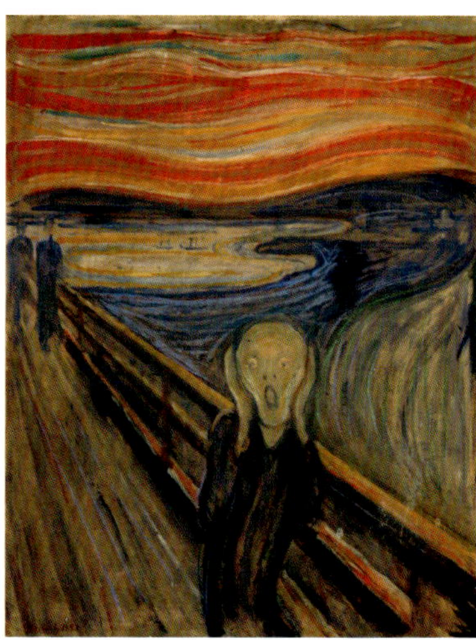

Fig. 1.
Edvard Munch, *The Scream,* 1893. Tempera and pastels on cardboard, 35¹³⁄₁₆ × 28¹⁵⁄₁₆ in. (91 × 73.5 cm). National Gallery, Oslo

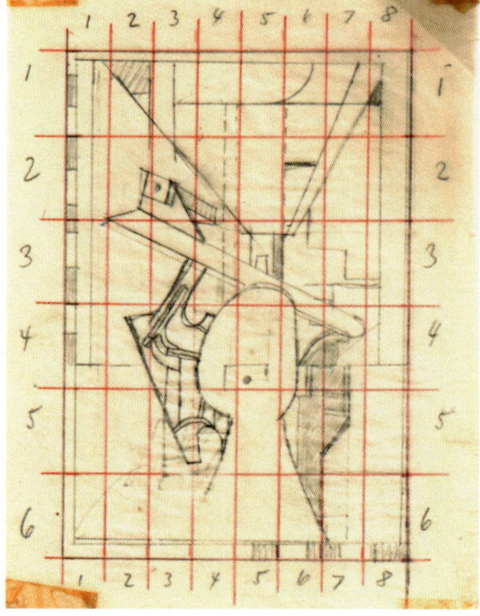

Fig. 2.
Richard Lindner, sketch for *The Scream,* 1958. Pencil and colored pencil on tracing paper, 8⅛ × 5¾ in. (20.5 × 14.6 cm). Private collection

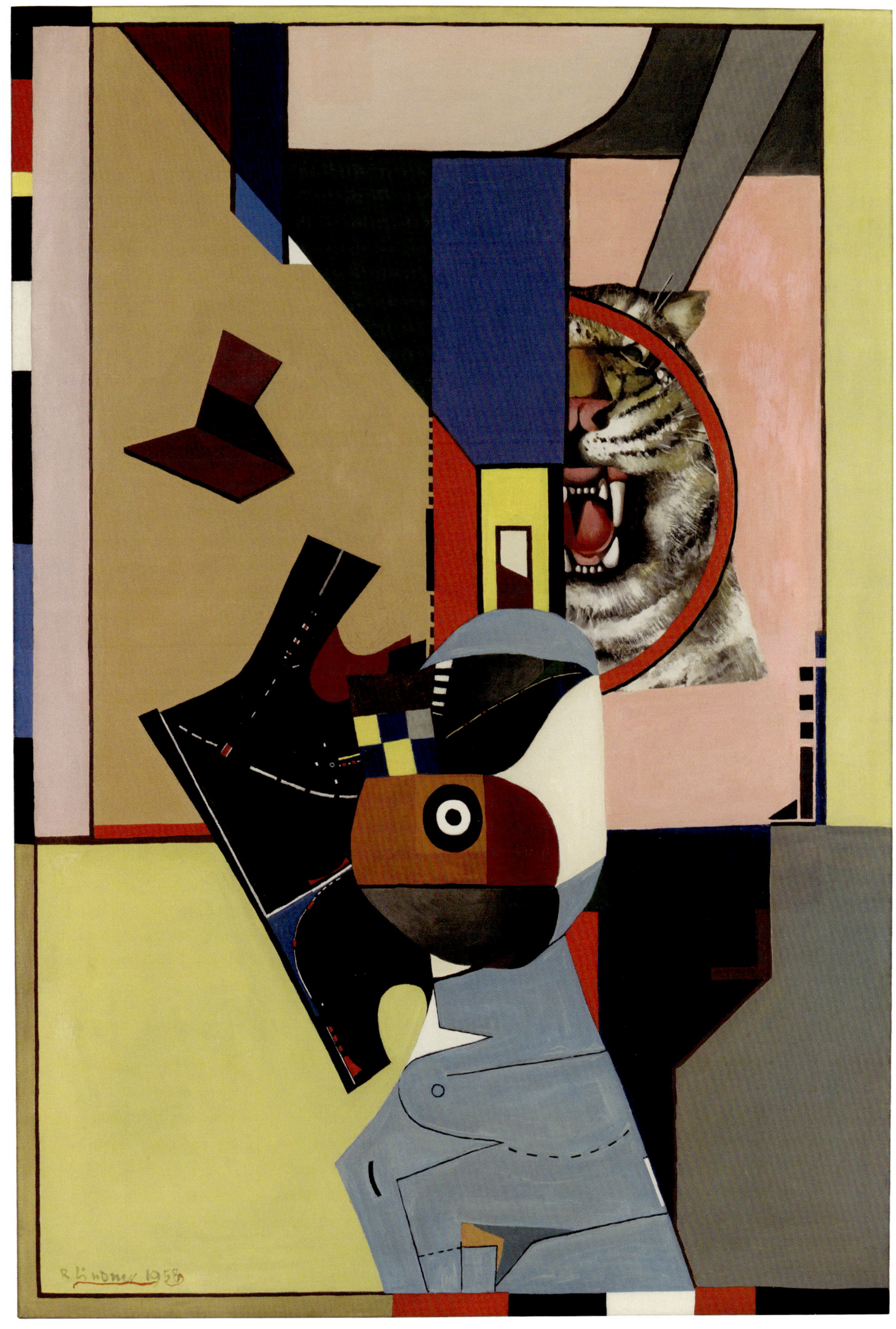

Jean (Hans) Arp

French, born Germany, 1886–1966

22
***Resting Leaf,* 1959**
Bronze, edition 2/5, 23 × 24 × 7 in.
(58.4 × 61 × 17.8 cm)
2006.52.97

The work of the visual artist and poet Jean (Hans) Arp is often considered within the dialogue and history of the Dada movement in Europe. While certainly a significant part of his history, Arp's involvement with the groundbreaking Dada enterprises at Zurich's Cabaret Voltaire in 1916 and his collaboration and exhibition with Dada artists in Cologne, New York, and Paris were not the source of the poetic expression that was his lifelong passion.

Arp conceived of this practice, which he believed to be distinct from natural forms yet coextensive with nature's own expression, as early as 1910–11, while living alone in Switzerland. His work in sculpture, constructed reliefs, prints, drawings, and the written word was directly inspired by forms he discovered in the world.

In 1915 in Zurich, Arp met Sophie Taeuber, a visual artist and dancer whom he married in 1922. Her works in textile and assemblage encouraged him to pursue his first constructed pictures—reliefs made by layering abstract forms cut from wooden planks. Under the influence of Surrealist writers and artists with whom he and Taeuber-Arp became familiar while living on the outskirts of Paris in the late 1920s, Arp interpreted his three-dimensional work using language. In both his writing and visual art, Arp pursued an intuitive and abstract expression. Sculptures could originate in the imagery of his dreams, but Arp nonetheless indicated their association with concrete forms through rational descriptive titles such as *Mountain, Navel, Bird,* and *Torso.*

Although a prolific artist, Arp is primarily known for his creation of multilayered, biomorphic, painted wood reliefs, which often possess an aura of whimsy and joy. Yet in his later years the artist primarily modeled three-dimensional, nonlinear shapes in plaster, which he then translated into materials such as stone and bronze. The medium of plaster enabled Arp to feel his way toward discovering form and to realize unique shapes that he could free from gravity by subsequently mounting them on pedestals. *Resting Leaf* exemplifies this practice. Although this work was ultimately realized as a three-dimensional study of form in space, the frontal view of the work is dominant: one experiences the undulating front surface as the artist's primary concern. This demonstrates Arp's continued fascination with the space between two and three dimensions occupied by relief forms. *Resting Leaf* is memorable for the delicate void that animates its center and from which its organic mass radiates. Arp made other examples of *Resting Leaf,* including a larger-scale bronze and a version in white marble.

—**Jennifer R. Gross**

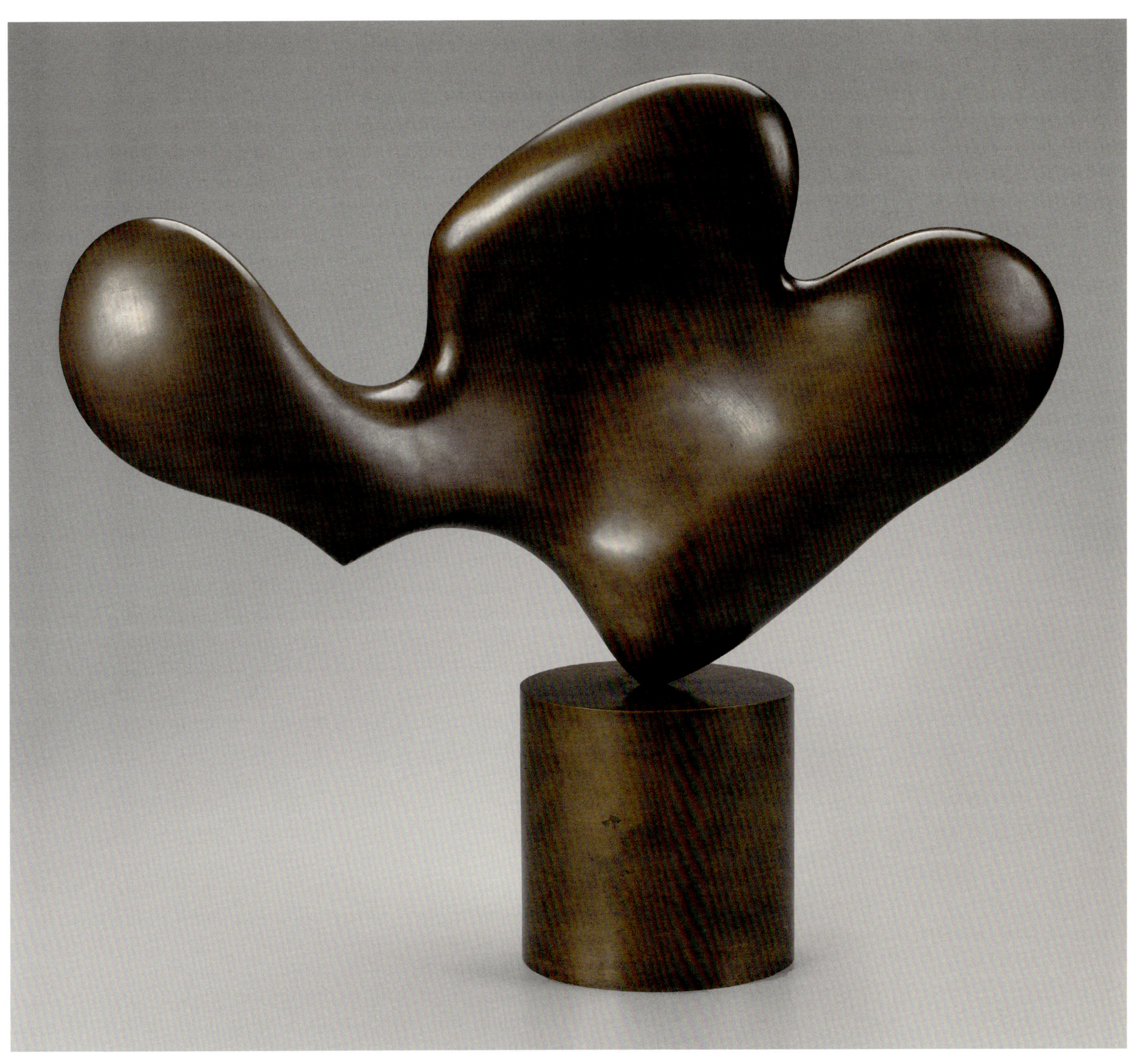

Alicia Penalba

French, born Argentina, 1913–1982

23
***Faune des mers* (Sea Fauna), 1959**
Bronze, edition 5/6, 17½ × 33⅛ × 10¼ in.
(44.5 × 84.1 × 26 cm)
2006.52.120

Faune des mers (Sea Fauna) is a quintessential example of Alicia Penalba's signature works: dynamic ensembles of clay slabs shaped on metal armatures and cast in bronze that suggest constructions found in nature. Though *Faune des mers* evokes an avian creature in the process of settling gently into a resting position, it is not specific or directly representational. Like Constantin Brancusi's *Bird in Space* (1923, Metropolitan Museum of Art, New York), Penalba's *Faune des mers* seeks to capture the essence of flight while avoiding its depiction. But whereas Brancusi eliminated the wings and features of a bird to emphasize its body mass, Penalba presents only a series of carefully balanced, winglike forms that appear caught in an instant of unfurling and contracting.

Vibrant, nature-based abstractions such as *Faune des mers* and *Bird in Space* are characteristic of the sculpture of the inter- and postwar École de Paris, a school defined less by a particular style—its members variously adhered to Cubism, Surrealism, and Art Informel abstraction, among other tendencies—than by the characteristics of its members. Like Penalba, who was born in Argentina, and the Romanian Brancusi, the majority of these artists had migrated to Paris from other parts of the world.[1] Penalba arrived from Buenos Aires in 1948 on a French government grant to study printmaking, but abstract sculpture soon captured her interest. She began studying with Russian-born sculptor Ossip Zadkine and paying visits to Brancusi's studio; by the early 1950s she declared her commitment to a sculptural practice grounded in abstraction.[2]

Apparent references within Penalba's works to her South American roots, combined with her Parisian artistic pedigree, positioned her as a prime representative of Argentina's cultural sophistication on international art exhibition circuits of the 1950s and 1960s.[3] In 1961 she was awarded the grand prize for sculpture at the sixth Bienal de São Paulo for works included in the official Argentine pavilion. Penalba's works also anchored the exhibition *New Art of Argentina*, organized by Argentina's Museo Nacional de Bellas Artes (National Museum of Fine Arts), which toured art museums in the United States in 1964.

Penalba remained in Paris until her death in 1982, and her work emerged from and corresponded to Parisian, rather than Argentine, traditions. Nonetheless, her complex, carefully balanced arrangements of wedges and planes strongly suggest the jagged rock formations and native flora and fauna of Patagonia, the mountainous region of Argentina's and Chile's south, where she spent long periods as a child. *Faune des mers* is a case in point: although cast in a hard, dark bronze, it retains the earthy warmth of the clay in which it was modeled, and evokes a creature that could not be indigenous to a crowded European metropolis.

Faune des mers stands as a monument to a distant childhood encounter with the power of nature: its details long since lost, only the potent experience of form and movement remains.

—Jennifer Josten

1. Ionel Jianu, *Zadkine* (Paris: Arted, 1964), 15–17.
2. Luce Hoctin, "Trois jeunes sculpteurs," *L'Oeil*, March 1960, 48–50; and Roger van Gindertael, *Penalba: Sculptures*, exh. cat. (New York: Galería Bonino, 1966), n.p.
3. Argentina was foremost among developing nations in deploying contemporary artworks in the service of diplomacy and economic growth during these decades; see Andrea Giunta, *Avant-Garde, Internationalism, and Politics: Argentine Art in the Sixties* (Durham, N.C.: Duke University Press, 2007).

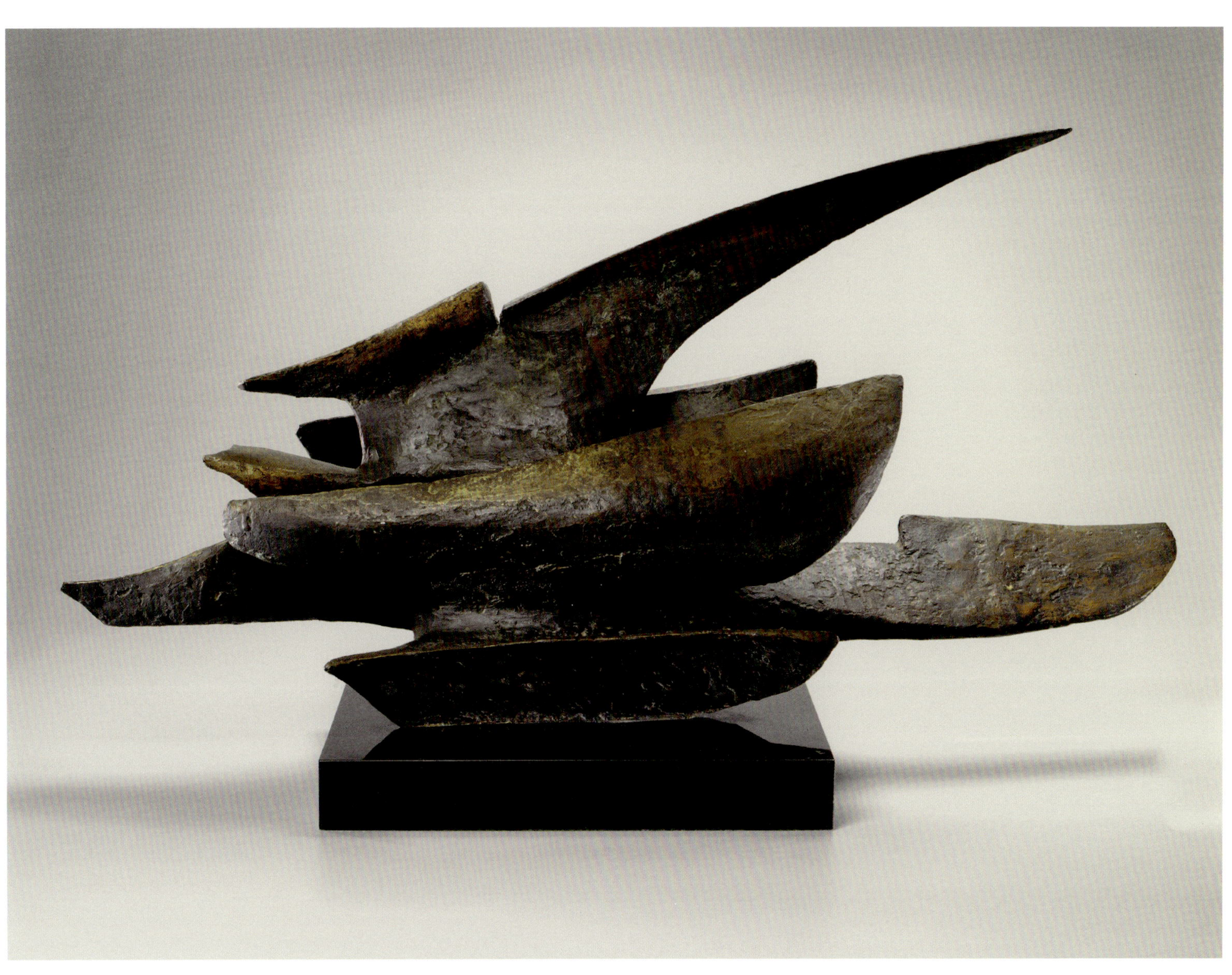

Richard Stankiewicz

American, 1922–1983

24
***Astrological Surprise*, 1959**
Rusted steel, 26½ × 22 × 33 in.
(67.3 × 55.9 × 83.8 cm)
2006.52.113

25
***Untitled*, ca. 1980**
Rusted steel, 72 × 42 × 30 in.
(182.9 × 106.7 × 76.2 cm)
2006.52.70

26
***Untitled*, ca. 1980**
Rusted steel, 70 × 44 × 36 in.
(177.8 × 111.8 × 91.4 cm)
2006.52.69

After training briefly as a painter in New York following his service in World War II, in 1950 Richard Stankiewicz returned to Europe, where he stayed until the following year, working with artists Ossip Zadkine and Fernand Léger. Zadkine's expert use of volumetric voids in his sculpture had an impact on Stankiewicz's future approach to assemblage, as did Léger's machine-aesthetic paintings that celebrated industry's potential beauty. On returning to the United States in 1951, Stankiewicz was impressed by the visual interest of rusty metal scrap he found in his overgrown garden. Quickly learning to weld, he began transforming such junk materials—examples of America's burgeoning culture of disposable consumer goods—into sculptures.

In Stankiewicz's hands, fragments from heavy machinery like exhaust pipes, bent steel rods, grates, and steel drums became animated creatures. Although frequently compared to three-dimensional Cubist works and to David Smith's tack-welded sculptures, Stankiewicz's playfully anthropomorphic early works also display an awareness of Picasso's Surrealist sculpture and of the biomorphic assemblages of sculptors such as Max Ernst. His preferred description of these figural sculptures was penned by Eleanor C. Munro, who called Stankiewicz's practice "close to a child's game of monster building in the vacant-lot."[1]

The earliest Stankiewicz work in the Charles B. Benenson Collection belongs to a small series of sculptures from 1958 and 1959 that reference cosmology. *Astrological Surprise* (cat. 24) combines pipes and grillwork with a wheel resembling a navigational, or a zodiacal, chart. Art historian Emmie Donadio has suggested that the flying lessons Stankiewicz was taking in the late 1950s, as well as the Soviet launch of Sputnik in 1957, may have proved an inspiration for this body of work, which was also "reminiscent of the artist's powerful dream while he was still in the Navy, of creating a universe in which all the parts related to the whole."[2] Indeed, Stankiewicz was never drawn to the entropic or diffuse qualities of the junkyard. Rather, his sculptural groupings relied on cohesion and internal tension.

In 1951, just as he was developing the formal strategies that would anchor his entire career, Stankiewicz helped cofound the celebrated artist-run collective Hansa Gallery in New York. This offered an important leg up in the relatively small New York art world of the early 1950s. Partially because of Hansa, small assemblages like *Astrological Surprise* quickly brought public attention, which was often divided between those who saw Stankiewicz as a truly innovative sculptor and those who debated how much an artist needed to *transform* materials—be they paint or scrap metal—for the result to be considered art. Such debate died down as Stankiewicz and other artists using found materials were codified in the groundbreaking 1961 exhibition at the Museum of Modern Art, New York, *The Art of Assemblage.*

The scale of Stankiewicz's work grew in the ensuing years. Early works such as *Astrological Surprise* were relatively small and could be displayed on a pedestal or a tabletop. The freestanding vertical sculpture from around 1980 (cat. 25) in the Benenson Collection is slightly larger than human scale. In it, pipes, springs, and drum fragments spiral centripetally from a central core, in a seeming illustration of how Stankiewicz described his method of composition: "A common procedure for me is to make a pedestal . . . and stick something to it, like a post or a tube or something, and . . . I have to get nervous, panicky and eventually I have to make a move and I don't know what that leads to, so the whole thing is improvised."[3]

Stankiewicz's self-imposed challenge to innovate without plans or preparations had taken on a new dimension in the 1970s and 1980s. As scrap metal became more common in the work of other artists, he moved away from scavenging and began working with new, standardized steel forms. Although later works like the round sculpture in the Benenson Collection (cat. 26) were still composed of rust-colored industrial fragments, a kind of lyrical formalism replaced the biomorphism and animated juxtapositions of Stankiewicz's earlier works. In that sculpture, a large steel circle frames the landscape, and it is echoed by a smaller circular fragment of a steel drum. Strips of steel traction plates or grippers have been transformed into geometric planes that jut forward and then recede backward in space.

Taken as a group, the Stankiewicz sculptures in Benenson's collection exemplify different phases in an artistic career marked by the search for compositional harmony and invention among industry's diverse materials.

—Cathleen Chaffee

1. E. C. M. [Eleanor C. Munro], "Reviews and Previews: Richard Stankiewicz," *Art News*, January 1956, 51.
2. Emmie Donadio, *Miracle in the Scrap Heap: The Sculpture of Richard Stankiewicz*, exh. cat. (Andover, Mass.: Addison Gallery of American Art, 2003), 33.
3. Oral history interview between Robert Brown and Richard Stankiewicz, June 26, 1979, unpublished transcript and sound recording, Archives of American Art, Smithsonian Institution.

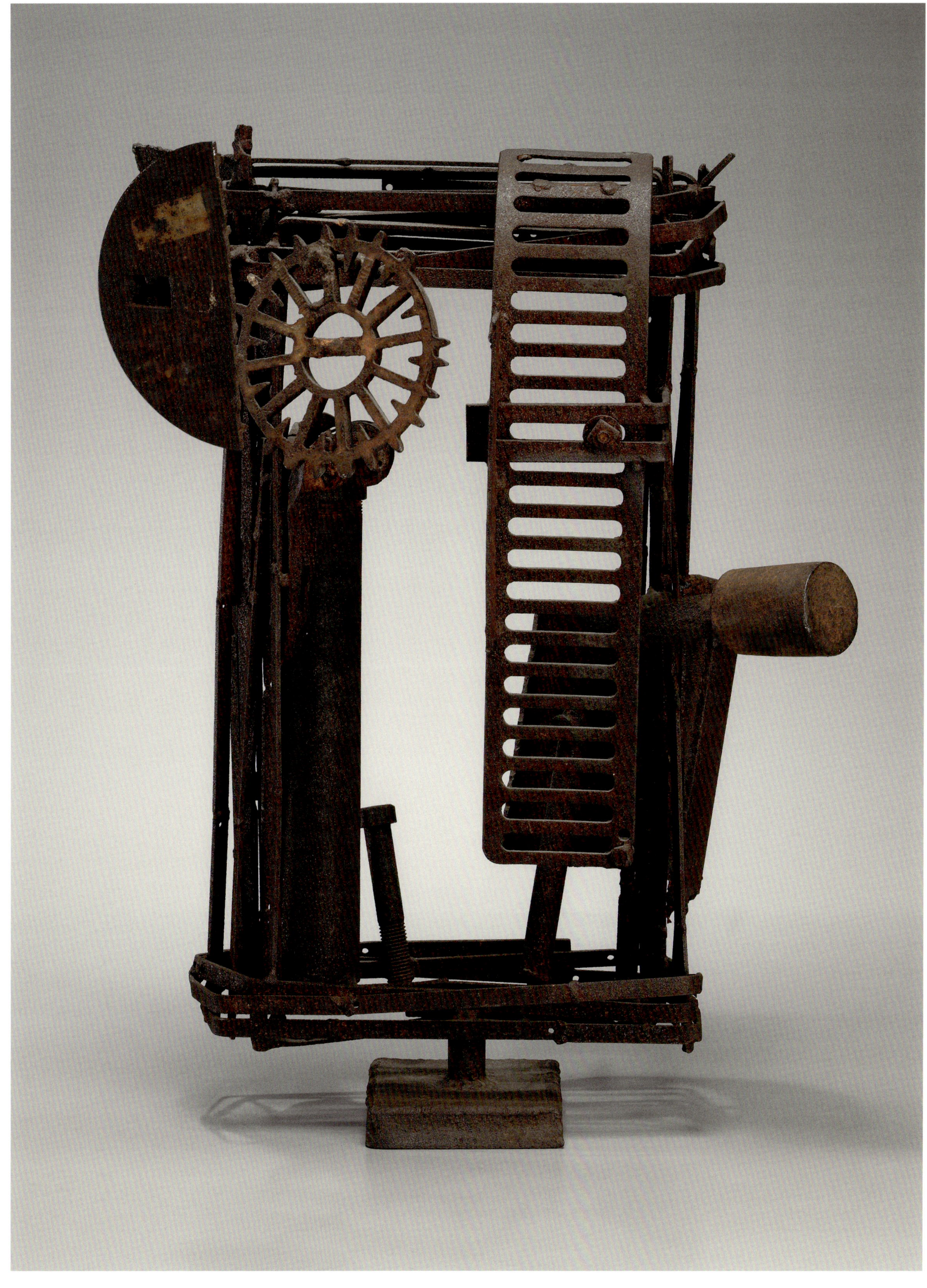

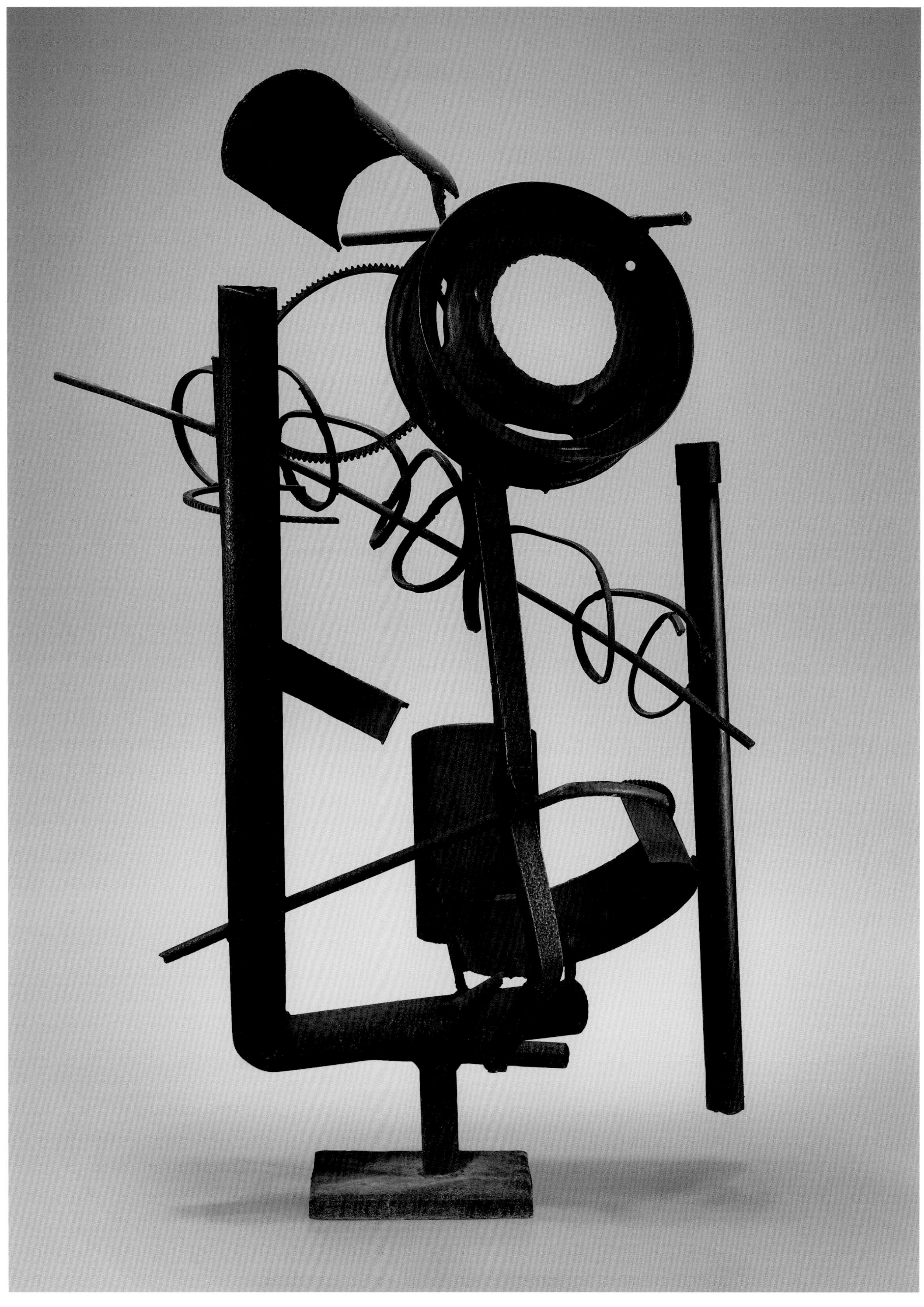

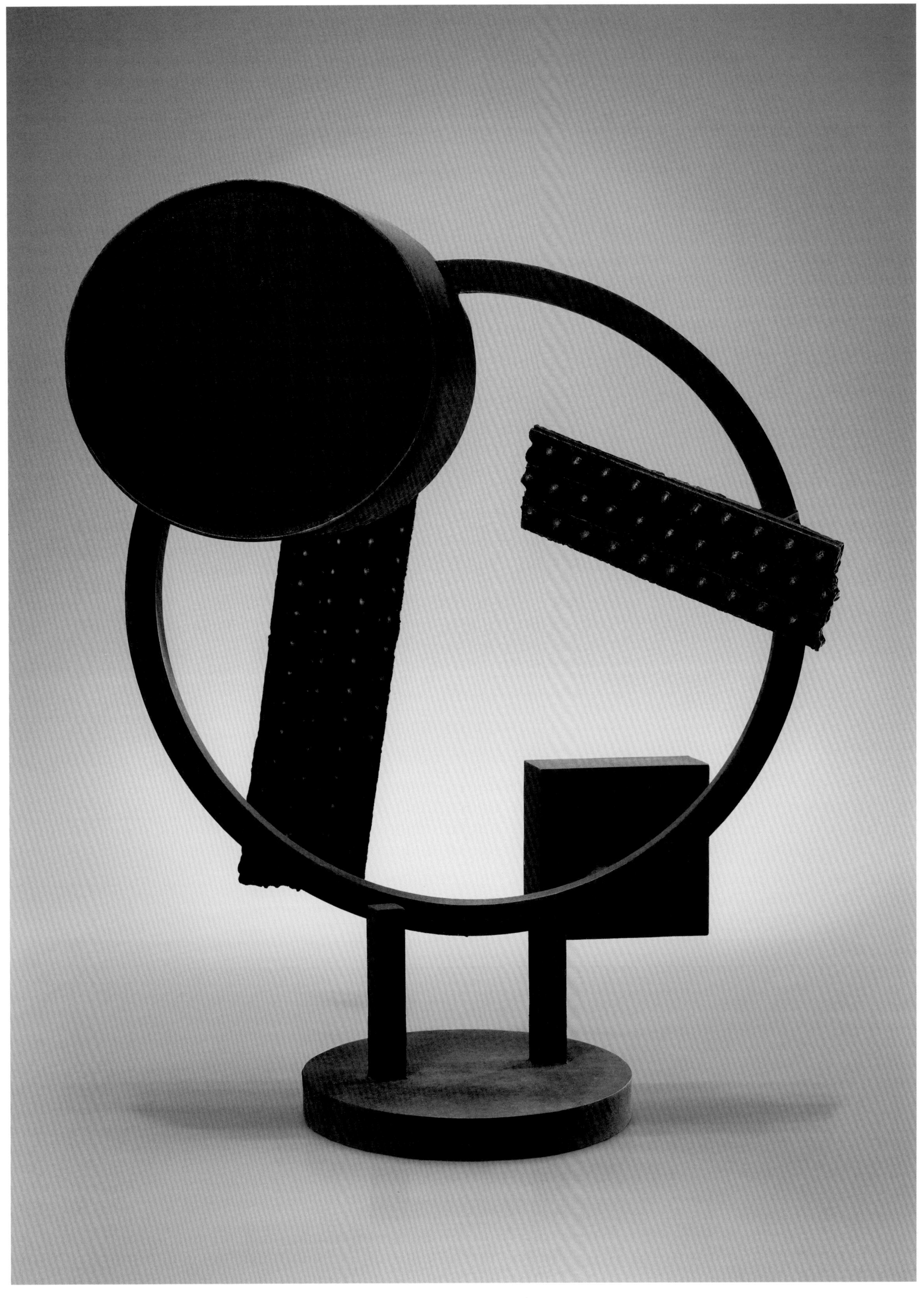

Jean Dubuffet

French, 1901–1985

27
Personnage avec chapeau dans un paysage
(Figure with a Hat in a Landscape), 1960
Black ink, 13¼ × 9 ¹⁵⁄₁₆ in. (33.7 × 25.3 cm)
2006.52.27

28
Dessins (Drawings), 1960
Black ink, 12⅞ × 9⅞ in. (32.7 × 25.1 cm)
2006.52.33

29
Paysage avec quatre personnages
(Landscape with Four Figures), 1960
Black ink and wash, 9³⁄₁₆ × 11¼ in.
(23.3 × 28.6 cm)
2006.52.26

The drawings by Jean Dubuffet in the Charles B. Benenson Collection occupy a special place in the history of Dubuffet's draftsmanship, as the artist likely produced them as visual comments on the very medium of drawing.

Early in 1960, Dubuffet was approached by his gallerist, Daniel Cordier, with an idea for a special project: an album that would reproduce one hundred exemplary drawings made by the artist between 1942 and 1960.[1] The timing of the volume was important, as it was to accompany a retrospective of Dubuffet's drawings with which Cordier would open his first American exhibition space that December (for this reason, the catalogue would appear in both French and English simultaneously).[2] Cordier hoped to include original lithographs in forty of the books, effectively converting them into luxury editions. Dubuffet balked at that idea, and instead suggested that he provide some new drawings to be published for the first time in the Cordier volumes. Two of the Dubuffet works in the Benenson Collection—*Personnage avec chapeau dans un paysage* (Figure with a Hat in a Landscape; cat. 27) and *Dessins* (Drawings; cat. 28)—are particularly important in that they were among the six drawings that were included in the Cordier volumes as works expressly produced for those books.

As adornments to a compendium of his drawings, these two drawings serve as meta-images through which Dubuffet could summarize and comment on his approach to drawing. Of particular interest in this respect is the *Personnage*; the figure marks the end of Cordier's text and the beginning of the appendices (lists of titles, dimensions, and locations of the other drawings). In other words, the *Personnage* transitions the reader to that section of the book devoted to organizing empirical information.

Notably, the figure and his surroundings defy such an organizational burden. This fellow might seem like a respectable bourgeois; his fedora serves as a mark of propriety, as do his wing-tip shoes. His positioning is ambiguous, however. He does not stand so much as hover at an odd angle within an atmosphere of dispersing particles and vaporous strands. His seemingly boneless arms lack conviction in their gestures; he could be flailing to dispel the fog, but his smile suggests that he might be reveling in the chaos, flapping his arms to better stir up the stuff. So, while this image adorns a section of the book dedicated to ledger-book accuracy, this character personifies the project of drawing as something in which chaos prevails. Indeed, we might even consider this personage a surrogate for Dubuffet, who, as the artist himself frequently expressed, preferred a kind of drawing that seemed unprofessional and even anticultural— a kind of drawing that would transgress the very priorities of mastery and virtuosity on which the history of drawing was based.[3]

The topmost portion of *Dessins* intensifies Dubuffet's investigation of drawing as a sort of entropic enterprise.[4] This densely packed rectangle is unlike any other work that Dubuffet made. Typically, in drawings and paintings that he packed with dots and threads—such as *Paysage avec quatre personnages* (Landscape with Four Figures; cat. 29)—the artist relied on the physical frame or edge of the field proper to supply the boundaries of the work; the bottom and the two sides of the composition terminate at the edge of the support. Yet here Dubuffet uncharacteristically supplied a palpable outline, asserting a rectangle separate from that of the page. That edge bulges from the pressure of the figures crowded within, and lines spring out of the rectangle like sparks of energy.

The lower half of *Dessins* seems to convey what happened next—the figures and their visceral surroundings tumbled out after the dam of the rectangular boundary burst. It is almost as if the Cordier book, and its claim to containing Dubuffet's drawings in a scholarly publication, mandated an image that would declare such containment impossible. In the process, the very nature of drawing, in particular its historical privileging of uncorrupted contours, was thoroughly abolished by Dubuffet, who cherished corruption and dispersal.

—Sarah K. Rich

1. Dubuffet was the first artist for whom Cordier served as a broker; eventually Cordier would become Dubuffet's exclusive gallerist in Paris after 1957 (and after 1960 in the United States). See Daniel Cordier, *Huit ans d'agitation* (Paris: Galerie Daniel Cordier, 1964). See also Bénédicte Ajac, *Donations Daniel Cordier: Le regard d'un amateur*, exh. cat. (Paris: Musée national d'art moderne, Centre Georges Pompidou, 1989). For a brief description of Dubuffet's drawings from 1960, see the volume of Dubuffet's catalogue raisonné dedicated to the drawings of this period: Max Loreau, *Catalogue des travaux de Jean Dubuffet: Dessins, 1960*, Fascicule 18 (Geneva: Weber, 1969), esp. 7–11, 33.
2. Daniel Cordier, *Les dessins de Jean Dubuffet* (Paris: Frédéric Ditis, 1960); Daniel Cordier, *The Drawings of Jean Dubuffet*, trans. Cecily Mackworth (New York: George Braziller, 1960).
3. Cordier's text frequently dwells on the indecorous, unruly aspects of Dubuffet's line. Dubuffet's own comments regarding his admiration for "raw" art are legion. Among the most useful and accessible summaries of his work are Jean Dubuffet, "Anti-cultural Positions," 1951, reprinted in Mildred Glimcher, *Jean Dubuffet: Towards an Alternative Reality* (New York: Abbeville, 1987), 127–32; and Jean Dubuffet, "Memoir on the Development of My Work from 1952," trans. Louise Varèse, in *Dubuffet*, ed. Peter Selz, exh. cat. (New York: Museum of Modern Art, 1962), 63–137.
4. This drawing was omitted from the French edition, possibly by mistake. Instead a different drawing was (perhaps inadvertently) reproduced twice, once right side up (after pl. 82) and once on its side (before pl. 100). In the English edition this repetition is eliminated, and the top, rectangular portion of *Dessins* is instead reproduced before pl. 82.

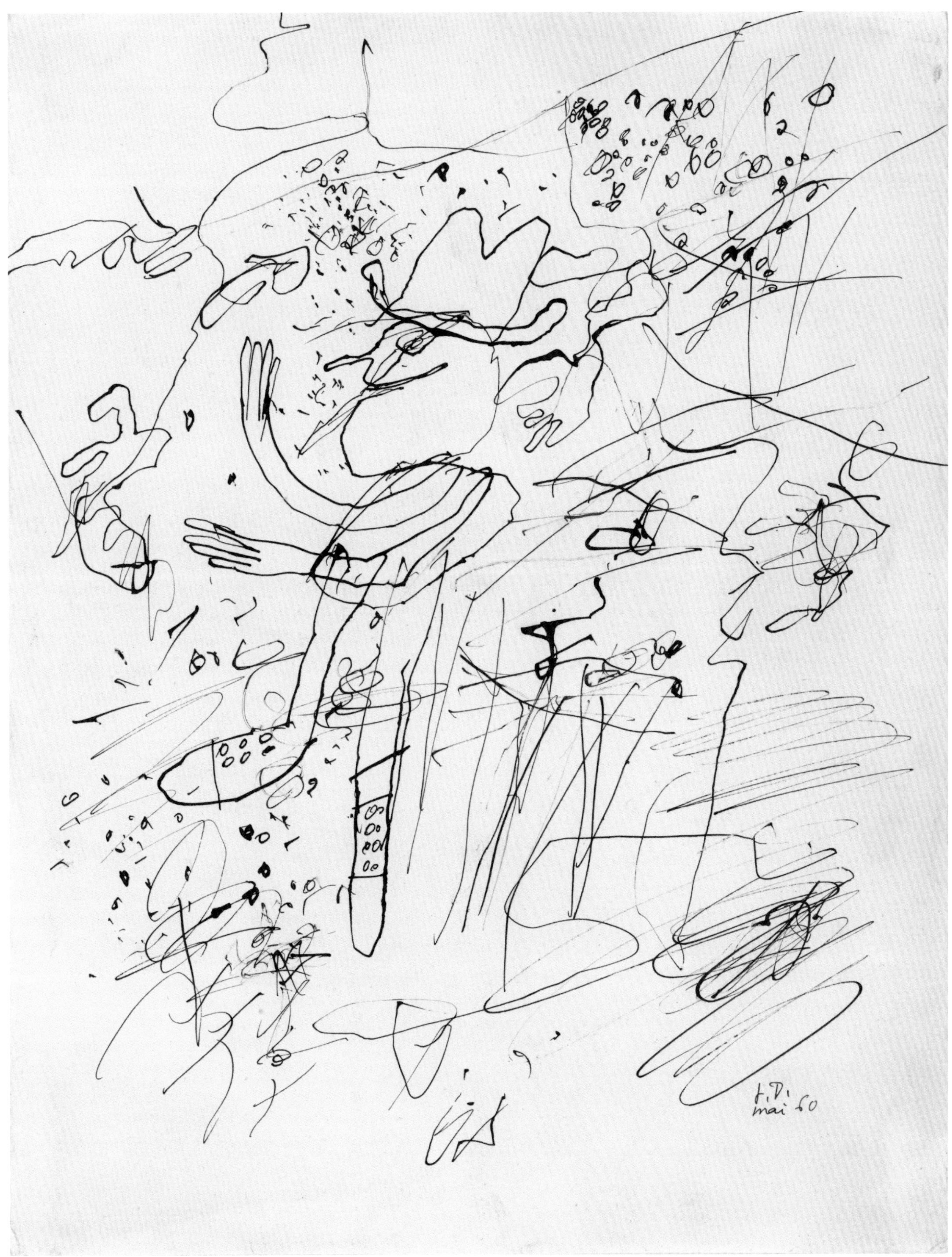

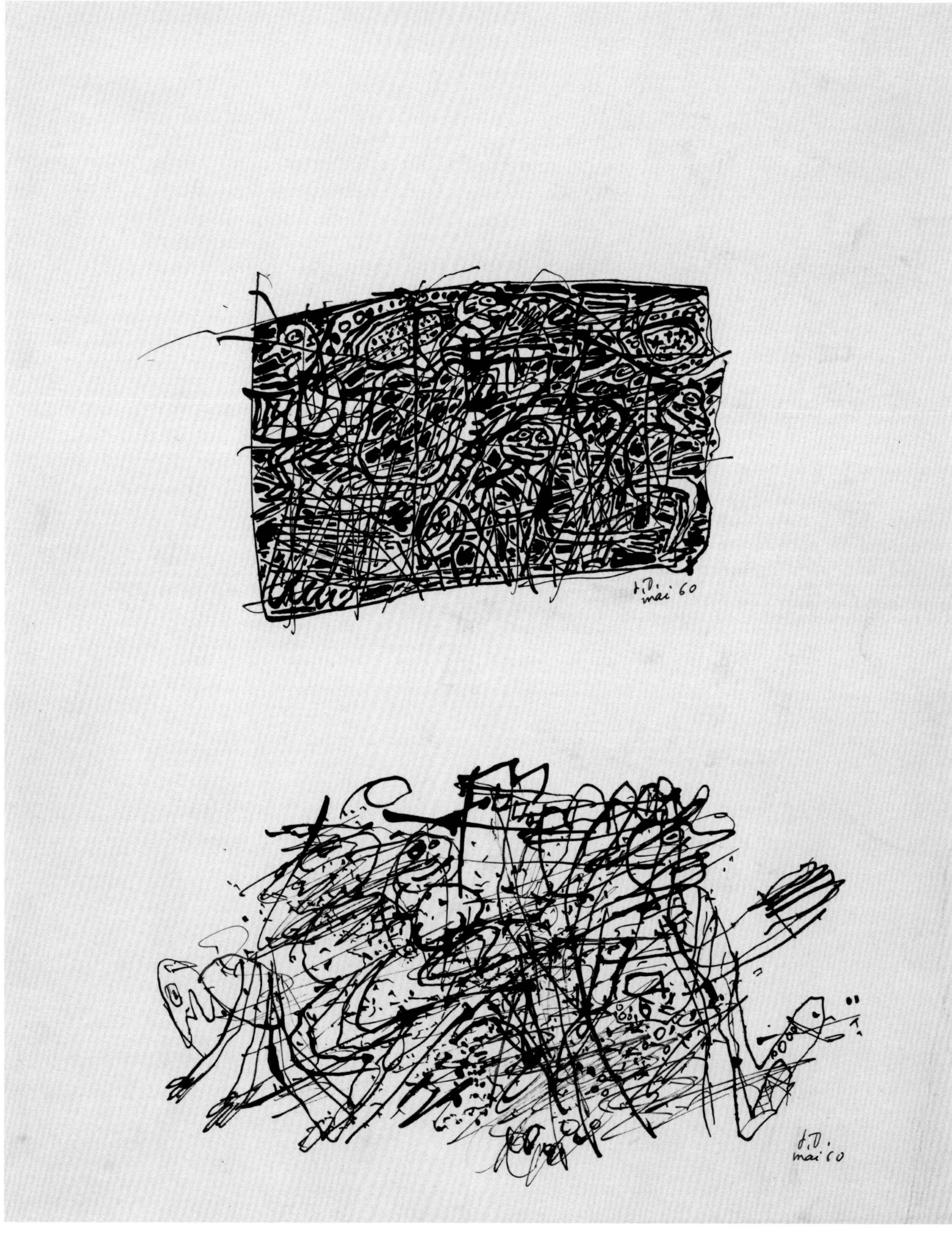

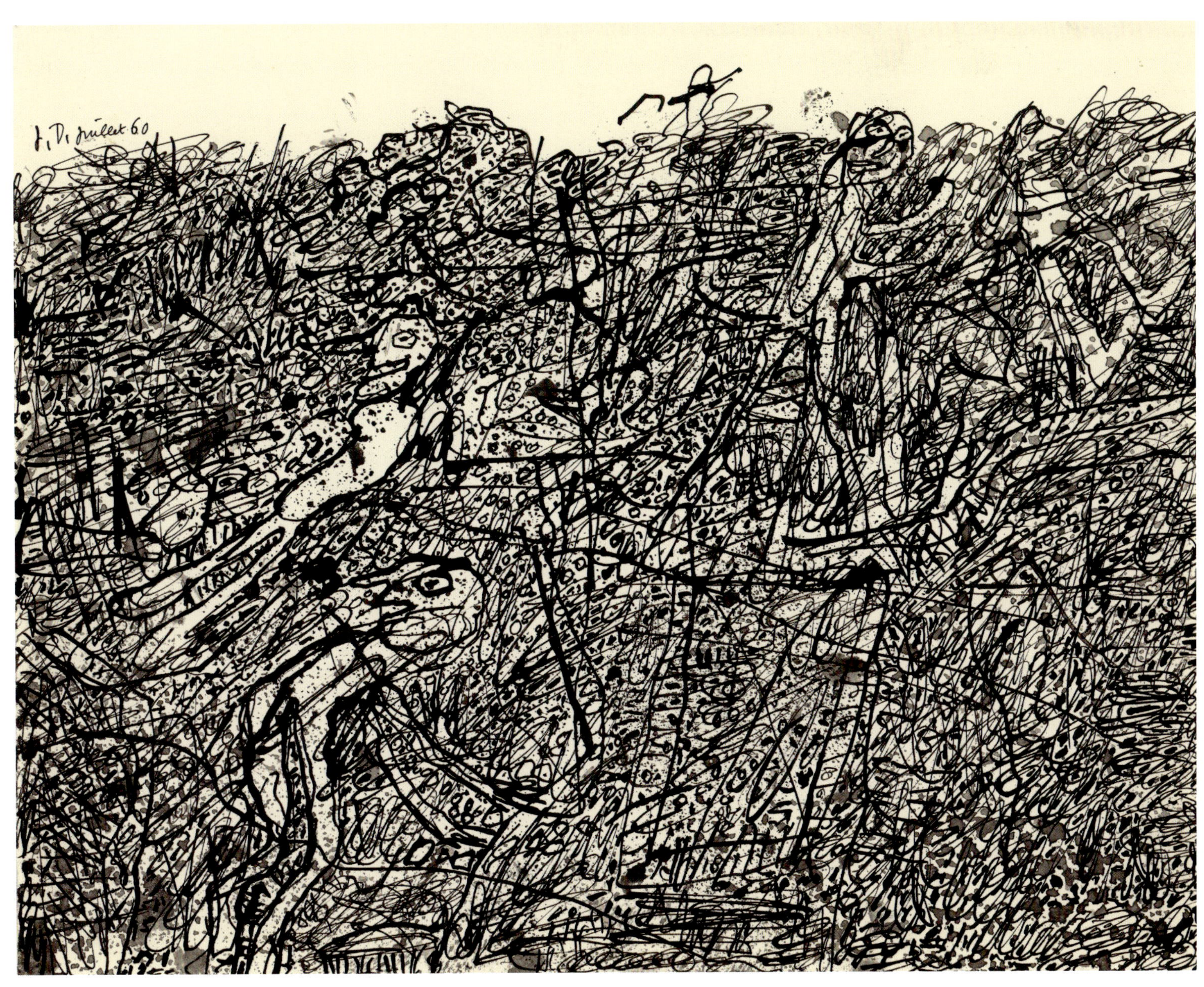

29

Jean Paul Riopelle

Canadian, 1923–2002

30
Plage (Beach), 1960
Oil on canvas, 39 × 38 in. (99.1 × 96.5 cm)
2006.52.96

Although Canadian by birth, Jean Paul Riopelle spent most of his life in Paris. At the Thirty-First Venice Biennale, in 1962, he was the first Canadian artist to be awarded a prize; it was also the first time in the Biennale's history that Canada was represented by just one artist. Painted only two years before this honor, *Plage* (Beach) is an arresting example of Riopelle's mature work.

Striking in its energetic eruption of vigorous facture and vibrant color, *Plage* retains all the immediacy of the artist's active bodily engagement with his artwork. Riopelle himself related his painting method to the terms of combat—an attack on the blank canvas. Art historian Patrick Waldberg likewise seized on the aggressive aspect of Riopelle's art, describing it as exploding "with the crash of a bomb blast and the light of a rocket causing everything around it to disappear." [1]

Riopelle's physical exuberance when painting is evident in the formal structure of his work. The thickly layered impasto in *Plage* assumes a tactile three-dimensionality. It was Riopelle's practice to squeeze paint out of the tube directly onto the canvas, and then to spread and sculpt it with a palette knife. In *Plage*, many of the white and gray color patches still retain the imprint of the knife blade. The artist never made sketches or preliminary designs, refusing all premeditation and calculation in his belief that "the painting must work itself out." [2] The final effect is one of perpetual flux. Color planes overlap, and fluid strokes of paint slide toward one another in seemingly continuous movement. The potential for transformation seems ever present, as if the paint were still wet.

Although Riopelle's early development was shaped by his association with André Breton and the Parisian Surrealist circle, he refused to be pinned down by labels, theories, or movements, subsequently remaining outside both the European Art Informel and the American Abstract Expressionist groups, despite his affinity with their art and ideas.

Riopelle attributed his development of a unique abstract painterly language to a particularly memorable encounter with nature. While vacationing on the Canadian coast in 1945, the artist was struck by the strange and unfamiliar patterns created by ripples of water and moving marine life in a sinkhole. Later, while trying to reproduce his initial visual impression, Riopelle became aware of the potential for nonfiguration in the natural world. Consequently, the artist maintained that his was not an abstract art, but a representational one. Likening his works to Claude Monet's *Nymphéas*, Riopelle claimed that he was relentlessly moving closer toward nature, rather than away from it. It is therefore not coincidental that like *Plage*, the majority of Riopelle's titles from the 1960s refer to the sea. These constitute a retrospective homage in the middle of his career to his initial artistic breakthrough.

—Maria Taroutina

---

1. Patrick Waldberg, "Le salon des surindépendants," *Paru*, December 1949, 130–31; quoted in Monique Brunet-Weinmann, "Birth of a Signature," in *Jean Paul Riopelle: Catalogue Raisonné, 1939–53*, ed. Yseult Riopelle, French with English translations by René Detroye, Lisa Leblanc, and Stephen Wright (Montreal: Hibou, 1999), 1:132.
2. Jean Paul Riopelle, quoted in Michel Waldberg, "Riopelle, the Absolute Gap," in *Jean Paul Riopelle*, ed. Riopelle, 1:51.

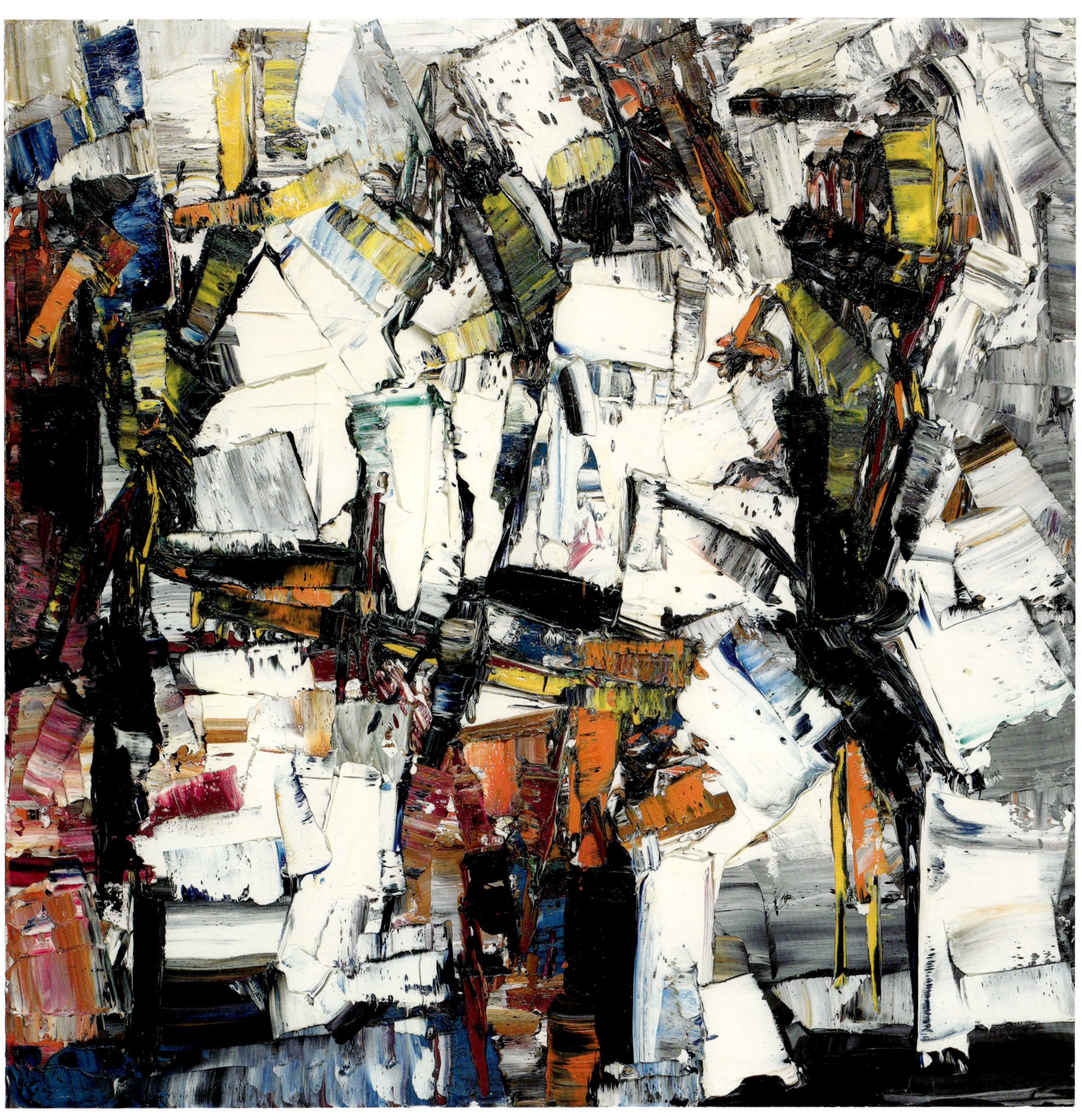

Marisol (Escobar)

American, born France 1930

31
Mayflower, 1961–62
Wood with paint and glass,
75 × 41¼ × 11 ¼ in.
(190.5 × 104.8 × 28.6 cm)
2006.52.71

Marisol Escobar, born in Paris to Venezuelan parents in 1930, settled in New York in 1950 to study painting with Hans Hofmann but was soon drawn to North and South American folk sculpture. By the end of the decade she had caught the attention of the New York art world with tiny terracotta and bronze figures, arranged into larger groupings or displayed in antique printer's boxes.[1] In 1960, Marisol (by then known by her first name alone) happened on a discovery that would transform her artistic practice. In the garage of her friend Conrad Marca-Relli's East Hampton home, she found a potato sack filled with old wooden hat forms that the painter's wife, a hatter, had used in her craft.[2] These discarded shapers offered Marisol a means of working on a human scale. Five of them are positioned atop *Mayflower*, which forms part of the first group of larger-scale assemblages that brought Marisol widespread recognition in the emerging Pop movement in 1962.[3]

Here the hat forms, transformed into human heads through the addition of carved and plaster-cast faces, preposterously large wooden noses, and painted hats, eyes, and lips, preside over dozens of carved, painted, and assembled faces encased in a glass-fronted wooden cabinet. Whereas the solid, thick-necked hat-form heads radiate the staunchly middle-class Protestant sensibility echoed in the work's title, the encased faces appear ungrounded and ghostly: a cacophony of glass eyes, open mouths, wrinkled skin, mismatched plaster-cast noses and chins, and the occasional painted halo of yellow, blue, or red hair.[4] In keeping with other works based on hat forms that Marisol produced between 1960 and 1962, *Mayflower* may be understood as a commentary on the enduringly provincial values and fixed hierarchies of the post–World War II United States. The regularity of the dominant heads contrasts with the diversity of the individuals enclosed below them, highlighting the rigid political, racial, and class structures through which the United States continued to be controlled.

Marisol's use of plaster-cast facial features reveals a close dialogue with Jasper Johns's *Target with Four Faces* (1955, Museum of Modern Art, New York), a work widely known and considered representative of a more generalized shift in New York galleries and museums from Abstract Expressionist painting to assemblage and Pop art by 1960.[5] By encasing four identical casts of a friend's lower face above a painted target, Johns underscored a relationship between mass production and the homogenization of identities in mainstream culture. In contrast, Marisol cast her own facial features and distributed them among the faces of *Mayflower*, indicating a personal identification with a broad spectrum of experiences and values.[6] An outsider in the postwar New York avant-gardes by virtue of her gender and her South American and European upbringing, Marisol combined folk-art techniques with a highly developed observational capacity to produce oblique, original commentaries on American society at midcentury.

—**Jennifer Josten**

1. Marina Pacini, "Tracking Marisol in the Fifties and Sixties," *Archives of American Art Journal* 46, nos. 3-4 (Fall 2007): 62–64.
2. Nancy Grove, "A Point of View: The Portraits of Marisol," in *Magical Mixtures: Marisol Portrait Sculpture*, exh. cat. (Washington, D.C.: National Portrait Gallery, Smithsonian Institution, 1991), 15.
3. Grace Glueck, "It's Not Pop, It's Not Op—It's Marisol," *New York Times Magazine*, March 7, 1965, 50; and Vivien Raynor, "Exhibition at Stable Gallery," *Arts Magazine*, September 1962, 44.
4. The sculpture's title may refer to the ship that brought the first English Protestant settlers to New England in 1620.
5. Marisol and Johns both exhibited with the Leo Castelli Gallery, in New York.
6. Marisol's pale, wide-eyed visage is present in many of her works, beginning in 1961; see, for example, the Yale University Art Gallery's *Dinner Date* (1963; gift of Susan Morse Hilles, 1973.86), in which two likenesses of Marisol join each other at a table over a meal on cafeteria trays. In the early 1960s, Marisol offered a practical rationale for casting her own face and body for her works: "I'm usually the only person around to use as a model." Quoted in Glueck, "It's Not Pop, It's Not Op—It's Marisol," 34. As Nancy Grove observes, however, she "later came to see her use of self also as a search for identity." Grove, "A Point of View," 15.

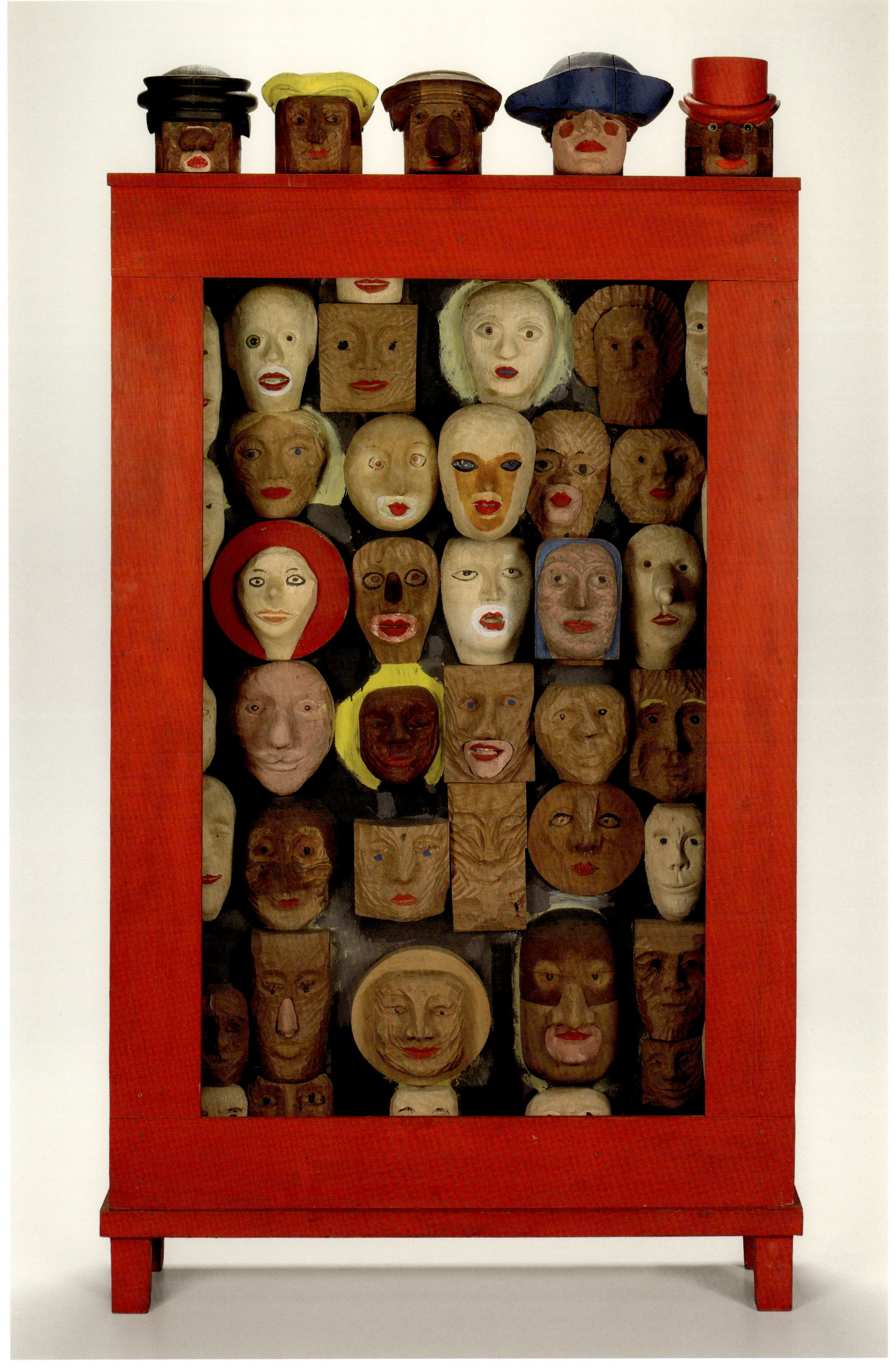

Oskar Kokoschka

Austrian, 1886–1980

32
***View of the Thames from the Vicker's Building, Millbank,** 1962*
Oil on canvas, 35⅝ × 49½ in.
(90.5 × 125.7 cm)
2006.52.15

Although primarily known as a portraitist, Oskar Kokoschka painted numerous landscapes and cityscapes throughout his life, producing a series of arresting views of London, Berlin, Prague, Venice, Paris, and Amsterdam, among others. Like many artists of his generation, Kokoschka was adversely affected by the two world wars, and his highly wrought Expressionist style speaks to his personal ordeals. Having experienced firsthand trench warfare and the mutilated, ravaged landscapes it produced, Kokoschka came to regard his radiant, sweeping views of cities as symbols of a politically free and prosperous Europe. Remembering World War I, he recalled, "[T]hen I thought . . . if ever I come out of this rat-existence alive, I will paint landscapes . . . the roots of my culture, of my civilization."[1]

View of the Thames from the Vicker's Building, Millbank, is one such example of an affirmative, redemptive painting. It depicts a broad panorama of London seen from the Millbank Tower on the north bank of the river Thames, south of the Palace of Westminster. Kokoschka's choice of vantage point was not merely dictated by the aesthetic desire to capture a beautiful view but was rooted in deeper symbolism. During World War II, more than a million homes were destroyed in London by Nazi aerial bombardments. Millbank Tower— at the time London's tallest skyscraper— symbolized Britain's postwar economic and construction boom. Furthermore, the elevated viewpoint allowed Kokoschka to produce an extensive, far-reaching vista with a high horizon line, creating the pictorial illusion of an infinite expanse. London was thus portrayed as an immense, boundless metropolis, fully recovered from the Nazi onslaught.

In contrast to the heavy, foreboding colors and anxious, furrowed lines of many of Kokoschka's earlier landscapes, the present work is executed in brighter, luminous tones and is suffused with a warm, atmospheric light. The thick impasto and vigorous brushwork activate the surface of the canvas, producing an almost anthropomorphic quality that makes the buildings appear to be in constant motion. Kokoschka rarely made preparatory sketches, and often used his fingers, as well as his paintbrush handle, to scratch forms into the wet paint. This active bodily engagement with the work generates a dynamic, emotional charge.

In the middle ground, the pronounced verticality of the Victoria Tower—the Palace of Westminster's most prominent architectural feature—punctuates the horizon line, drawing attention to its neo-Gothic façade. Together with the Thames, which Kokoschka described as London's "artery of life flowing from century to century," the Victoria Tower evokes England's rich past and survival despite repeated outside threats to its stability.[2]

—**Maria Taroutina**

1. Oskar Kokoschka, interview with Andrew Forge, quoted in Richard Calvocoressi, *Kokoschka: Paintings* (New York: Rizzoli, 1992), 17.
2. Oskar Kokoschka, *My Life*, trans. David Britt (London: Thames and Hudson, 1974), 123.

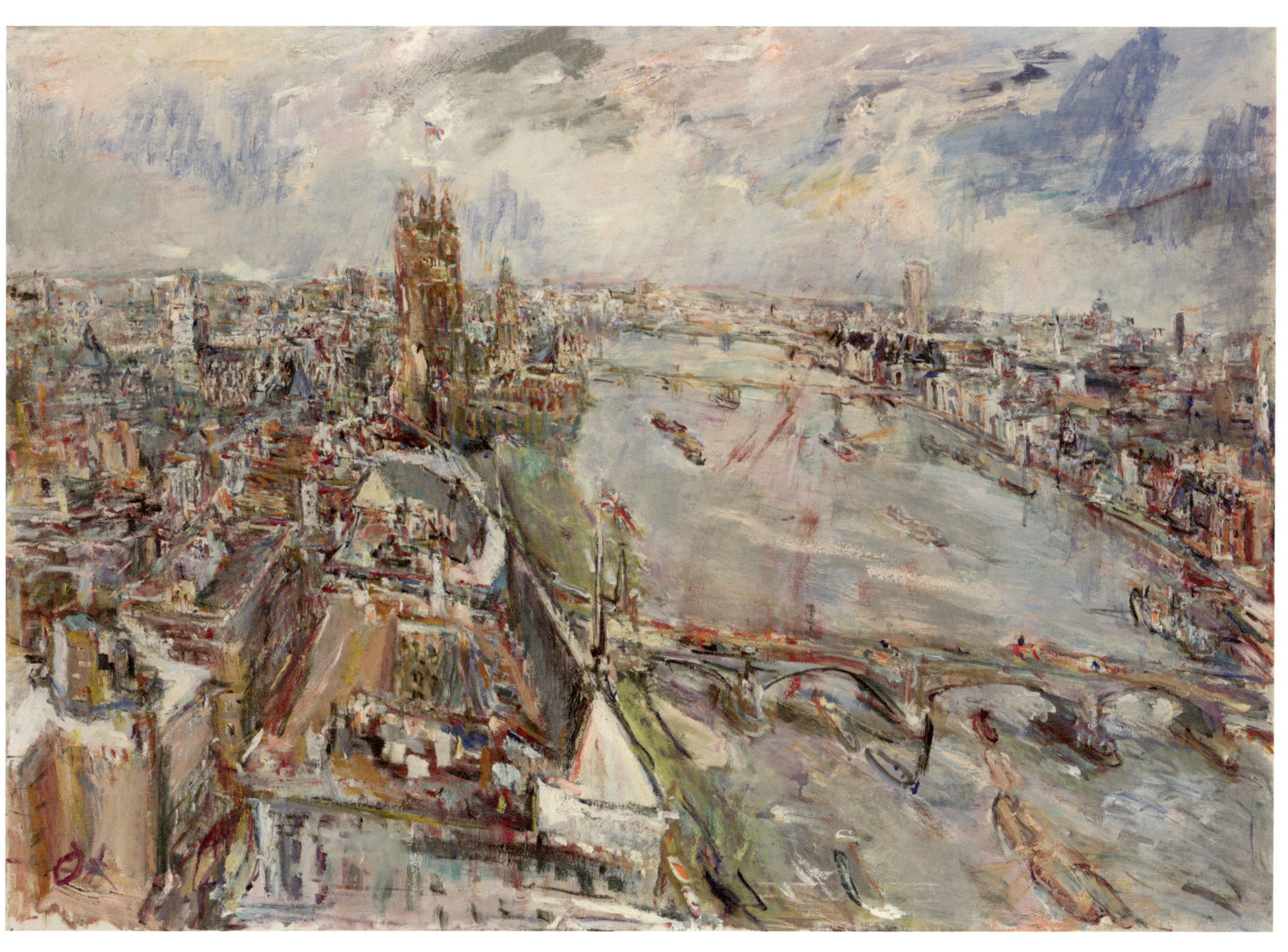

Larry Rivers

American, 1923–2002

33
Double French Money, 1962
Oil on canvas, 72 × 60 in. (182.9 × 152.4 cm)
2006.52.52

Larry Rivers painted *Double French Money* during his stay in Paris in 1962. The work represents both sides of a one-hundred-franc note. In the top register, a bust of Napoléon Bonaparte is depicted in front of barely visible traces of French flags. The general looks right toward an obliterated image of Les Invalides, France's military history museum. In the bottom register, the same image of Napoléon is reversed and shown looking left toward a pencil drawing of the Arc de Triomphe. Stenciled French words, "BANQUE DE F" (Bank of F[rance]) and "CENT NOUVEAUX" (one hundred new), as well as the number one hundred in the top left and right corners, are combined with expressive passages of paint. Both the words and the images appear half finished or half erased and are at a distant remove from the crisp graphics of the original banknote (fig. 1). The work abounds with visible pencil underdrawing, drips, smudges, and traces of deletions and overpainting. Instead of a faithful duplicate of the banknote, Rivers produced a highly personalized image characterized by disjunction, omission, and fragmentation, akin to the modern urban landscape—a theme that the artist explored at length in much of his oeuvre.

Although typically—and reductively—considered to be proto-Pop art, Rivers's work stands in stark contrast to the polished, mechanical rendition of Andy Warhol's and Roy Lichtenstein's mature Pop paintings, in which many of the vestiges of process were purposely eliminated. Having been trained in abstraction at the Hans Hofmann School of Fine Arts in New York from 1947 to 1948, Rivers maintained the importance of a sensual, painterly, and personal art, even as he rejected many tenets of Abstract Expressionism. Thus, in *Double French Money* he provocatively merges nonobjective and non-narrative abstraction with careful draftsmanship and figuration. He also brings together two traditionally opposed registers by using a painterly abstract style to depict the mundane materials of everyday life.

Similarly, Rivers is playfully ironic in his choice of subject matter. On the one hand, *Double French Money* mocks the use of France's glorious symbols to elevate the banal aesthetic of a banknote; on the other hand, this usage underlines their sublimation into the most powerful signifier of late capitalism: money. In a more self-referential gesture, Rivers implicitly critiqued the growing commodity status of art in the 1960s by making money the literal subject of his painting. As an investment, art has the potential to multiply money, "doubling" in value through time. Rivers himself regarded the *French Money* paintings as part of his most successful series. He painted at least fifteen variations, claiming that he "was able to repeat these subjects without getting tired of them."[1]

—**Maria Taroutina**

1. Larry Rivers and Carol Brightman, *Drawings and Digressions* (New York: Crown Publishers, 1979), 151.

One-hundred-franc note, 1959

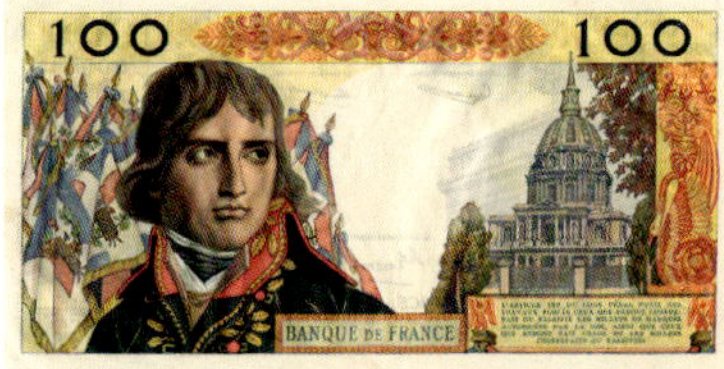

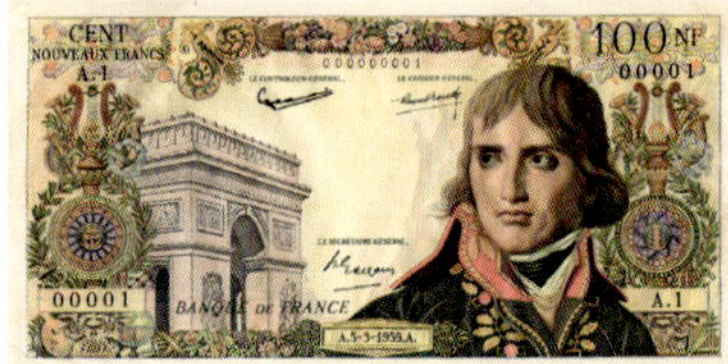

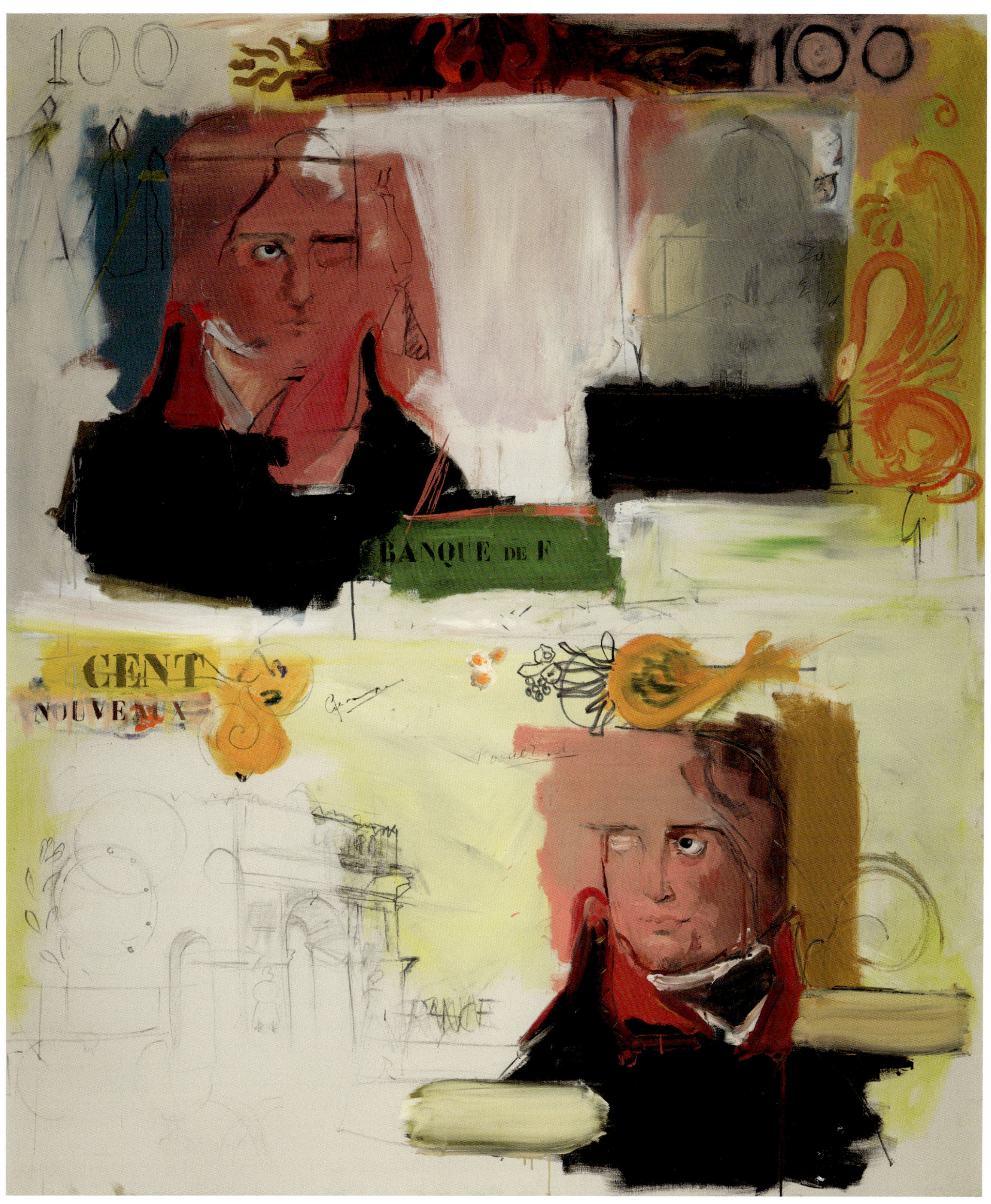

100
100
BANQUE DE F
GENT
NOUVEAUX
FRANCE

David Smith

American, 1906–1965

34
Bec-Dida Day, 1963
Steel with paint, 89 × 65 × 18 in.
(226.1 × 165.1 × 45.7 cm)
2006.52.68

35
Untitled, 1953
Black ink and tempera, 17 11/16 × 24 1/16 in.
(45 × 61.1 cm)
2006.52.87

36
Untitled, 1954
Black ink and wash with tempera, 17 9/16 ×
22 5/8 in. (44.6 × 57.4 cm)
2006.52.89

37
Untitled, 1960
Brown ink, 41 1/8 × 26 1/8 in. (104.4 × 66.4 cm)
2006.52.88

Although renowned as an accomplished sculptor and draftsman, David Smith began his artistic life as a painter, moving to New York in 1926, where he enrolled at the Art Students League. Premonitions of Smith's future as a remarkable innovator in three dimensions first became manifest when he adhered objects to the surfaces of his paintings and began assembling small, painted wood constructions. Impressed by the iron sculptures of Picasso and Julio González in the early 1930s, Smith began to weld metal forms together to weave a syntax of Surrealist-inspired images into a skein of associative imagery. Smith found inspiration in the machine aesthetic of U.S. industry. He used the skills he developed working as a riveter on car-frame assembly in an Indiana Studebaker plant to create works that re-imaged the landscape and the human figure as powerful abstractions. He would later hone his mastery of the oxyacetylene torch as an art-making tool in a Schenectady defense plant during World War II, where he worked as a welder of M7 tanks and locomotives. Smith used these skills to assemble a vocabulary of found machine and farm equipment parts and cut iron and steel elements into freestanding sculptures.

In 1940 Smith moved permanently to his summer studio at Bolton Landing in upstate New York, where he would work until his death. In the intervening twenty-five years he was remarkably productive. The influence of painting never left Smith's work. He would compose his sculptures on the floor of his studio, laying cut shapes in proximity to one another. Once he had a satisfying composition, he would weld these forms together. The Surrealist-inspired works of the 1940s led to the stunning series of landscape-informed works of the 1950s, such as *Australia* (1951, Museum of Modern Art, New York). Smith's sculpting vocabulary in the mid-1950s was embodied in flat forged pieces and steel stamped into slender bars and flattened silhouettes. It was in this decade that he made the works that constitute the *Tanktotem* series (1953–60). These abstract shapes took the human form as their point of reference and often incorporated boiler-tank ends to evoke the head or torso of a figure. *Bec-Dida Day* (cat. 34) can be viewed as an extension of the original *Tanktotem* series. Like most of the works in that series, *Bec-Dida Day* strongly suggests the abstract form of a running figure.

Bec-Dida Day is named after the artist's two daughters, Rebecca and Candida, who spent two months every summer with Smith at Bolton Landing. According to his daughters, the work was inspired by the shared birthday party the girls celebrated with him each August.[1] The application of a vibrant palette of paint to the form imbues it with a lively energy evocative of the sense of celebration and childlike joy such an occasion elicits. *Bec-Dida Day* is an exemplary work by one of the most important sculptors of the twentieth century.

In addition to *Bec-Dida Day*, Charles B. Benenson gave four drawings by Smith to the Yale University Art Gallery, three of which are illustrated here. Dating from 1953, 1954, and 1960, these untitled works (cats. 35–37) offer fine examples of how Smith used drawing to study the image that his three-dimensional forms would make against a flat plane.

The untitled drawing from 1953 (cat. 35) strongly relates to the landscape sculptures of the same period in Smith's oeuvre. In it, forms flow around and across the surface of the paper and into one another, much as the welded forms he assembled would be viewed against the sky or a landscape. The drawings from 1954 and 1960 were made much more quickly. The calligraphic marks captured on these pages are assembled into compositions rather than flowing loosely across the page.

—**Jennifer R. Gross**

1. Candida N. Smith, "The Fields of David Smith," in *The Fields of David Smith*, exh. cat., by Smith, Irving Sandler, and Jerry L. Thompson (Mountainville, N.Y.: Storm King Art Center, 1999), 35.

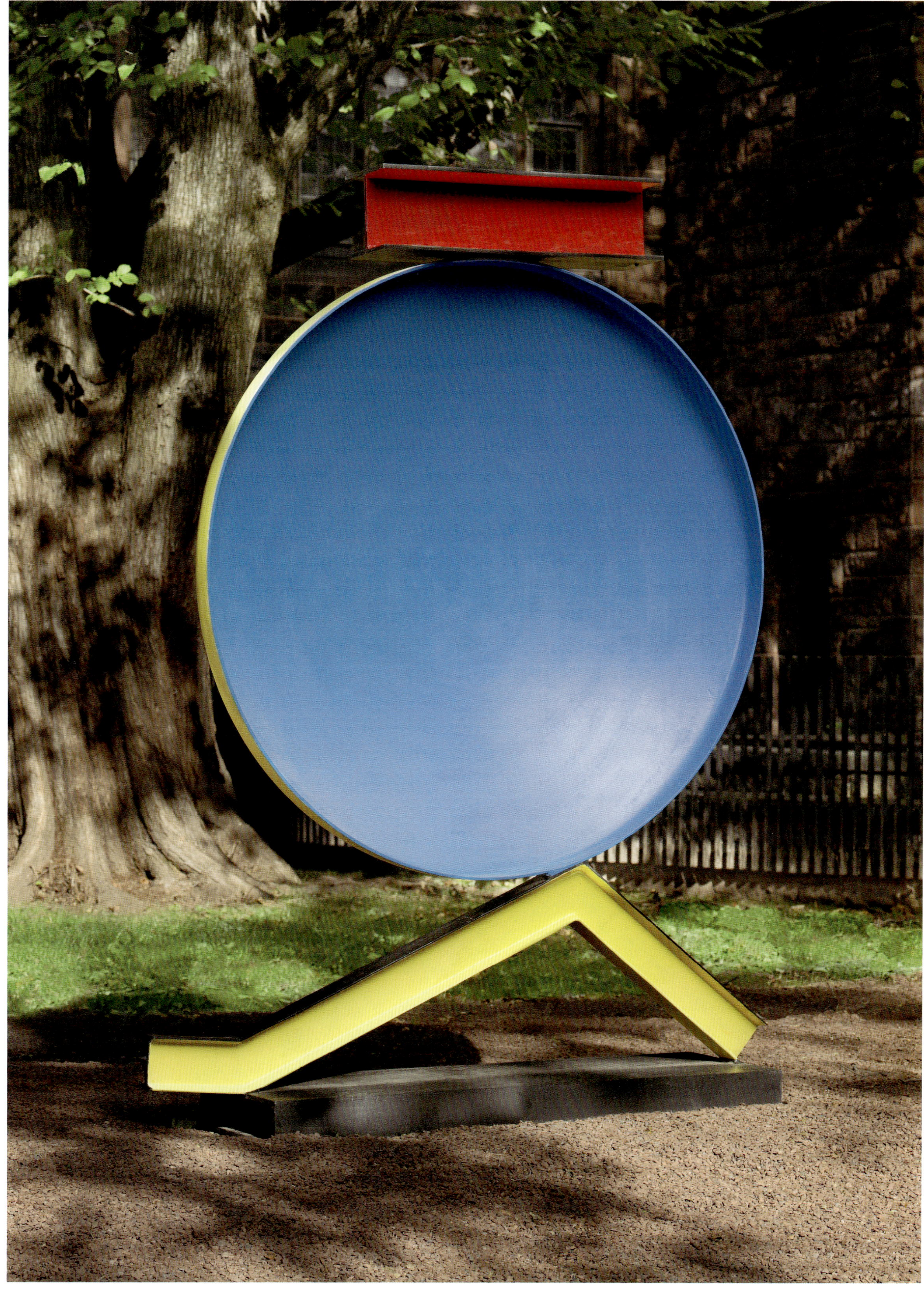

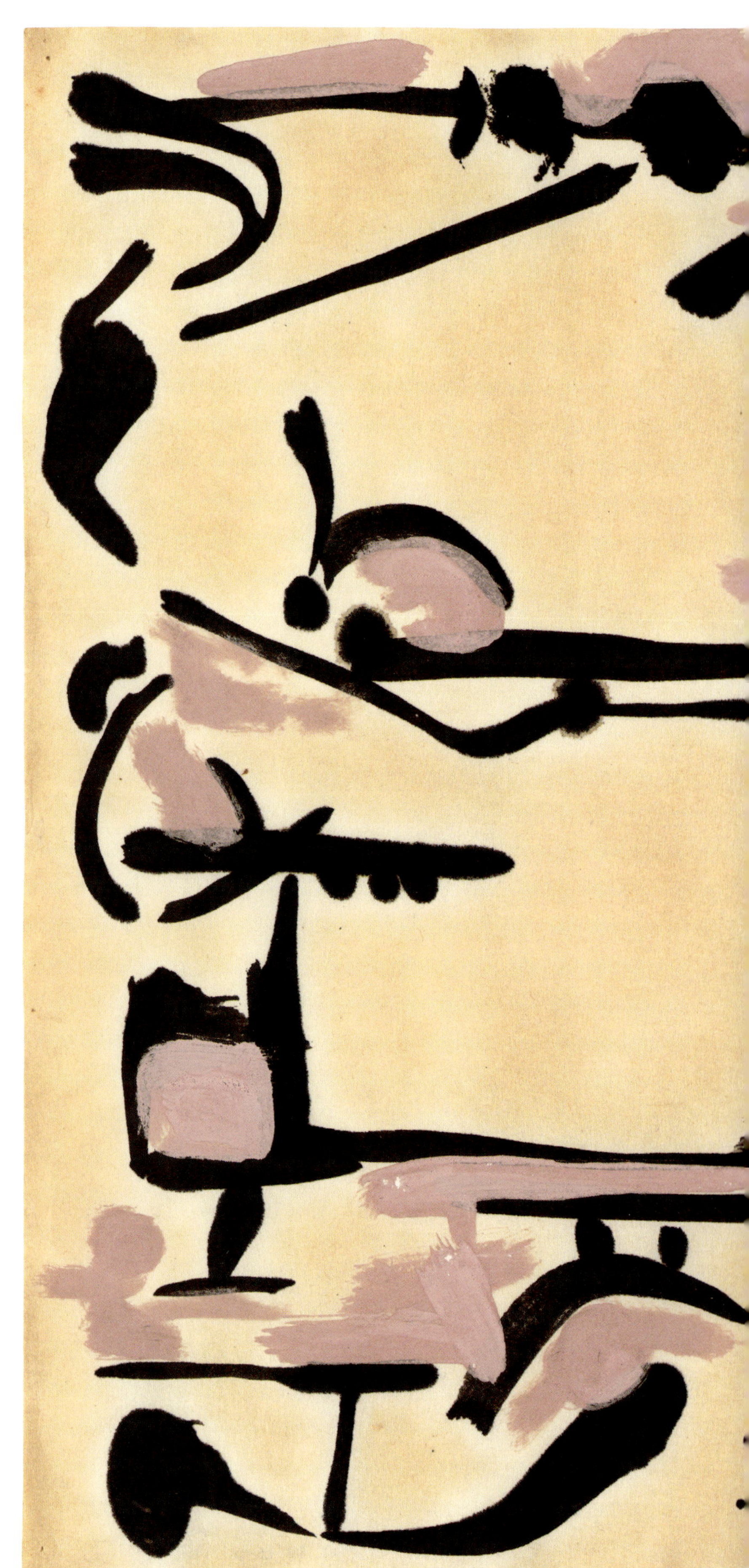

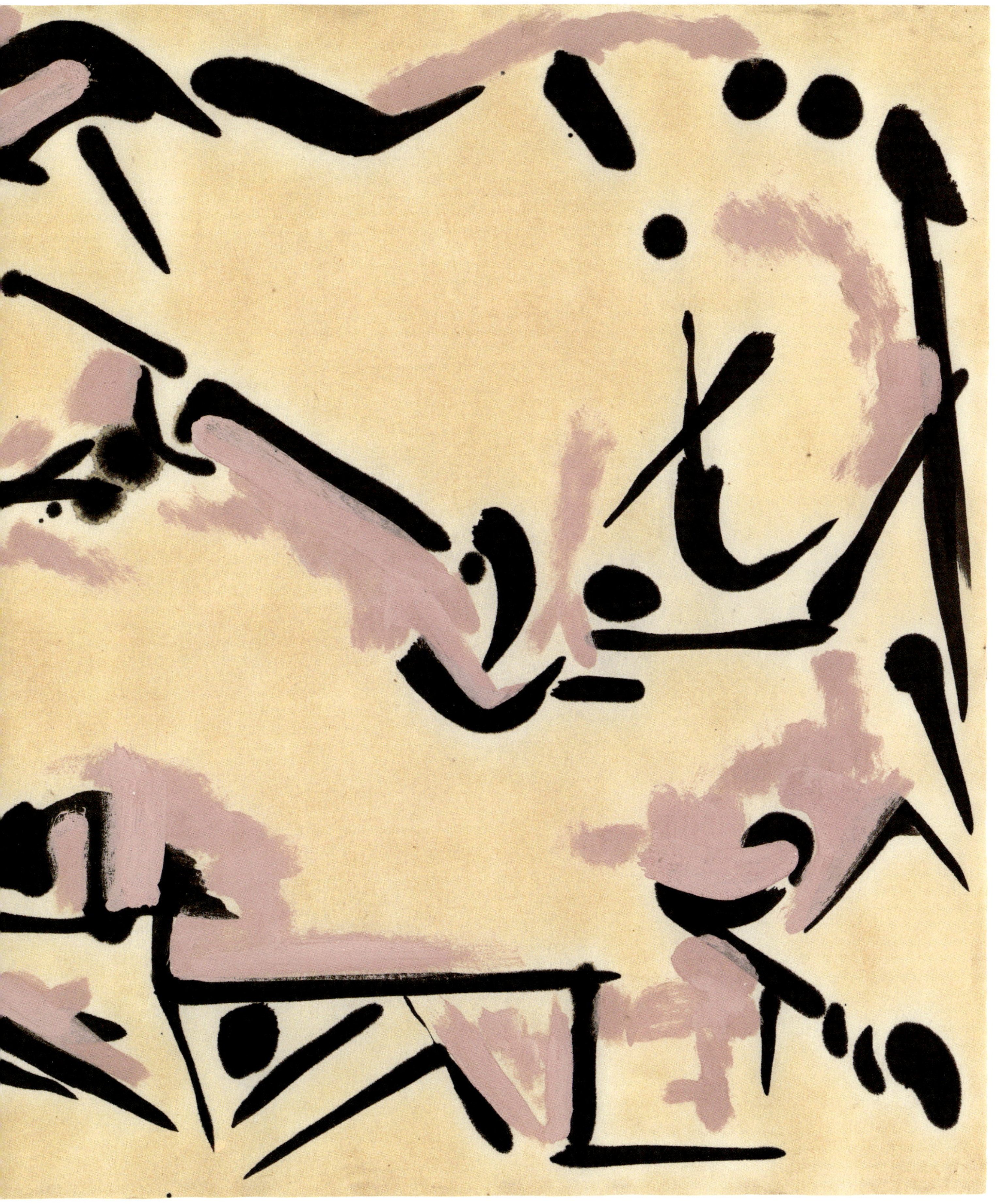

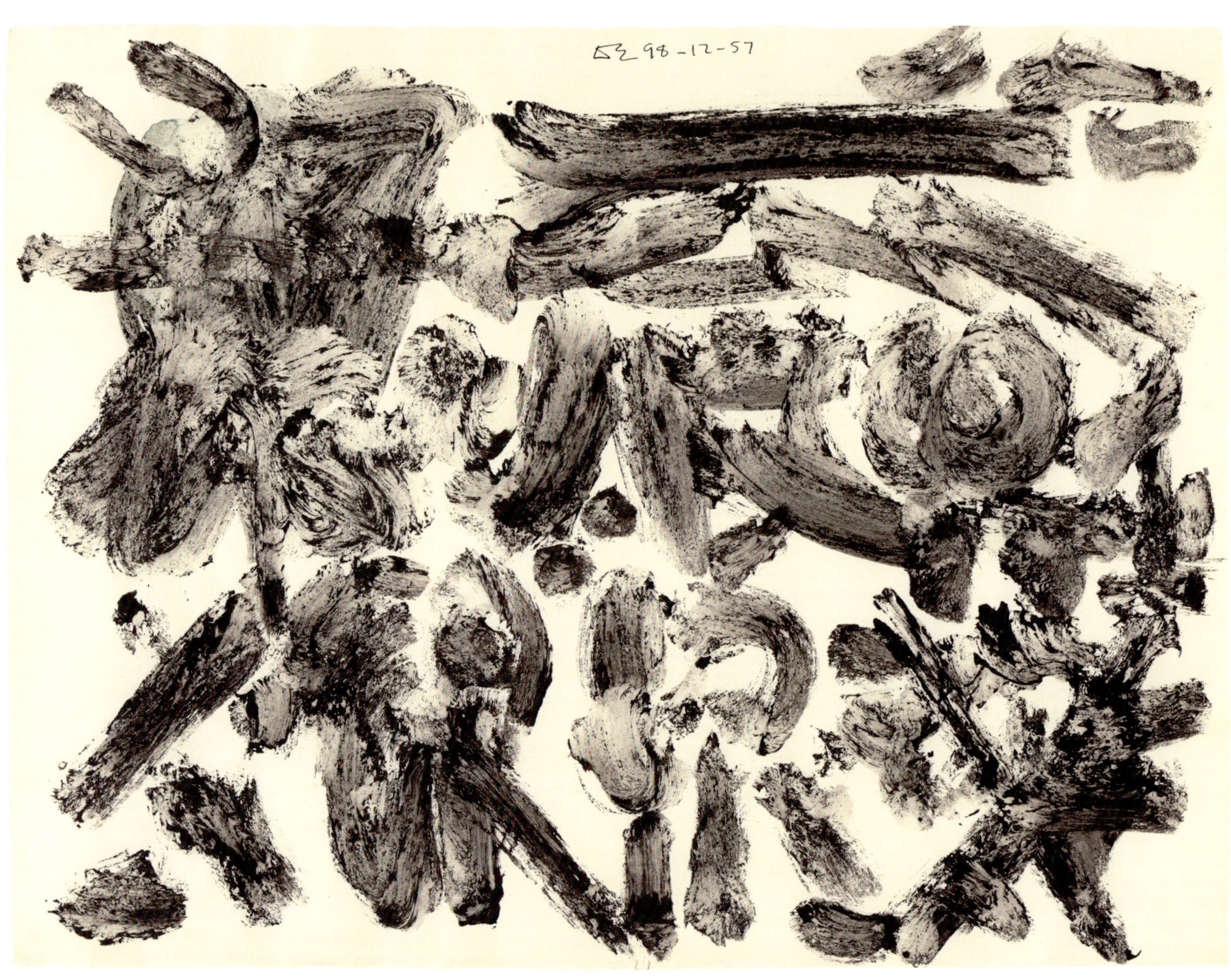

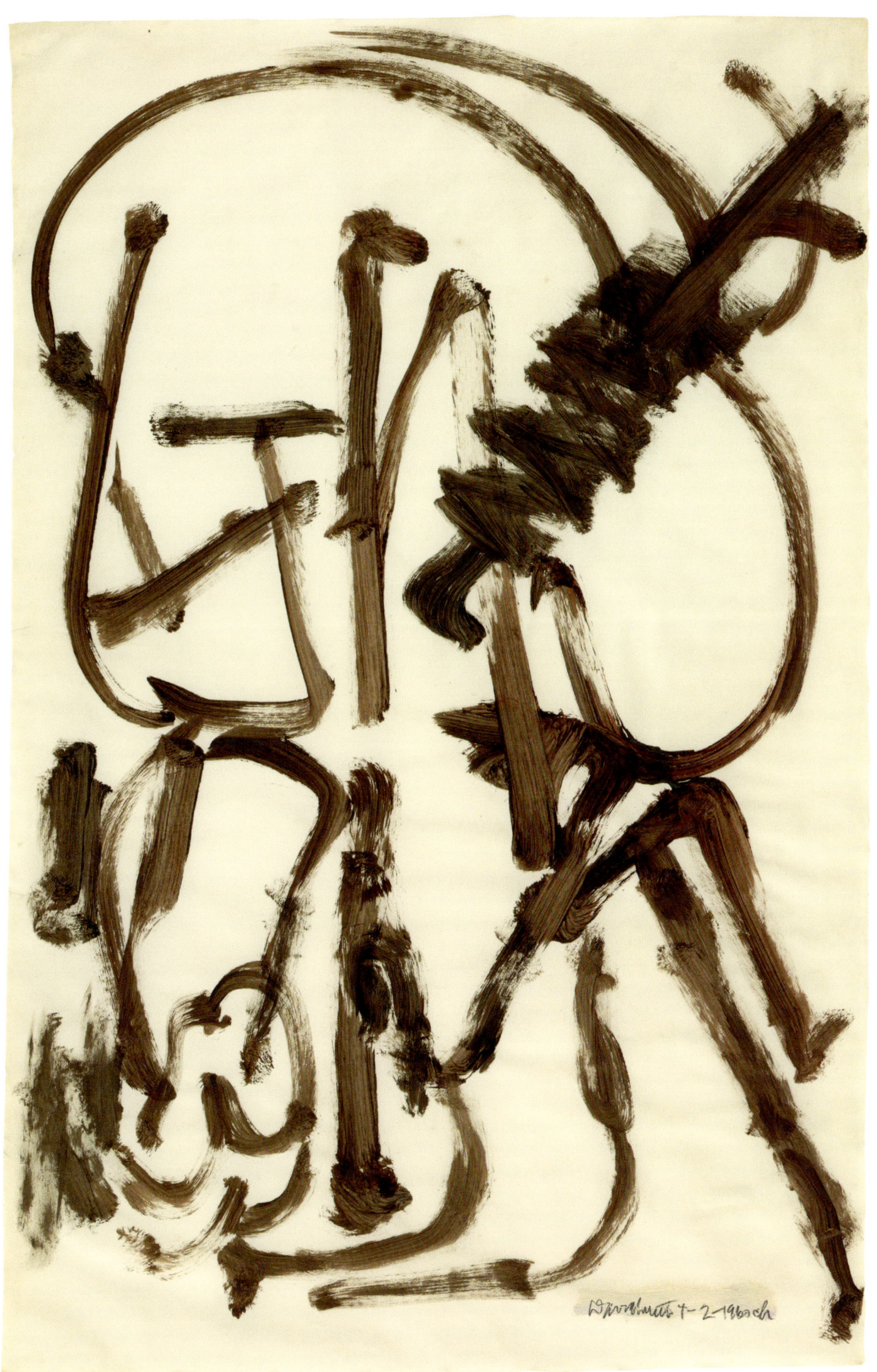

Jiří Kolář

Czech, 1914–2002

Although he first exhibited his artworks in 1937, Czech artist Jiří Kolář spent the ensuing decades alternating between his work as a poet and as a visual artist.[1] While active as a writer within the Prague-based avant-garde Group 42 from 1942 to 1948, Kolář was inspired by the painters of that group to add images to his poems. Then, in an echo of Theodor Adorno's suspicion of expressive art after the Holocaust, Kolář emerged from the war disillusioned with writing: "[W]hen I managed to sift through a number of authentic eyewitness reports [from concentration camps], it was a wonder I did not feel compelled to put on gloves when I had to read a book of poems."[2] Drawn to the dry, bureaucratic language of contracts, receipts, and protocols, Kolář began making typewriter poems and treating found text as fragments for collage.[3]

Kolář was a critical witness to the effects of government authority: from the early optimism of communism in the Czech Republic, to 1953, when he was imprisoned and banned for a decade from publishing his "dissident" poetry, to the failure of the Prague Spring in 1968, which he captured in daily diaristic collages.

Kolář wrote, "The world attacks us directly . . . and assembles and reassembles us again. Collage is the most appropriate medium to illustrate this reality."[4] The three Kolář collages in the Charles B. Benenson Collection are dated soon after the artist's solo exhibition in 1962 at the Klub VU Mánes in Prague, which led to his international recognition. The first, an untitled collage of a woman, is an example of what Kolář called an "object chiasmage": glued surfaces made up of small paper scraps and often labyrinthine in their use of referents.[5] Here a cow's head adorned with flowers veils the face of a lingerie model, transforming her into a harvest or fertility goddess (cat. 38). The collage includes images of artworks such as Leonardo da Vinci's *Mona Lisa* (ca. 1503–6, Musée du Louvre, Paris) and Max Ernst's 1959 bronze sculpture *Daughter and Mother*, an example of which was also owned by Benenson. An oversized woman's hand wears a car steering wheel in place of a ring, and the fragmentary legs, breasts, and lips of other women fill the panel. A three-dimensional sculpted arm is attached on top of the composition, which adds a disquieting dimension to the frenetic images, as does Kolář's inclusion of a woodblock print of a woman praying before a multiheaded demon, an illustration of how devils could change into animals to trick humans. This collage may caution against hedonistic surrender to 1960s commodity culture.

Kolář's other two works in the Benenson Collection are also planar collages supplemented by object chiasmages. Here, however, the artist creates an overall compositional field, rather than a juxtaposition of recognizable images. The untitled collage of canceled stamps (cat. 39) is connected to the origins of collage in nineteenth-century trompe l'oeil painting. There, stamps frequently made an appearance as symbols of currency and collecting. For Dada artist Kurt Schwitters, the inclusion of a canceled postage stamp in a collage could serve as a critique of the imperial issuing power, whereas Pop artists from Andy Warhol to Arman used stamps in the 1960s as readymade, reproduced, and reproducible images. By then, the accessibility of silkscreen technology had irreversibly brought photography into the painter's studio. Art historian Brandon Taylor has noted that although enlarged photographic silkscreens marked a rupture between early and late twentieth-century collage aesthetics in the work of artists from Warhol to Robert Rauschenberg, the work of Kolář proved an exception.[6] His collages are a bridge between Futurist writing, Dada and Surrealist collage, and the Pop art of the 1950s and 1960s.

The collage with a knife and a rolling pin (cat. 40) belongs to a group of mid-1960s works by Kolář that incorporate common household goods such as spatulas, washing boards, and cutting boards. These collages of domestic objects are connected to a body of writing Kolář developed from 1954 to 1957 called the "poetry of instructions," which he based on his reading of food cans, cookbooks, and technical manuals, texts that inspired his assertion that "[s]omeday, it will become possible to make poetry out of anything at all."[7]

Kolář's rephrasing of popular images from the history of art, his use of text fragments, and his incorporation of three-dimensional objects into two-dimensional collage appealed to American audiences, and he was the subject of a solo exhibition at the Guggenheim Museum in New York in 1975. It is likely that Charles B. Benenson, like many collectors of his generation, was introduced to Kolář's work following that exhibition's resounding success.

—**Cathleen Chaffee**

1. This practice paralleled contemporaneous connections between poetry and visual images made by the French Letterism movement, founded in 1945.
2. Jiří Kolář, *Jiří Kolář*, trans. Paul Wilson (Milan: Giancarlo Politi Editore, 1986), 21.
3. He also penned an elaborate dictionary to describe each new technique he developed, becoming one of the most productive postwar theorists of the formal characteristics of collage.
4. Jiří Kolář, quoted in Charlotta Kotik, *Jiří Kolář: Transformations*, exh. cat. (Buffalo: Albright-Knox Art Gallery, 1978), 9.
5. The term is derived from the Greek letter chi (x).
6. Brandon Taylor, *Collage: The Making of Modern Art* (New York: Thames and Hudson, 2004), 181.
7. Jiří Kolář, quoted in Wieland Schmied, "Der Weg des Jiří Kolář," in *Jiří Kolář*, exh. cat. (Hanover: Kestner-Gesellschaft, 1969), 8; excerpted and translated in Thomas Messer, "Introductory Collage," in *Jiří Kolář*, exh. cat. (New York: Solomon R. Guggenheim Museum, 1975), 13.

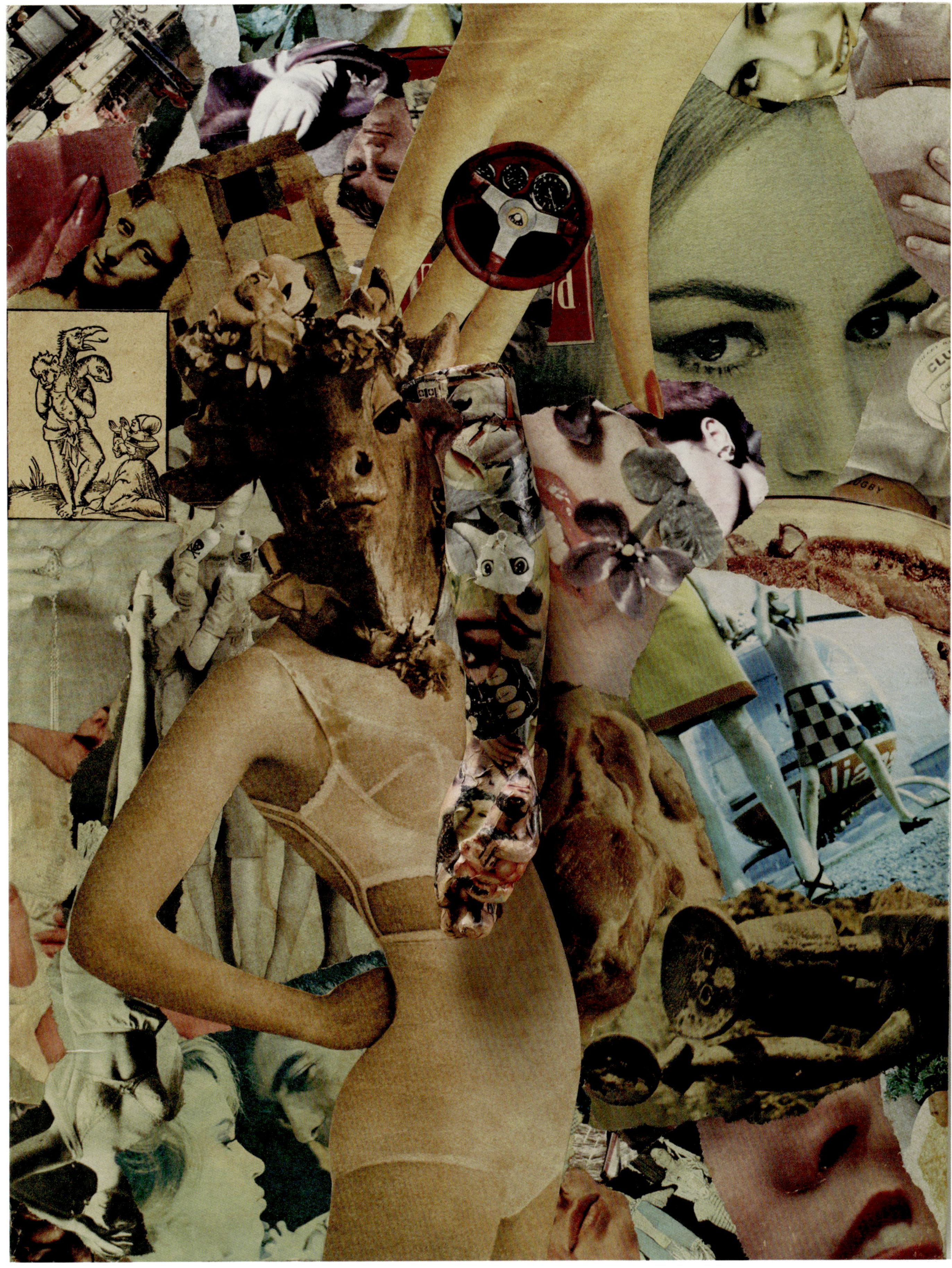

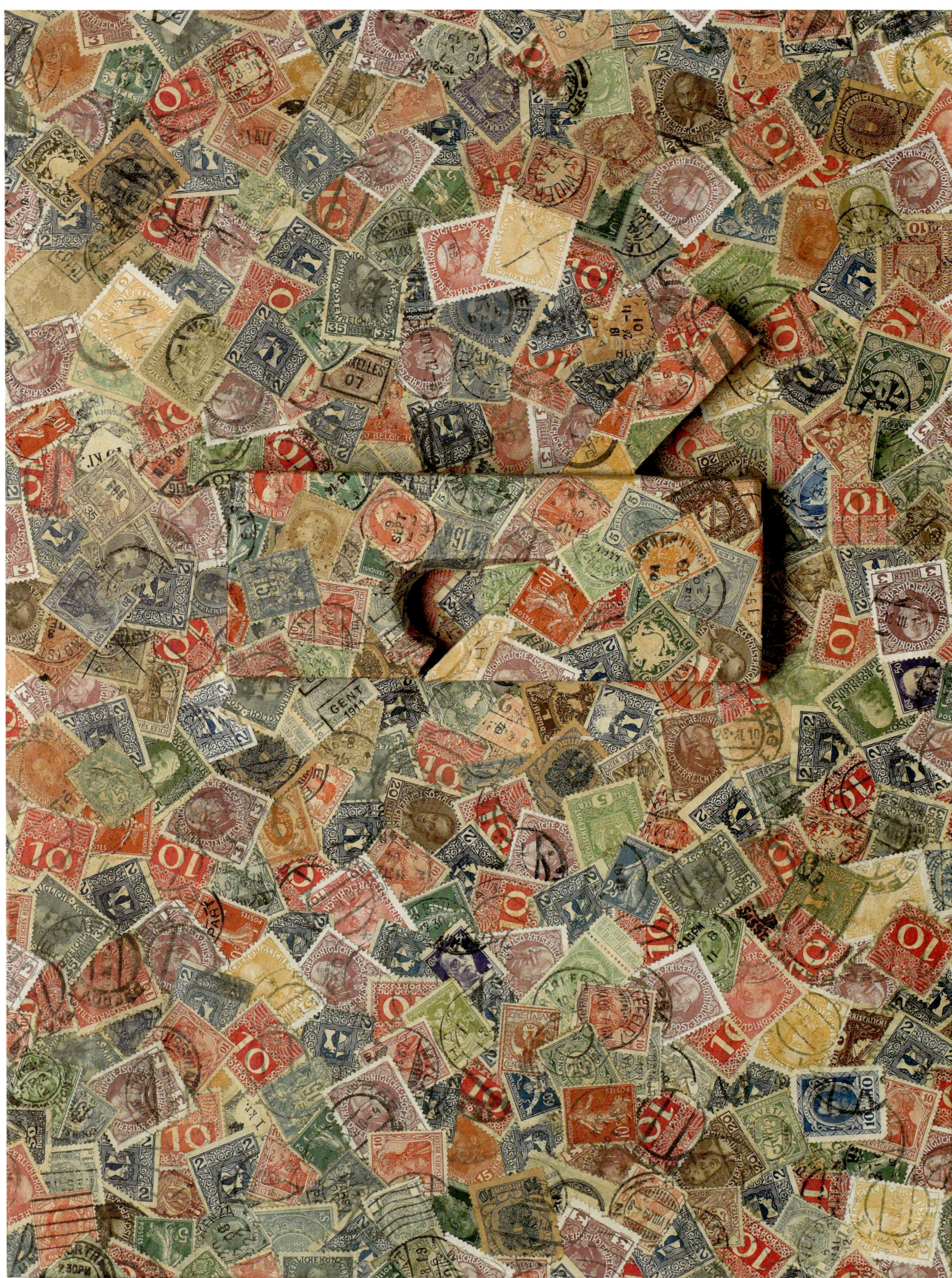

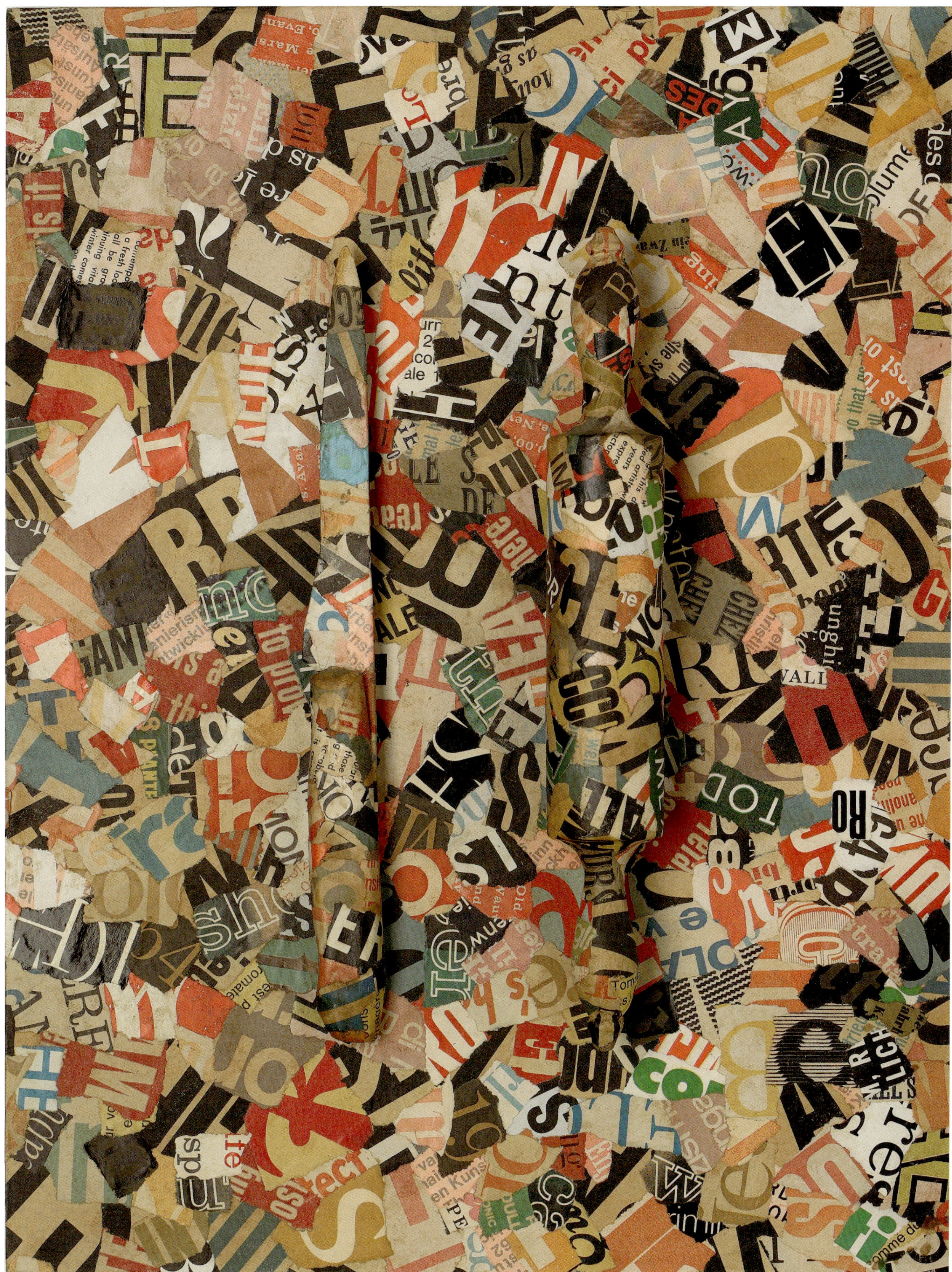

Alexander Calder

American, 1898–1976

41
***Numbered One to Nine**, 1967*
Sheet metal with paint and wire, installed
approximately 45½ in. × 9 ft. 4 in.
(115.6 × 284.5 cm)
2006.52.54

In 1960, Alexander Calder flatly declared that he had "more or less retired from the smaller mobiles," the constellations of colored shapes and wire that had earned him international fame. He had come to characterize these works dismissively, even disparagingly, as "fiddling."[1] Later in the decade, when *Numbered One to Nine* was made, critics encouraged Calder's ongoing production of mobiles but seemed to challenge galleries and museums to find fresh and surprising contexts for these works. Accordingly, the Perls Galleries in New York organized an exhibition displaying the genesis of Calder's hanging constructions, which dated to the early 1930s.[2] The effort was rewarded with renewed critical enthusiasm for Calder and his work. "It's a revealing show," one critic lauded. "Obviously the simple movement of the mobile is based on any number of complexities."[3] The mobile's enduring popularity was therefore credited to its ability to suggest a deeper meaning. It also succeeded in maintaining the undercurrent of whimsy that permeated Calder's exploration of materials in newer formats.

Mobiles always retained some appeal for the artist as well. Even as Calder preoccupied himself with static sculptures, he still grappled with a formal question that the "stabiles" and "wallmobiles" could not answer: how does one produce endless harmonies from constantly shifting geometries? A visit to Piet Mondrian's studio in 1930 had proven to be a moment of genesis for Calder.[4] He believed that real movement was the essential component that distinguished his work from Mondrian's painted interplay of black lines and red, blue, yellow, and white rectangles.

This notion of origin was one of several elementary principles on which Calder based his art, from the simple palette of primary colors (plus black and white) that he employed to the organic structures from which his forms were abstracted. Given their ubiquity in the vast "system of the Universe," spheres represented to Calder the "ideal source of form."[5] He crowned opposite sides of the mobile from the Charles B. Benenson Collection with flattened versions of such forms—one golden yellow and one pure black disc—calling to mind the sun and its nocturnal counterpart, the moon. This sphere's cosmic associations fascinated Calder, who wrote about his trip to a planetarium to observe the movements of "detached bodies floating in space."[6] He also recounted his experience aboard a ship when he witnessed a blazing sunrise and a full moon on each end of the horizon.[7] Inhabiting the open space below, Calder and the other passengers on deck must have appeared like the lower stratum of red discs in the mobile: dispersed in an asymmetrical but somehow precise position between two endpoints, in concert with the entities looming overhead.

—**Keely Orgeman**

1. Geoffrey T. Hellman, "Onward and Upward with the Arts: Calder Revisited," *New Yorker*, October 22, 1960, 169; quoted in Marla Prather, *Alexander Calder, 1898–1976*, exh. cat. (Washington, D.C.: National Gallery of Art, 1998), 279.
2. The Perls Galleries served as Calder's exclusive dealer in the United States. Art critic William Berkson noted that the mobiles in one of their exhibitions appeared "their old ingratiating selves," whereas "Calder's most interesting works are nowadays his stabiles." Berkson's remarks, though harsher than those of other critics during this period, show an indifferent attitude toward the mobile style, which he seemed to regard as outmoded or overexposed. William Berkson, "Exhibition at Perls Gallery," *Art News*, February 1966, 14. See also Diane Waldman, "Exhibition at Perls Gallery," *Arts Magazine*, April 1966, 62.
3. Noel Frackman, "Alexander Calder," *Arts Magazine*, September 1968, 60.
4. Calder's retelling of this story appears in the following texts, all of which are reproduced on the Calder Foundation's website, www.calder.org/historicaltexts. html (accessed January 13, 2010): Alexander Calder, "Mobiles," in *The Painter's Object*, ed. Myfanwy Evans (London: Gerald Howe, 1937); Calder, "What Abstract Art Means to Me," *Museum of Modern Art Bulletin* 18, no. 3 (Spring 1951): 8; and Katherine Kuh, "Interview with Alexander Calder," in *The Artist's Voice: Talks with Seventeen Artists* (New York: Harper and Row, 1962), 39–51.
5. Calder, "What Abstract Art Means to Me," 8.
6. Ibid.
7. Jean Lipman, *Calder's Universe* (New York: Viking, 1980), 17. See also Alexander Calder and Jean Davidson, *Calder: An Autobiography with Pictures* (New York: Pantheon, 1966), 54–55.

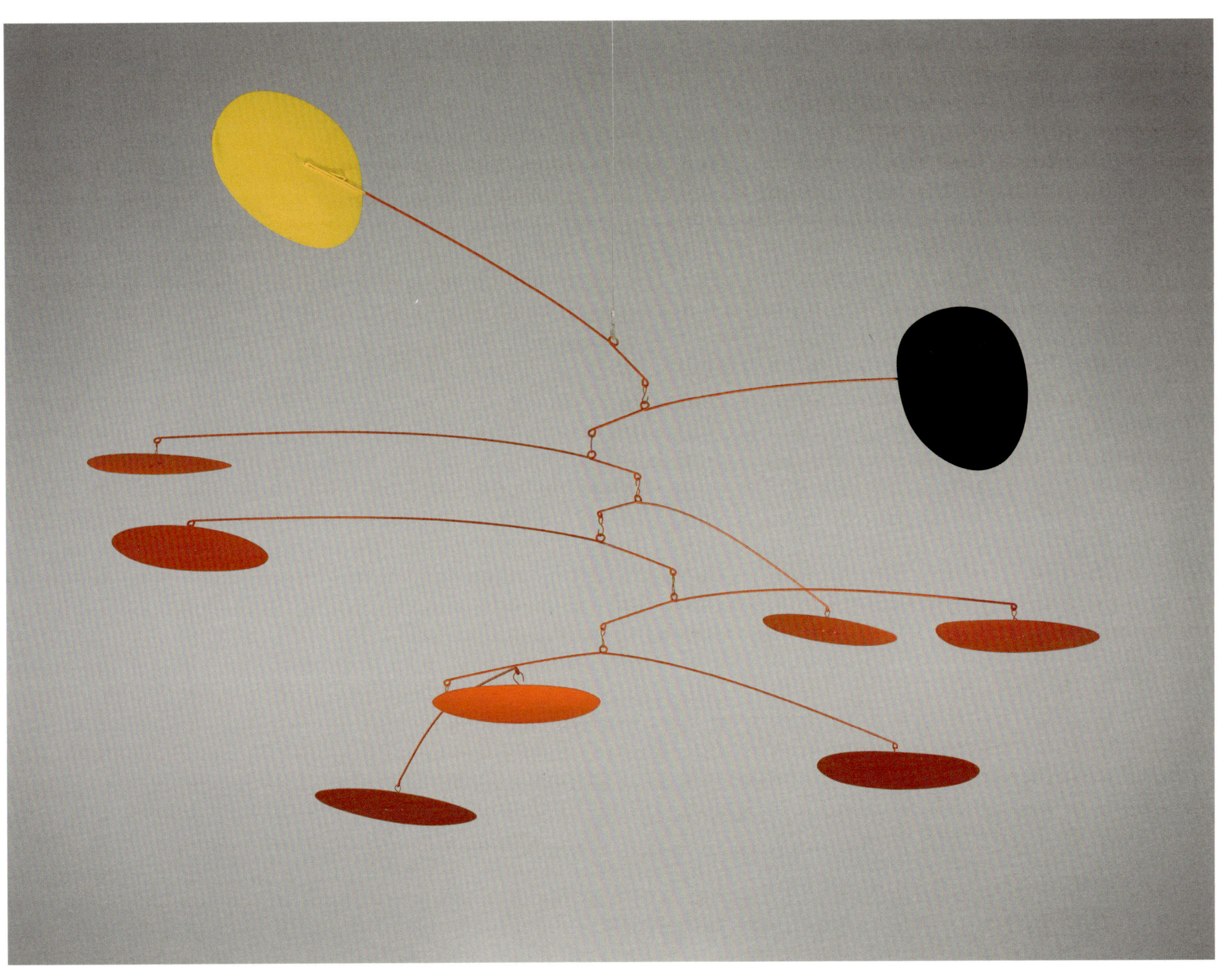

Joan Miró

Spanish, 1893–1983

42
Jeune fille s'évadant (Girl Escaping), 1968
Bronze with paint, edition 2/4, 80⁷⁄₁₆ × 16⅝ ×
28 ¼ in. (204.3 × 42.2 × 71.8 cm)
2006.52.20

43
Personnage et oiseau (Figure and Bird), 1970
Bronze with brown and green patina, edition
2/4, 63 × 48¹⁄₁₆ × 11¹⁄₁₆ in. (160 × 122 × 28 cm)
2006.52.67

At the opening of his 1974 retrospective at
Paris's Grand Palais, an eighty-one-year-old
Joan Miró claimed that he was "an established
painter, but a young sculptor." [1] Although Miró
intermittently experimented with three-
dimensional forms throughout his career,
sculpture did not become his focus until the
1960s. Miró was commissioned to produce thirteen monumental sculptures for the Fondation
Maeght in the South of France in 1964. He
immersed himself in this new medium for the
following two decades, producing a variety of
large and small sculptures in bronze, plaster,
resin, fiberglass, and concrete.

Although Miró never considered himself
an exponent of Surrealism, his work was
continually informed by Surrealist ideas and
practices, even late in his career. Much of his
sculpture, for example, relied heavily on the
Surrealist concept of using found objects.
Miró would explore the sculptural possibilities of found items in drawings and sketches,
which he then used to create plaster and
wooden maquettes. These were subsequently
cast into bronze and often painted with
Ripolin, an industrial house paint.

Jeune fille s'évadant (Girl Escaping) is built
around two found objects: a pair of mannequin legs and a water spigot, both of which
are painted vibrant red (cat. 42). A series
of drawings executed between November
25, 1964, and February 1, 1965, capture the
sculpture's gestation. Miró began the sculpture with the mannequin legs and gradually
built it in an additive fashion. The figure's
voluptuous legs and buttocks are offset by her
coquettish faucet "hat." Miró modeled the
torso and head in clay, and they are composed
of a square and a circle crudely marked with

two eyes, a nose, and a mouth. The girl's
midsection reads both as a second face and
as a chest with prominent white breasts and
two vertically aligned buttons. Miró clearly
intended this doubling as a visual pun; the
majority of his painted sculptures from the
1960s and 1970s are similarly playful.

The discontinuity between the figure's
sensuous lower half and her clumsy upper
body creates what Miró called "a poetic shock
. . . an original formal impact," and it recalls
Surrealist "exquisite corpse" drawings from
the late 1920s. [2] These works were assembled by
collaborators who would each add to a composition in sequence, producing jarring and
visually disjunctive images.

By contrast, Miró's second sculpture
in the Charles B. Benenson Collection,
Personnage et oiseau (Figure and Bird), was
originally envisioned in 1963 as a patinated
bronze (cat. 43). It was not until 1982 that it
was re-created on a monumental scale in
bright yellow, red, blue, and green after its
selection as the model for a large-scale public
sculpture in the United Energy Plaza in
Houston (fig. 1).

The present work was cast at the Clé-
menti foundry in 1970, and its unpainted
bronze surface appears timeless and precious,
characteristics traditionally associated with
this medium. However, the dynamic composition conveys the same levity and fragmentary qualities of *Jeune fille s'évadant*. *Personnage
et oiseau* is an arrangement of found objects
depicting a woman with a bird perched on her
head. The large, hollow pyramid replaces the
woman's body, and a protruding cylinder at
its center functions either as a navel or as an
evocation of ambiguous sexuality. A sphere
with two hollow cavities and an attached
crescent shape signify a head, eyes, and a
nose. The entire ensemble is crowned by a set
of rods attached to three flat blades, evoking a
bird's feathery form.

Although Miró's work engaged with
abstraction, it almost always referenced
figuration. A poet of humble objects, Miró
based his sculptures on everyday things
that reflected the world around him,
claiming that he wished his work to exist

"in a human and living way, with noth-
ing literary or intellectual about it." [3] The
vitality and humor of *Jeune fille s'évadant* and
Personnage et oiseau successfully encapsulate
these goals and demonstrate Miró's inven-
tiveness and originality.

—**Maria Taroutina**

1. Joan Miró, quoted in Joan Punyet Miró, "Catalan
and Mallorcan Aspects of Miro's Painted Sculpture,"
in *The Shape of Color: Joan Miró's Painted Sculpture*, by
Laura Coyle, William Jeffett, and Miró, exh. cat.
(Washington, D.C.: Corcoran Gallery of Art, 2002), 15.
2. Miró, letter to Pierre Matisse, September 28,
1936; published in *Joan Miró: Selected Writings and
Interviews*, ed. Margit Rowell, translations from the
French by Paul Auster, translations from the Spanish
and Catalan by Patricia Mathews (Boston: G. K. Hall,
1986), 126.
3. Ibid.

Fig. 1.
Joan Miró, *Personnage et oiseaux* (Figure and
Birds), 1982. Bronze and stainless steel with
paint, H. 55 ft. (16.76 m). Installed in Houston

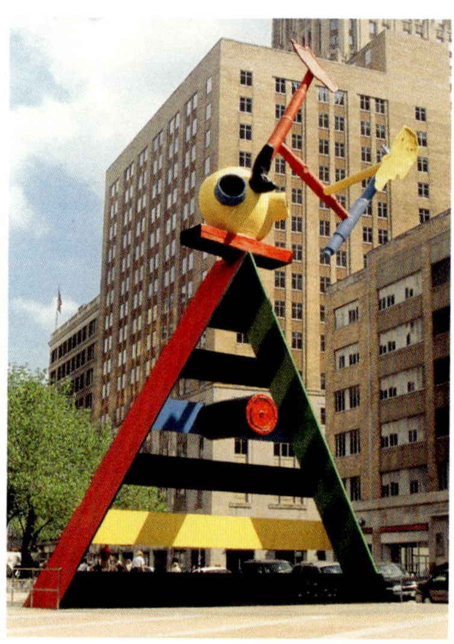

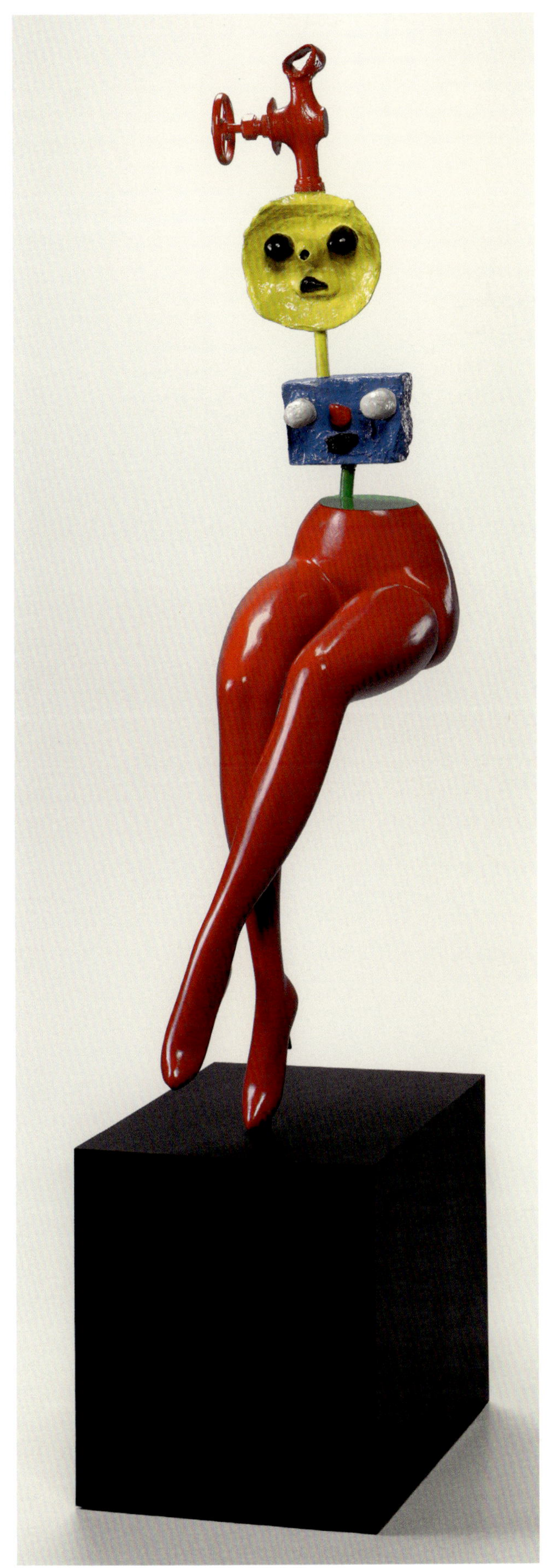

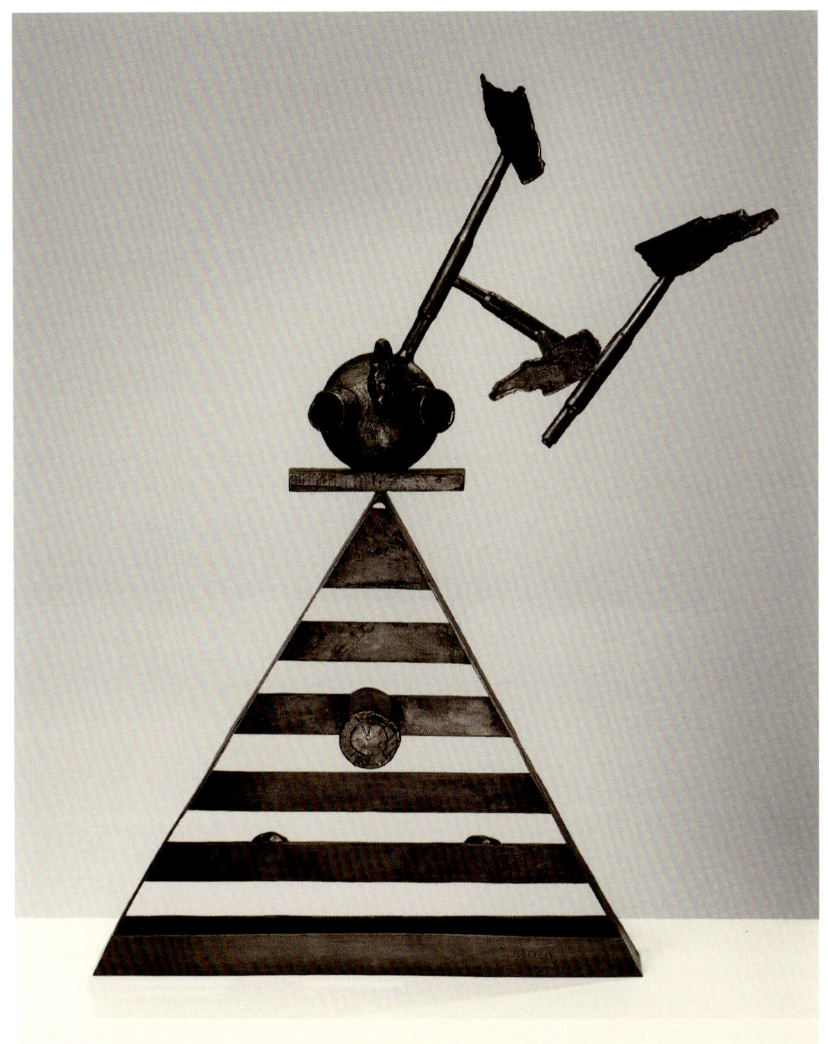

Mary Frank

American, born 1933

44
Sundial in Winter, **1970**
Ceramic, 29¼ × 17 × 8½ in.
(74.3 × 43.2 × 21.6 cm)
2006.52.86

Mary Frank began working in clay in the 1960s, a time when figurative art had largely fallen out of favor. Before becoming a ceramic sculptor, Frank, the daughter of the painter Eleanor Lockspeiser, explored painting, drawing, sculpting with wood, and casting in plaster and concrete. By the late 1960s Frank was channeling her early efforts into a series of clay sundials made using the slab construction method.[1]

The two-part *Sundial in Winter* belongs to this early period, and it is composed of a rectangular "sundial" resting at an angle on a vertical base. At the center of the dial's face is a dark recess from which two horned animals seem to have emerged. Inside this space, Frank roughly cut out the shapes of stars and a lightning bolt, suggesting the firmament surrounding the sun. The tiny animals and a nude female rider are attempting to summit the dial's steep slope, as if in search of a sunnier high ground. From their precarious perch on the sloping surface, the figures act as the sundial's gnomon or indicator, casting shadows and keeping time. Another small horse appears to have recently conquered the set of steep, narrow steps built into the sculpture's base. Frank's works often possess an archaic quality, and here the pedestal resembles an ancient Mayan temple. Irregular slash marks on the sides and back of the pedestal suggest petroglyphs, while the horses resemble those in prehistoric cave painting. Because of their small size, these figures give Frank's otherwise modestly scaled sculpture a feeling of monumentality, while their lyricism reflects Frank's own interest in movement and dance, a childhood passion that she pursued in studies with the choreographer Martha Graham. In the words of Margaret Moorman, Frank's sculptures are from a "timeless world . . . a realm where joy, grief and the simplest sort of wonder go unmasked."[2]

Frank's love of clay stemmed in part from its flexibility. She declared it to be the most impressionistic material and often left behind evidence of her working methods that a ceramicist making more functional objects would deem unsightly.[3] The interior of the pedestal in *Sundial in Winter* bears the imprint of the textile Frank used to roll the clay into flat sections, and her fingerprints are clearly visible on the sides of the sculpture. Frank felt that such visible proof of construction allowed the viewer to experience concrete signs of the artist's presence. She described her work as displaying a "range of human emotions that is just staggering, from the most quixotic and oddly curious and touching kinds of feelings to the most powerful and basic."[4] However, Frank declined to further specify what personal experiences informed her work, wishing it to remain open, with meanings as malleable as the clay from which it was constructed.

—**Diane C. Wright**

1. Another example of the *Sundial* sculpture was exhibited at the Whitney Biennial in 1970, where Charles B. Benenson may have seen it.
2. Margaret Moorman, "In a Timeless World," *Art News*, May 1987, 90.
3. Hayden Herrera, *Mary Frank* (New York: Harry N. Abrams, 1990), 10.
4. Fleur Weymouth, "An Interview with Mary Frank," *Helicon Nine* 9 (1983): 24.

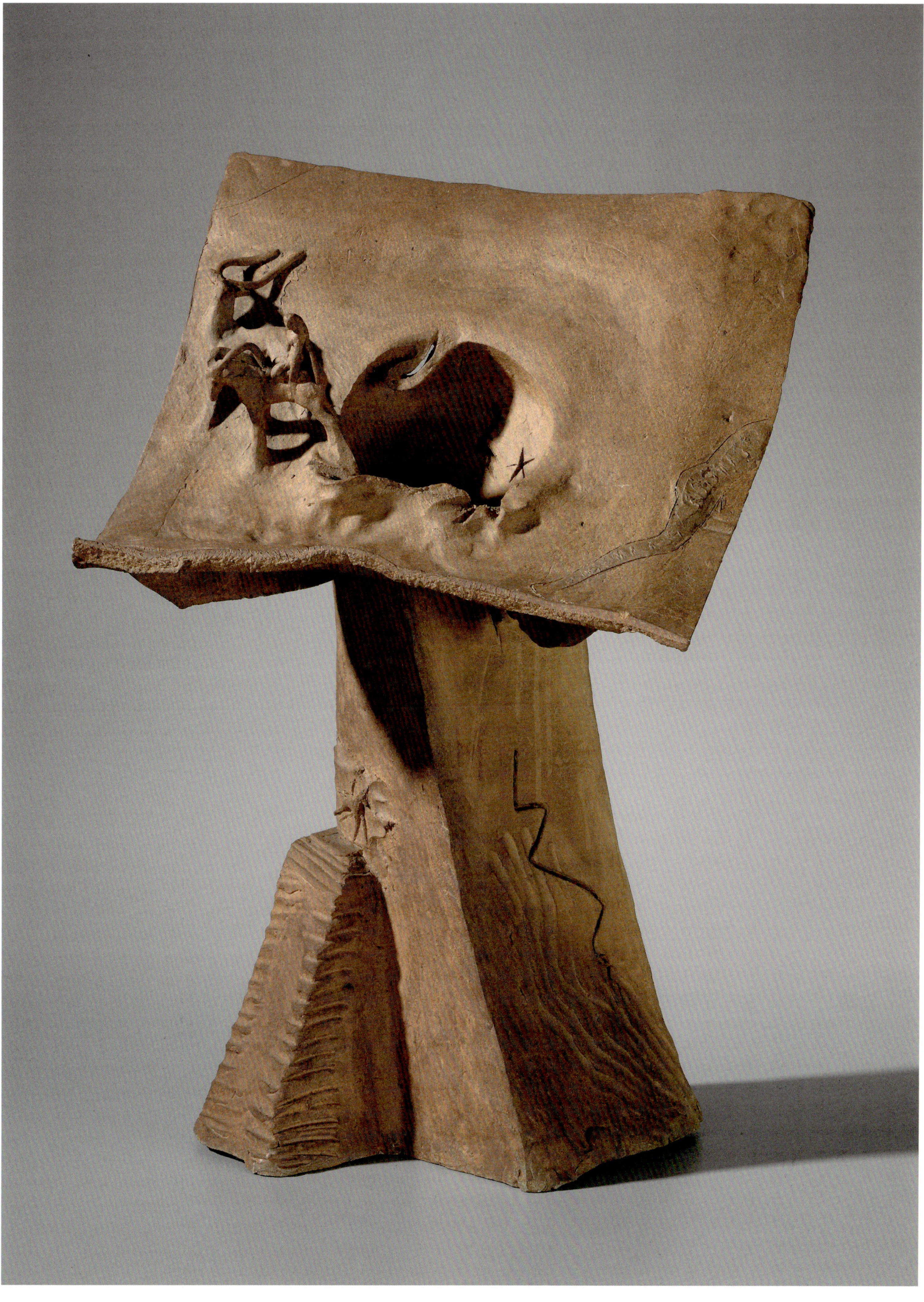

Saul Steinberg

American, born Romania, 1914–1999

45
Lambrate, 1971
Pen and black ink, colored crayon, and graphite, 19¾ × 25⅝ in. (50.1 × 65.1 cm)
2006.52.104

46
Empire State Building, 1970
Pen and black ink, brush and black ink, waxy black crayon, black pencil, and graphite, 23³⁄₁₆ × 29⅛ in. (58.8 × 74 cm)
2006.52.32

47
Civil War (High School), 1970
Graphite and colored pencil, 22³⁄₁₆ × 27 in. (56.3 × 68.5 cm)
2006.52.30

48
Evolution, 1967
Graphite, watercolor wash, pen and colored ink, colored crayon, white watercolor, and oil pastel, 23¹⁄₁₆ × 28¾ in. (58.5 × 73 cm)
2006.52.102

49
The Administration Building, 1969
Rubber stamping and graphite, 41¼ × 71¹³⁄₁₆ in. (104.7 × 182.4 cm)
2006.52.46

50
Untitled, 1966
Pen and black ink and graphite on printed paper, 19¹⁄₁₆ × 12⁹⁄₁₆ in. (48.4 × 31.9 cm)
2006.52.107

51
Cacographer, 1968
Graphite, pen and blue, red, and black ink, and gray, blue, and brown colored pencil, with blind stamp and rubber stamping, 20¹⁄₁₆ × 29⁷⁄₁₆ in. (51 × 74.8 cm)
2006.52.106

Charles B. Benenson's collection of Saul Steinberg drawings spans the length of Steinberg's career in the United States, during which the artist not only provided illustrations for periodicals such as the *New Yorker* but also exhibited regularly with the Betty Parsons and Sidney Janis galleries in New York and Galerie Maeght in Paris. The bulk of Benenson's collection is concentrated in the period from the mid-1960s to the early 1970s, an important phase in Steinberg's career.

In his art, Steinberg adapted existing cultural stereotypes and clichés, calling attention to the idiosyncrasies of language, culture, and humanity. "What I am playing with," Steinberg wrote, "is the voyage between perception and understanding."[1] Just as playfully, Steinberg referenced a vast array of artistic styles and elements of popular culture, such as comics and advertisements. He recorded as influences children's drawings, folk art, icons, and graffiti.[2]

Steinberg was born and raised in Romania before moving to Milan in 1933 to study architecture. Works such as *Lambrate* (cat. 45) depict the Bauhaus-inspired architecture with which the artist became familiar in Italy. While there, he began producing drawings for humorous journals to earn money. On the completion of his degree, rendered useless by the Fascist government's racist stipulations and with World War II underway, Steinberg fled Italy for the United States in 1941. His immigrant experience permeated his later work, where official-looking stamps, signatures, and fingerprints often serve to "document" his drawings. He was fascinated by the authority such simple marks carry.

Steinberg began to produce drawings for U.S. publications while awaiting a visa in the Dominican Republic. Between 1941 and 1999, he provided the *New Yorker* with artwork that included eighty-five cover designs.[3] Producing art for literary periodicals such as the *New Yorker* allowed Steinberg to thoroughly investigate the relationship between word and image and to infuse his drawings with witty and philosophical meaning. In 1942 he moved to New York, a locale that would embed itself in his work for the following fifty years. In *Empire State Building* (cat. 46), for example, the building's Art Deco spire rises ominously above a dark ink wash representative of the night sky.

The political and social turmoil of the late 1960s, recalling the strife of Balkan hostilities, German Nazism, and Italian Fascism, provoked a strand of cynicism in Steinberg's work. He grew frightened by the violence of the U.S. government's actions in Vietnam and by the unrest of its citizenry. This anxiety

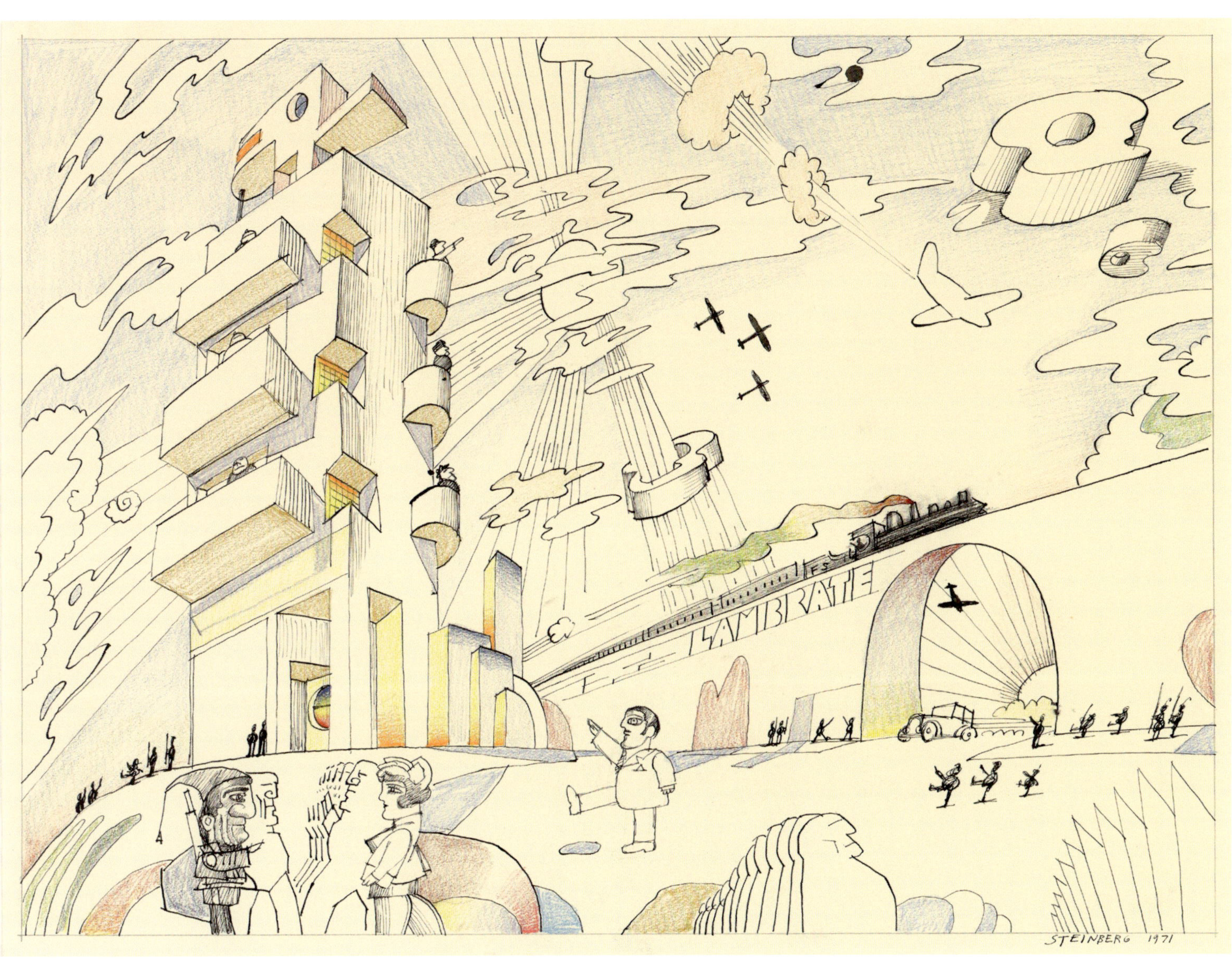

LAMBRATE
FS
STEINBERG 1971

manifested itself in the armies of robotic, marching figures that began to populate his drawings, such as *Lambrate*. Likewise, *Civil War (High School)* (cat. 47) exhibits this national unrest; it depicts a building being destroyed, expelling rubble and flames while mounted police officers charge onto the page. Two enigmatic masked figures in the extreme foreground stare blankly at the viewer.

Mounted police, heroes on horseback, sphinxes, crocodiles, and cats are all elements of the visual vocabulary Steinberg developed and referenced throughout his career. Some of these elements are seen in *Evolution* (cat. 48). This watercolor features a *Lebenstreppe* (staircase of life), which displays the ages of humankind or phases of life—a motif Steinberg adapted multiple times.[4] Here, a boy rendered in the manner of a child's sketch ascends to adolescence and manhood before turning into a suit-wearing dog, a golden eagle, and then descending into the form of a crocodile, a fish, an insect, and, finally, a snail. In this drawing, power and fame become dangerous, corruptive forces.

In the late 1940s Steinberg began using rubber-stamp impressions in his drawings. At first he used store-bought stamps, but by 1965 he was commissioning custom designs depicting cyclists, Native Americans on horseback, painters at easels, and lines and hatching. These allowed him to duplicate imagery, and to repeat it, often filling the sheet. He referred to this type of stamp drawing as "a computerized form of art" that removed the hand, and thus the ego, of the artist.[5] *The Administration Building* (cat. 49) was created entirely from rubber-stamp impressions that together construct a city in the International Style. It includes buildings on a hill, inhabited by stationary and striding figures, soldiers with rifles who leave supine bodies in their wake, and Steinberg's ubiquitous crocodiles, hardly surreal within such a scene. Steinberg's representational shorthand anticipated the return to figuration that occurred in the New York art community in the 1970s.

The way Steinberg frequently employed the visual substrate of the page within his drawings is evident in his untitled drawing on staff paper of 1966 (cat. 50). The upper register of the work is made of unembellished staff paper, whereas, in the lower half, Steinberg has vertically oriented and drawn over the paper's parallel lines, which provide the foundation for a musical scene. Such drawings are often self-referential, indicating their very material formation and turning the act of drawing into the subject of their compositions. "What I draw is drawing, [and] drawing derives from drawing," Steinberg stated. "My line wants to remind constantly that it's made of ink."[6] In drawings Steinberg called "stenographic" or "hieroglyphic," he used stylistic variations in line to indicate differences in voice, ideology, or personality.[7] Such reference to substrate and attention to writing can be observed in *Cacographer* (cat. 51), where various illegible scripts break the bounds of the flat surface on which they are projected by a writer. Elements in Steinberg's work often break through boundaries, passing from one plane to another. Steinberg's personal experience as an immigrant and as an artist who bridged the divide between high and low art finds an echo in his boundary-defying work.

—Katherine D. Alcauskas

1. Saul Steinberg, quoted in Joel Smith, *Saul Steinberg: Illuminations*, exh. cat. (New Haven, Conn.: Yale University Press, 2006), 156.
2. Grace Glueck, "The Artist Speaks: Saul Steinberg," *Art in America*, November–December 1970, 114.
3. *March to April*, for example, which depicts a cat riding a bike across a bridge that links two plains labeled March and April, respectively, closely resembles a cover of the *New Yorker* published on March 26, 1966. For an illustration of this work, see the collection checklist in the present volume.
4. This is a common emblem present in European visual representation from the sixteenth century onward.
5. Glueck, "The Artist Speaks," 112.
6. Saul Steinberg, quoted in Harold Rosenberg, *Saul Steinberg*, exh. cat. (New York: Alfred A. Knopf, 1978), 19.
7. Joel Smith, *Steinberg at the New Yorker* (New York: Harry N. Abrams, 2005), 172.

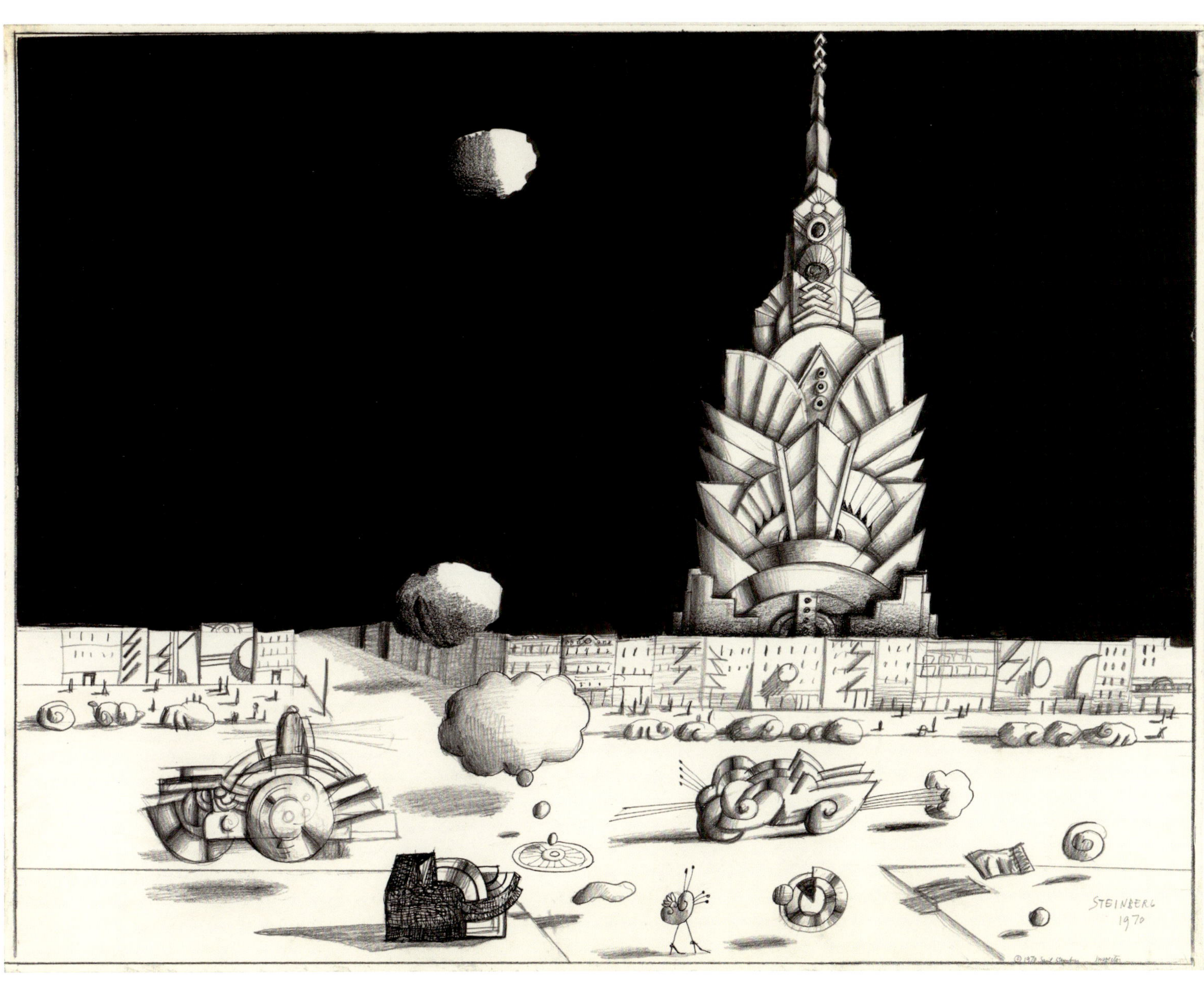

STEINBERG
1970

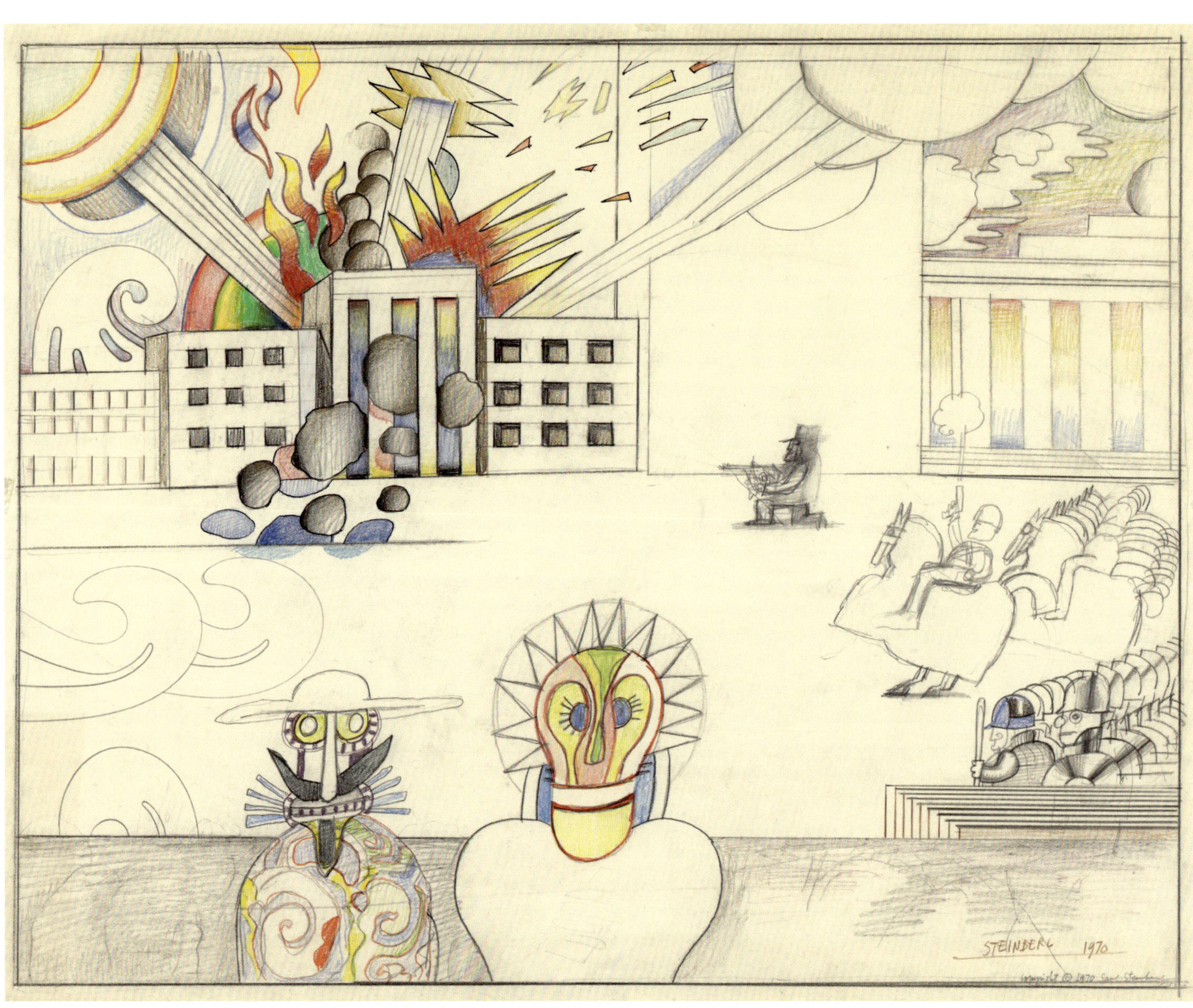

STEINBERG   1970
copyright © 1970 Saul Steinberg

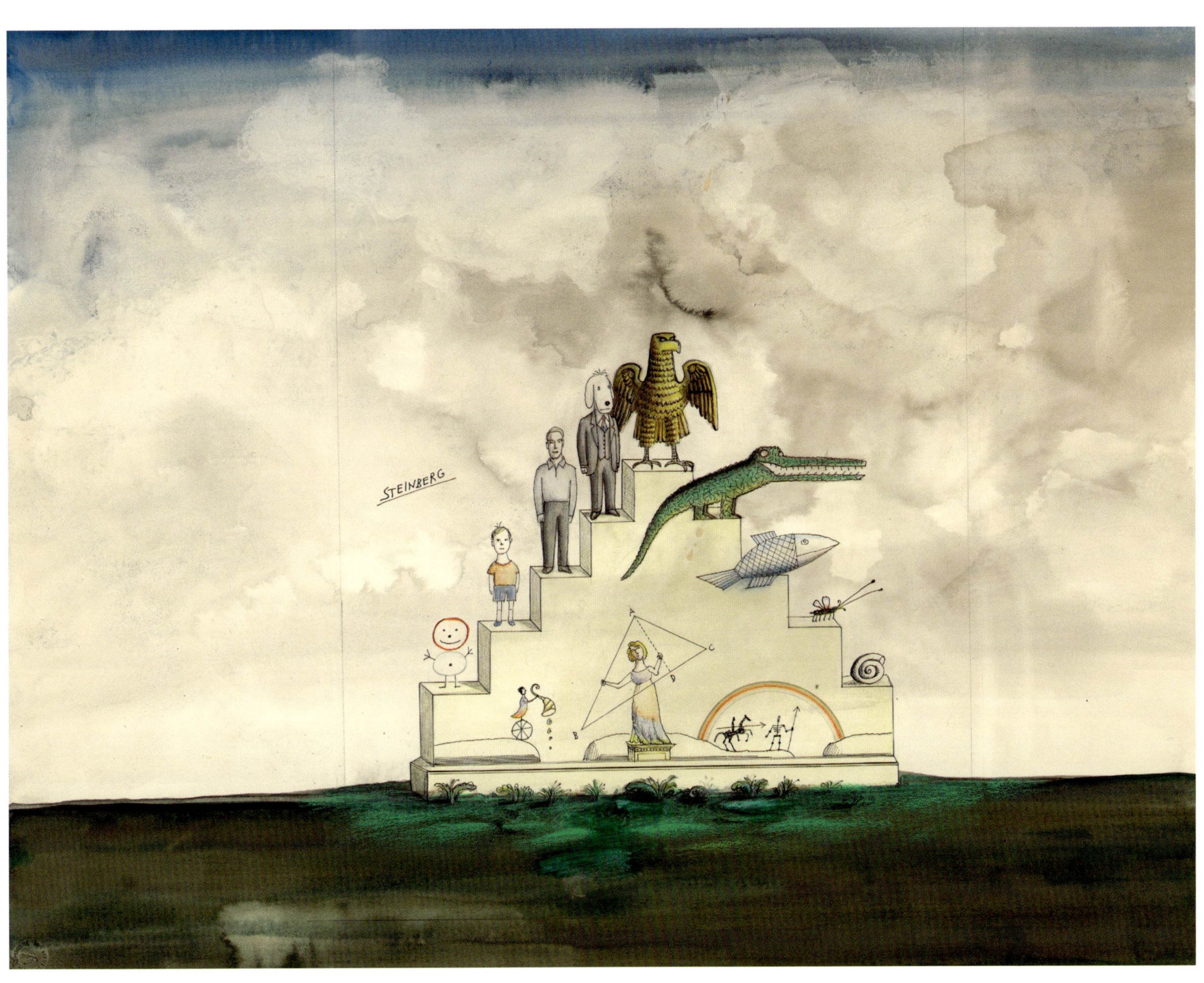

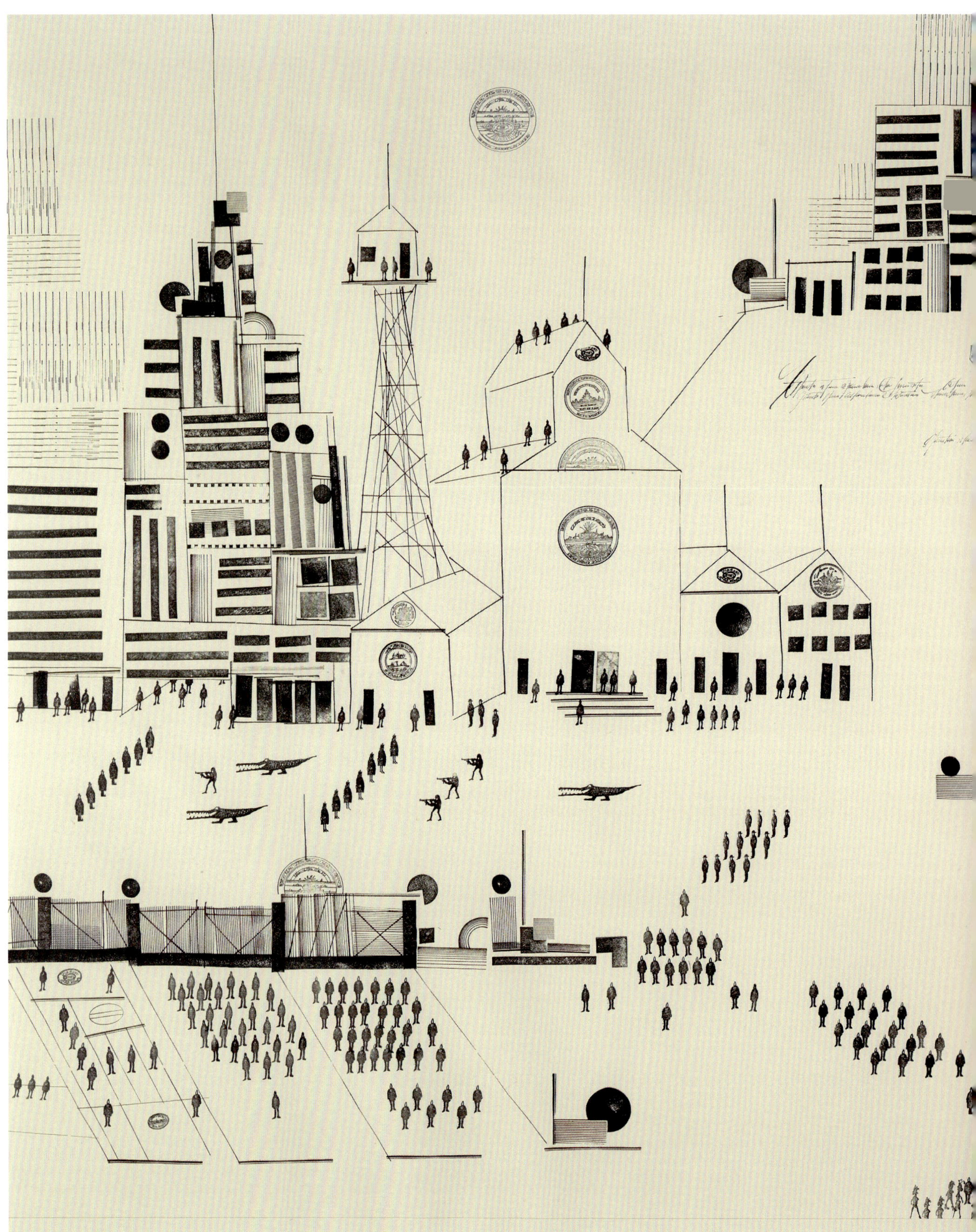

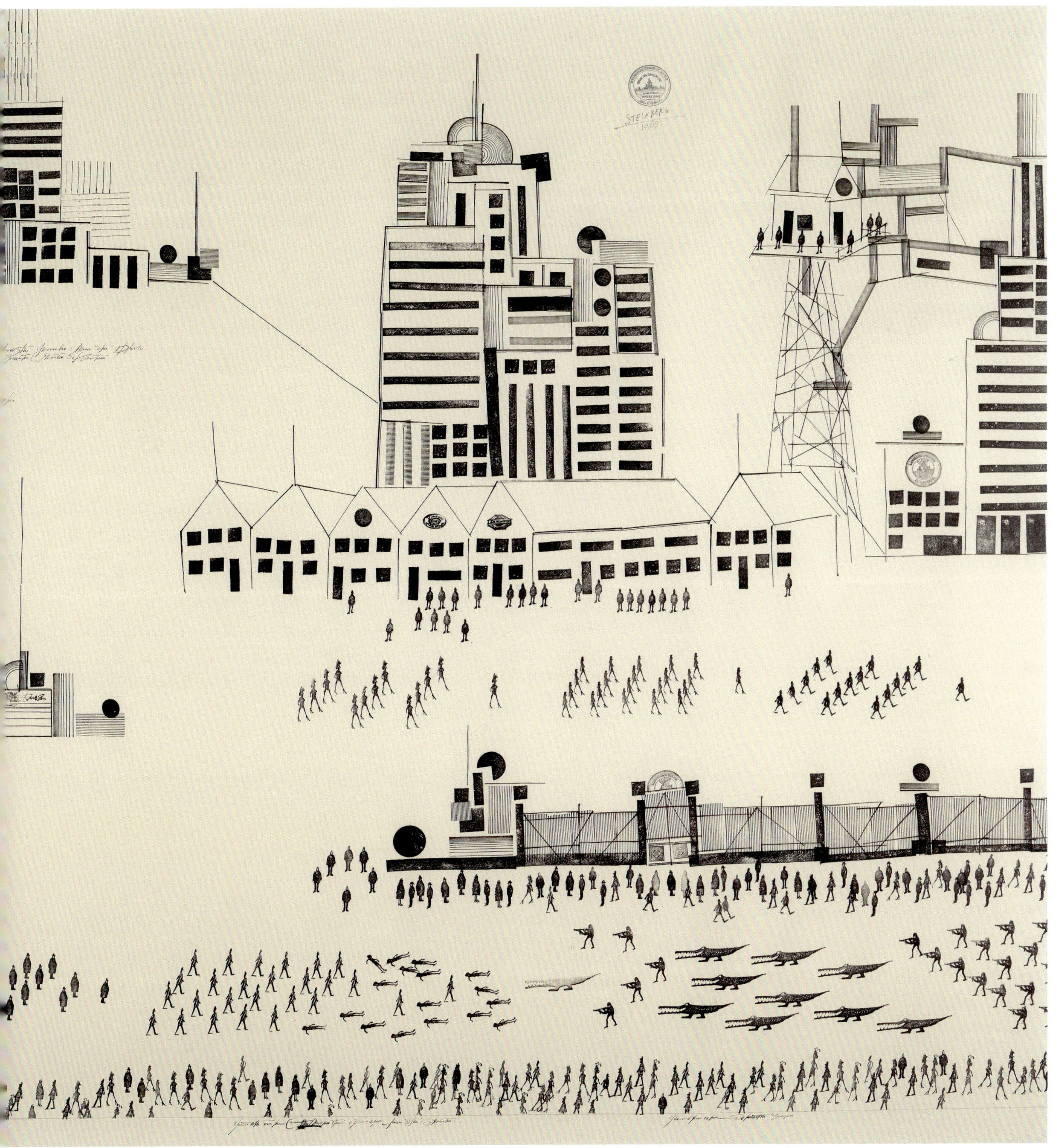

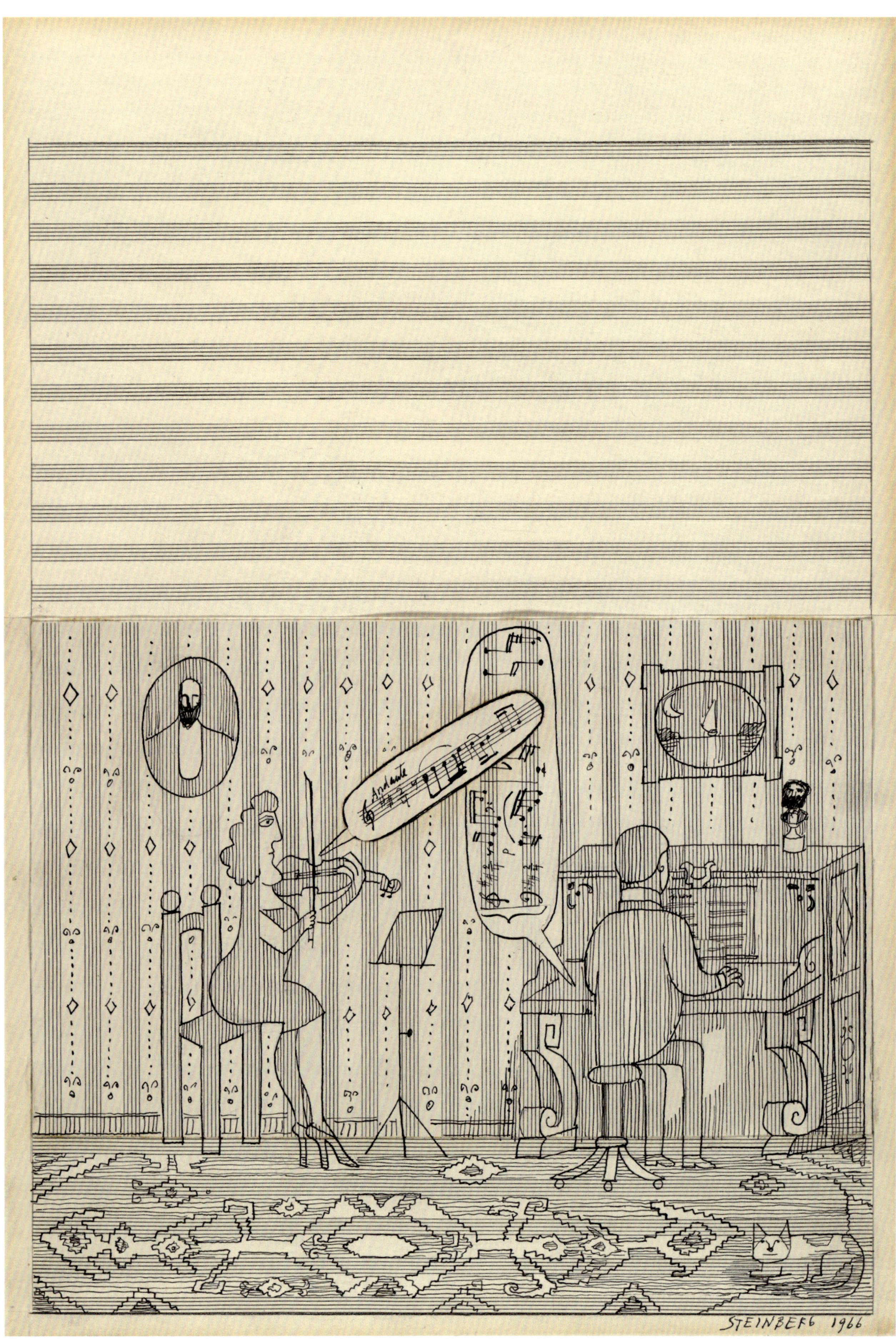
Andante
STEINBERG 1966

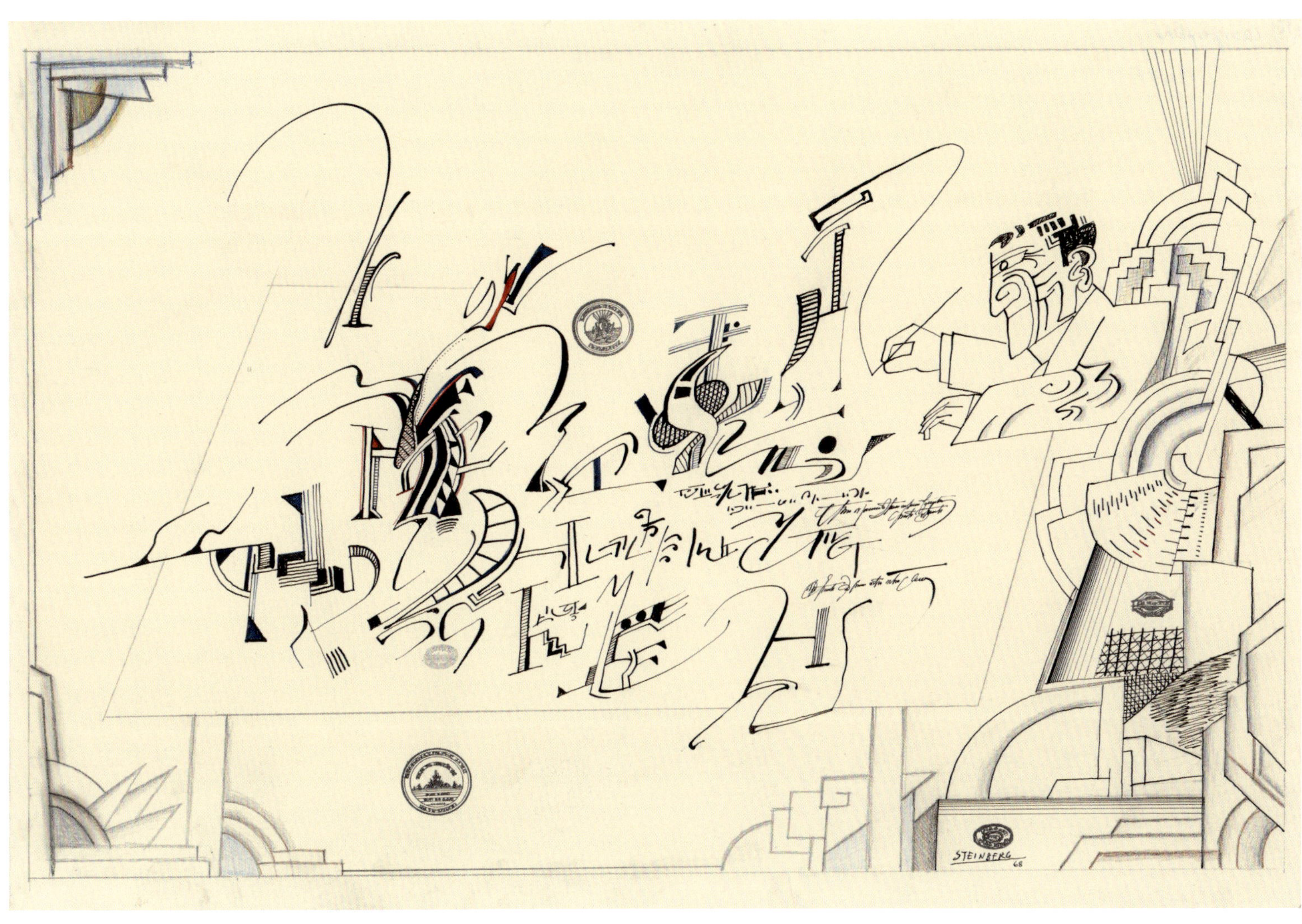

51

Red Grooms

American, born 1937

52

***Picasso Goes to Heaven,* 1973**
Acrylic and charcoal on paper laid down
on canvas; six panels, overall 15 ft. 2½ in. ×
16 ft. 4 in. (463.6 × 497.8 cm)
2006.52.42

53

Studio at the Rue des Grands-Augustins,
1990–96
Acrylic on canvas; six panels, overall
10 ft. 3 in. × 18 ft. 3 in. (312.4 × 556.3 cm)
2006.52.3

54

***Cedar Bar,* 1986**
Colored pencil and crayon on paper
mounted to board; five panels, in artist's
frame, overall 9 ft. 11½ in. × 27 ft. × 3 in.
(303.5 × 823 × 7.6 cm)
2006.52.56

Art history and its heroes are major themes in Red Grooms's exuberant oeuvre. In addition to portraying Modernist artists such as Henri Matisse, Jackson Pollock, and Willem de Kooning alongside the Old Masters, he also produced imaginative sculptural reconstructions of artists' studios and gathering places, such as Les Deux Magots in Paris. Three of the Grooms works in the Charles B. Benenson Collection wittily revisit the great figures of twentieth-century art history in affectionate and humorous anecdotal portraits.

Grooms developed his signature "comic book" style in the 1960s and 1970s, following on the tongue-in-cheek playfulness often present at Happenings (in which he participated) and in Pop art. However, unlike the relatively restrained surfaces of Andy Warhol's and Roy Lichtenstein's Pop paintings, Grooms's style is highly expressive and characterized by a bright palette and gestural brushwork.

Picasso Goes to Heaven (cat. 52) is one of many works that Grooms painted in 1973 to commemorate the older artist's death. At the center of a monumental summation of his life, Pablo Picasso dances around in a cockeyed party hat, seeming to celebrate his ascension into the chorus of "immortal artists" waiting above: Michelangelo, Leonardo da Vinci, Titian, Rembrandt, and Velázquez. The work

is filled with depictions of the artists, writers, critics, dancers, composers, collectors, and lovers in Picasso's life. On the left are members of the Ballets Russes: his ballerina wife Olga Khokhlova, dancer and choreographer Vaslav Nijinsky, and impresario Serge Diaghilev. In the bottom right are artists Henri Rousseau and Paul Cézanne, accompanied by Picasso's patrons: art dealer Ambroise Vollard, Leo Stein, Gertrude Stein, and her partner, Alice B. Toklas. Hovering directly above Picasso are his close friends Jaime Sabartés and Jean Cocteau, as well as the composer Igor Stravinsky. In the top left corner Grooms paints Picasso's intimates from his early 1900s Paris studio circle called Le Bateau-Lavoir: Georges Braque, Max Jacob, Guillaume Apollinaire, Marie Laurencin, and Matisse. The painting's bright colors, bold patterns, and caricatured faces create the impression of a raucous celebration.

By contrast, *Studio at the Rue des Grands-Augustins* (cat. 53), painted twenty years later, is a more restrained depiction of Picasso at work on his masterpiece *Guernica* (1937, Museo Reina Sofía, Madrid). Grooms explained that his work reflected the contemporary strife of the world in the early 1990s, namely, the Gulf War, Somali conflict, and the fall of the USSR: "I was affected by the current situation just like [Picasso] was with the bombing of Guernica in Spain by the Nazis."[1] In addition to iconic elements of *Guernica* such as the screaming horse and woman with a candle, Grooms included references to contemporary politics. For example, Picasso is shown painting the Manhattan skyline, with the Soviet newspaper *Pravda* at its center.

Additionally, Grooms recreated the objects and people who surrounded Picasso while he was painting *Guernica,* such as the large brown stove famously photographed by Brassaï in Picasso's studio, the artist's chambermaid Inez, and his lover Dora Maar, who is portrayed on the right side of the canvas with a lit cigarette. In the context of the early 1990s, the painting's somber palette expresses an uncertainty about the new post–Cold War world order.

Cedar Bar (cat. 54) is more satirical than Grooms's Picasso paintings. Grooms was

a regular at the Greenwich Village bar in the 1950s when it was a favorite haunt for Abstract Expressionist artists, and Grooms himself briefly experimented with abstract painting during a 1957 summer course taught by Hans Hofmann. In the center of the work, Pollock fights with de Kooning while Ruth Kligman, the sole survivor of Pollock's fatal 1956 car crash, applies a fresh coat of lipstick. To the right, art critic Clement Greenberg and painter Franz Kline, who wears a yellow suit, greet critic Harold Rosenberg, while painter Ad Reinhardt somberly observes from his bar stool as artists John Chamberlain and Norman Bluhm fight on the floor. Mark Rothko converses with art critic Dore Ashton at a table in the bottom right corner, and at left, Elaine de Kooning smokes a cigarette with Lee Krasner, who is fondled by artist Aristodemos Kaldis. Grooms twice depicts himself as the redheaded bartender, serving drinks to artists Budd Hopkins, Philip Guston, and John Hultberg.

Grooms's lighthearted excursions into the annals of art history recall those of his great hero, Picasso, who similarly engaged with past masterpieces at the end of his life as a way of exploring his own place in the history of art. By revisiting the distinguished personalities of Modernism, Grooms also inserts himself into the lineage of twentieth-century art as one of its most original and versatile proponents.

—Maria Taroutina

1. Red Grooms, "Conversation with Susan Greenberg Fisher: Contemporary Artists on Picasso," Yale University Art Gallery, February 26, 2009, transcript, 1. A copy is on file with the Gallery's Department of Modern and Contemporary Art.

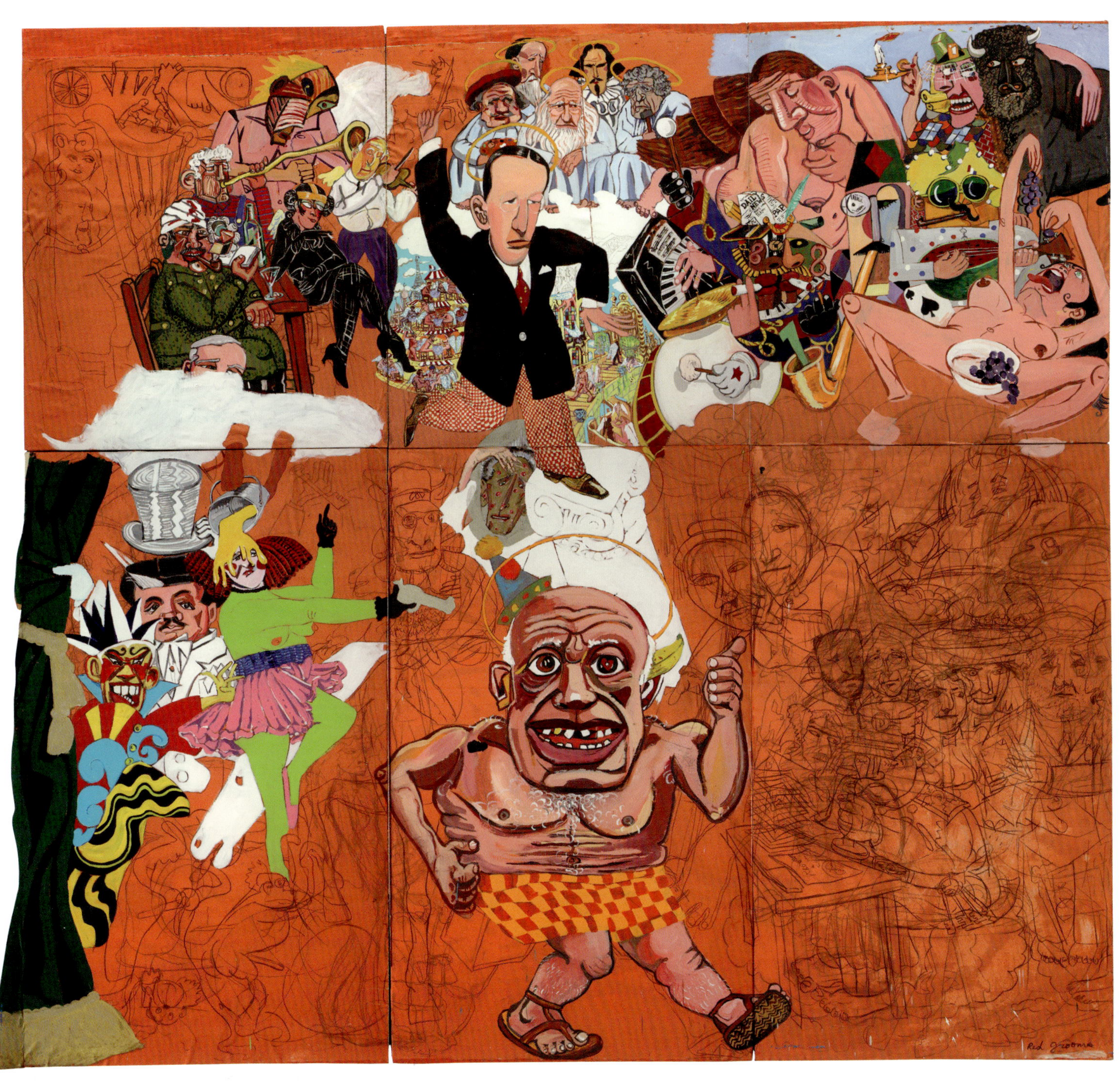

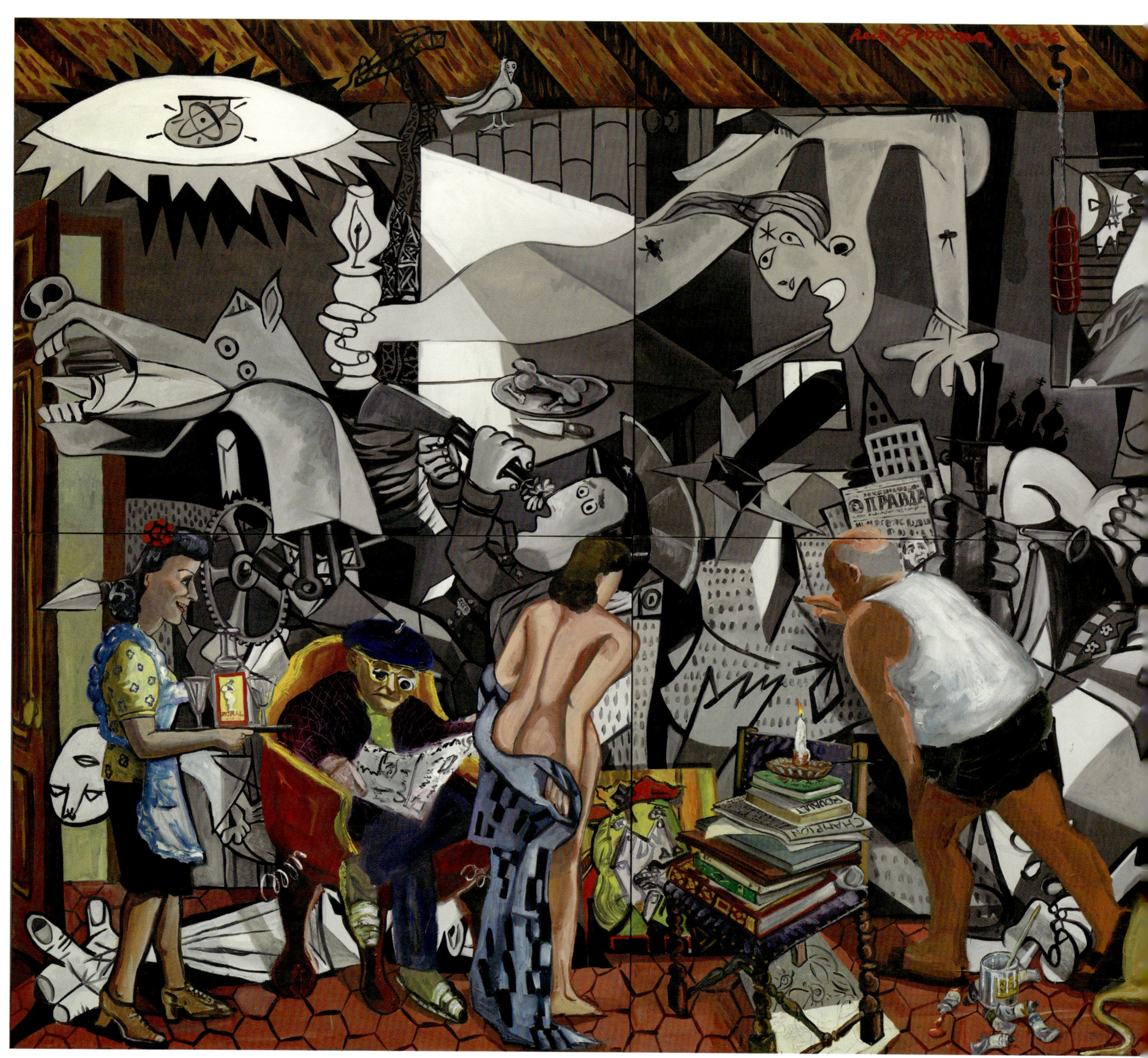

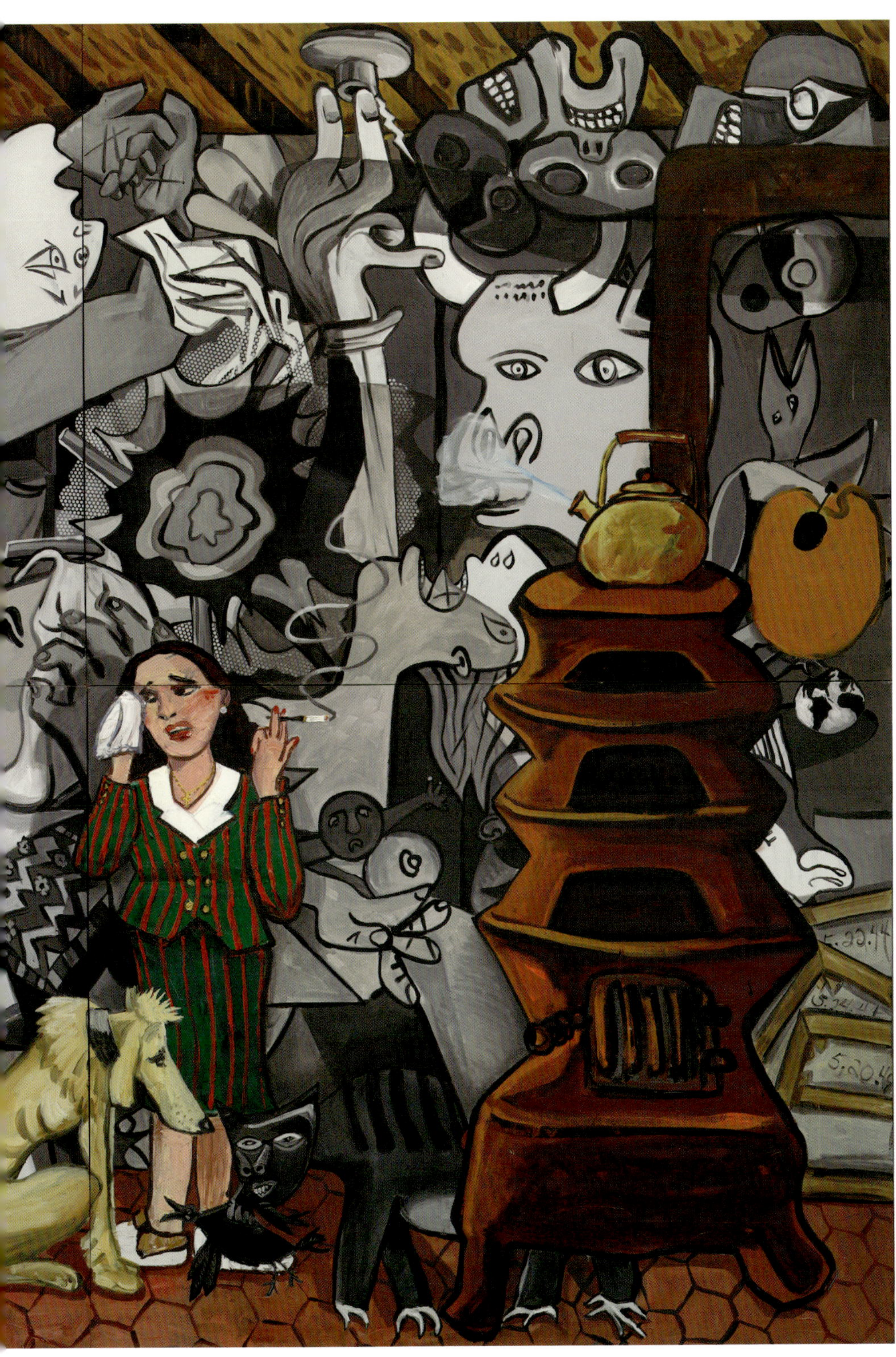

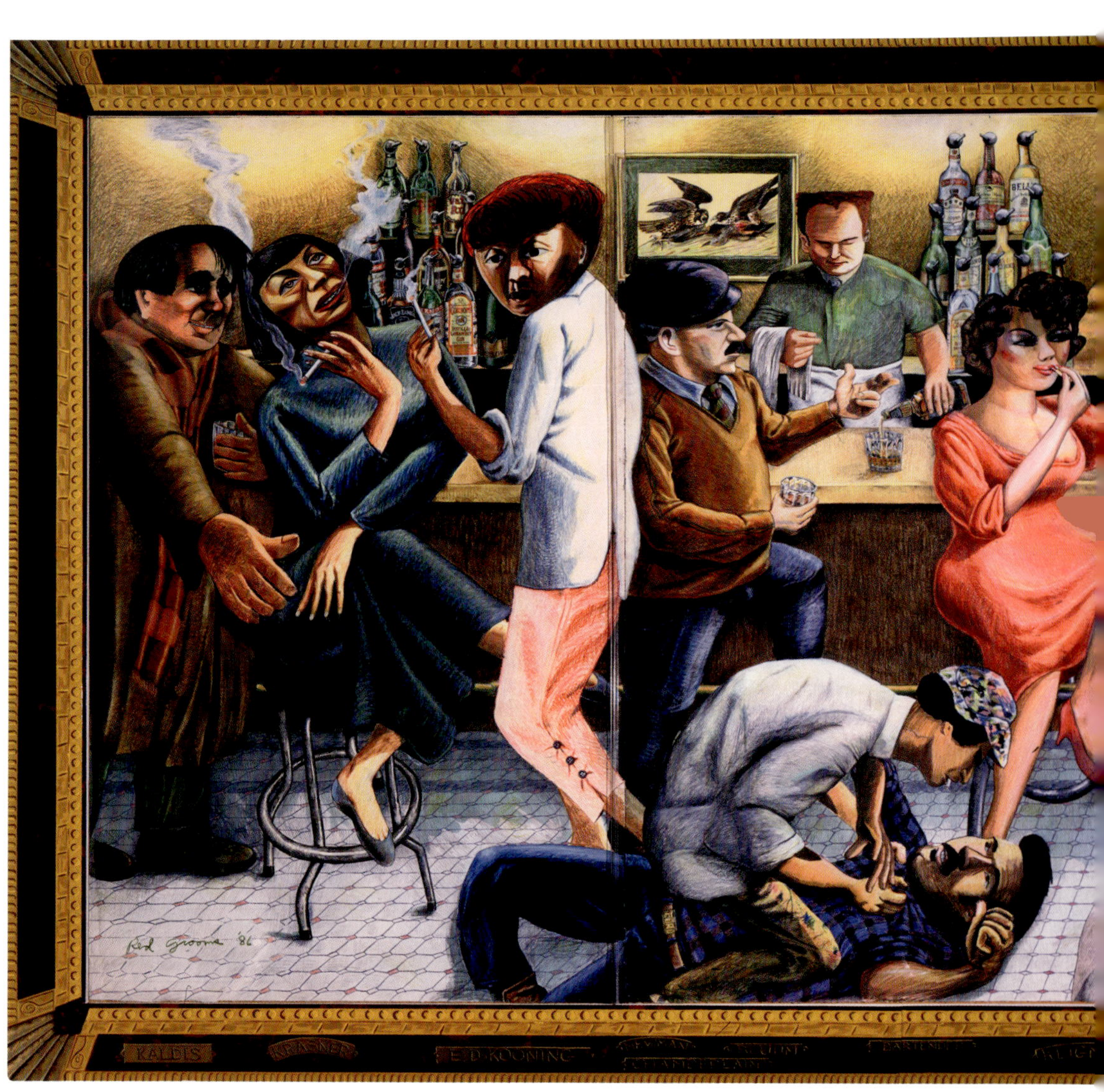

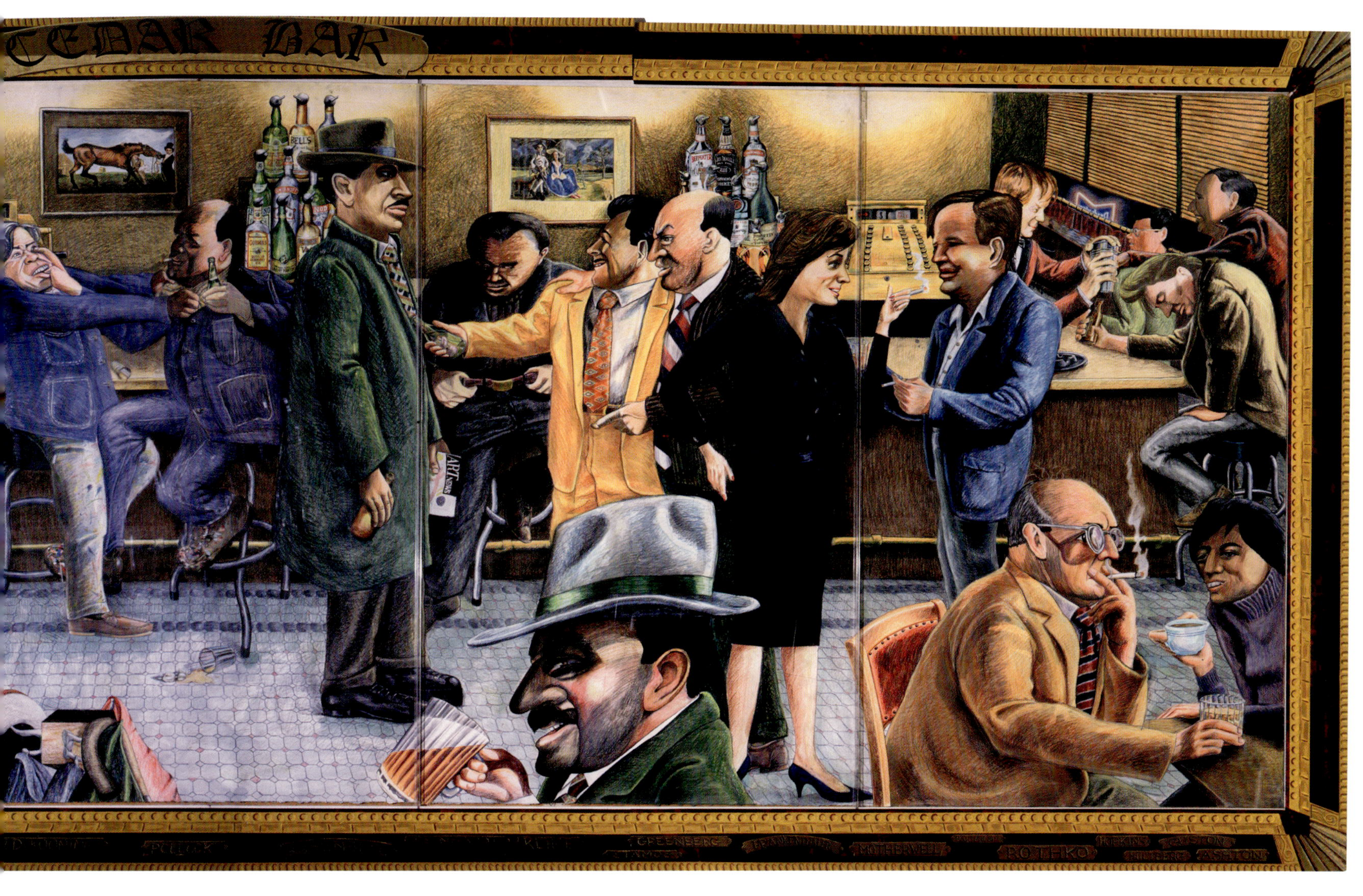

CEDAR BAR

Jim Dine

American, born 1935

55
***Model on the Gloucester Road*, 1976**
Charcoal and pastel, 45 %₁₆ × 31½ in.
(115.8 × 80 cm)
2006.52.13

56
***The Studio at Night in the Woods*, 1977**
Acrylic on canvas, 36 in. × 13 ft. 2 in.
(91.4 × 401.3 cm)
2006.52.99

57
***July—The Swedish Sea*, 1985**
Oil and charcoal on canvas with metal tools
and a seashell; three panels, overall 72 in. ×
16 ft. 10¼ in. (182.9 × 513.7 cm)
2006.52.55

58
***Crommelynck Gate with Tools*, 1983**
Bronze, edition 2/6, 9 ft. × 11 ft. × 36 in.
(274.3 × 335.3 × 91.4 cm)
2006.52.64

After making his career in the 1950s as an instigator of Performance art Happenings and the creator of Dada-inspired paintings, Jim Dine left New York for London in the late 1960s, and he only returned in 1971. *Model on the Gloucester Road* of 1976 (cat. 55) belongs to a series of overtly figural drawings that Dine began around 1974–75 that acknowledged the important influence of those early years in London when he was first exposed to European art, especially to the figurative works made in France between the two world wars by artists such as André Derain.

During this period, Dine drew in charcoal, which he then erased until only the traces absorbed by the paper remained. Describing that point in the process, Dine said, "I know where to go from there, and I start to work on an area and just keep working until finally I have to fix it. Then I take an electric sander or sanding blocks and take out part of it."[1] In *Model on the Gloucester Road*, Dine's sanding disintegrated the paper in the area of his model's pudenda. The lacuna here may mean that this area was the one Dine remained convinced could be improved through repeated efforts of erasing and redrawing.

Although separated by a number of years, Dine's monumental paintings *The Studio at*

Night in the Woods (1977; cat. 56) and *July—The Swedish Sea* (1985; cat. 57) share several themes. The first work combines two traditional categories of painting: the studio interior and the still life. An expansive accumulation of glasses, vases, and mugs are interspersed with small classical statues, gesturing disembodied hands, and a skull.[2] Classical sculptures and skulls were often included in seventeenth-century Dutch still-life painting as a way of positioning art's permanence relative to other, more transient accomplishments. By virtue of such memento mori the elements became lessons on the fleeting nature of life and its pleasures. In *July—The Swedish Sea* the skull again appears as one of three iconic images forming a triptych. Dine had often included real objects alongside his painted ones, but he ceased to do so from 1975 to 1982. Here, a large shell is attached to the left panel, the exoskeleton of the dead crustacean perhaps echoing the skull's bone, and the junctures of the triptych are emphasized by a pair of baling hooks embedded on either side of the middle canvas.

Although Dine's work underwent dramatic stylistic changes, as evidenced by the difference between *Model on the Gloucester Road* and the other three works in the Charles B. Benenson Collection, the artist remained surprisingly consistent in his personal interests. The poet Robert Creeley, in a meditation on Dine, wrote about five unifying subjects throughout the artist's work: tools, robes, hearts, trees, and gates.[3] Indeed, the heart is central both to the composition of *July—The Swedish Sea* and to Dine's oeuvre. As the artist noted, the heart as an abstract yet symbolic form "strikes a primitive chord."[4] If the heart suggests love, and the skull represents death, the raised gloved hand implies basic human action—perhaps that of the artist.[5] The work's themes are those of art and life itself, rendered here with richly textured, graphic sensibility.

In *Crommelynck Gate with Tools* (cat. 58) Dine combines tools with another significant theme: the gate.[6] The Dine family owned a hardware store in Cincinnati where the artist sometimes worked as a young man, and tools appear in his artworks from the beginning—as referents to his family as well as to potency

and potential.[7] A testament to the friendship and collaboration between Dine and the French master printer Aldo Crommelynck (1931–2009), *Crommelynck Gate with Tools* is loosely based on the nineteenth-century wrought-iron gate to Crommelynck's Paris studio and residence. The printmaker—who helped artists from Pablo Picasso to Jasper Johns realize their ambitions in a wide range of print media—had worked with Dine since 1973. The basic structure of Crommelynck's gate is reproduced in Dine's sculpture at double the original's scale, and cast tree branches and tools such as wrenches, hammers, and clamps replace its more elaborate scrollwork. The bronze cast tools' bent torsion becomes an analogue of the decorative flourishes on the original grillwork. As a reference to an actual gate—one leading to an inspiring studio where Dine went to collaborate and innovate—the sculpture represents a route to a place of artistic creation. For viewers, Dine's personal journey joins with the larger symbolic implications of gates as transitional spaces and as markers of passage—from public to private space, or from one world to the next.

—**Cathleen Chaffee**

1. Interview with Constance Glenn in *Jim Dine Figure Drawings, 1975–1979*, exh. cat. (New York: Harper and Row, 1979), n.p.
2. The painting belongs to a series of still lifes by Dine that were shown in the exhibition *Jim Dine: New Paintings*, April 29–June 9, 1978, at the Pace Gallery, New York.
3. Robert Creeley, "Tools," "Robes," "Hearts," "Trees," and "Gates," in Graham W. J. Beal et al., *Jim Dine: Five Themes*, exh. cat. (New York: Abbeville, 1983), 48, 70, 94, 118, 134.
4. The heart first emerged as a theme after a series of sets Dine designed for Shakespeare's *A Midsummer Night's Dream* in 1965. See ibid., 36
5. Formally, *July—The Swedish Sea* is related to a small series of heart-and-hand diptychs titled *The Death at South Kensington* that Dine made in 1983 to commemorate a friend.
6. The origins of the gate sculpture can be traced to a series of paintings Dine began in 1981. Each example from the edition of *Crommelynck Gate with Tools* is unique, as Dine bent the tools in different ways for each sculpture. Additionally, both one example from the edition and an artist's proof were brightly painted.
7. In a painting such as *Black Garden Tools* (1962), Dine attached a rake, a pitchfork, and shovels to an otherwise abstract work's surface, echoing Jasper Johns's use of mechanical objects such as wooden slats or rulers in his *Device Circle* paintings beginning in 1959.

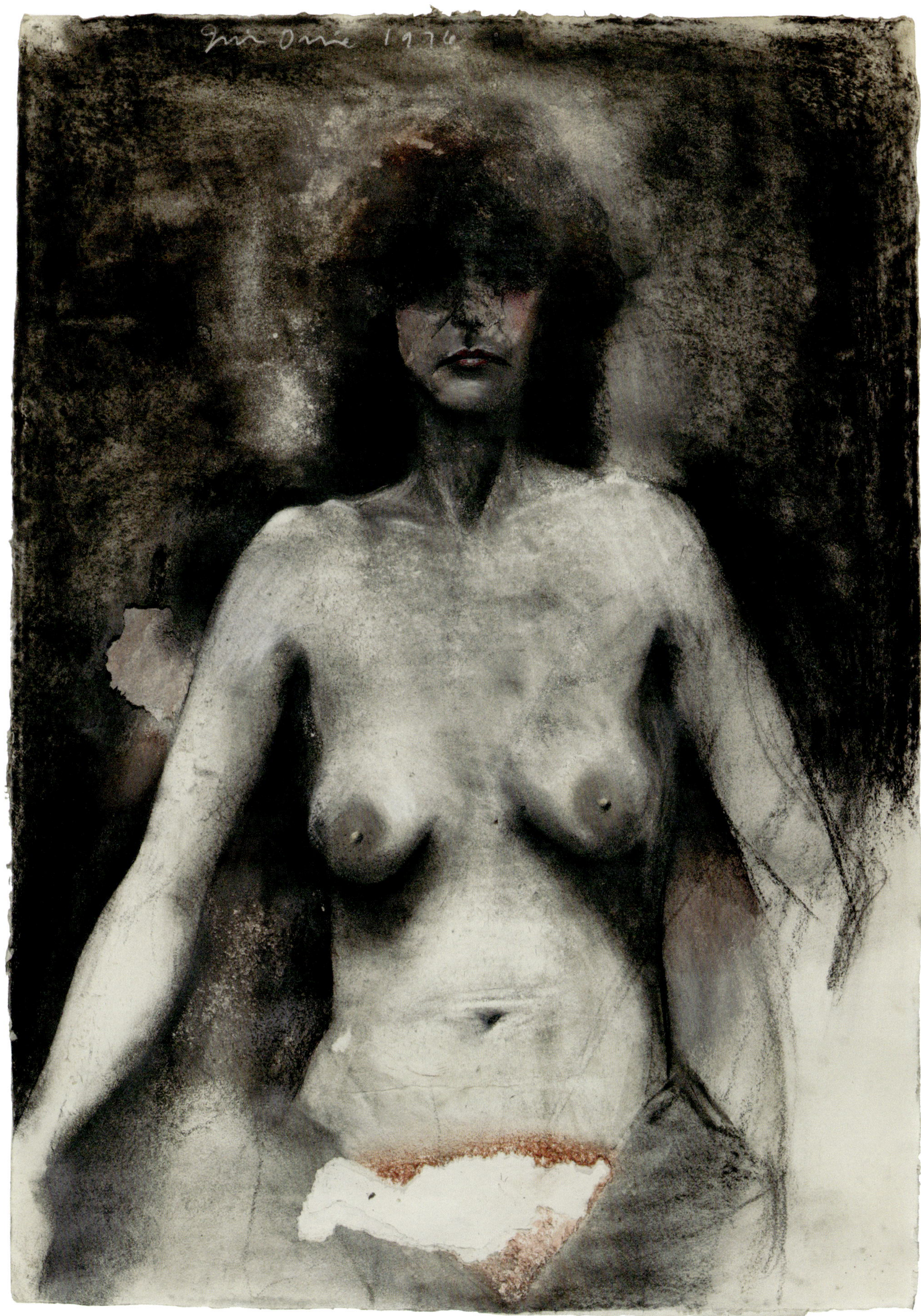

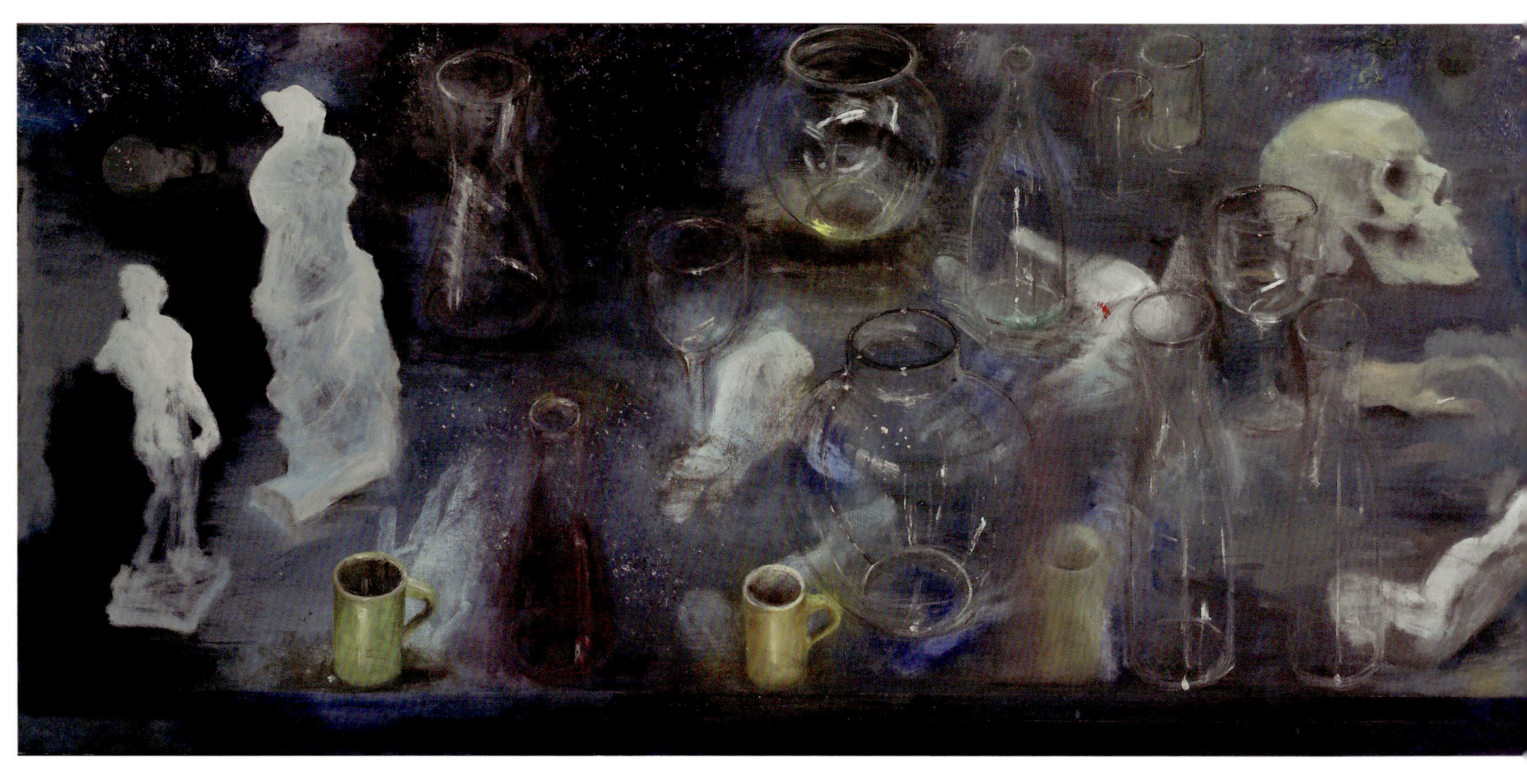

56

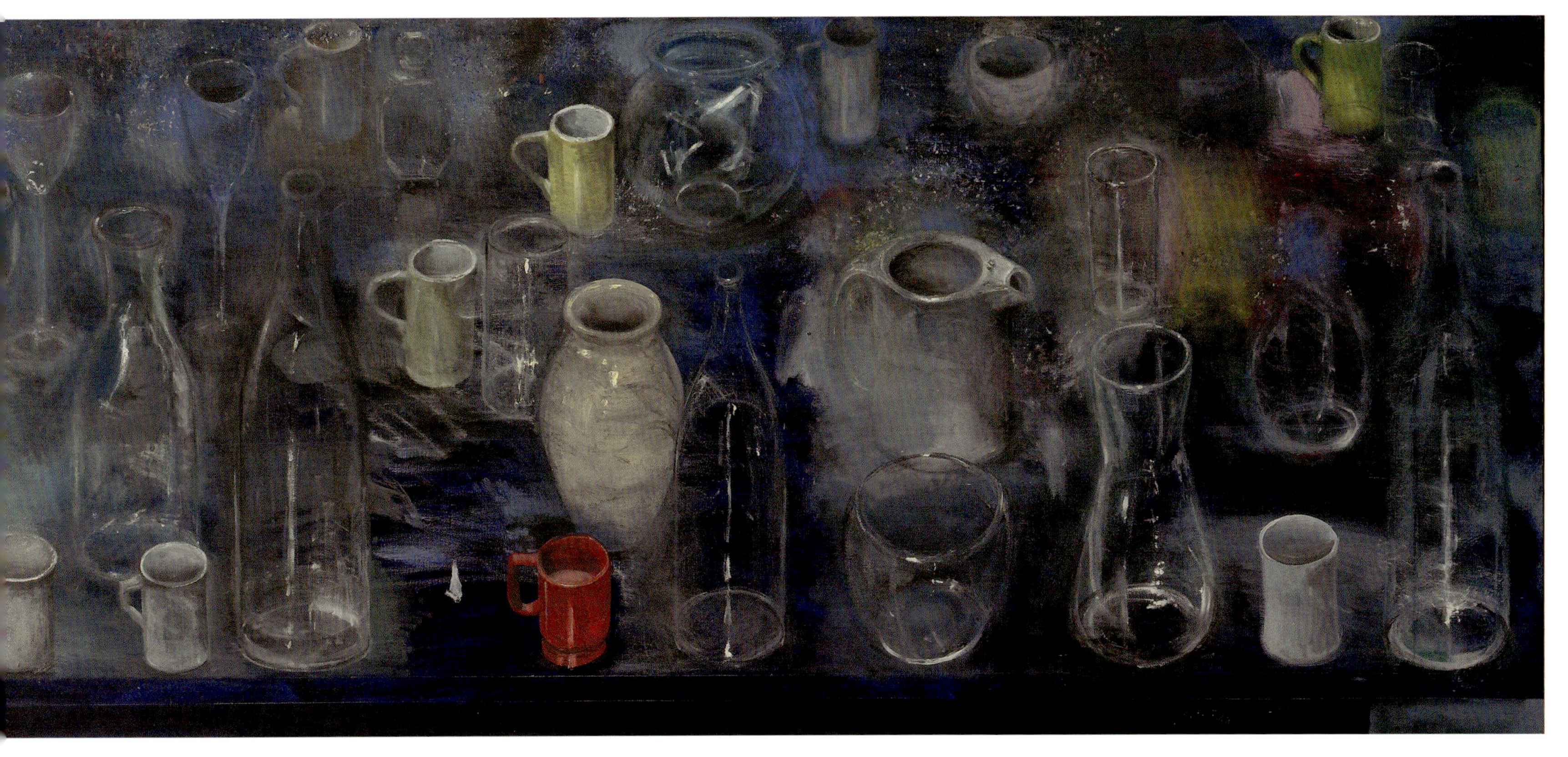

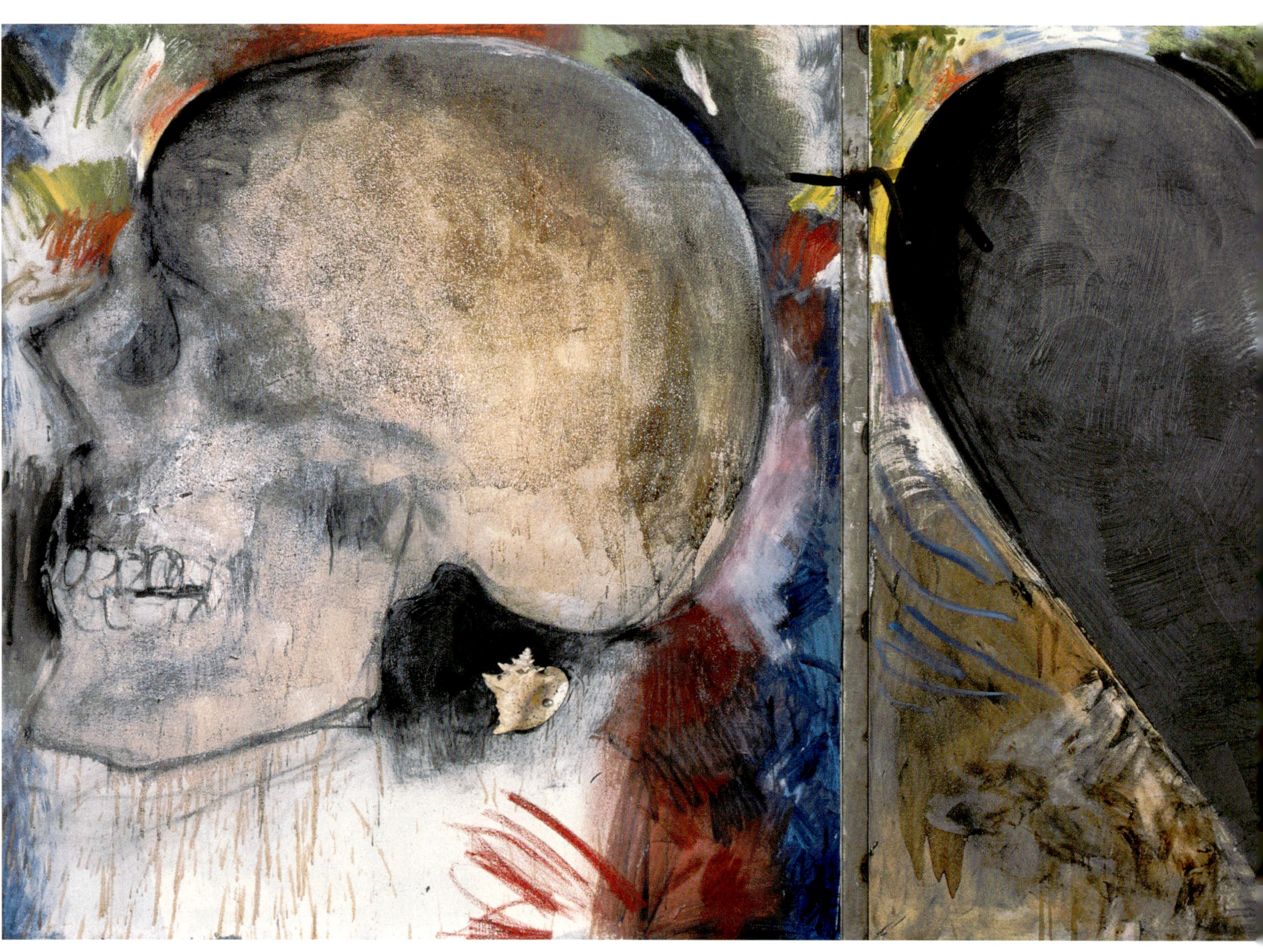

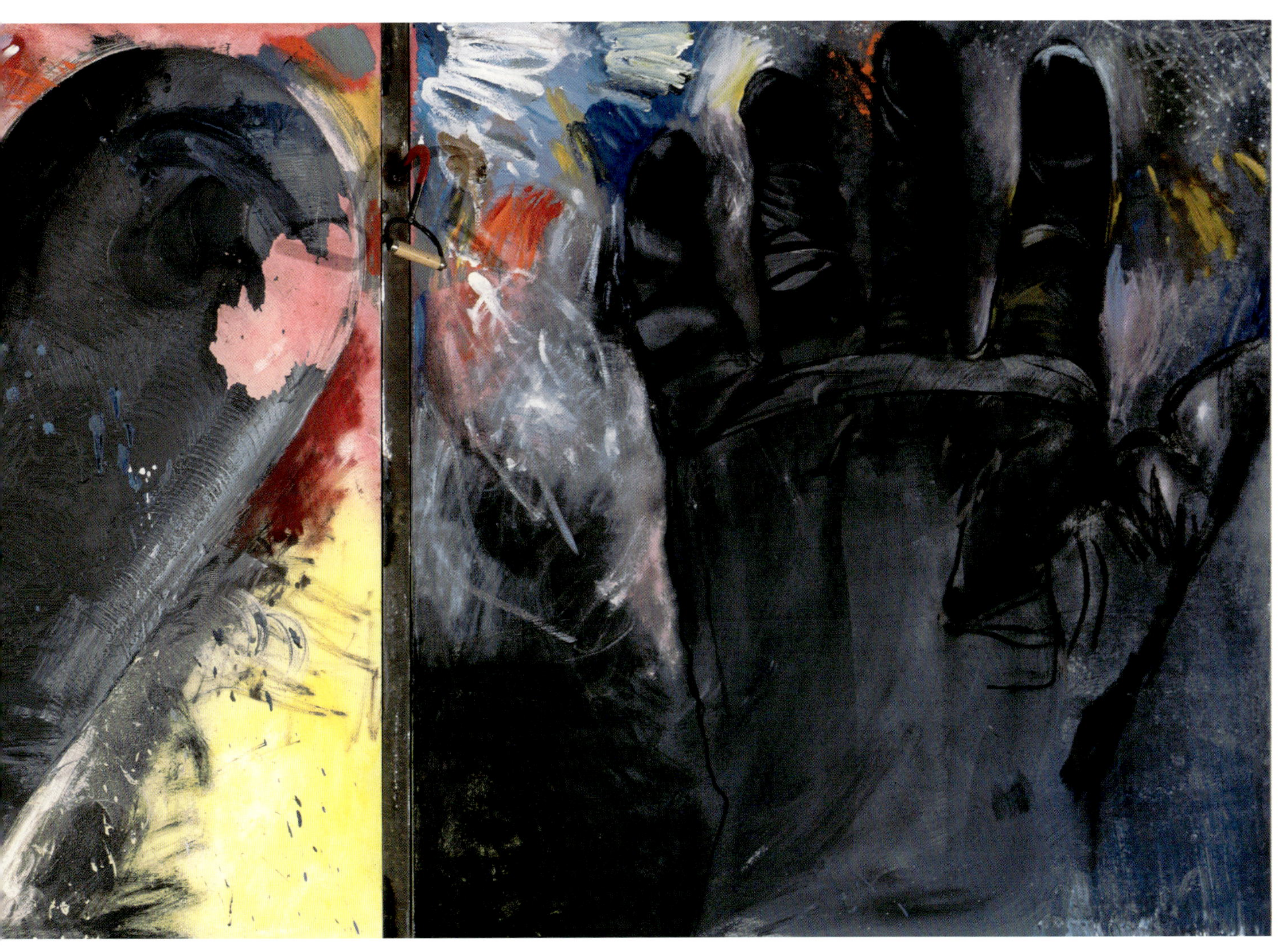

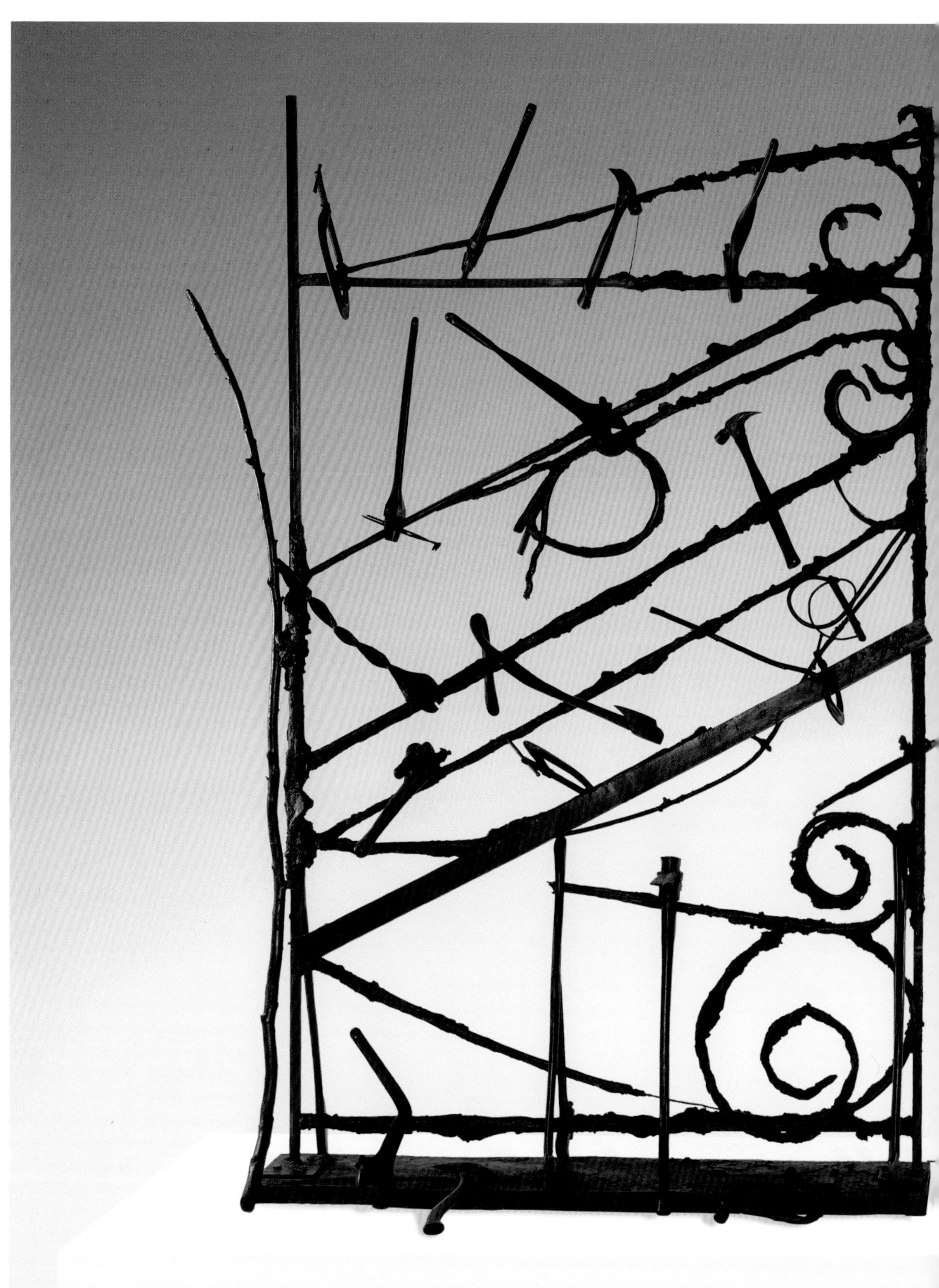

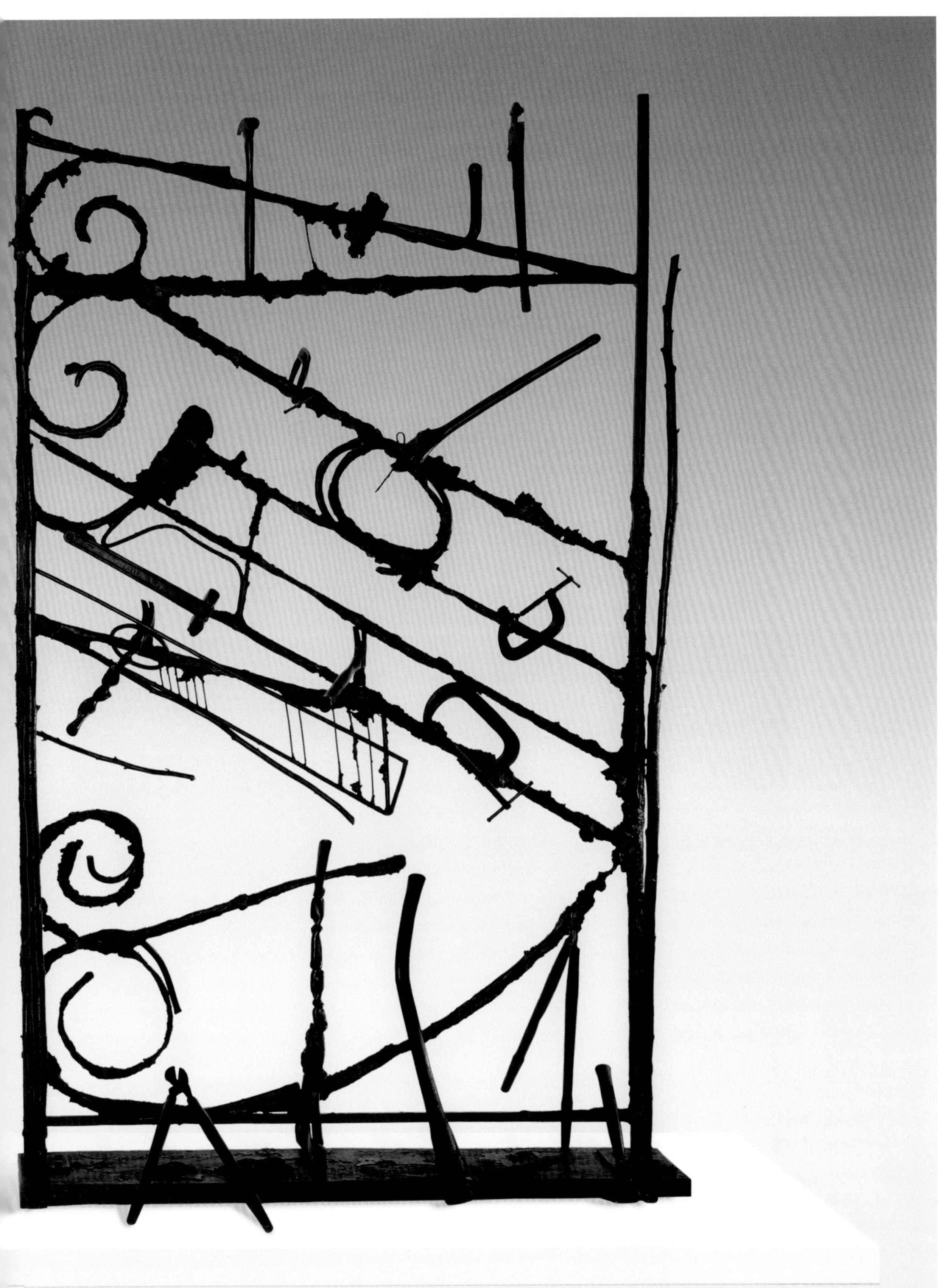

Mark di Suvero

American, born China 1933

59
***Thataway*, 1976**
Wrought and cast iron and steel with paint,
13 × 19 × 13 ft. (396.2 × 579.1 × 396.2 cm)
2006.52.65

Mark di Suvero's 1960 debut solo exhibition at New York's Green Gallery included large sculptures made of railroad ties and scrap metal that threatened to burst through the walls of the space, inspiring the critic Sidney Geist to write, "[N]othing will be the same. . . . Large, generous and dazzlingly pure, [di Suvero's] work is the opposite of the cynicism and small ideas that clutter the world of art."[1] While these early works had been directly inspired by the scale and gesturalism of Abstract Expressionist painting, di Suvero soon introduced kinetic and interactive elements into his sculptures and began openly exploring how sculptural tension could speak to human and environmental interdependency. In 1967, the scale of his sculpture began moving toward the monumental, beginning a new phase of his career. After a number of trenchant protests against the U.S. government at the end of the 1960s, including the celebrated 1966 *Peace Tower*, a fifty-five-foot-high steel structure onto which four hundred other artists attached protest paintings and placards, di Suvero embarked on a self-imposed exile in Europe for the duration of the war in Vietnam.

In France, di Suvero worked with large industrial equipment to create sculptures on an ever-increasing scale. *Thataway* is one of the first works he made after his return to the United States in 1975, when the Whitney Museum of American Art offered him a retrospective exhibition. For the Whitney, di Suvero sited his large-scale sculptures throughout the five boroughs of New York City. Taking art out of the confines of the museum and directly to the community was in keeping both with the artist's liberal politics and with populist institutional aspirations in the 1970s that led New York museums to open branches in the Bronx and in Harlem.

Standing thirteen feet tall, *Thataway* belongs to a large number of sculptures

ranging from tabletop-sized to twice life-sized that di Suvero has made throughout his career alongside the monumental commissions for which he is best known. In this sculpture, a metal sea buoy evoking a planetary model pivots from a middle point and is counterbalanced by a torqued pipe "drawing" in space. The sculpture's energy emanates from its central core, and from its implied potential for movement or change. Balance and tension are foregrounded here, as is the interdependency of sculptural elements. The playful title *Thataway* suggests directionality even as the sculpture itself undermines it: the pointed "arm" of the work's red-painted I-beam signals no particular route. On the contrary, the path it calls on viewers to follow continually returns them to the sculpture, evoking di Suvero's statement, "I think that the art that is . . . the most life-giving, is the one that makes you realize where you are. It concentrates your existence. It makes this compendium and it turns it from a lot of grapes to a very pure wine."[2]

—**Cathleen Chaffee**

---

1. Sidney Geist, "A New Sculptor: Mark di Suvero," *Arts Magazine*, December 1960, 40.
2. *Mark di Suvero*, exh. cat. (Barcelona: Instituto Valenciano de Arte Moderno Centre Julio González, Generalitat Valenciana, Conselleria de Cultura, 1994), 123.

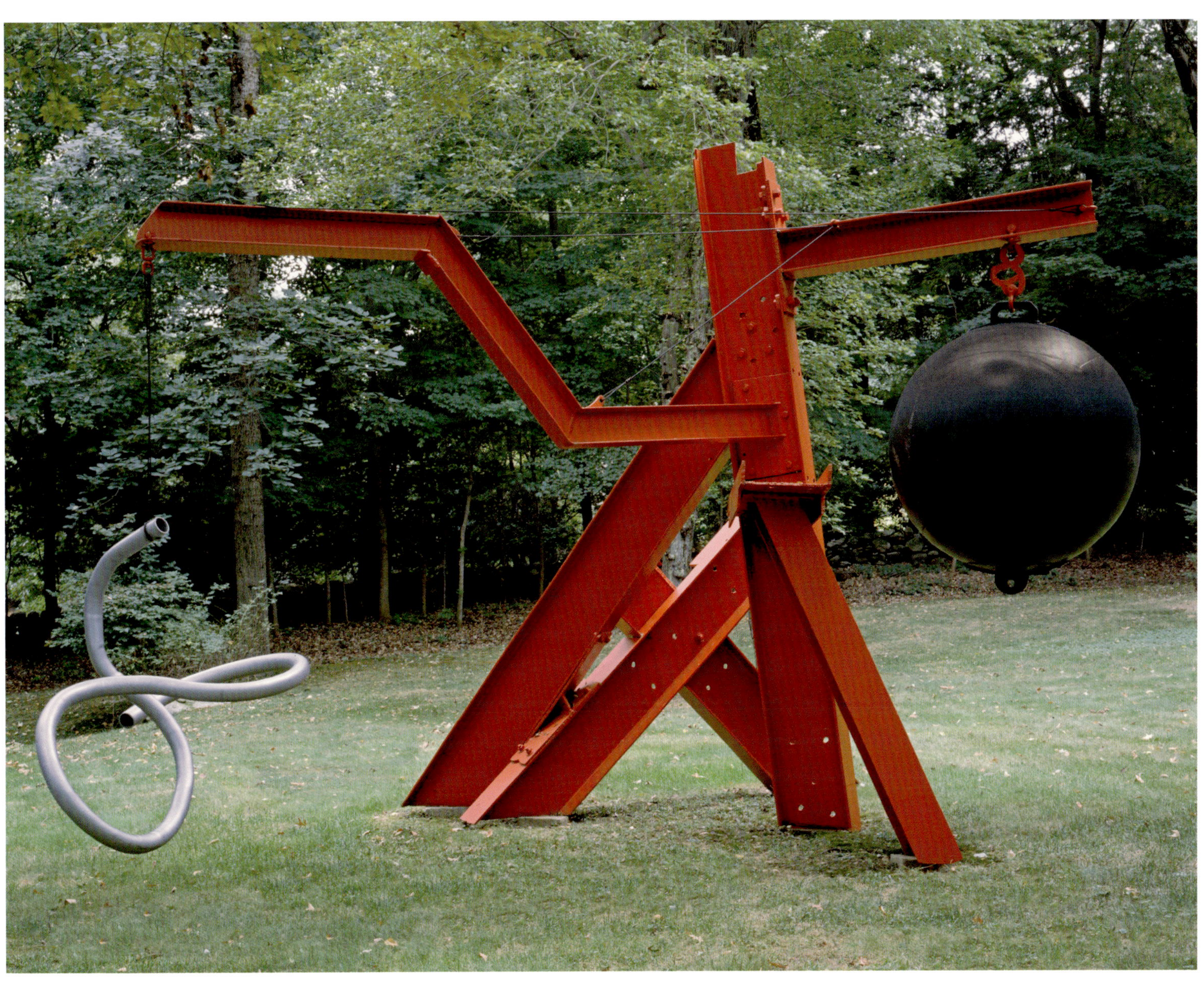

Peter Campus

American, born 1937

60
***Man's Head*, 1978**
Gelatin silver print, 31¹⁵⁄₁₆ × 26⁷⁄₁₆ in.
(81.2 × 67.1 cm)
2006.52.92

Peter Campus first made his artistic reputation in the early 1970s as a pioneer of video art. His closed-circuit installations and video environments produced distortions of space and the human form that could prove perceptually disturbing and that posed difficult questions about the fragility of fixed identity. Yet despite the rapid critical acclaim such works garnered, at the close of the decade Campus temporarily abandoned video in favor of still photography. The artist explained this shift saying that he wished to create "something less electronic, more permanent."[1] Indeed, the works he made in the following years possess a timeless, iconic quality.

Man's Head from 1978 belongs to a series of monumental photographic enlargements of human faces against monochromatic backgrounds that Campus produced in the late 1970s and early 1980s. In most cases, the final image was selected from a number of Polaroid photographs made during successive sittings, where pose and lighting were varied. The likeness was then either enlarged into a silver print photograph or it was transferred to a Cibachrome transparency and projected onto a wall, its final dimensions dictated by the gallery space in which it was shown. The Polaroid on which Campus based *Man's Head* was subjected to both treatments in different exhibitions.

Campus used the present model in several works, likely attracted by the man's arresting, even paralyzing, gaze. Having studied experimental psychology at Ohio State University from 1955 to 1960, Campus was particularly interested in exploring the human psyche under duress or in situations of phenomenological uncertainty. At first Campus used disorienting video technology to unsettle his audience, and subsequently he did so by staging head-on encounters with an alienating, frightening treatment of the human face.

In *Man's Head* the dark, brooding face emerges from a sea of blackness. The close-up viewpoint and striking frontality of the head set up a direct, dramatic confrontation with the viewer. The image conveys an uncanny agency: the man appears to be fully conscious of the viewer's presence. The partly obscured right side of the face further amplifies the menacing quality of the portrait by limiting the onlooker's view—it is as though Campus's subject can fully see us, but we can only partially see him. This effect would undoubtedly have been augmented in exhibitions where the image was projected in a completely dark room.

The somber mood of this and other works in the sequence reflects a moment of personal crisis in Campus's life in the late 1970s, which began what the artist considered his "dark age."[2] Consequently, his work from the late 1970s reveals a sustained meditation on temporality and permanence, as well as a profound questioning of the individual self. For the viewer of *Man's Head*, the figure's presence is constituted only by the temporary moment of illumination, which the artist described as the only "difference between void and non-void. It's basically my understanding that we are temporally just a flash of light in the void."[3]

—Maria Taroutina

1. Peter Campus, "Artist's Statement," in *Peter Campus, Photographs, and David Deutsch, Paintings and Drawings*, exh. cat. (Cambridge, Mass.: Hayden Gallery, Massachusetts Institute of Technology, 1983), n.p.
2. Campus, quoted in Wulf Herzogenrath, "External Images as Internal Portraits," in *Peter Campus: Analog and Digital, Video and Foto, 1970–2003*, exh. cat., ed. Herzogenrath and Barbara Nierhoff (Bremen, Germany: Kunstverein in Bremen, 2003), 19.
3. Marjory Supovitz, interview with Peter Campus, *Peter Campus: Mask Projections*, exhibition flyer (Cambridge, Mass.: Hayden Gallery, Massachusetts Institute of Technology, 1976).

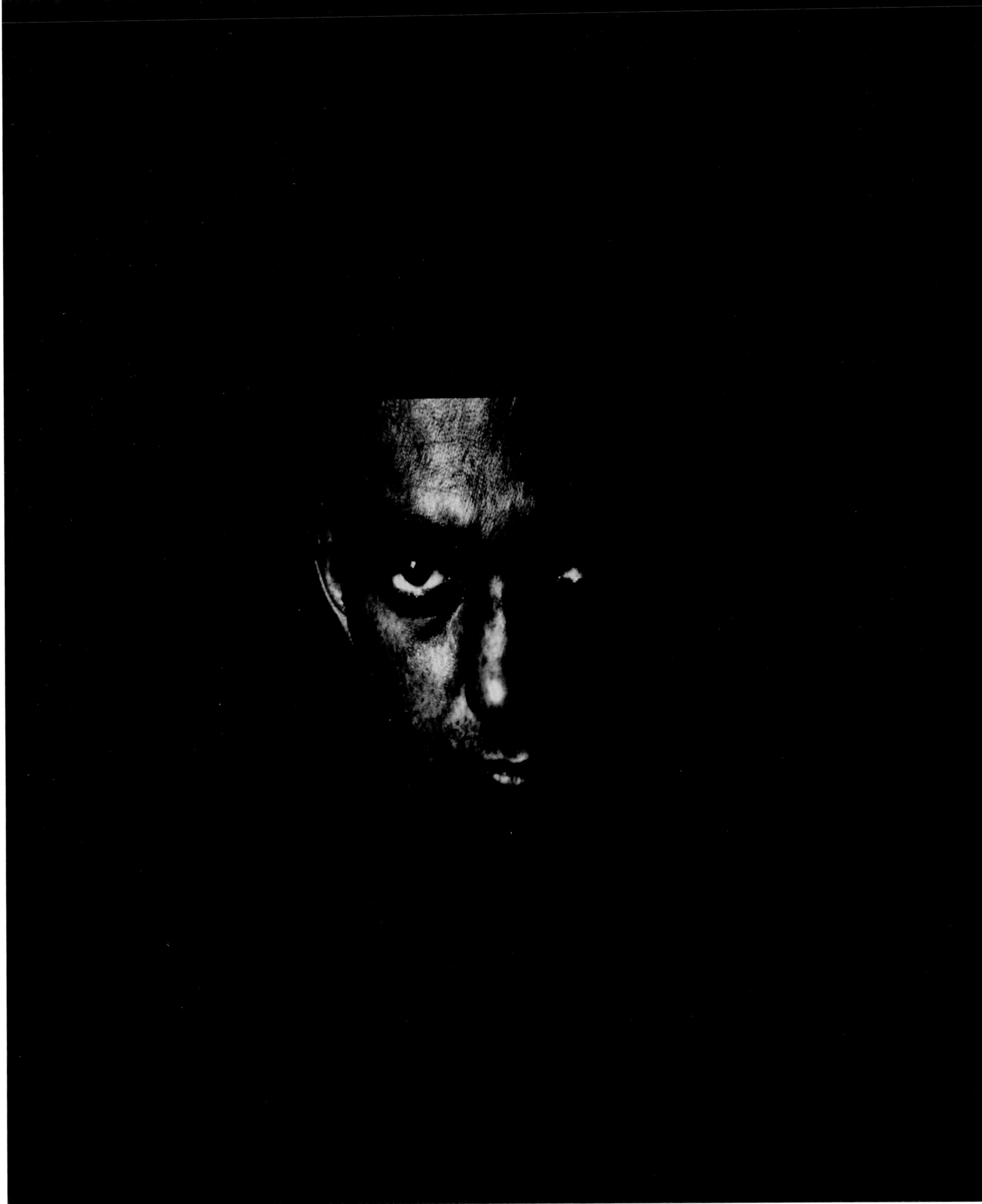

Philip Pearlstein

American, born 1924

61
***Male and Female Models on a Kilim Rug,*
1978
Acrylic on canvas, 60 × 72 in.
(152.4 × 182.9 cm)
2006.52.45

Philip Pearlstein's *Male and Female Models on a Kilim Rug* is representative of American painting's New Realist wave, in the 1970s. This decade saw a reassertion of the human figure as a central motif in art after the widespread dominance of abstraction in the preceding decades. Moreover, the rise of Performance art in tandem with the Civil Rights movement and feminist activism placed the human body at the forefront of dialectical and philosophical debates. Although trained as an abstract artist, Pearlstein anchored his formalism in figuration.

In *Male and Female Models on a Kilim Rug*, Pearlstein depicts two nearly life-size figures stretched out on his studio floor atop a vibrantly patterned carpet. The female model lies on her stomach with her right leg slightly raised, while the male model reclines on his back with his head and shoulders falling outside the picture plane. In this work Pearlstein accents pictorial structure rather than subject matter. He is essentially a formalist who resists narrative and emotion, preferring to focus on pattern, color, and composition: "I have deliberately tried to not be expressive about the models . . . not to make any kind of comment, but just to work at the formal problems of representational painting in relation to picture structure."[1]

Pearlstein's working method clearly underscores this objective. He begins by zooming in on a model's foot or hand, and then works outward in an additive fashion, ignoring the canvas edge. This unconventional methodology is especially obvious in the abrupt cropping of this work, which truncates the male model's head just below the shoulders and barely contains the female model's body. The poses of the models are equally spontaneous, adopted randomly without interference from the artist. Consequently, the structure of the finished work is largely dictated by chance—a type of

analytical or observational automatism—with Pearlstein relinquishing much of his control over the appearance of the final painting.

Adopting the large dimensions of Abstract Expressionist canvases, Pearlstein replaces those earlier artists' gestural, expressive, abstract subject matter with a tight, highly finished representation of the human form. Despite this ostensible "return" to Realism, New Realist artists like Pearlstein did not negate the intervening Modernist developments. As art historian Linda Nochlin has pointed out: "One would never confuse a Pearlstein nude with one by Courbet."[2] The artist's use of artificial lighting, crisp, unmodulated patterns, and synthetic colors engages a twentieth-century sensibility, while his abrupt cropping and irregular composition responds to a photographic aesthetic. In a typically Modernist move, Pearlstein plays with painting's spatial logic by depicting the figures from above in a work intended for vertical display on a wall. Consequently, although the viewer seems to look down at the models, it is in fact the models who loom large over the viewer, frustrating visual logic.

The work can be compared to Jack Beal's *Reclining Nude on Couch* of 1974 (fig. 1), also in the Charles B. Benenson Collection. Beal uses dramatic lighting to heighten the contrast between light and dark values, and he juxtaposes clashing colors and conflicting textures to produce visual dissonance. Unlike Pearlstein's objective transcription of external phenomena, Beal's painting is a self-consciously manipulated and modified version of reality. In this way, the two works by Beal and Pearlstein are opposed in both their intentions and results, although they share a monumental approach to the human figure. In both paintings, looming human bodies are dramatized and brought close to the canvas surface.

—**Maria Taroutina**

1. Philip Pearlstein, "Philip Pearlstein," in *Art of the Real: Nine American Figurative Painters*, ed. Mark Strand (New York: Crown, 1983), 101.
2. Linda Nochlin, *Bathers, Bodies, Beauty: The Visceral Eye* (Cambridge, Mass.: Harvard University Press, 2006), 214.

Fig. 1.
Jack Beal, *Reclining Nude on Couch*, 1974. Oil on canvas, 67 × 62 in. (170.2 × 157.5 cm). Yale University Art Gallery, Charles B. Benenson, B.A. 1933, Collection, 2006.52.41

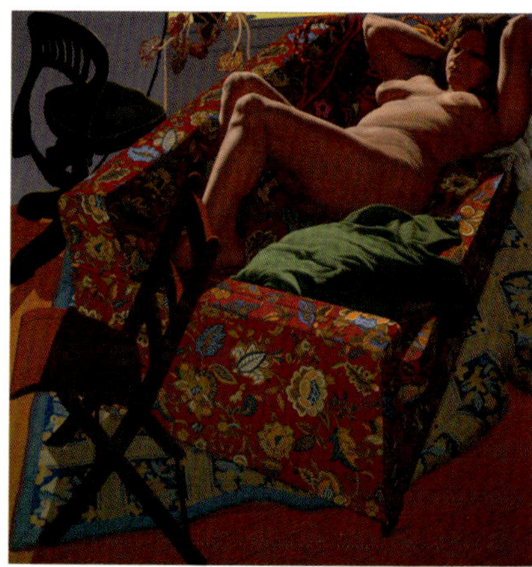

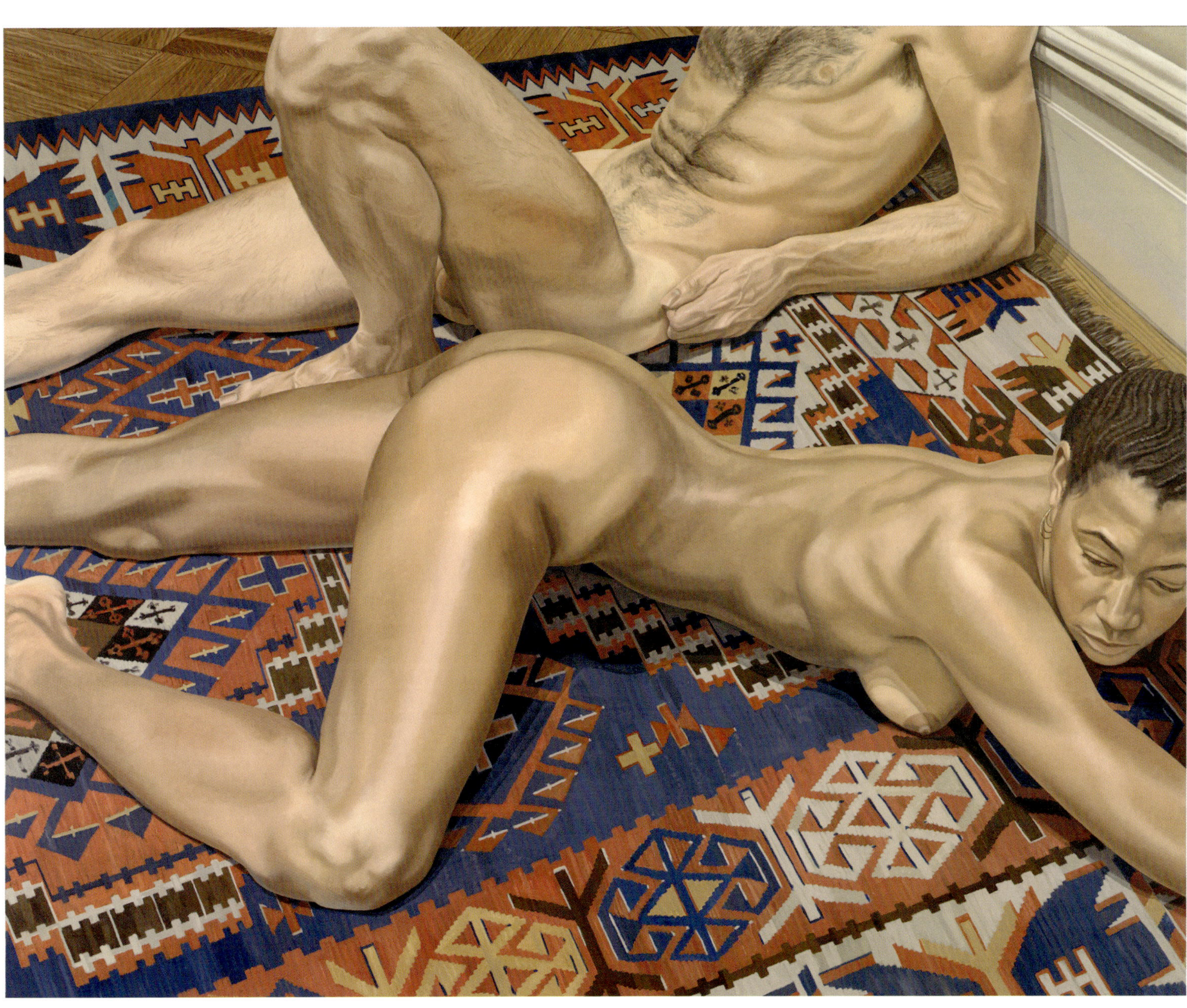

Jean-Michel Basquiat

American, 1960–1988

62
Diagram of the Ankle, 1982
Xeroxed paper, oil stick, and acrylic on
canvas; two hinged panels, overall 60 in. ×
10 ft. (152.4 × 304.8 cm)
2006.52.11

The frenetic exuberance delivered by Jean-Michel Basquiat's *Diagram of the Ankle* is conveyed through the artist's signature techniques of swift diagrammatic drawing, the expressionistic application of paint, and his use of an idiosyncratic, highly keyed palette.

Basquiat was a self-taught artist whose career aspirations and mature painting style were well developed by the time he was in his early twenties. Adapting street graffiti's uniquely succinct delivery system of images and words to canvas, Basquiat created a powerful and fresh body of work that became emblematic of the raw energy of New York's East Village art scene in the 1980s. The aggressive scale and energetic slang in Basquiat's paintings made them unparalleled in capturing this heady period in American art, when the art market collided with street culture. These works presaged the advent of the explosive hip-hop music scene and the rising awareness of African American culture as a formative component in the national identity and visual culture of the United States.

The young artist's meteoric rise to fame in both the United States and Europe led him to almost instantaneous success. He was befriended by Andy Warhol, with whom he would also collaborate as they shared an admiration for and joy in the tradition of painting. While Warhol's late imagery was more refined than Basquiat's in its execution, the two artists both understood that bold iconography married to expressionistic paint handling could be a powerful force in effecting emotional engagement with their work. To Warhol's supreme skills Basquiat added his own vibrant integration of wordplay, which imbued the visual saturation of his paintings with aural inference. The resulting works were remarkable hybrids of both Pop art's and Abstract Expressionism's legacies.

The diptych format of *Diagram of the Ankle* often occurs in the artist's oeuvre. Basquiat used it to create a polarized energy between two panels he made separately and later hinged together. In the painting's left-hand panel, the surface is composed of Xeroxes of a sketch of a maple leaf, lists of anatomical parts, and the artist's diagrams of a shoe and an ankle. The composition of these elements on the panel reads in its final form as an oversized notebook that Basquiat "corrected" with agitated editorial markings.

These primitive directional arrows and their texts were also applied to the surface of the more painterly right-hand panel, bringing the two distinct grounds into reconciliation. While on the left-hand panel he traces the anatomical associations and literal steps of the ankle in question, on the right-hand panel Basquiat humorously adds to this narrative through visual association by painting the large and threatening jaws of a canine. This caricature of an angry junkyard dog reads as the nemesis of the painting's enigmatic cipher: the ankle. The artist also endowed the body of a chicken with the face of a man, creating a possible protagonist for the painting. This "chicken man," who has lost his "halo" through Basquiat's editorial correction with a large "X" and a red scrawl, reads as a hapless interlocutor within the context of these other visual cues, complicating the work's already subjective narrative.

Basquiat's unique contribution to art history was the means by which his work voiced the vernacular of African American culture while embracing Modernist traditions in painting. Despite the brevity of his life, his vibrant and engaging oeuvre stands as a testimony to his singular vision, which helped insert cultural difference into the mainstream of contemporary art discourse.

—**Jennifer R. Gross**

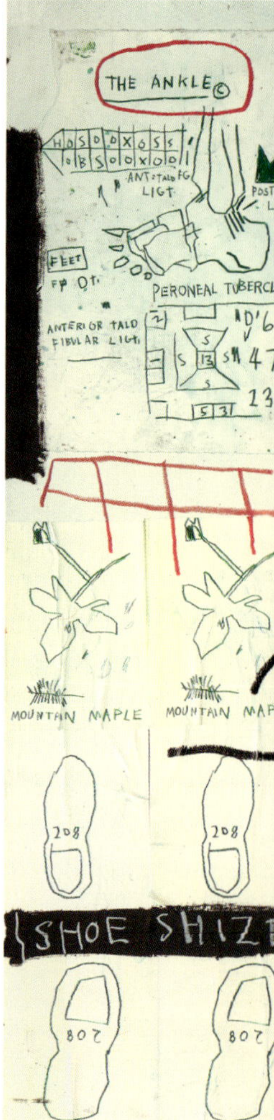

62

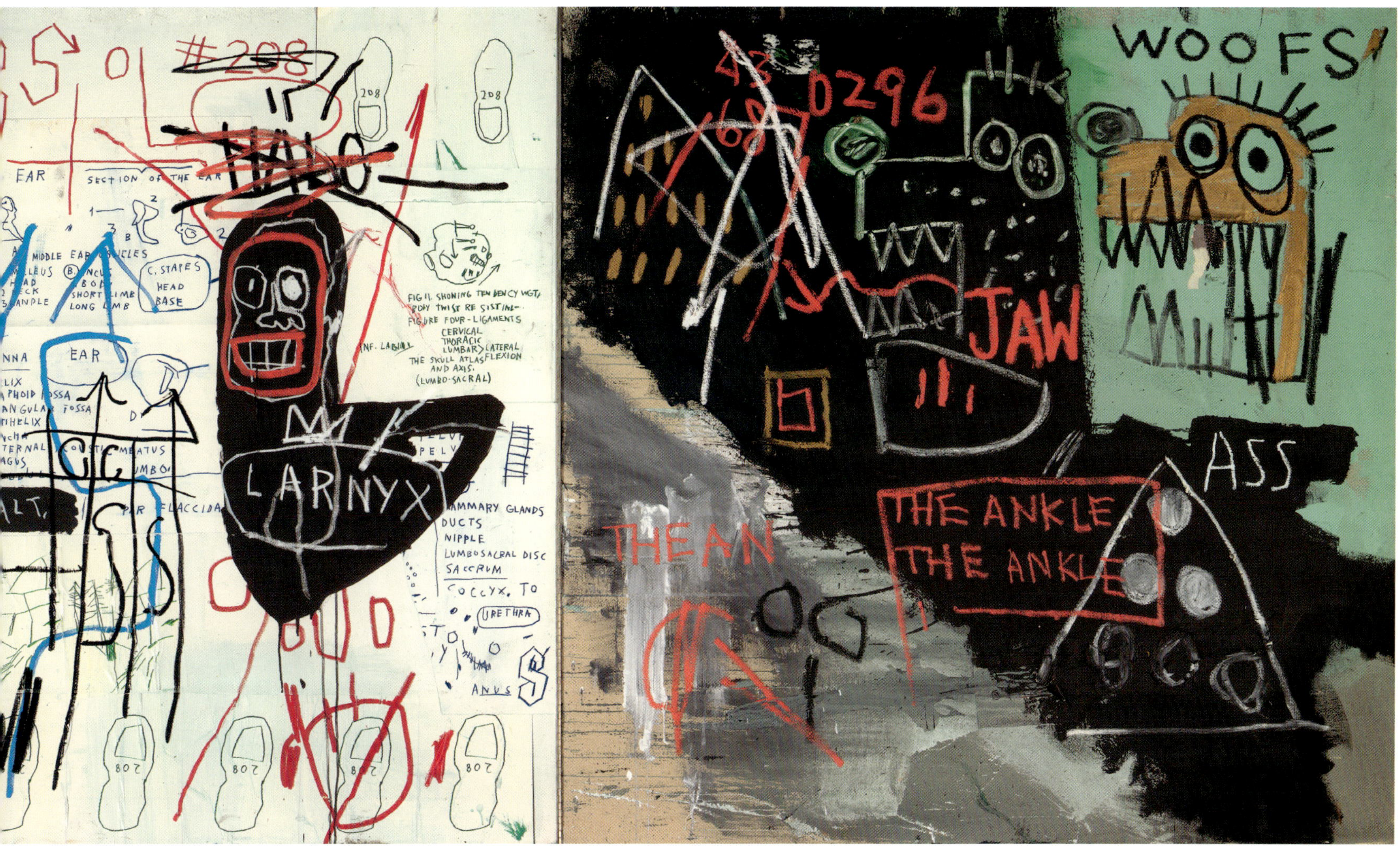

#208
208
208
208
EAR
SECTION OF THE EAR
HALO
MIDDLE EAR
C. STAPES
HEAD
BASE
EAR
LARNYX
LARYNX
FIG II SHOWING TENDENCY OF
BODY TO RESIST
FIGURE FOUR - LIGAMENTS
CERVICAL
THORACIC
LUMBAR
THE SKULL ATLAS
AND AXIS.
(LUMBO-SACRAL)
LATERAL
FLEXION
INF. LABIAL
MAMMARY GLANDS
DUCTS
NIPPLE
LUMBOSACRAL DISC
SACCRUM
COCCYX, TO
URETHRA
ANUS
208
208
208
208
WOOFS
0296
JAW
THE AN
THE ANKLE
THE ANKLE
ASS

Gilbert & George

British; Gilbert Proesch, born Italy 1943, and George Passmore, born 1942

63
***Urinight,* 1982**
Mixed media, 9 ft. 10⅞ in. × 9 ft. 10½ in.
(302 × 301 cm)
2006.52.50

Measuring almost ten by ten feet and with its nearly life-size human figures, *Urinight* appears uncannily animate. "We like it very much when the pictures take over. . . . You go to a museum to look at a picture, but we like it when the picture looks at you," affirm Gilbert & George.[1] Although created in two dimensions, *Urinight* draws on the artists' past legacy of Living Sculpture, still manifest in the images' dramatic address.

Gilbert & George entered the international art scene in 1969 with a series of so-called Living Sculptures. In the best-known of these, *The Singing Sculpture,* the two artists, covered in multicolored metallic powder, stood on a table, moving and singing along to a recording of the 1930s British popular song "Underneath the Arches." In the following decade, Gilbert & George became increasingly concerned by the rigid classification of their art as life. Consequently, by 1971, they had moved on to making figurative large-scale pictures: monumental, mural-like assemblages of individually framed panels.

Typical of the 1980s works, *Urinight* is polemical. It portrays seeming adolescents urinating into foliage, their hands suggestively positioned over their groins. Four of the boys are depicted from the back, while a fifth is shown in three-quarter view with eyes closed, raising his shirt in an eroticized gesture. The acidic urine-yellow color of the figures underscores their activity. Above them, twelve dramatically lit black-and-white heads float against a night sky. If we can treat urinating outdoors as a form of marking territory, the figures are at the same time available to the gaze of those alongside them. The sexually charged images provoke associations of public urination with public sex and subversively twin the heteronormative camaraderie of a pissing contest with seduction, as underlined by the male spectators above the youths. Gilbert & George consider titles crucial parts of their pictures, elements integral to their overall impact. *Urinight,* a pun on the word *urinate* pronounced in a Cockney accent, gives a voice to the image.

The consumption and excretion of fluids figure extensively in Gilbert & George's repertoire—particularly in pictures from the series *Drinking Sculpture* (1973–74) and in *Thirst* (1982, Tate Collection and National Galleries of Scotland). These biological activities are given a transgressive edge in *Urinight* by making the viewer into a voyeur. This perhaps underscores the artists' mission to shock their refined, museum-going audience out of disengagement or complacency.

In the London East End neighborhood where their studio is located, Gilbert & George have recorded gritty urban scenes since the 1980s. They insist, however, that their pictures are not documents but an "invented" art.[2] According to them, the carefully orchestrated manipulations in scale, composition, and color produce symbolic and emblematic, rather than simply documentary, images. Consequently, *Urinight* is not just a trace of a voyeur's gaze, or a fragment of everyday life; it has an independent presence in its own right.

—**Maria Taroutina**

1. Gilbert & George, quoted in Carter Ratcliff, "Gilbert and George: The Fabric of Their World," in *Gilbert & George: The Complete Pictures, 1971–1985* (New York: Rizzoli, 1986), x.
2. Gilbert & George, "What Our Art Means," in *Gilbert & George,* vii.

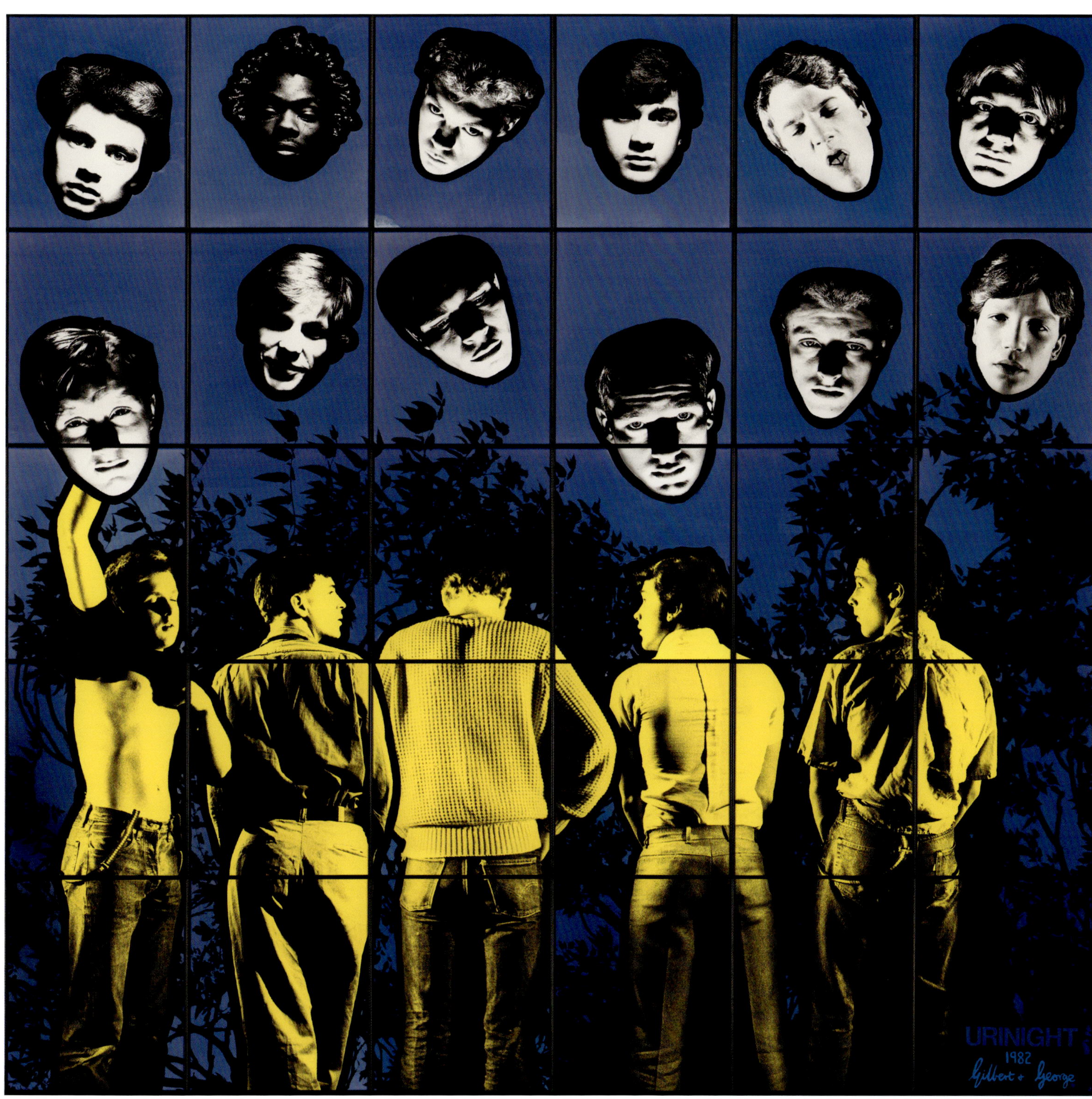

63

James Rosenquist

American, born 1933

64
***While the Earth Revolves at Night*, 1982**
Acrylic on canvas; three panels, overall
78 in. × 16 ft. 6 in. (198.1 × 502.9 cm)
2006.52.53

After his training at the Art Students League in New York, James Rosenquist took work as a billboard painter in the late 1950s, an experience that not only codified his illusionistic painting style but also gave the young artist an intimate understanding of advertising's logic. In his 1960s paintings, Rosenquist juxtaposed cropped images of popular icons like President John F. Kennedy or Marilyn Monroe with erotically charged body parts, airplanes, and candy-colored speeding cars. Food also frequently turned up in these painted collages as exemplars of the cycle of attraction and consumption in which objects of desire are easily obtained—and then exhausted just as quickly. Most of his paintings were based on appropriated photographs—often from familiar advertisements—found in slightly out-of-date newspapers and magazines. These mural-sized paintings elevated emblems of American consumerism and technology to the scale of history painting, approaching them with conflicted fascination. Rosenquist's was a potentially violent Cold War America, one in which industrial progress functioned both as a promise and as a threat.

In the left panel of *While the Earth Revolves at Night*, a gloved female hand appears to have dropped a bag of groceries. The image of clumsiness or anger abuts a panel in which a woman's red lacquered fingernail juts beneath venetian blinds. The oversized nail is dangerously filed into the razor-sharp nib of a fountain pen and surrounded by arcing star trails, such as those captured in time-lapse photography of the night sky. In the right panel, a series of interlocking gears—perhaps those of a clock—echo this astral rotation.

The idea that painting should be truthfully representational, that it should function as a "window on the world," was a central tenet of Western art for centuries. In Symbolist paintings that experimented

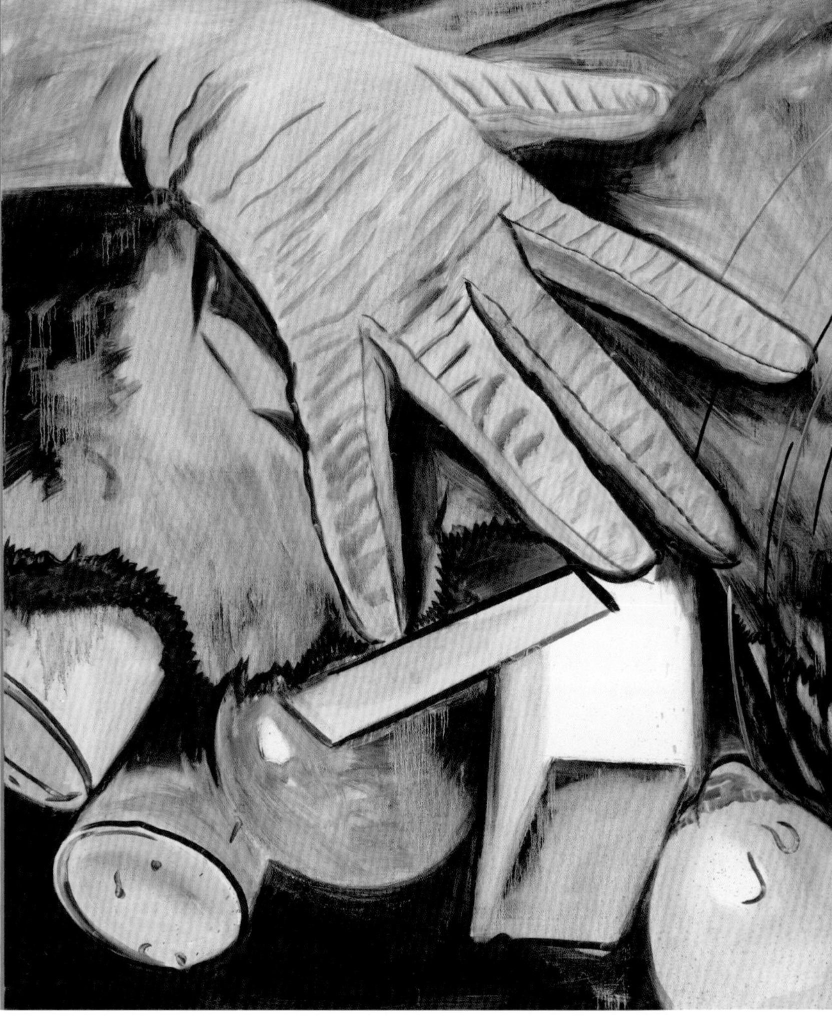

64

with illustrating the ineffable, and abstract paintings that rejected recognizable subject matter altogether, modern artists in the nineteenth and twentieth centuries moved steadily away from representational fealty to the known world. The phallic fingertip in *While the Earth Revolves at Night* blocks off the stars beyond it, seemingly asserting that while it is rendered in a photo-realistic manner, the painting's central window offers no portal to cosmic truths.

While the Earth Revolves at Night belongs to a celebrated group of monumental triptych paintings from the 1980s, which includes *House of Fire* (1981, Metropolitan Museum of Art) and *Fahrenheit 1982 Degrees* (1982, private collection). In these works, Rosenquist moved away from the collagelike overlap that characterized his juxtapositions of imagery in the 1960s; instead, he abutted relatively unfragmented scenes, creating incongruous adjacencies. The venetian blinds and the erotically charged red fingernail in the painting exemplify 1980s fashion, while the subject matter resonates with tropes from 1980s film, such as that decade's re-appraisal of 1930s film noir. If the painting's central femme fatale and its nocturnal palette evoke such filmic themes, Rosenquist's use of multiple viewpoints and his defiance of cogent narrative are more evocative of channel surfing than of cinematic montage.

—**Cathleen Chaffee**

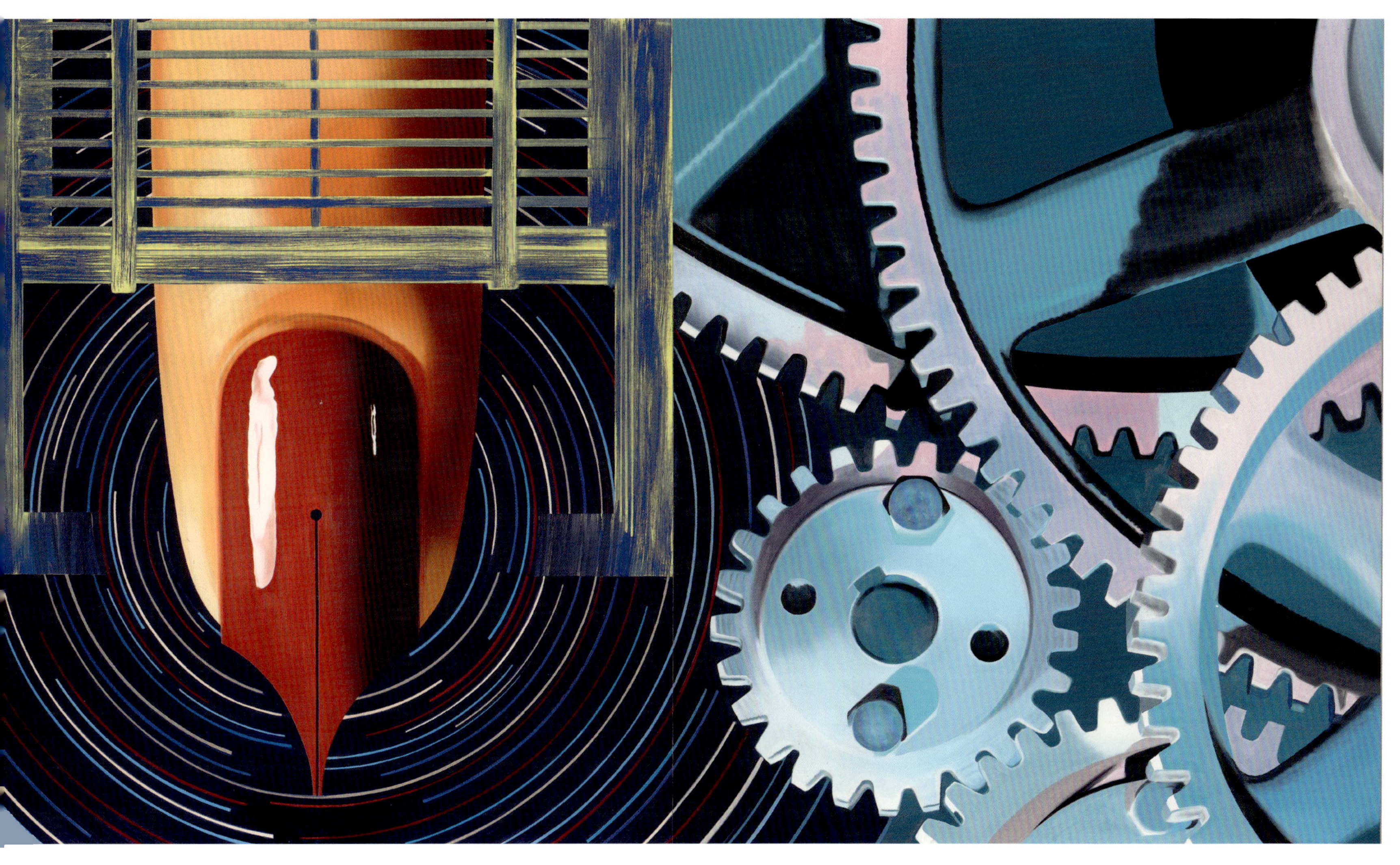

Anthony Caro

British, born 1924, HON. 1989

65
Ocean, 1982–83
Rusted steel, 8 ft. 4 in. × 11 ft. 10 in. × 79 in.
(254 × 360.7 × 200.7 cm)
2006.52.63

British sculptor Anthony Caro is primarily known for the painted sculptures of welded steel he began making in the United States in the 1960s while teaching at Bennington College in Vermont. Influenced by the dialogue he had there with his artist colleagues—the painters Kenneth Noland and Jules Olitski, as well as the critic Clement Greenberg, who championed their work and articulated their aesthetic values—Caro reconsidered the more traditional definitions and aspirations of art in which he had been trained.

The sculptures that resulted from Caro's reassessment explored perspective and space through the juxtaposition of welded planar forms that were unified and given expressive life through the application of surface color. These works were groundbreaking, pushing beyond the totemic and constrained assemblages of David Smith, whose work Caro greatly admired. Caro's pursuit of formal sculptural inquiry has since produced an even more significant body of work that has transformed traditional considerations of sculpture within and in response to architectural space.

Ocean exemplifies Caro's interest in exploring the primary elements of sculptural practice: mass, form, and particularly volume within a prescribed spatial theater. This somber and condensed yet open form conveys a presence of mass and volume through an assembling of disparate elements. These engage the viewer in an unfolding visual narrative as he or she moves around the work. The composite elements of *Ocean* roll out in a sequence unanticipated by the viewer due to Caro's abrupt layering and framing of broad planes, restrained gesture, and succinctly articulated details that expressively punctuate this framed sequence.

Presented directly on the ground, the work's compact structure is welded from Caro's principal medium: unfinished steel. The artist cannibalized industrial forms and bisected spheres with real and implied planes of steel to create a tableau of sculptural abstraction. *Ocean* is confrontational; its heavy, blunt forms are rendered on a slightly larger-than-human scale from bulky steel goods, such as buoys salvaged from the maritime industry. The unwieldy, rounded forms that resulted from Caro's scavenging of industrialization's by-products helped him to match the sculptural volume and scale that originally compelled the artist to pursue this series of raw steel sculptures.

These works stand in contrast to the light, open vistas created by Caro's rectilinear sculptures from the 1960s, which were composed of fragmented I-beams, lean steel piping, and planes of wire mesh. Unlike in the work of sculptors to whom he is often compared, such as Henry Moore, Richard Serra, or David Smith, there is no implication that landscape or the figure inspired this later series by Caro. Rather, he articulates abstraction as its own end, a delicate interplay of indelicate material fact.

—**Jennifer R. Gross**

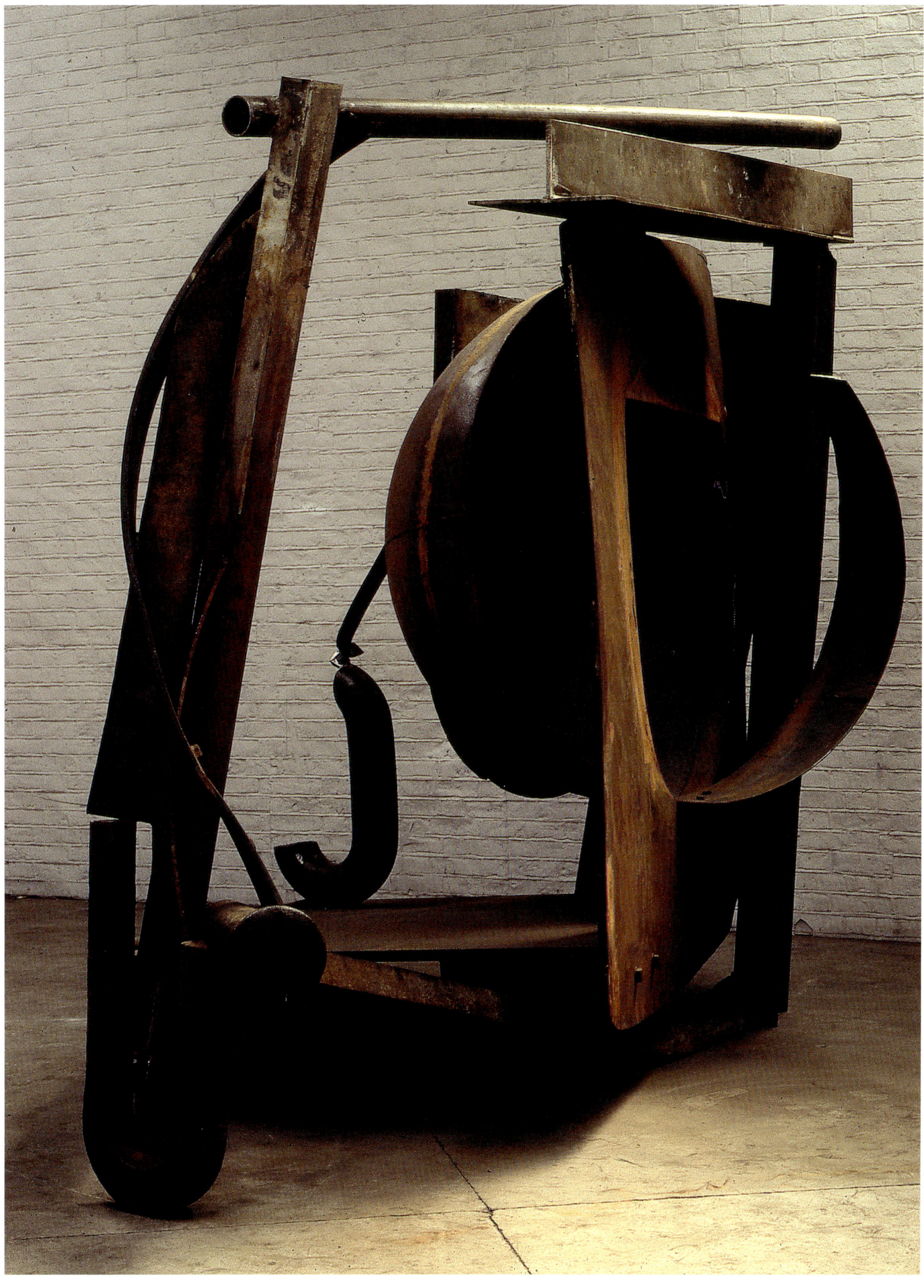

Louise Bourgeois

American, born France, 1911–2010

66
Shredder, **1983**
**Wood and metal, 96 in. × 9 ft. × 9 ft.
(243.8 × 274.3 × 274.3 cm)
2006.52.62**

In 1924, the critic Robert Fry argued that art historians did not need to apply psychoanalytic interpretations to artists because the process of making art had allowed them to sublimate sexual energies, aggression, or trauma.[1] Louise Bourgeois, whose practice more consistently resembles the worrying of a scab than the resolution of a psychic wound, fundamentally opposed such an argument. For more than sixty years, Bourgeois plumbed her personal history—and other sources such as biology, psychology, politics, and sexuality—to create works that share an expressive narrative force, if rarely a consistent aesthetic. Her open communication about some of her referents, which include her own family, has made it tempting to "read" a richly symbolic artwork by Bourgeois as if it were a rebus. To do so, however, is to miss a chance to be unnerved by her subversive alternation between recognizable forms and those that decline either to resolve into abstraction or to fully represent known objects in the world.

In the late 1960s, along with a number of other artists such as Eva Hesse and Yayoi Kusama, Bourgeois began making sculptures that alluded to body parts and biomorphic forms. Such fragmentary references to the human body represented a departure from the clean geometries of Minimalism and seemed to challenge the purity and autonomy of traditional sculpture.[2]

Such biomorphic sculpture also sometimes appeared to suggest that the creative act itself constituted a kind of violence. Bourgeois apparently encouraged this reading, noting that "[i]n my art I'm the murderer. . . . The guillotine appears all the time in my work."[3] Indeed, she frequently positioned knives and scissors in menacing proximity to representations of, or surrogates for, the human form. Among other things, her references to violence suggest that good art is often dangerous. Here, it can undermine our perception of the human body as a unified, indissoluble entity. Looming large over viewers, *Shredder* does not just imply menace; it embodies it. Five immense wooden discs harvested from enormous cable spools appear to grind vertically against a horizontal beam, into which corresponding wedges have been carved. The sculpture transforms abstract shapes—five circles and a line—into an object that seems almost animate. Inspired, according to the artist, by hearing a lecturer interpret her work, *Shredder* appears to answer the critic's interlocution with an aggressive threat.[4]

Shredder was Bourgeois's contribution to the 1983 Whitney Biennial in New York, and it remained a prominent fixture in her studio for at least a decade afterward. She underlined its potential destructive power with the photo she selected to represent the sculpture in progress for the Biennial catalogue (fig.1). In it, *Shredder* appears to roll over a pair of dismembered mannequin legs. Known for carefully staging her interactions with sculptures for the camera, Bourgeois posed a decade later for a photograph with *Shredder* immediately behind her and one of her oversized sculptures of a spider directly in front. The photograph seems to imply that *Shredder* was being held in reserve—ready and waiting to carry out the artist's bidding in the world.

—**Cathleen Chaffee**

1. Robert Fry, quoted in Griselda Pollock, "Old Bones and Cocktail Dresses: Louise Bourgeois and the Question of Age," *Oxford Art Journal* 22, no. 2 (1999): 88–89.
2. See Leslie Jones, "Transgressive Femininity: Art and Gender in the Sixties and Seventies," in *Abject Art: Repulsion and Desire in American Art*, exh. cat., ed. Craig Houser (New York: Whitney Museum, 1993), 43n.13.
3. As quoted in Irving Sandler, *Art of the Postmodern Era: From the Late 1960s to the Early 1990s* (New York: Icon, 1996), 121.
4. Kay Larson, "All-American Energy," *New York Magazine*, April 11, 1983, 62.

Fig. 1.
Louise Bourgeois, *Shredder*, 1983, in progress

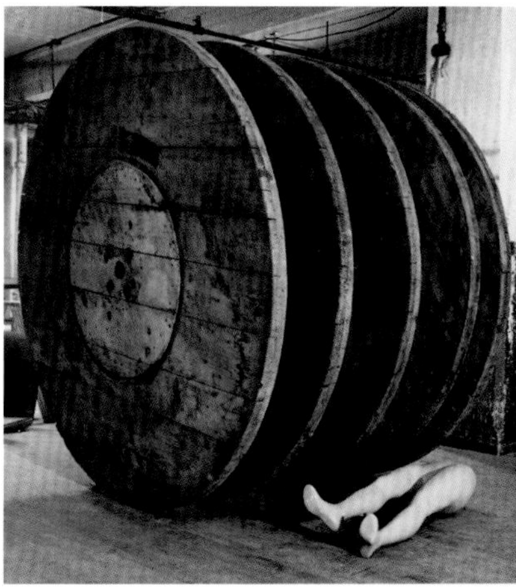

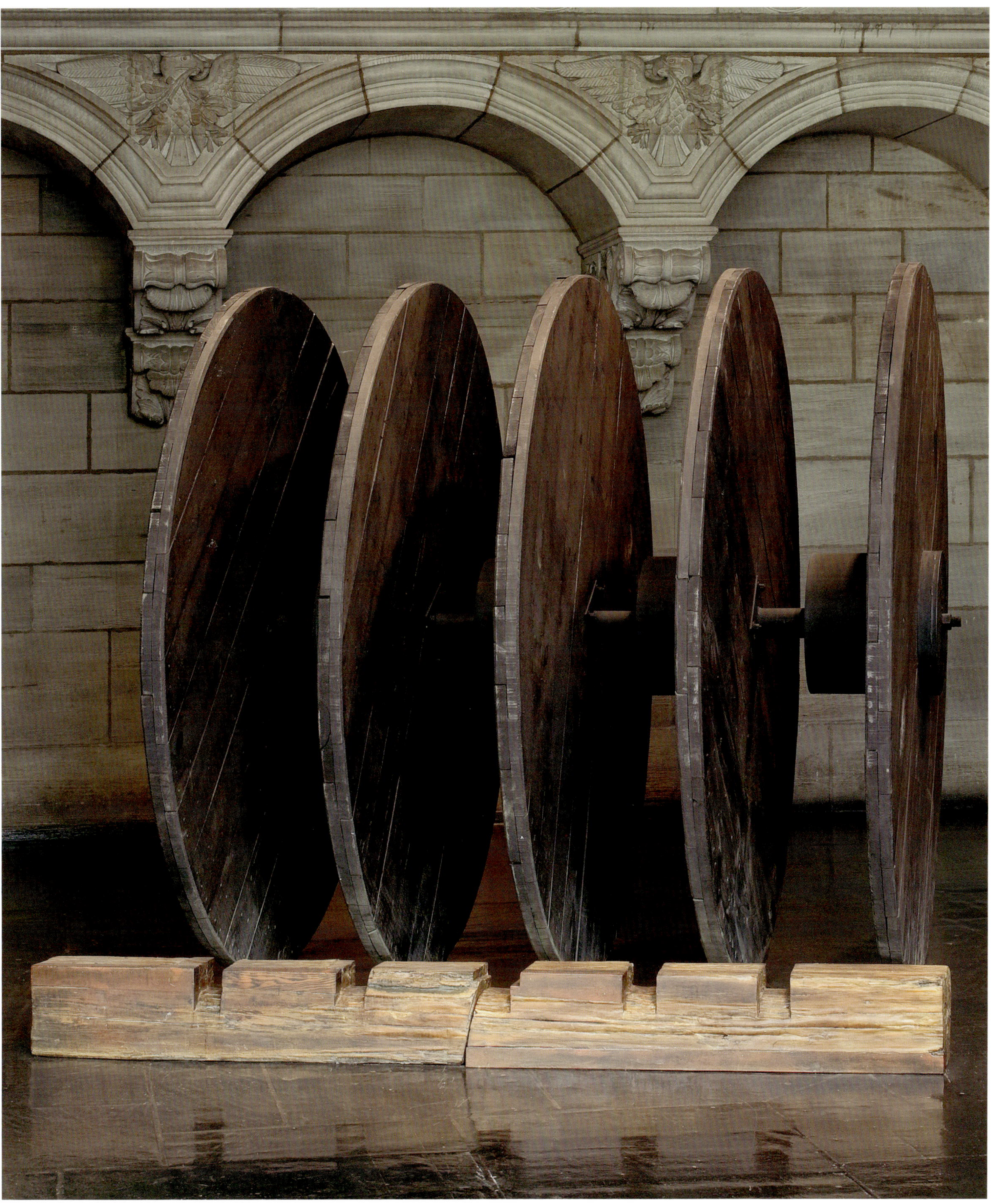

Ed Paschke

American, 1939–2004

67
***La Bomba* (The Bomb), 1983**
Acrylic on canvas, 50 × 85 in. (127 × 215.9 cm)
2006.52.60

The intense green, violet, and blue hues of Ed Paschke's painting *La Bomba* (The Bomb) submerge the viewer's eye in a radiant atmosphere, suggesting the familiar haze of a television screen's vibrant pixilation. The abstracted profiles of a man wearing glasses, or of a group of five men, that increase in size and definition from left to right give the painting its sense of depth and mystery. As in many of Paschke's late works, the subject's generalized features are evoked through the interplay of contrasting dark and light colors that mimic positive and negative articulations of skin, nose, lips, and eyes. Bisecting rays of color cleave and join the individual profiles across the surface of the canvas and render these masked figures as cool, ominous caricatures. The title, *La Bomba*, may indicate Paschke's interest in the controversial punk/ new wave musician Tonio K (Steve Krikorian), who often wore oversized Ray-Ban sunglasses. The title track of Tonio K's 1982 Capitol Records album *La Bomba* was a rant against the international weapons race.

As a young artist, Paschke was originally known for his focused interest in popular culture. His subjects—as wide-ranging as Lee Harvey Oswald, Abraham Lincoln, and Elvis Presley—were known to the public only as composite characters created by the media. An assessment of Paschke's life's work reveals, however, that his sights were set on the periphery of cultural norms and the means by which commodity culture can fuel and distort desire.

There have been few winning subjects in Paschke's oeuvre; his was a jaundiced view of the seamy side of humanity. Paschke rose to recognition in the 1960s and 1970s with provocative paintings that imaged then-transgressive subcultures, places where the boundaries of identity could be explored alongside the limits of tolerance. Confrontationally cropped and posed life-sized images of pimps, prostitutes, and transgendered men and women garbed in offensively patterned costume confections were lavishly rendered in garish colors. Specific identities were concealed by sunglasses or tattooed masks that the artist used to stylize his characters' features.

Paschke's paintings remind us that we can neither escape our own perverse curiosity nor prevent our gaze from being tainted by judgment. His sumptuously painted works give us the virtuosic technique we want from painting but serve it up on a platter of confrontational imagery garnished with a sordid palette. This "bait and switch" denies viewers the satisfaction of passively consuming Paschke's painterly product.

Paschke's later works, such as *La Bomba*, address the distortion of meaning and identity that occurs in a culture imaged through mass media, as well as our difficulty in grappling with the media's truths and mistruths. Their radiant hues catch us in a Svengali-like hold between attraction and repulsion.

—Jennifer R. Gross

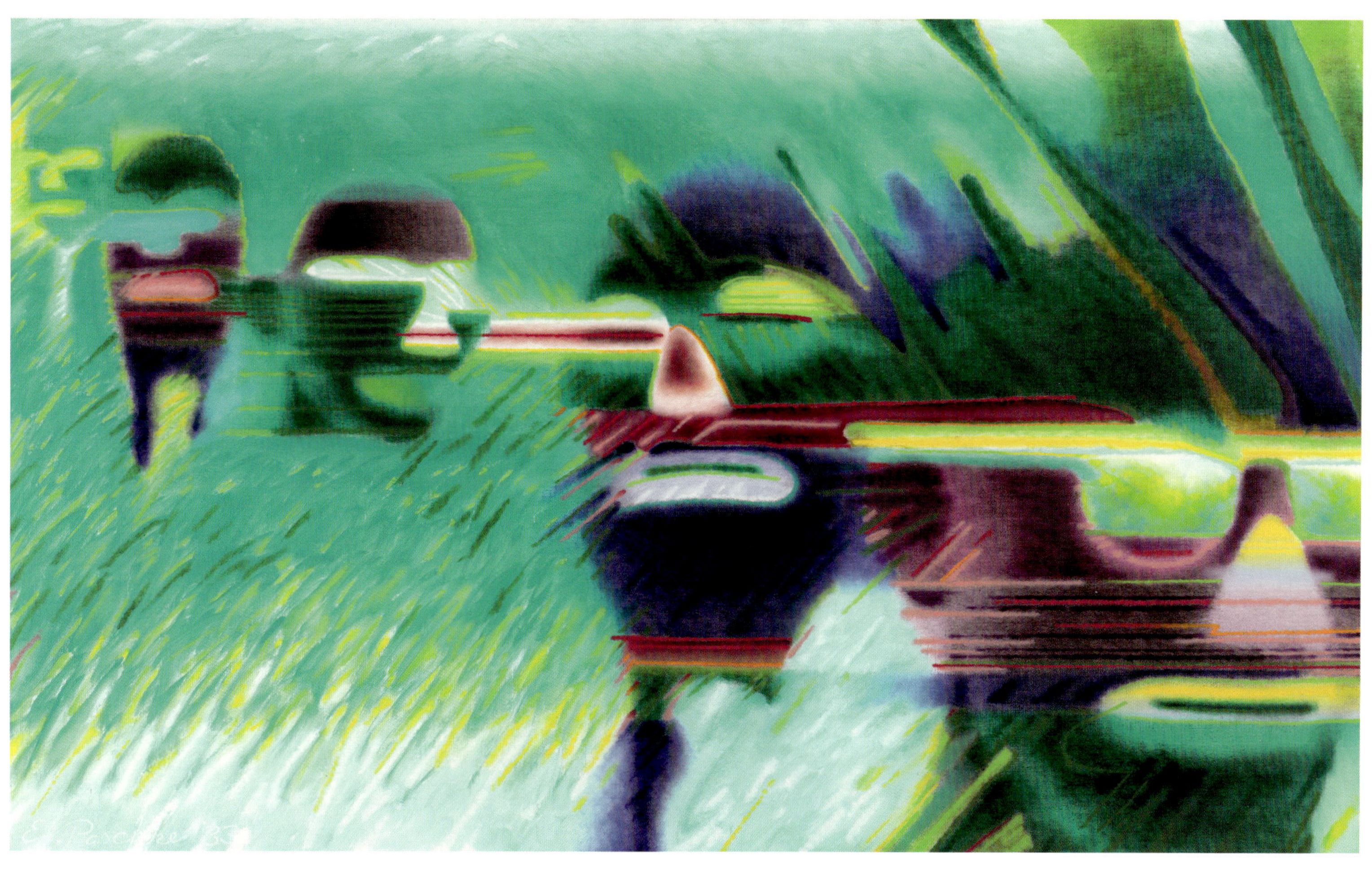

R. B. Kitaj

American, 1932–2007

68
Amerika (Baseball), 1983–84
Oil on canvas, 58 × 58 in. (147.3 × 147.3 cm)
2006.52.14

69
China and Russia, 1980
Pastel and charcoal, 30 ³⁄₁₆ × 28½ in.
(76.6 x 72.4 cm)
2006.52.100

Born in Ohio to a Russian Jewish mother and a Hungarian father, Ronald Brooks Kitaj spent the majority of his career in England, returning to the United States shortly before his death in 2007. Kitaj thematized notions of belonging, estrangement, and persecution in his art. His complex and subtle works question the idea of a distinctive, fixed identity and probe deeply into the major political, social, racial, and ethnic divides that have plagued the twentieth century.

Amerika (Baseball) (cat. 68) was painted in England and is one of Kitaj's many works that reference the sport. An avid baseball fan, the artist associated the game with his carefree childhood in the United States. Although at first glance the work seems to celebrate U.S. culture, its title hints at another, darker layer of potential meanings. By calling the work *Amerika* rather than *America,* Kitaj referred to the incomplete novel of his favorite author, Franz Kafka. In *Amerika: The Man Who Disappeared* (1927), Kafka related the strange wanderings of Karl Rossmann, a European emigrant who travels to the United States. In a particularly symbolic passage, the Statue of Liberty is described as ominously holding a sword instead of a torch. The promise of freedom and deliverance is thus converted by Kafka into an emblem of hostility and persecution. Kitaj's repeated mining of referents from literary and philosophical texts constituted a major part of his artistic practice, and in *Amerika,* the artist's allusion to Kafka underscored his own conflicted feelings toward his immigrant status and Jewish identity.

Visually, this sense of alienation is captured in the male figure in the bottom right-hand corner of the canvas, whose profile and blond beard resemble those of the artist. His scale and elaborate hat and bow tie separate him from the rest of the composition; he is literally on the margins of the painting. More of a detached observer than an active participant, he turns his back on the field and looks away, lost in his own reverie.

By contrast, the other figure in the foreground is wholly absorbed by the players on the field, who are portrayed in different attitudes of pitching, batting, and catching the ball. Their energetic movements are expressively captured by Kitaj's agitated, gestural brushstrokes, while the vibrant, contrasting colors activate the surface of the painting. A highly accomplished draftsman, Kitaj would first draw his entire composition on canvas, and would then apply thin glazes of paint with a dry brush. He called this technique "drawing-painting" and claimed that he drew inspiration from the late works of Paul Cézanne and Edgar Degas, executed in a similar style.

Structurally, *Amerika* was based on Diego Velázquez's *Philip IV Hunting Wild Boar (La Tela Real)* (fig. 1), which Kitaj saw at the National Gallery in London. The broad perspective, high horizon line, and numerous tiny figures were all adopted by Kitaj from the Spanish original, as were the atmospheric sky and oval arena. Just as baseball had become the modern American equivalent of the age-old tradition of the hunt, so Kitaj was positioning himself as the contemporary successor to the lyrical, painterly tradition of the Old Masters, a tradition that he vehemently defended as the repository of human passions, intellect, and history: a bulwark against what he saw as the sterility of nonrepresentational and conceptual art.

These views meant that the human form played an important role in Kitaj's art, as evidenced by *China and Russia* (cat. 69), a small pastel depicting two allegorical figures. Having been greatly impressed by an exhibition of Degas's pastels in Paris in 1975, Kitaj increasingly turned to pastels as his preferred medium in the late 1970s and early 1980s. In the present work, *Russia* has pronounced Slavic facial features and is dressed in white, while *China* wears a red and green garment and stands upright behind *Russia.* As in many of Kitaj's historical allegories, the precise meaning of this composition remains elusive. The vulnerable, hunched figure of Russia, trapped

Fig. 1.
Diego Velázquez, *Philip IV Hunting Wild Boar (La Tela Real),* probably 1632–37. Oil on canvas, 71¹³⁄₁₆ in. × 9 ft. 11 in. (182 × 302 cm). National Gallery, London

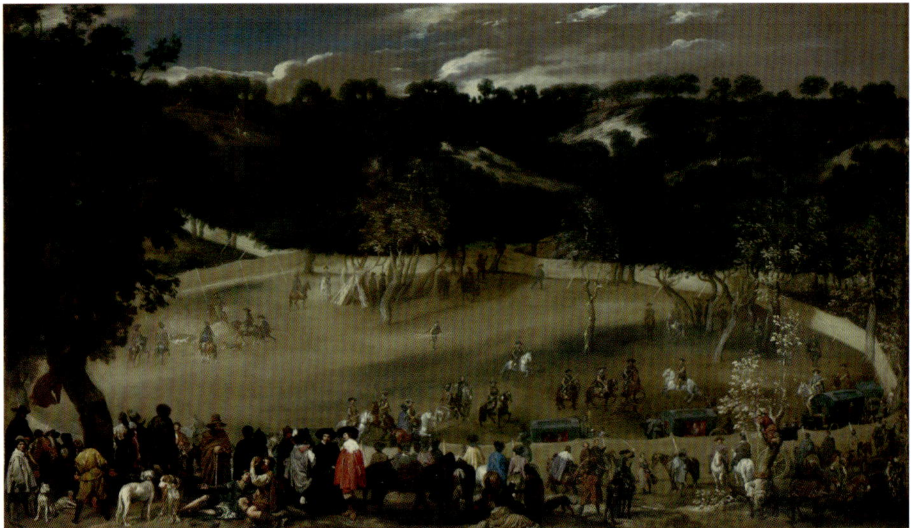

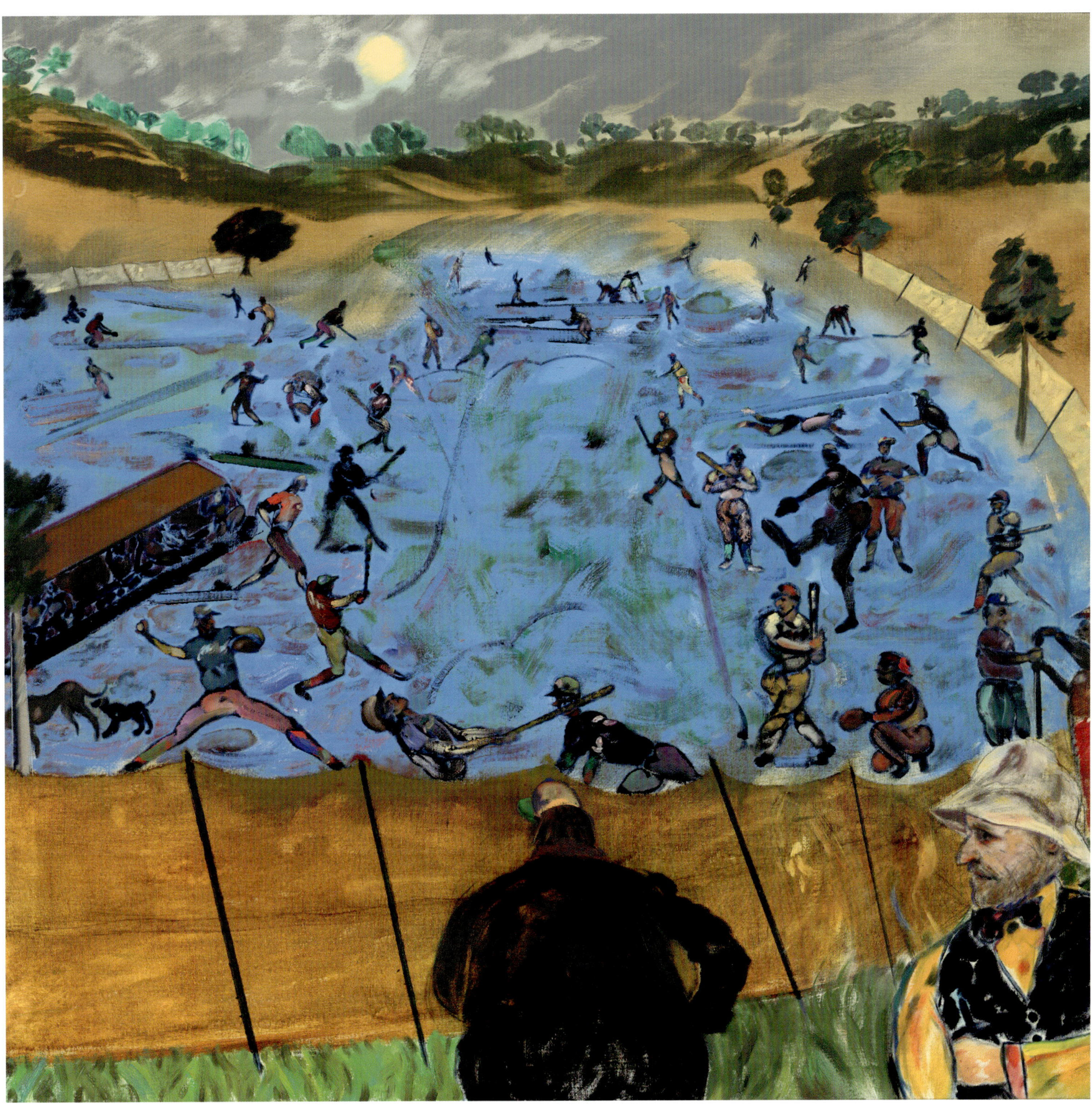

in a corner, seems to suggest defeat or helpless-
ness. Yet it remains unclear whether the work
is a commentary on contemporary politics or a
broader philosophical statement on the socialist ideals Kitaj publically espoused.

The intimate nature of *China and Russia*
suggests that it may also have had a personal,
coded meaning for the artist. In Russian Kitaj
means "China." It is possible that Kitaj not
only allegorically associated himself with
the socialist ethos but likewise created a
self-portrait, continuing his deconstructive
project on identity.

—Maria Taroutina

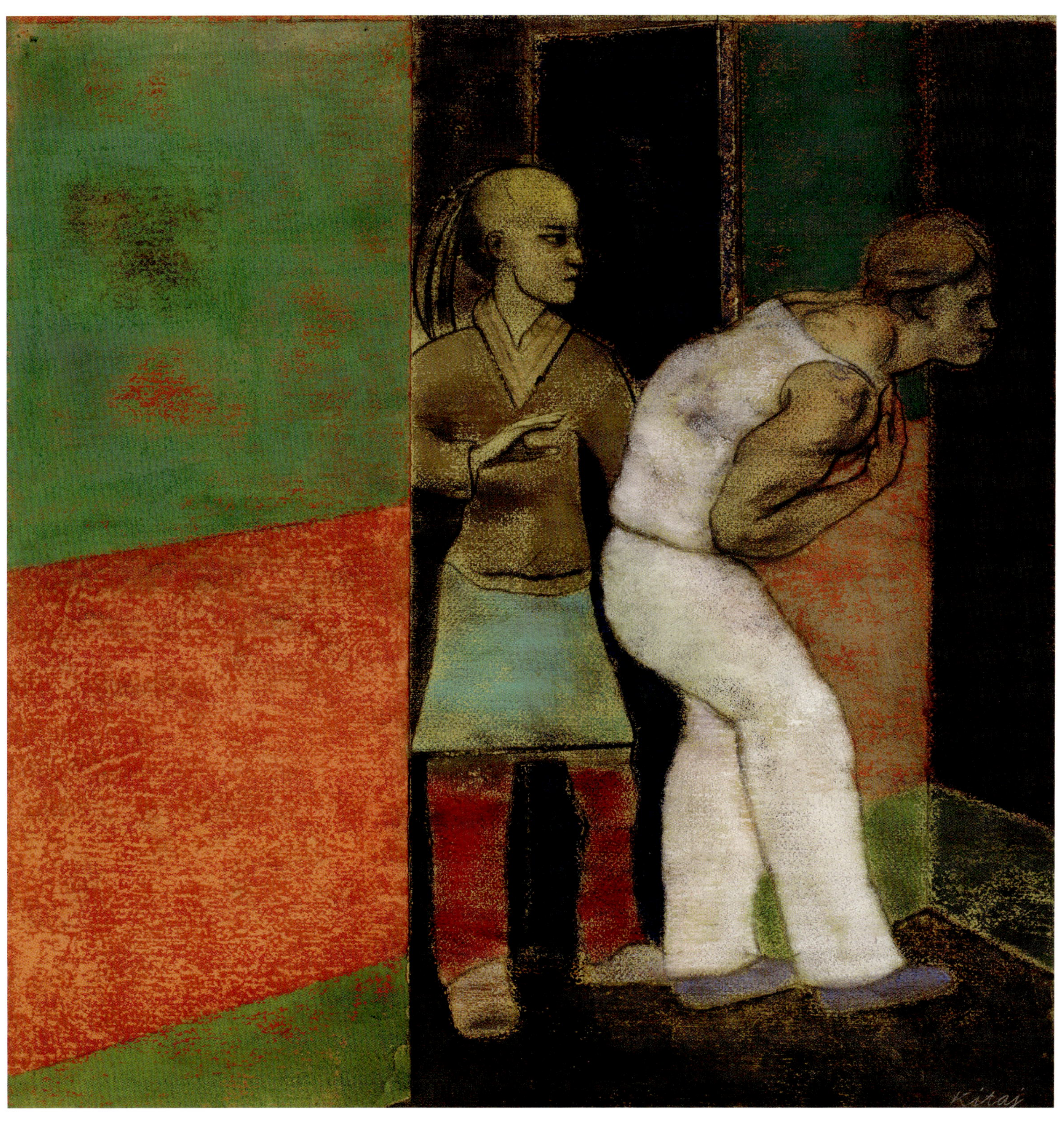

69

Magdalena Jetelová

Czech, born 1946

70
Boban, 1986
Oak, 11 ft. × 11 ft. 2 in. × 10 ft. 10 in.
(335.3 × 340.4 × 330.2 cm)
2006.52.74

Magdalena Jetelová's *Boban* provokes an unsettling disruption of space, functionality, and scale. Viewers are dwarfed by the uncanny oak sculpture, which resembles a hulking chair but lacks a seat and balances unsteadily on three legs while a long, cantilevered arm accentuates its instability.

Jetelová, a Prague native, began to explore and deform commonplace domestic structures such as chairs, houses, and staircases in the late 1970s. In these works, she distorts the objects' scale and stability: her houses often contract in size, while her chairs swell. *Boban* is more abstract and rudimentary than Jetelová's earlier chair pieces, and it consists simply of six oak trunks that have been stripped of bark.[1] In 1987, two years after Jetelová immigrated to West Germany, the Museum of Modern Art, New York, introduced her work to the American public. That exhibition included *Boban* and *Crossing* (1986, Walter Storms Galerie, Munich), a sprawling oak stairway perched atop thin sticks. Both works are rough-hewn and appear to be either unfinished, or in disrepair. And, as curator Diane Farynyk noted, "both works generate uneasiness about their stability and symbolically instill a vague angst over man's survival."[2] If chairs in art often function as surrogates for the body, *Boban* is a body on the brink, simultaneously vulnerable and menacing. Additionally menacing is the anthropomorphic thrust of *Boban*'s arms, which suggests that the structure could monstrously lurch forward. Such qualities demonstrate the capacity of familiar structures to provoke strong psychological responses in viewers.

Jetelová developed her artistic vocabulary largely independent of Western influence, and critics have consistently read her warped and precarious forms as metaphors for the totalitarian regime under which she came of age in the former Czechoslovakia. The 1970s and 1980s belonged to a period of "normalization," when the Czech Communist Party reasserted tight control and revoked the freedoms that had been granted in 1968 during the brief liberalization known as the Prague Spring. In this interpretation, Jetelová's monumental, nonfunctioning chairs operate as stand-ins for bloated power structures.[3] Shaky where it should be stable, *Boban* appears unable to support the weight of any body, whether individual or collective.

Jetelová's destabilized objects unnerve her viewing subjects by challenging us to see everyday forms in a new way, and they ignite a fresh perception of a seemingly familiar world.[4] Initially, we may mentally correct the awkward angles and fill in the missing parts to form a chair. Yet the powerful form of *Boban* does not submit to such adjustments. Its instability underlines the gap between the object's insistent reality and our expectations. In its capacity to radically reposition the viewer in the world, Jetelová's work also realizes its political potential, throwing assumed truths out of balance.

—**Amy Canonico**

1. Diane Farynyk, "Projects 5: Magdalena Jetelová," brochure (New York: Museum of Modern Art, 1987), n.p.
2. Ibid.
3. Eleanor Heartney, "Magdalena Jetelová: The Pathos of Contingency," in *Magdalena Jetelová: Recent Work*, by John Weber Gallery, exh. cat. (New York: John Weber Gallery, 1990); and Pavel Liska, "From Spatial Sculpture to Sculptured Space," in *Magdalena Jetelová: Orte und Räume (Locations and Spaces): 1990–1996* (Ostfildern, Germany: Cantz Verlag, 1996), 22.
4. The Russian author Victor Shklovsky developed the idea of *ostranenie* (defamiliarization) and its significance for art (particularly for writing) in his 1917 essay "Art as Technique." An excerpt can be found in Charles Harrison and Paul Wood, eds., *Art in Theory, 1900–2000: An Anthology of Changing Ideas* (Malden, Mass.: Blackwell, 2003), 277–81.

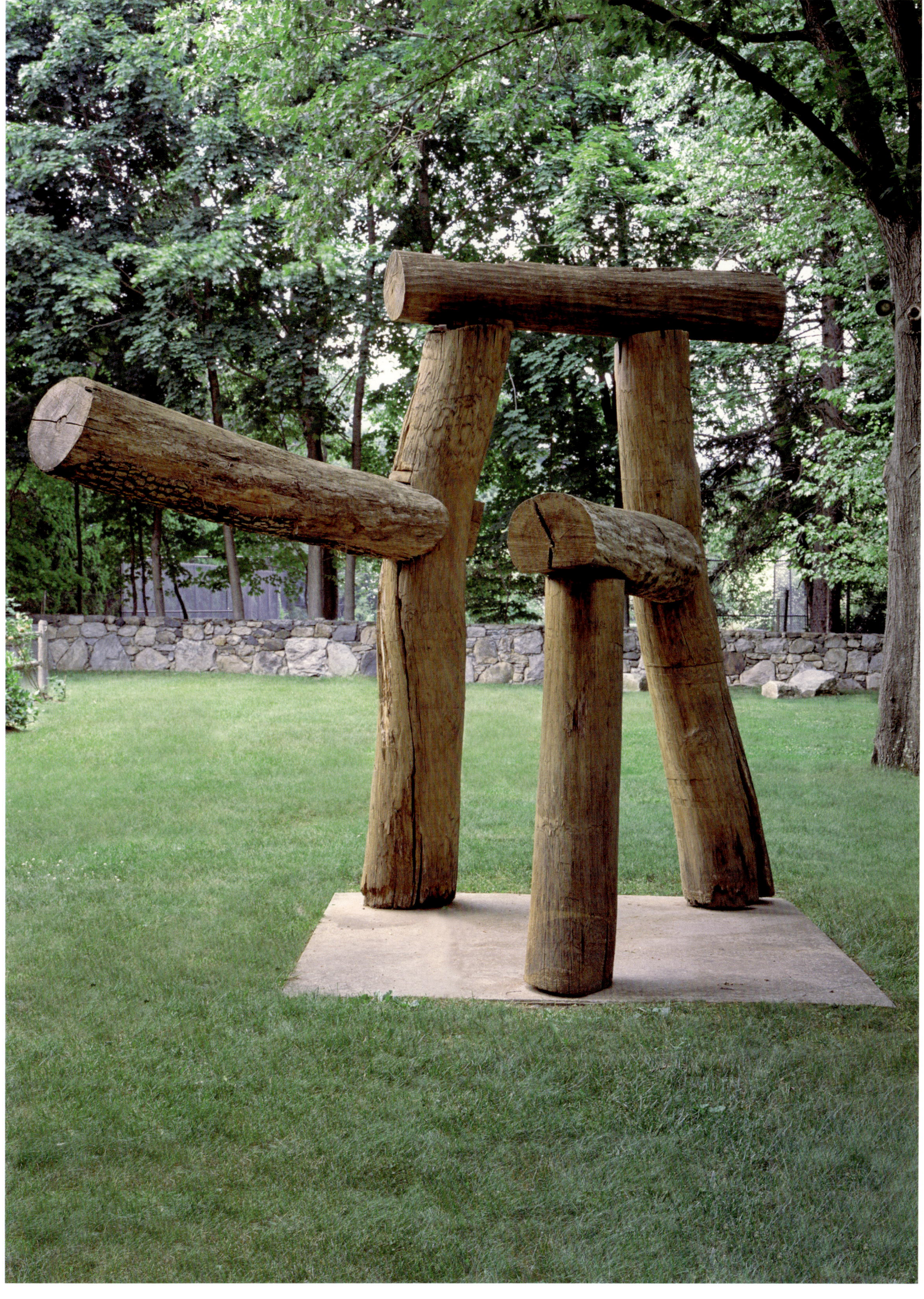

Al Held

American, 1928–2005

71
***Pan North XI*, 1987**
Acrylic on canvas, 9 × 14 ft.
(274.3 × 426.7 cm)
2006.52.57

Pan North XI exemplifies the intensely architectural, spatial abstraction that Al Held pursued in his art during the last twenty years in the studio. Held, who was a professor of painting at the Yale School of Art from 1962 to 1980, came to recognition in New York in the early 1960s with small, richly colored abstract paintings, heavy with an impasto that asserted the surface of the picture plane and the viewer's position as a distant observer of the painting as object. In these early paintings, Held developed a vocabulary of flat, abstract forms: circles, squares, and triangles that played out across the surface. These characters would soon develop into the dynamic, three-dimensional forms that came to inhabit and course through the complex spatial fields of his mature work. In a 1958 issue of *It Is*, an art journal published in New York, Held stated that his project was an endeavor to move painting outward toward the viewer, to make real the space between the canvas and the spectator.[1] While Held would generate no new forms to occupy his painterly world, he would attempt throughout the following forty years to perpetually create new relationships between them and their viewers.

In the mid-1960s, Held increased the scale of his paintings to mural size, seizing and defining the architectural spaces in which these works were exhibited. His simple, flat depictions of colored shapes began to transform into complex matrices of lines that proposed three-dimensional form. From 1967 until the late 1970s, Held removed color from his work to master and see clearly the spatial complexities that the juxtaposition of line and form could afford. *Volta VIII*, in the Yale University Art Gallery's collection (fig. 1), is a fine example of the rigor and spatial vitality that Held was able to achieve in this series.

While he was in Rome at the American Academy in 1981, Held's general interest in Italian Renaissance painting and architecture blossomed into a keen enthusiasm for the complex interface of painted and real space that he observed in church frescoes and in museum collections throughout Italy. He returned home to New York and proceeded to pursue wildly complex nonobjective abstractions occupied with richly colored, crisp forms seated in deep spaces that receded in perspective. In these late works, opulent colors imbue the paintings with an illuminating, raking light. Through his interweaving of a complex skein of contrasting colors, Held was able to achieve a remarkable depth in these compositions that rolls away from the viewer toward a distant horizon. The palette in *Pan North XI* conveys the strong physical and emotional atmosphere asserted by these paintings. Its dusky twilight pulls the observer toward the sweet nostalgia normally affected by the observation of the setting sun. Here, Held has masterfully evoked the mysterious artifice of experience that begins on the near side of the picture plane, somewhere between the viewer's optic nerve and the place occupied by his or her own two feet.

—Jennifer R. Gross

1. Al Held, quoted in Irving Sandler, "A Series of Statements," *It Is* 2 (Autumn 1958): 78. He said, "I am not an all-over painter. The rigid logic of two-dimensional esthetics binds us to the canvas surface making it an end in itself, not a means to an end. I would like to develop from this not by going inwards toward the old horizon, but outward toward the spectator. The space between the canvas and the spectator is real—emotionally, physically, and logically, it exists as an actual extension of the canvas surface. I would like to use it as such and thus bridge the gulf that separates the painter from the viewer."

Fig. 1.
Al Held, *Volta VIII*, 1978. Acrylic on canvas, 48 × 48 in. (121.9 × 121.9 cm). Yale University Art Gallery, Richard Brown Baker, B.A. 1935, Collection, 2008.19.770

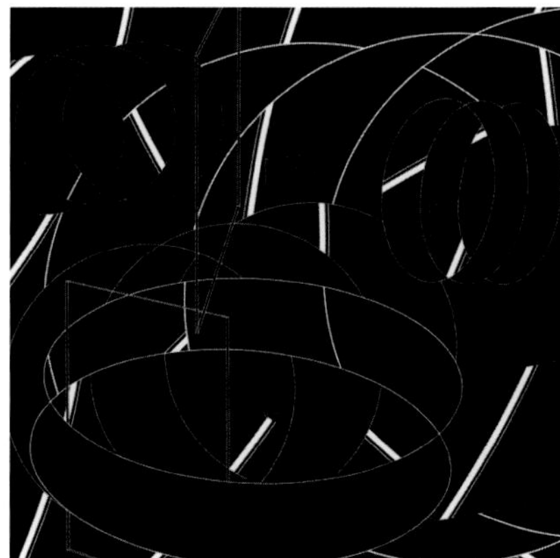

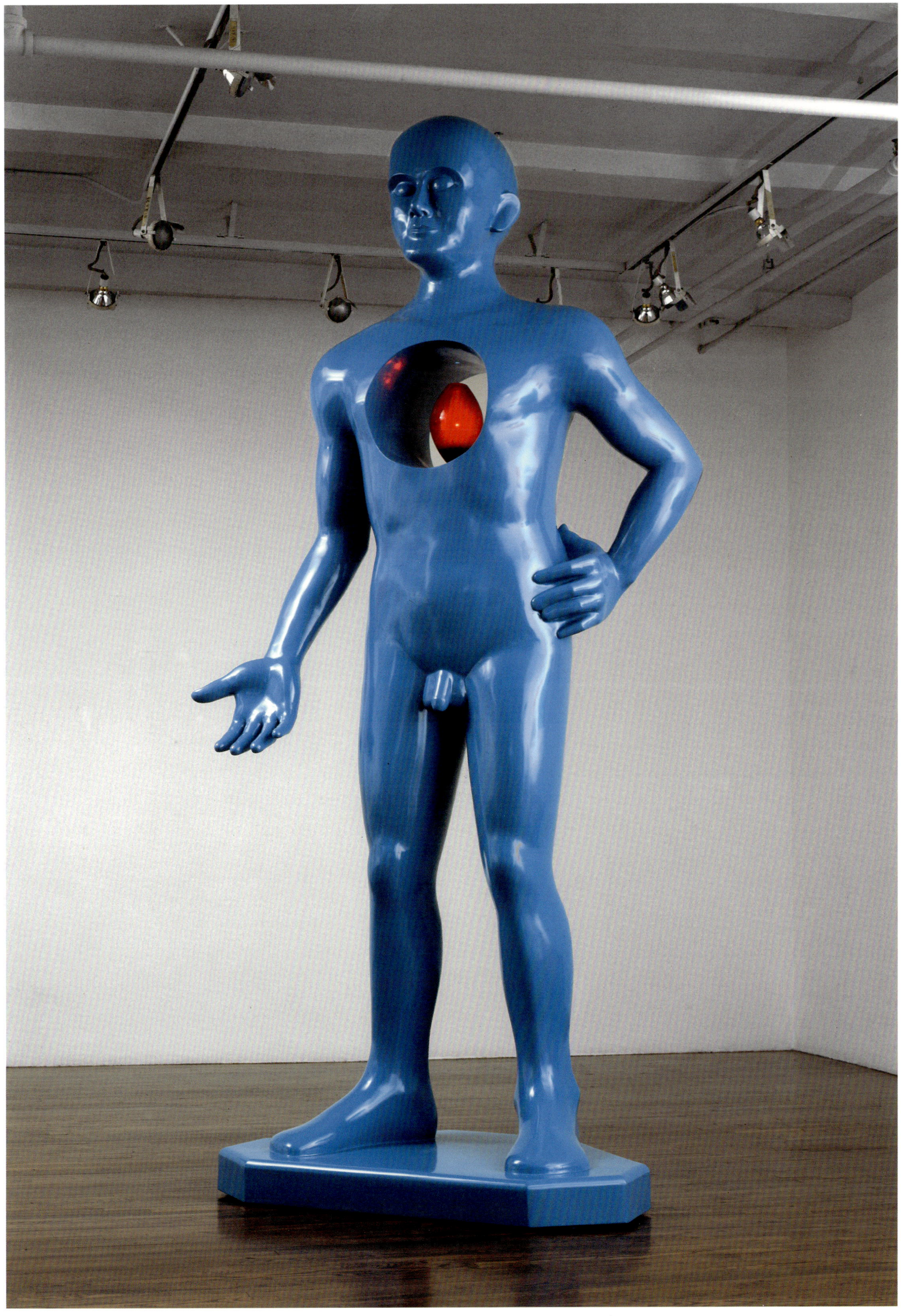

Martin Wong

American, 1946–1999

74
La Vida (The Life), 1988
Oil on canvas, 96 in. × 9 ft. 6 in.
(243.8 × 289.6 cm)
2006.52.47

Unlike many of Martin Wong's disaffected portrayals of urban decay and slum life, *La Vida* (The Life) is surprisingly vibrant and genial. The work depicts the red brick façade of a tenement building at Houston Street and Avenue B in Loisaida, a Hispanic and African American neighborhood on New York's Lower East Side. On the ground level, a conga band plays while children skateboard and jump in the gushing water of an open fire hydrant. Groups of friends drink on the stairwells, while hip-hop dancers, boxers, firemen, policemen, and embracing couples populate the windows of the six-story building. Divisions between the public and private spheres are blurred as life spills out onto the street and fire escapes.

In this work, Wong carefully details the wide range of ages, racial groups, and personalities that inhabit the building. In the bottom left window we see a smiling woman in traditional African dress, while diagonally to the right, a man wearing dark sunglasses and a thick gold chain holds a boom box. In the bottom right window we recognize the familiar face of pop icon Mr. T. The figures in the building include individualized depictions of Wong's friends and acquaintances, such as the graffiti artists Daze, Sharp, and LA2, as well as the poet Amiri Baraka. Most prominent of all is Miguel Piñero, whose portrait appears at least three times in *La Vida*. A well-known Nuyorican poet and author of the Pulitzer Prize–winning play *Short Eyes* (1973–74), Piñero became Wong's close friend and lover in the 1980s, and actively promoted the artist's work. Painted shortly after Piñero's untimely death earlier that year, *La Vida* poignantly commemorates his significant role in Wong's life. Wong, an openly gay artist, also included a veiled reference to gay desire in the leftmost window of the fifth floor. Here, the silhouettes of a pair of firemen echo Wong's *Big Heat* (Whitney Museum of American Art), painted in the same year, in which two firemen passionately embrace in front of a charred building.

Wong grew up in San Francisco's Chinatown, before moving to New York at the age of thirty to pursue a career as an artist. Although he studied ceramics at Humboldt State University, Wong was entirely self-taught in painting, and his figurative works are always somewhat naively executed. Here, disparities in scale and imprecise human anatomies contrast sharply with Wong's rendition of the façade, where each individual brick is painstakingly delineated. The visual grit of Wong's pictorial world resonates both with the actual graffiti of his neighborhood in New York and with the increasing prominence of graffiti art in SoHo art galleries in the 1980s.

Wong's large, almost caricatured paintings situate him at the vanguard of a new eighties aesthetic. The return to a raw painterly style in that decade marked a rupture with the intellectualism of the preceding years, which had been dominated by Conceptualism and installation and video art. In their simplicity and directness, Wong's works represent tumultuous city life, delivering emotionally charged depictions of racial, social, and sexual identity.

—**Maria Taroutina**

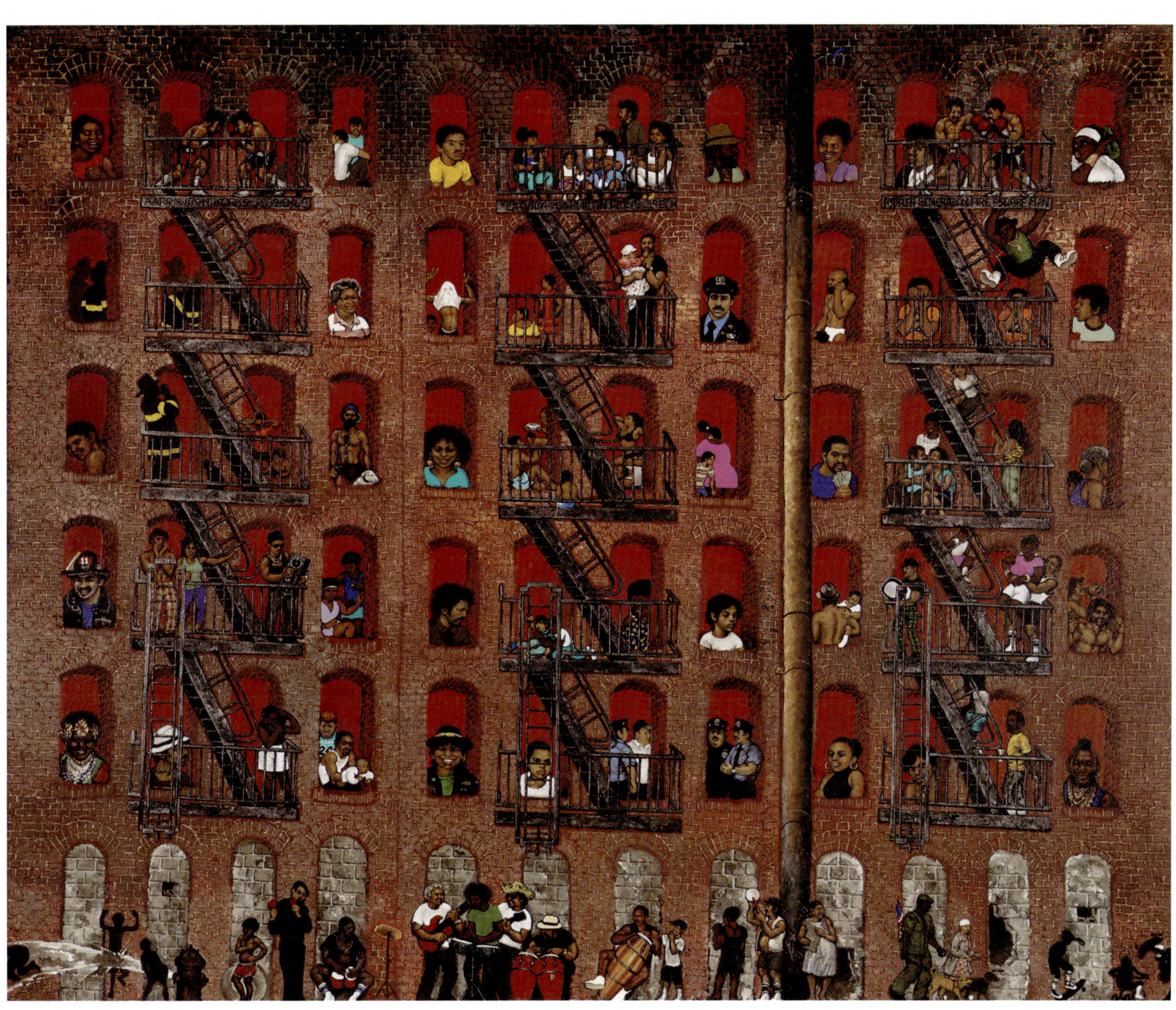

Viola Frey

American, 1933–2004

75
Pink Nude Woman, **1989**
Ceramic with colored glaze,
68 × 98 × 78½ in.
(172.7 × 248.9 × 199.4 cm)
2006.52.59

Viola Frey's polychromatic *Pink Nude Woman* is colossal for ceramic sculpture, a scale that defined Frey's practice since she was a student at the California College of Arts and Crafts in the 1950s. More than five feet tall when seated on the ground, the imposing recumbent nude diminishes its viewer to the size of a child. When growing up on her family's vineyard in Lodi, California, Frey developed a fascination with nature and an awe for strong female role models, particularly her mother and paternal grandmother. The artist designed her female nudes to embody organic growth, strength, and independence. Although *Pink Nude Woman* recalls a passive odalisque, a pose common to depictions of the female nude in Western art, the sculpture's brightly colored surface and monumentality deflect readings of the figure as sensual.

Indeed, the artist's use of the reclining position was more practical than symbolic. Frey began experimenting with the recumbent figure after encountering difficulties engineering large-scale works that stood upright. Beginning around 1984, she also held weekly sessions with a live model whose poses led her to approach the figure in a horizontal rather than vertical mode.[1]

Frey's monumental sculptures were created using a modular method of construction inspired by architecture, which allowed her hollow figures to grow far beyond the scale of traditional ceramics. Frey likened the growth of these figural sculptures to the life cycle of a plant that emerges from a seed.[2] Her use of additive assembly also recalls the work of her fellow West Coast ceramicist Peter Voulkos, who in the 1960s and 1970s built pots from stacked tiers that reached several feet in height. Frey herself began making slab compositions of life-sized classical torsos in the mid-1960s. To do so, she constructed the sculpture's entire form with wet clay.

When dry, it was sawed into eight-inch thick, double-walled jigsaw pieces that were successively fired in a kiln before reassembly.[3]

Study with the painter Richard Diebenkorn in Frey's undergraduate years and a workshop with Mark Rothko while a graduate student at Tulane University encouraged the artist in her development of the abstract and aggressive handling of color that are prominent features of *Pink Nude Woman*. Frey preferred to paint her ceramic figures in low-fire glaze, outdoors and in natural light. The artist's hand and process are visible on the surface in drips of glaze and ripples of clay. Frey trusted that "active color should, must, enable the viewer to participate in the piece."[4] Flashes of red and bright blue contour lines keep the viewer's eye roaming over the female body's exaggerated curves, inviting an exploration of its mottled topography. With monumental sculptures such as *Pink Nude Woman* Frey left a significant mark in the history of ceramics and figurative sculpture.

—**Emily M. Orr**

1. Davira Spiro Taragin and Patterson Sims, *Bigger, Better, More: The Art of Viola Frey*, exh. cat. (New York: Hudson Hills, 2009), 17.
2. Ibid., 33.
3. Richard Whittaker, "Interview with Viola Frey," in *The Conversations: Interviews with Sixteen Contemporary Artists* (Lincoln: University of Nebraska Press, 2007), 71–72.
4. Susan Wechsler, *Low Fire Ceramics* (New York: Billboard, 1981), 73.

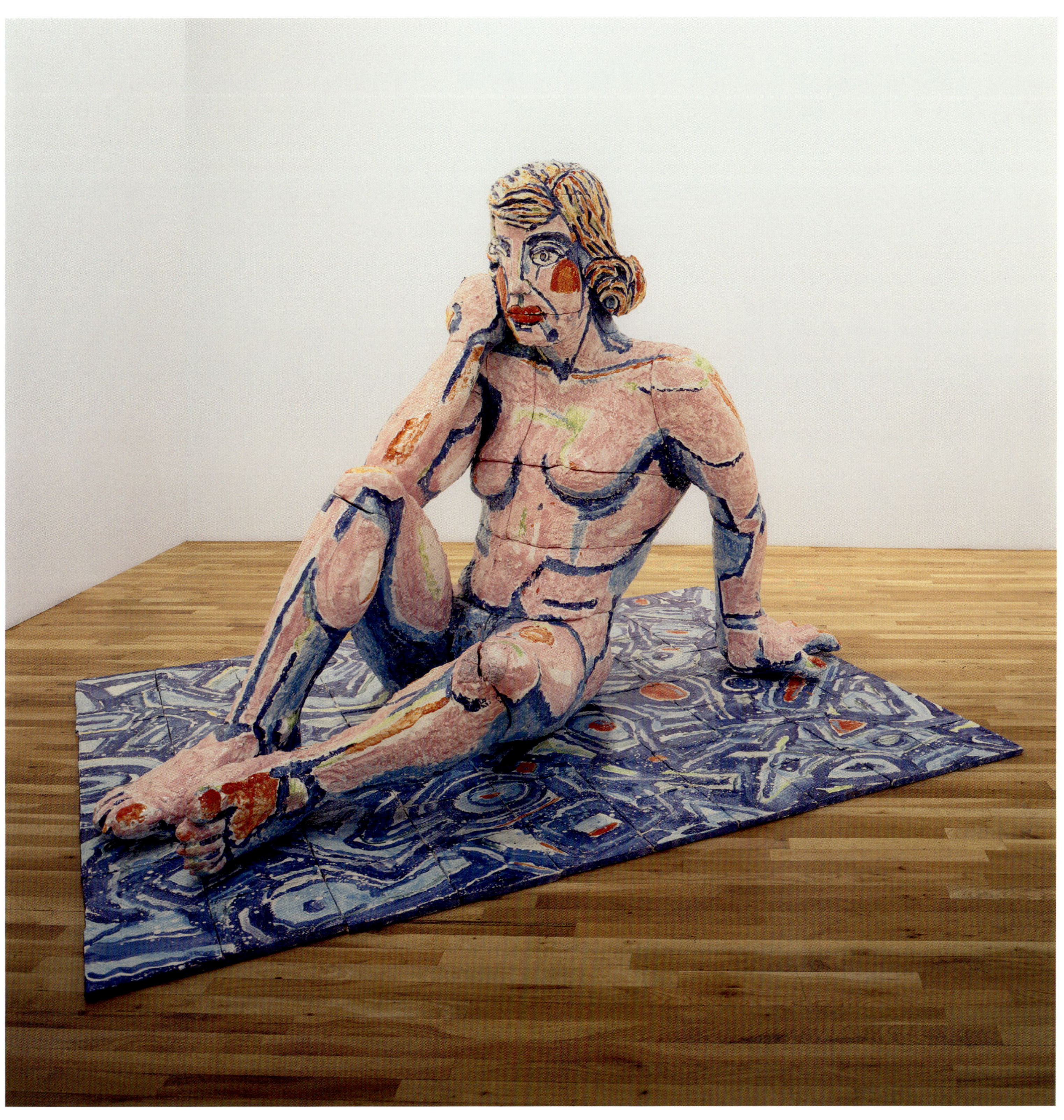

Pat Steir

American, born 1940

76
***At Sea after Gombrich,* 1989**
Charcoal and colored chalk,
60⁷⁄₁₆ in. × 9 ft. (153.5 × 273 cm)
2006.52.84

In *At Sea after Gombrich*, Pat Steir traces her body's gesture on the page with a diversity of materials, techniques, and energy, formally investigating the ways drawing can both express a sense of consciousness or selfhood and also create an image. In the drawing's range from abstraction to figuration, Steir explores one of her persistent interests: how mark-making develops into expression and image.

Steir attended the Pratt Institute in the mid-1950s, where she studied under Philip Guston and Richard Lindner. Steir's oeuvre grew from her attempts to distinguish herself from the dominant style of Abstract Expressionism, even as she worked to illustrate individuality and consciousness, fields of interest also pursued by artists of her professors' generation.[1]

In the 1970s, Steir used drawing to document her research into geometry and lettering as she explored how marks become lines, lines become words, and words become poetry. With these experiments, Steir contended with how mark-making is used in both art and language to record personal thoughts and consciousnesses; she often quotes her father, who told her when she was eight years old, "If you can learn to write, you can learn to draw." In 1983, after a period in which she mostly produced paintings, Steir began making large-scale drawings in graphite, ink, charcoal, and chalk. She pinned up long rolls of paper in her studio and drew with the full reach of her arm, capturing the entire momentum of her gesture on the page.[2]

At Sea after Gombrich is an example of one of these large drawings. A whorl of frenetic red and black lines arcs across the left side of the page in charcoal and colored chalk. On the right, Steir builds up thick layers of scribble and looping spirals, then intermittently covers the marks with swaths of translucent white chalk. The marks illustrate the communicative impulses at the origin of both art and writing, but they also depict a wave, like those in Gustave Courbet's series of wave paintings from 1869. Steir reinterpreted Courbet's paintings using a variety of techniques during the period in which she made *At Sea after Gombrich*. Here Steir's representation of her own art-making becomes an image of the ocean.

The drawing's title refers to the historian Ernst Gombrich; his 1969 book *Art and Illusion*, an influential text for artists and art historians, described how various cultures represented their three-dimensional world on a two-dimensional surface. Other drawings in Steir's *At Sea* series were named for artists including Katsushika Hokusai and J. M. W. Turner. The title of this work, however, points toward the imperfect, hand-drawn background grid over which Steir layered her gestural marks, a seeming parody of the grid's omnipresence in Renaissance perspectival drawing, where, as Gombrich discusses, it is a critical step in creating the illusion of three-dimensionality. Both the work's title and its grid suggest Steir's engagement with how art's subjective methods can, and cannot, capture objective reality.

—Elisabeth Thomas

1. Thomas McEvilley, *Pat Steir* (New York: Harry N. Abrams, 1995), 14–17.
2. Susan Harris and Jan Howard, *Pat Steir: Drawing Out of Line*, exh. cat. (Providence: Museum of Art, Rhode Island School of Design, 2010), 34.

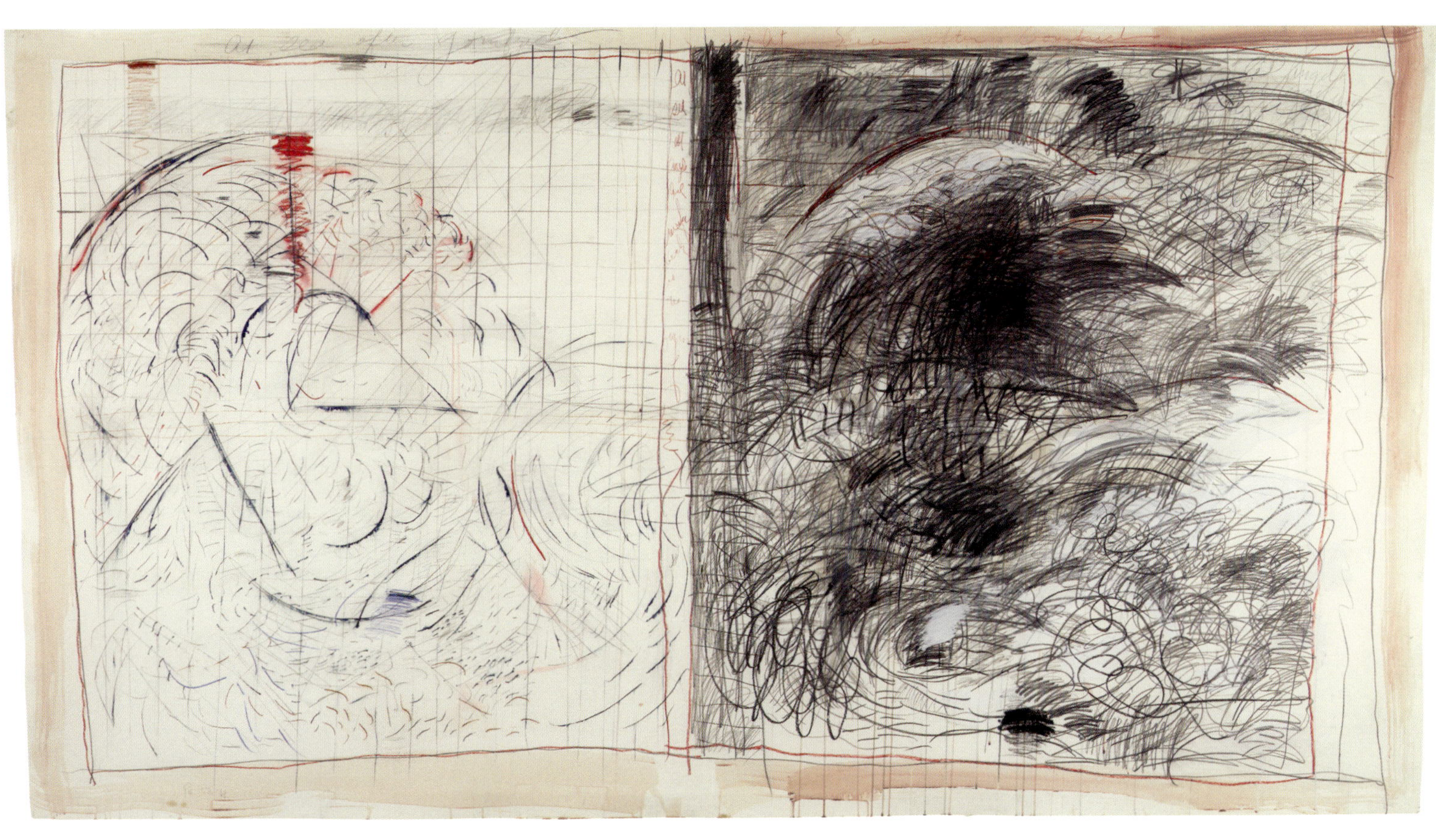

Ursula von Rydingsvard

American, born Germany 1942

77
Three Bowls, **1989**
Cedar and graphite, 56¾ in. × 9 ft. 8 in. ×
60 in. (144.1 × 294.6 × 152.4 cm)
2006.52.58

The structure of the bowl is a means by which I
can understand almost everything.
—Ursula von Rydingsvard

For three decades Ursula von Rydingsvard
has worked with the cedar four-by-fours that
comprise *Three Bowls.* Despite their bulk and
rigidity, she considers the milled lumber to
be as malleable as blank sheets of paper. The
wood evokes the time she spent as a child during World War II in a displaced persons camp
in Germany, as well as the Polish farms where
her ancestors lived. There, one could find
homes surrounded by wooden fences, homes
filled with wooden tools, cooking utensils,
and stacks of firewood. "There is, I guess, a
feeling of familiarity," she said of the cedar
in a 2001 interview, "a feeling of comfort and
grace. And at the same time, because of the
familiarity, I can really push it around."[1]

To produce works such as *Three Bowls,*
von Rydingsvard embarks on a labor-
intensive process that begins by cutting the
beams according to sketched guiding marks
and stacking them to realize the desired
form. She does not make preparatory drawings, emphasizing instead the importance
of openness and uncertainty.[2] She facets the
wooden planes with a power saw and then
rubs them with graphite to achieve a more
distressed and weathered texture. The rough
surface of *Three Bowls* suggests a connection
between nature and labor, one that is consistent with von Rydingsvard's mythologizing of
her peasant ancestors.[3]

While von Rydingsvard's aggressive
sawing and visible hand infuse this representational work with personal expression,
her sculptures are also rooted in Minimalist
precedents. Their serially repeated forms and
grids of four-by-fours link the work to 1960s
abstraction.[4] And like much Minimalist sculpture, which similarly confronts its viewers
on a large scale, von Rydingsvard's oversized

work challenges the traditional relationship between viewing subject and art object.
This trio of five-foot-tall bowls is presented
directly on the floor; without a base or plinth
to demarcate its space, it asserts itself as more
than an object for visual consumption.

As a vessel with an exterior and an
interior, the bowl can act as an analogue for
the body and the mind, and it reveals von
Rydingsvard's interest in the exploration
of psychological terrain.[5] Yet the sprawling topographies of many of her works also
correspond to landscape. After complet-
ing *Three Bowls,* von Rydingsvard received
a commission from the Walker Art Center
in Minneapolis. She recalls seizing this as
an opportunity to revisit this sculpture on
a larger scale that viewers could experience
as a vast landscape.[6] In the larger version of
Three Bowls the interior remains an imagined
one; in the smaller, Charles B. Benenson
Collection sculpture, a viewer can peer inside
and connect with the residual functionality of
the form. The bowls could be artifacts from a
past civilization, evoking personal or cultural
memory, while also appearing to contain
memories of their own. For von Rydingsvard,
these memories call her back to a premodern Europe in which pragmatism and labor
melded with organic, expressive form.

—**Amy Canonico**

Epigraph: Ursula von Rydingsvard, quoted in Arthur
Danto, "Beam, Bowl, and Paradox in the Sculpture of
Ursula von Rydingsvard," *Ursula von Rydingsvard: Cedar
Lace and Tossing Loops,* exh. cat. (Paris: Galerie Lelong,
2002), 22.
1. Ursula von Rydingsvard interviewed by Dede Young,
December 2001, in *Ursula von Rydingsvard: On an Epic
Scale,* exh. cat. (Purchase, N.Y.: Neuberger Museum of
Art, 2002), 32.
2. Ursula von Rydingsvard interviewed by Deborah
Emont Scott in *Ursula von Rydingsvard,* exh. cat., by
Michael Brenson and Scott (Kansas City, Mo.: Nelson
Atkins Museum of Art, 1997), 36.
3. On her first visit to Warsaw, von Rydingsvard
wrote in her journal in 1990, "I am almost afraid that
what I'm looking for is the human equivalent to my
bowls, shovels—that is peasant, earth working types
much like my parents but kinder." Quoted in Marek
Bartelik, "Reclaiming Spaces," in *The Sculpture of Ursula
von Rydingsvard,* by Dore Ashton, Bartelik, and Matti
Megged (New York: Hudson Hills Press, 1996), 89.
4. In a 1995 interview, von Rydingsvard said, "I feel
like a child of the minimalists. The regularity, the

repetitive regularity . . . there's a whole myth of perfection. My work is not sanitized and pure in terms of the
kind of layering they did. . . . In some ways, I combine
Abstract Expressionism and Minimalism. At one time,
I was in awe of both. I got my mixture using some of
the tools of both of these styles." Quoted in ibid., 77.
5. Ibid., 76.
6. "I had made a piece with three bowls that was quite
small, which I liked very much. When I received the
commission from the Walker Art Center I had this
small piece on my mind, and I felt that I now had
the opportunity to enlarge it, to allow it to evolve so
that it could develop a 'landscape' sense through to
its surfaces and edges. By making it larger I felt that I
could achieve a sense of plenty, or fullness that seemed
right for my initial idea. By spreading the surface of the
small piece over a much greater area in *Three Bowls,* it
became something very different." Von Rydingsvard
interviewed by Scott in Brenson and Scott, *Ursula von
Rydingsvard,* 34.

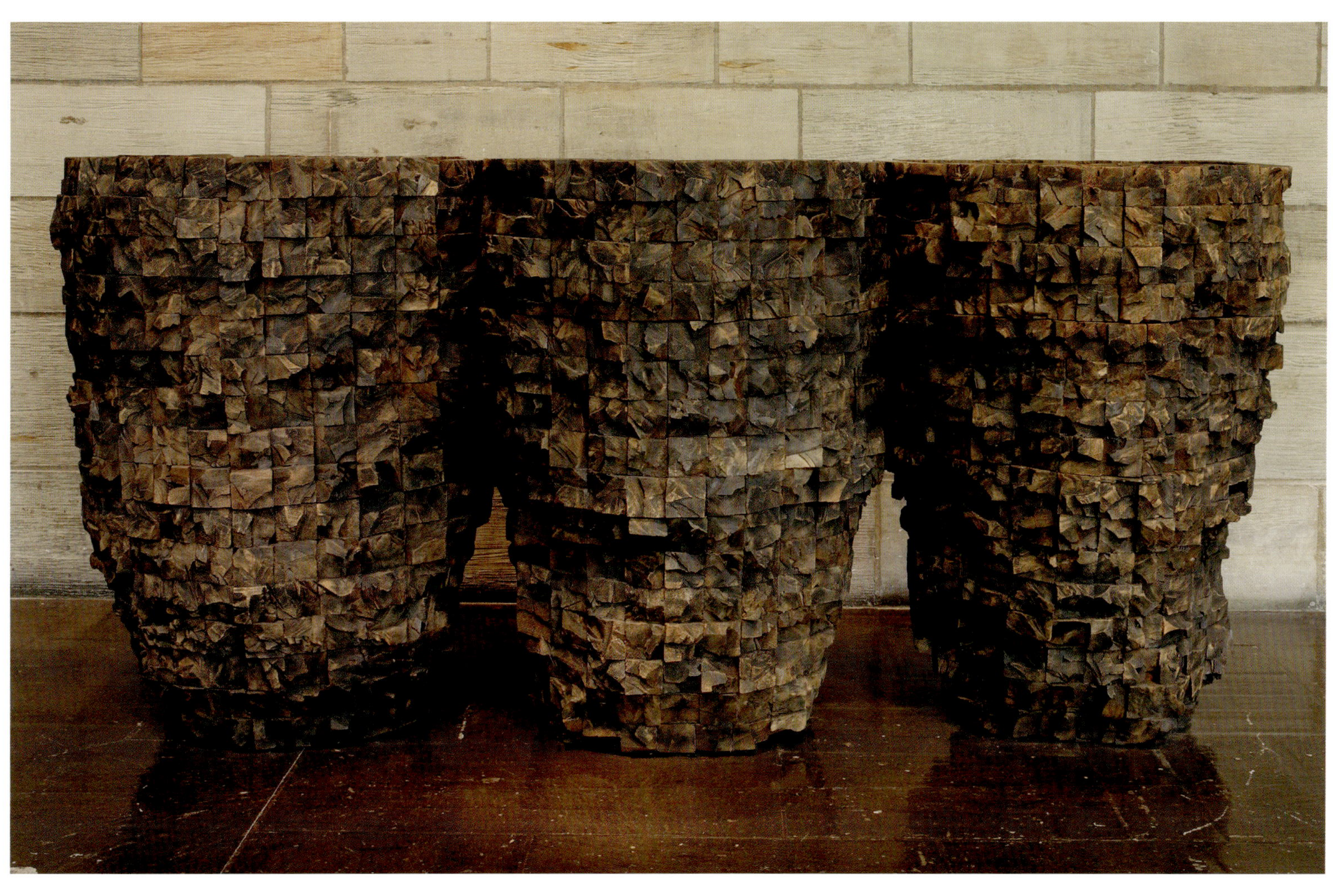

77

Alexander Liberman

American, born Russia, 1912–1999

78
***Lightweb*, 1991**
Welded steel with paint, 15 ft. × 52 in. × 52 in.
(457.2 × 132.1 × 132.1 cm)
2006.52.66

Although he made his living in New York as the editor in chief of Condé Nast, overseeing magazines such as *Vogue* and *Self*, the Russian émigré Alexander Liberman originally trained in Paris to be a painter, and he pursued art-making throughout his life. The genesis of his career as a sought-after creator of large-scale outdoor sculpture followed a welding lesson during a summer holiday. Liberman immediately began experimenting with found metal salvage and soon borrowed money to purchase scrap. He came to see nonrepresentational metal sculpture as a uniquely American breakthrough permitted by the enormity of the country's landscapes and its outsized confidence after World War II. His monumental three-dimensional works often possess an openness that belies the mass of his preferred sculptural materials: machinery and welded steel. Although he regarded the bronze forging of more traditional sculptors in metal such as Alberto Giacometti to be a higher form of art than his own, Liberman's carefully selected assemblages demonstrate how the industrial "art" of welding possessed a unique ability to unite disparate elements.

Liberman claimed that with his sculpture he tried "to create a solution in the spectator's brain by placing thesis next to antithesis."[1] The quest for a dialectic sculpture—built on thematic repetition and innovative variation—is evident in *Lightweb*. In this sculpture, Liberman chose, as he often did, one unifying color for his work. In other sculptures this use of a single color could bridge physical differences between the varied shapes of metal drums or steel I-beams. In addition to his use of color, Liberman's sense of compositional harmony and the repetition of subtly varied forms gave his work balance. In *Lightweb* Liberman used the linear qualities of his chosen metal forms to imitate gestural drawing in three dimensions. The dozens of identical steel ellipses are ebullient, roiling upward and ever threatening to overflow the columnar composition that appears to hold them in place. The sculpture's bright energy aptly illustrates Liberman's fascination with movement, one he described as "creating a mental gymnastic."[2]

While Liberman preferred his sculptures to evolve in an immediate relationship to their environment, and thus eschewed modeling them in advance, his drawings and paintings nonetheless demonstrate that he experimented and worked out related aesthetic concerns in parallel to the sculptures' creation. In a painting on paper such as *Untitled White V* (fig. 1), we see how Liberman also pursued his sculptural investigations of depth, illusion, and contrast in two dimensions. Here, dry charcoal lines and ellipses are hewn into wet acrylic on the paper's surface. The artist's interest in illustrating uncontainable energy is evidenced in the drawing's powerful lines, which the paper's edge only tenuously limits. As does Liberman's sculpture, this drawing suggests that art can at least record, if not contain, life's sublime characteristics and intoxicating force.

—**Cathleen Chaffee**

1. Marshall Blonsky, "Interview with Alexander Liberman," *Bomb*, Summer 1986, 22.
2. Ibid.

Fig. 1.
Alexander Liberman, *Untitled White V*, 1978. Acrylic and charcoal, 40 x 25⁵⁄₁₆ in. (101.5 x 64.2 cm). Yale University Art Gallery, Charles B. Benenson, B.A. 1933, Collection, 2006.52.119

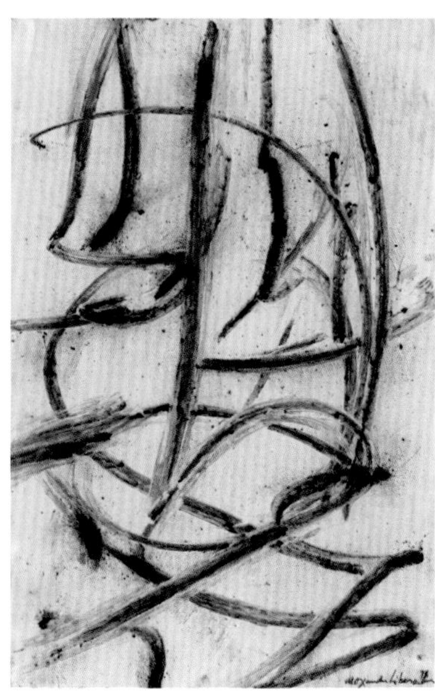

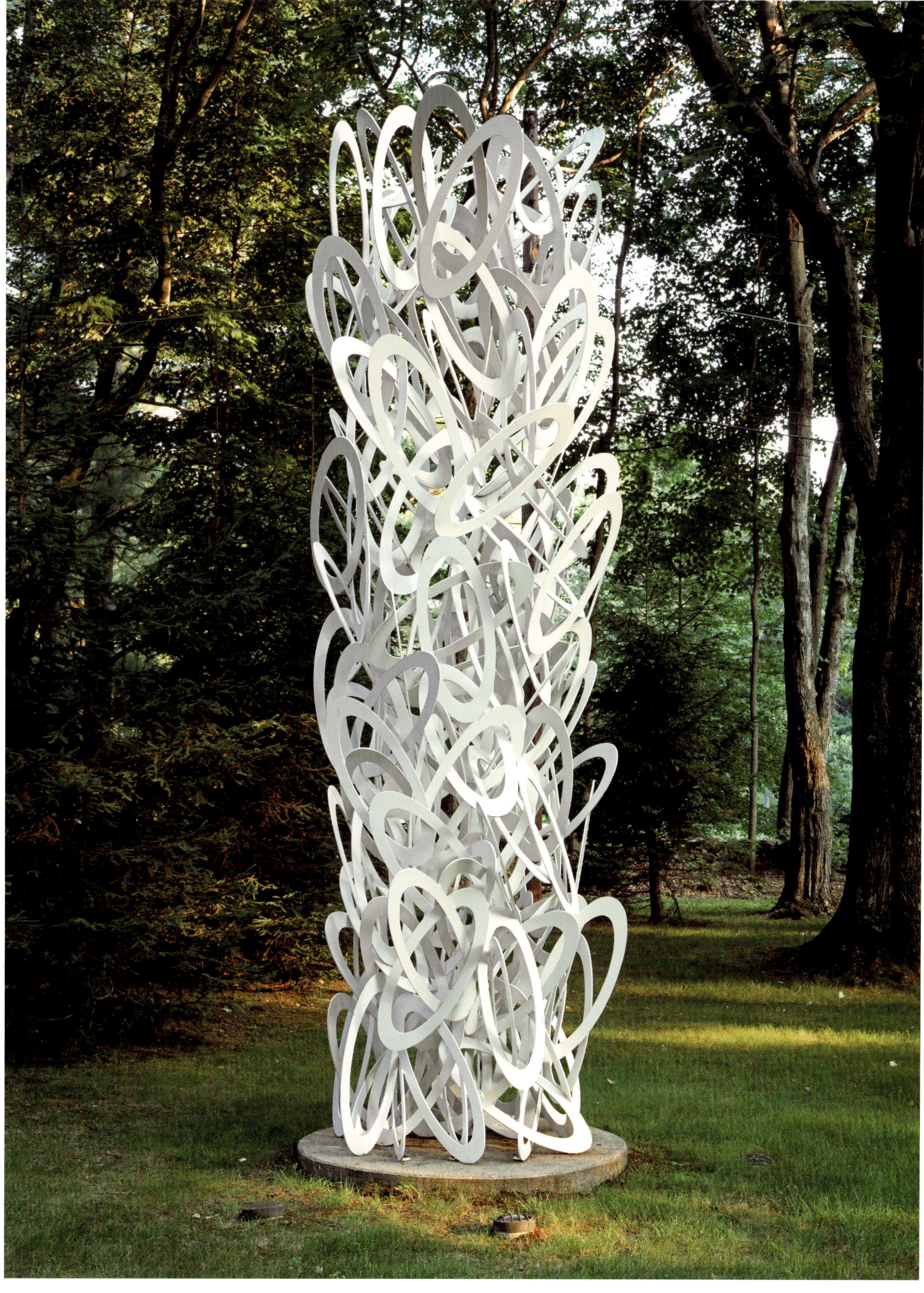

John Chamberlain

American, 1927–2011

79
***Ya Hoodie*, 1996**
Crushed metal with paint, 25 × 52 × 24 in.
(63.5 × 132.1 × 61 cm)
2006.52.49

Ya Hoodie is characterized by discontinuity and speed. Its vividly colored, undulating folds of crushed metal overlap, twist, and collide with each other, creating a porous body. The work replaces the solidity of traditional sculpture with momentum and perpetual flux. In many ways, the work's expressive arabesques and painted polychromatic surface have more in common with painting than with conventional sculpture.

John Chamberlain first developed this signature style in the early 1960s. His "automobile sculptures" consisted of imposing masses of crumpled, burnt, compressed, and disfigured metal. Then a struggling young artist, Chamberlain mostly relied on discarded car parts from junkyards for his raw material. The gritty, rusted appearance of his 1960s works clearly testified to their origins as found objects, and they were labeled "junk art" by critics. By the mid-1970s, however, Chamberlain had begun purchasing new, prepainted metal directly from manufacturers and employing a saturated palette of candy colors. He had also begun subjecting his works to increasingly complex formal manipulations, producing more intricate structures. By the early 1990s, Chamberlain's work had evolved from the relatively raw, hefty, and somber appearance of his early pieces to the lithe, baroque sculptural mode exemplified by *Ya Hoodie*.

The artist explained this stylistic shift as a pointed response to critics, who often interpreted his work as a critique of American consumer culture and fast-paced living: "I was tired of using automobile material because the only response I ever got was that I was making automobile crashes and that I used the automobile as some symbolic bullshit about our society."[1] Rather than making social commentary, the artist was interested in capturing in three dimensions the robust formal energy and raw improvisational quality of Abstract Expressionist painting.

In place of the tightly controlled techniques of conventional modeling and casting, Chamberlain's procedures were largely spontaneous. Employing a compactor, grinder, band saw, and even an acetylene torch, Chamberlain crushed, buckled, sliced, and burned readymade metal sheets, allowing the properties of the material and the creative impulse of the moment to dictate the final sculptural form. In many ways, this combination of artistic control and chance resembles the working method of Jackson Pollock, whose dynamic paintings were likewise determined by a mixture of artistic intention and gravity coupled with the viscosity of paint. *Ya Hoodie*'s "crumples" are thus not unlike Pollock's "drips," and they constitute an innovative translation of gestural painting into a sculptural idiom.

Ya Hoodie's painted surface of psychedelic yellow, pink, orange, and aquamarine further distances it from the monochromatic solemnity of traditional bronze and marble sculpture. Together with the playful title, this vivid palette suggests a certain levity, which is offset by the scratches, slashes, and paint loss on the sculpture's surface. Instead of retouching these brutalized areas with a fresh coat of paint, Chamberlain purposely left them in place as a testament to the violent means of the work's production. The result is a complex visual dialectic: *Ya Hoodie* is at once joyful and menacing, lyrical and opaque.

—Maria Taroutina

---

1. Julie Sylvester, "Auto/Bio: Conversations with John Chamberlain," in *John Chamberlain: A Catalogue Raisonné of the Sculpture, 1954–1985* (New York: Hudson Hills, 1986), 21.

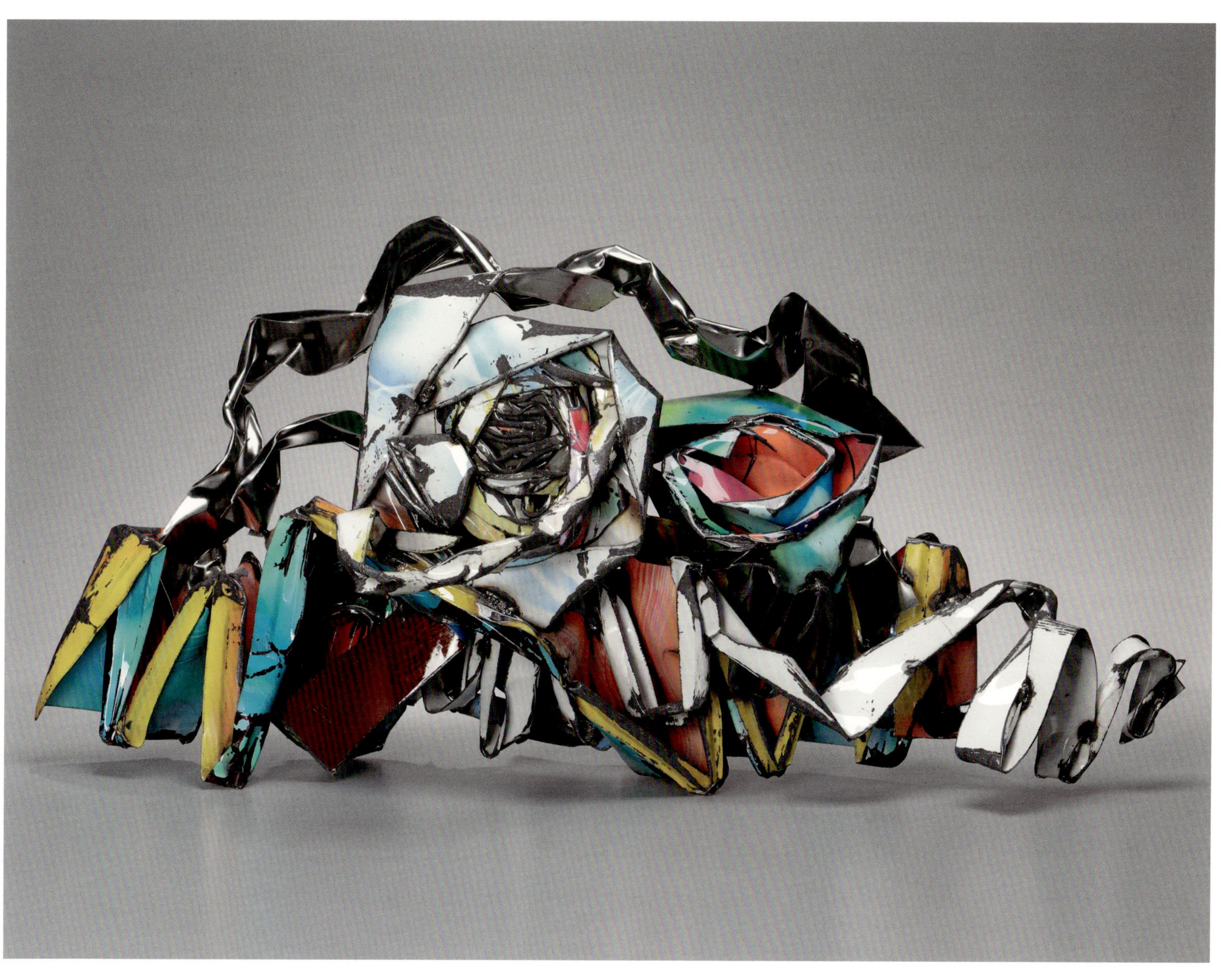

Collection Checklist

This checklist contains all works of modern and contemporary art from the Charles B. Benenson, B.A. 1933, Collection at the Yale University Art Gallery. The entries are arranged alphabetically by artist, then chronologically.

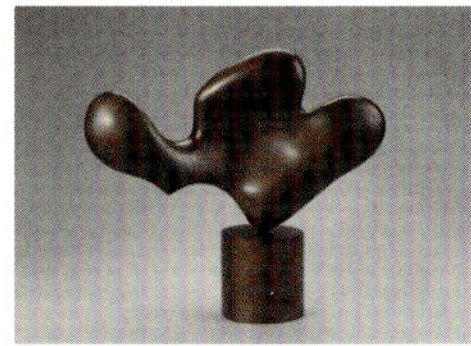

Cat. 22

Jean (Hans) Arp
French, born Germany, 1886–1966
Resting Leaf, 1959
Bronze, edition 2/5, 23 × 24 × 7 in.
(58.4 × 61 × 17.8 cm)
2006.52.97

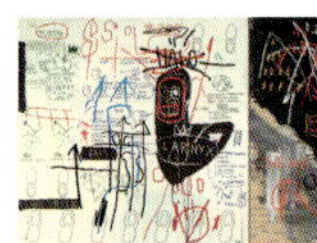
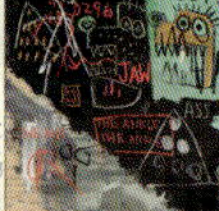

Cat. 62

Jean-Michel Basquiat
American, 1960–1988
Diagram of the Ankle, 1982
Xeroxed paper, oil stick, and acrylic
on canvas; two hinged panels, overall
60 in. × 10 ft. (152.4 × 304.8 cm)
2006.52.11

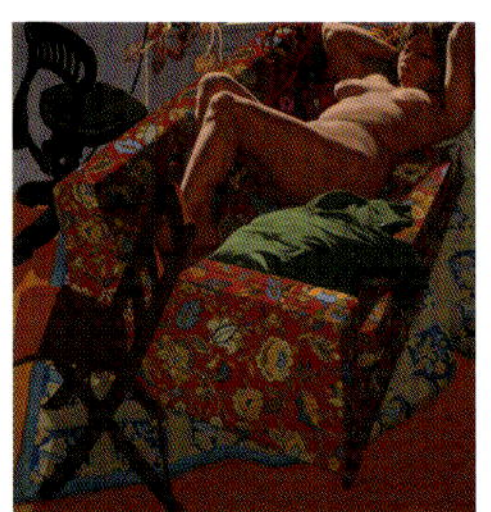

Jack Beal
American, born 1931
Reclining Nude on Couch, 1974
Oil on canvas, 67 × 62 in.
(170.2 × 157.5 cm)
2006.52.41

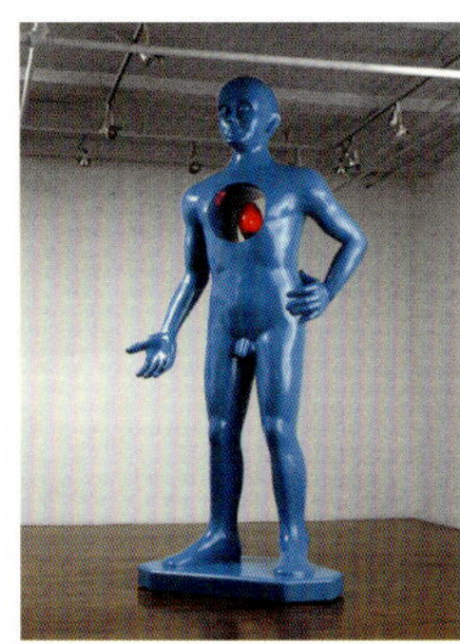

Cat. 73

Jonathan Borofsky
American, born 1942, M.F.A. 1966
Man with a Heart at 3,057,226, 1988
Fiberglass, cast resin, electric light,
digital recording of the artist's heart-
beat, and speaker, 12 ft. 4 in. × 70 in. ×
39 in. (375.9 × 177.8 × 99.1 cm)
2006.52.61a–c

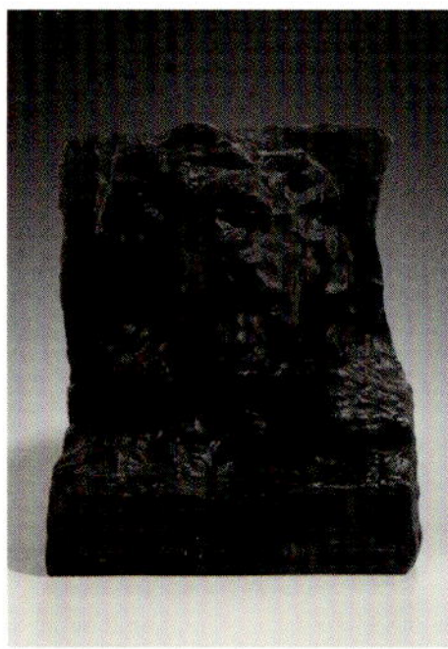

Émile Antoine Bourdelle
French, 1861–1929
Beethoven with Two Hands, 1908
Bronze with dark green patina,
20 ½ × 16 in. (52.1 × 40.6 cm)
2006.52.40

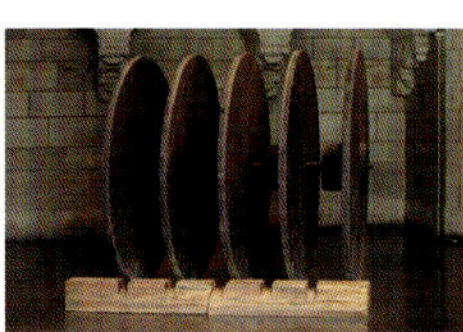

Cat. 66

Louise Bourgeois
American, born France, 1911–2010
Shredder, 1983
Wood and metal, 96 in. × 9 ft. × 9 ft.
(243.8 × 274.3 × 274.3 cm)
2006.52.62

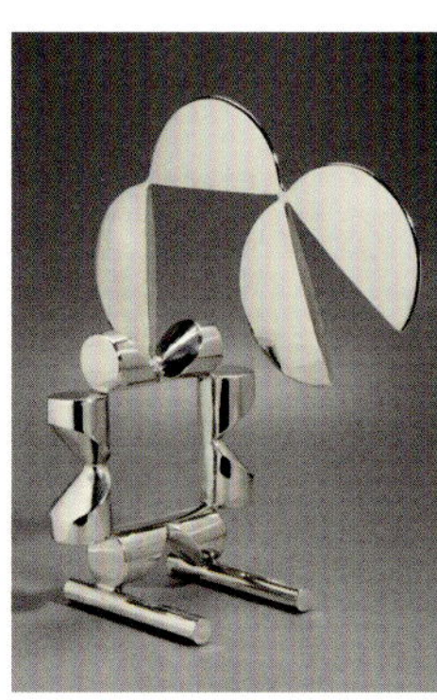

Antanas Brazdys
Lithuanian, born 1939
Split Discs, 1978–79
Stainless steel, edition 3/5, 19 ½ × 6 ¼ ×
7 ½ in. (49.5 × 15.9 × 19.1 cm)
2006.52.73

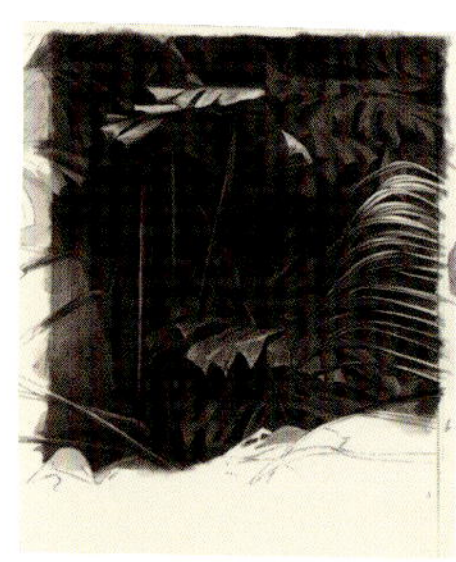

Elizabeth Butterworth
British, born 1949
Foliage Study (study for the series *Parrots
and Cockatoos*), 1977
Black ink and wash, 10 ¼ × 8 ¼ in.
(26 × 21 cm)
2006.52.85

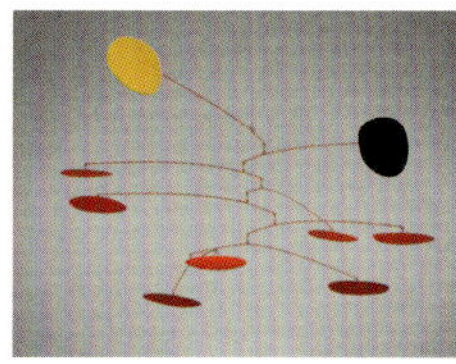

Cat. 41

Alexander Calder
American, 1898–1976
Numbered One to Nine, 1967
Sheet metal with paint and wire,
installed approximately 45 ½ in. ×
9 ft. 4 in. (115.6 × 284.5 cm)
2006.52.54

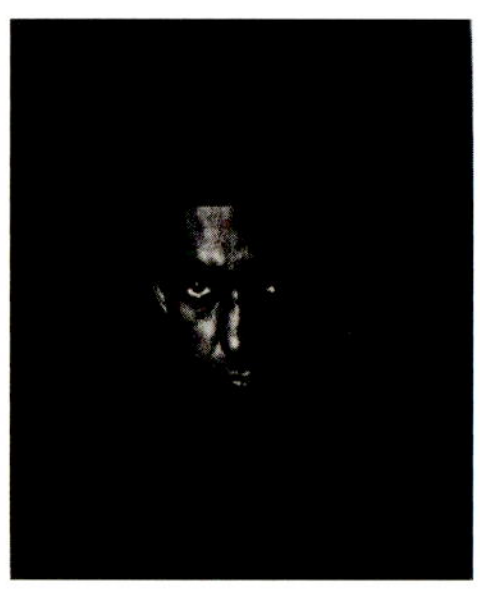

Cat. 60

Peter Campus
American, born 1937
Man's Head, 1978
Gelatin silver print, 31 ¹⁵⁄₁₆ × 26 ⁷⁄₁₆ in.
(81.2 × 67.1 cm)
2006.52.92

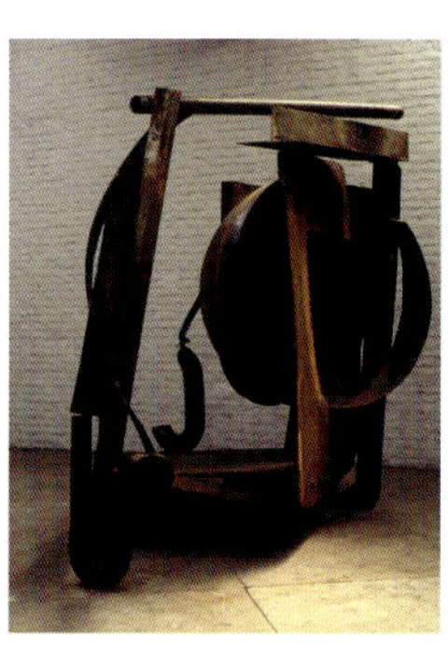

Cat. 65

Anthony Caro
British, born 1924, HON. 1989
Ocean, 1982–83
Rusted steel, 8 ft. 4 in. × 11 ft. 10 in. ×
79 in. (254 × 360.7 × 200.7 cm)
2006.52.63

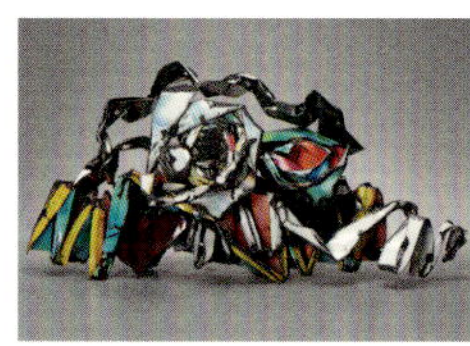

Cat. 79

John Chamberlain
American, 1927–2011
Ya Hoodie, 1996
Crushed metal with paint, 25 × 52 ×
24 in. (63.5 × 132.1 × 61 cm)
2006.52.49

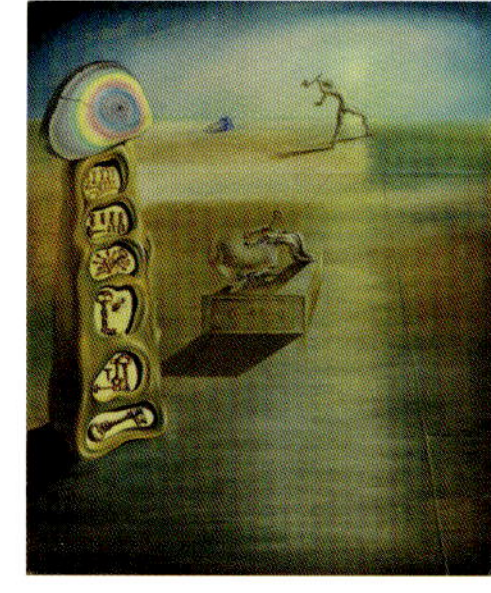

Attributed to Salvador Dalí
Spanish, 1904–1989
Untitled, 1930
Oil on board, 15 ½ × 12 in. (39.4 × 30.5 cm)
2006.52.98

This painting was acquired by
Charles B. Benenson from the April
20, 1966, sale of the Collection of
Helena Rubinstein, Sotheby Parke-
Bernet, New York (lot 66), where it was
described as having been acquired by
Rubinstein directly from Dalí. Since
then, the vibrancy of the rainbow's
colors and the figure of the man with
an axe, anomalous in Dalí's oeuvre,
have led some experts to question
the work's attribution, but none has
reached a definitive conclusion. At
this time it is the opinion of the Yale
University Art Gallery that further
research is required to attribute this
work with certainty.

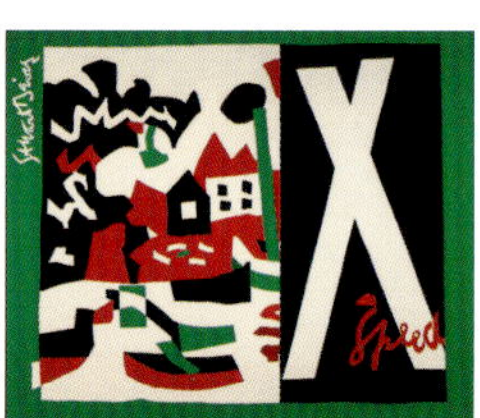

Cat. 18

Stuart Davis
American, 1892–1964
Lesson One, 1956
Oil on canvas, 52 × 60 ⅛ in.
(132.1 × 152.7 cm)
2006.52.2

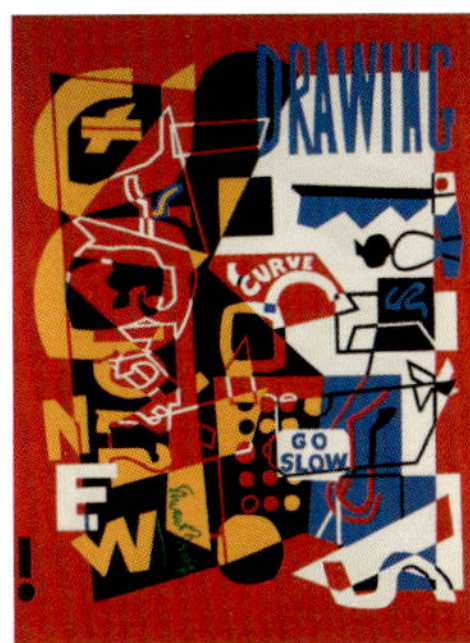

Cat. 19
Stuart Davis
American, 1892–1964
Combination Concrete #2, 1956–58
Oil on canvas, 71 × 53 in.
(180.3 × 134.6 cm)
2006.52.1

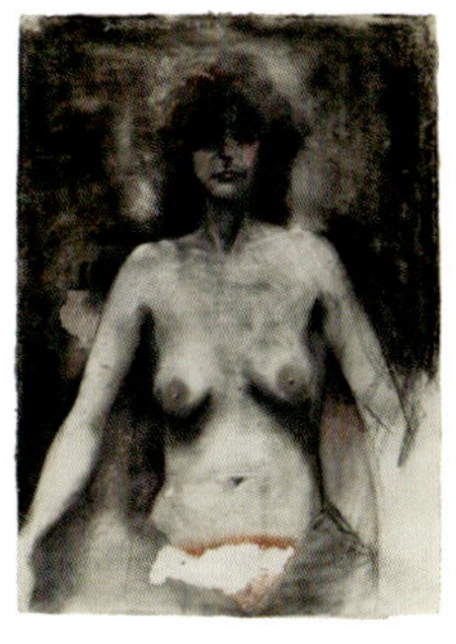

Cat. 14
Paul Delvaux
Belgian, 1897–1994
The Forest, 1935
Oil on canvas, 59 × 79 in.
(149.9 × 200.7 cm)
2006.52.12

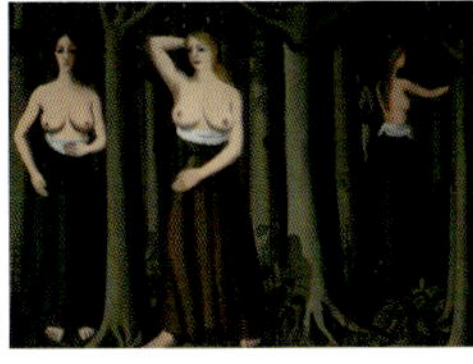

Cat. 55
Jim Dine
American, born 1935
Model on the Gloucester Road, 1976
Charcoal and pastel, 45 ⁹⁄₁₆ × 31 ½ in.
(115.8 × 80 cm)
2006.52.13

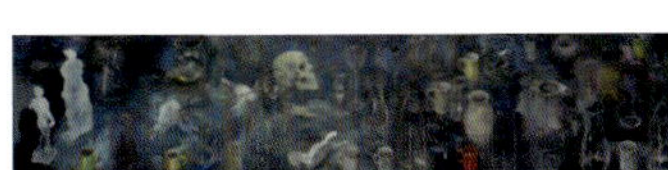

Cat. 56
Jim Dine
American, born 1935
The Studio at Night in the Woods, 1977
Acrylic on canvas, 36 in. × 13 ft. 2 in.
(91.4 × 401.3 cm)
2006.52.99

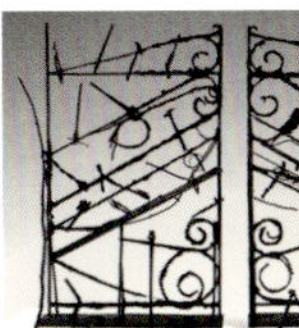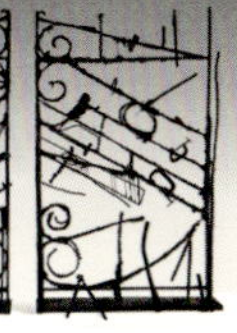

Cat. 58
Jim Dine
American, born 1935
Crommelynck Gate with Tools, 1983
Bronze, edition 2/6, 9 ft. × 11 ft. × 36 in.
(274.3 × 335.3 × 91.4 cm)
2006.52.64

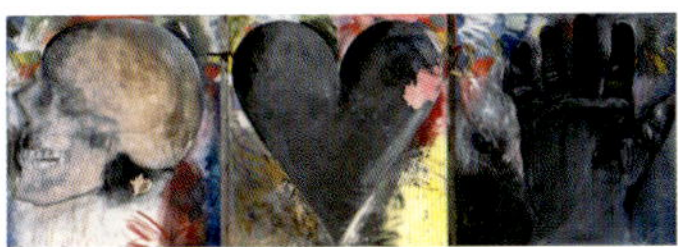

Cat. 57
Jim Dine
American, born 1935
July—The Swedish Sea, 1985
Oil and charcoal on canvas with metal
tools and a seashell; three panels, over-
all 72 in. × 16 ft. 10 ¼ in. (182.9 × 513.7 cm)
2006.52.55

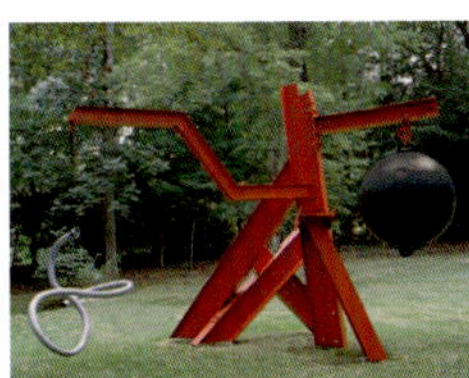

Cat. 59
Mark di Suvero
American, born China 1933
Thataway, 1976
Wrought and cast iron and steel with
paint, 13 × 19 × 13 ft.
(396.2 × 579.1 × 396.2 cm)
2006.52.65

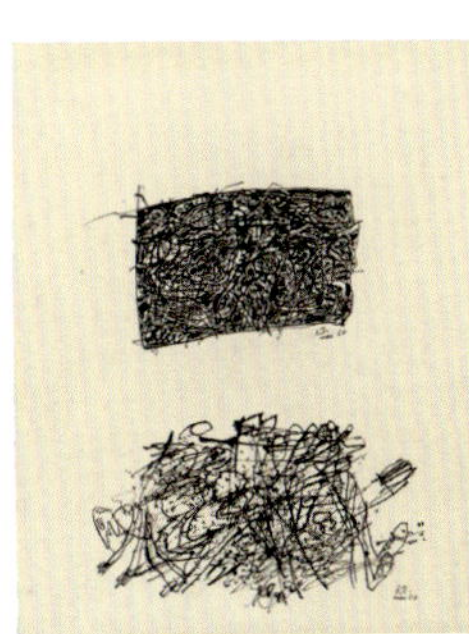

Cat. 28
Jean Dubuffet
French, 1901–1985
Dessins (Drawings), 1960
Black ink, 12 ⅞ × 9 ⅞ in.
(32.7 × 25.1 cm)
2006.52.33

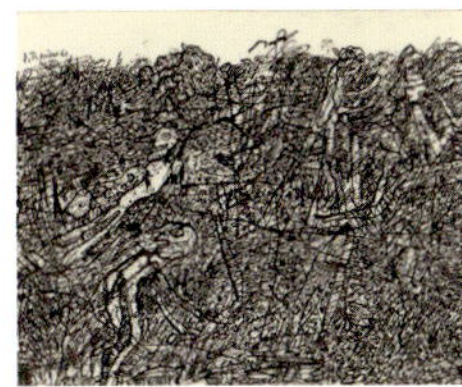

Cat. 29
Jean Dubuffet
French, 1901–1985
Paysage avec quatre personnages
(Landscape with Four Figures), 1960
Black ink and wash, 9 ³⁄₁₆ × 11 ¼ in.
(23.3 × 28.6 cm)
2006.52.26

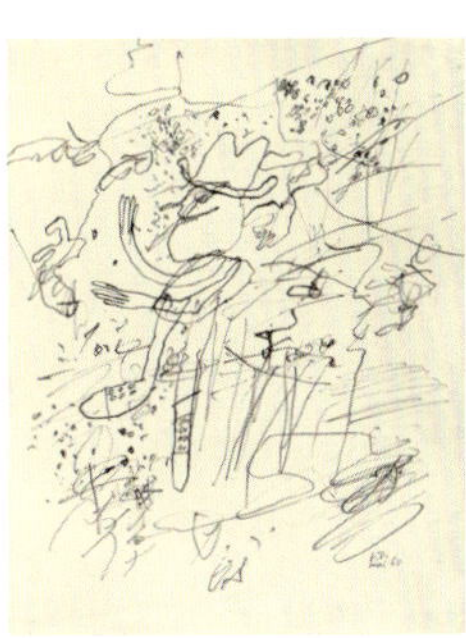

Cat. 27
Jean Dubuffet
French, 1901–1985
Personnage avec chapeau dans un paysage
(Figure with a Hat in a Landscape), 1960
Black ink, 13 ¼ × 9 ¹⁵⁄₁₆ in. (33.7 × 25.3 cm)
2006.52.27

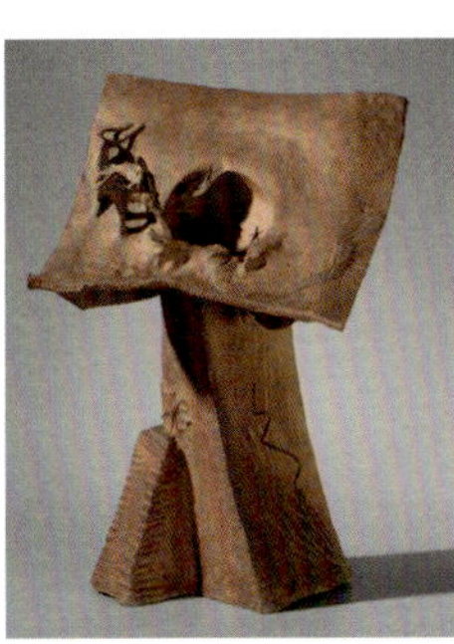

Cat. 44
Mary Frank
American, born 1933
Sundial in Winter, 1970
Ceramic, 29 ¼ × 17 × 8 ½ in.
(74.3 × 43.2 × 21.6 cm)
2006.52.86

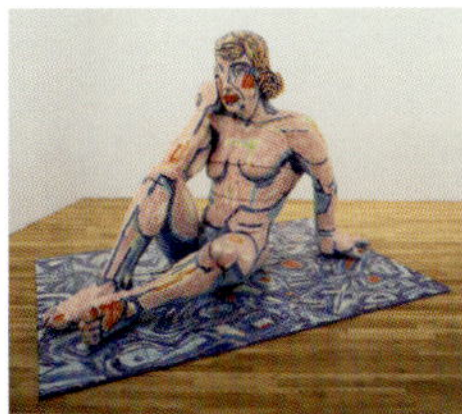

Cat. 75
Viola Frey
American, 1933–2004
Pink Nude Woman, 1989
Ceramic with colored glaze, 68 × 98 ×
78 ½ in. (172.7 × 248.9 × 199.4 cm)
2006.52.59

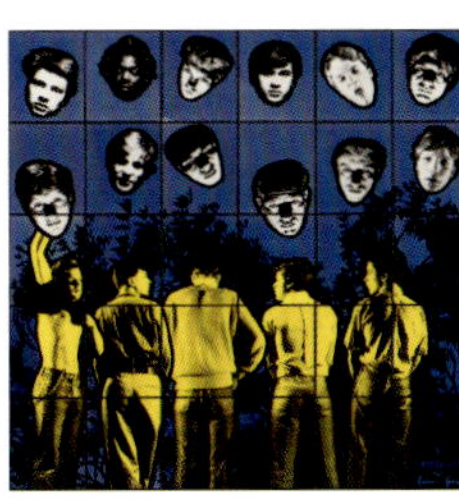

Cat. 63
Gilbert & George
British; Gilbert Proesch, born Italy
1943, and George Passmore, born 1942
Urinight, 1982
Mixed media, 9 ft. 10 ⅞ in. × 9 ft. 10 ½ in.
(302 × 301 cm)
2006.52.50

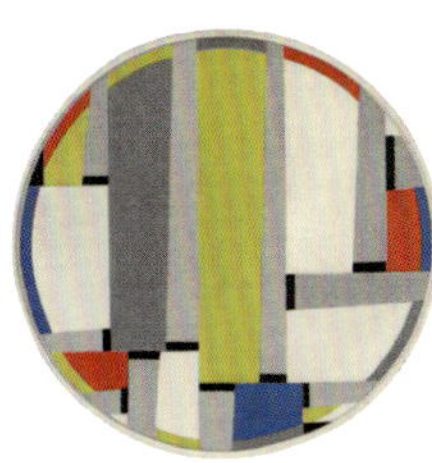

Fritz Glarner
American, born Switzerland, 1899–1972
Relational Painting, Tondo #48, 1958
Oil on wood, DIAM. 21 in. (53.3 cm)
2006.52.101

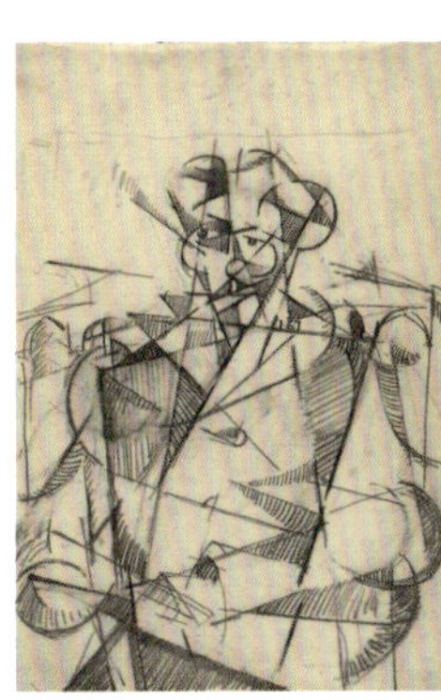

Albert Gleizes
French, 1881–1953
Untitled, 1914–15
Graphite, 12 ¼ × 8 ¹⁄₁₆ in. (31.1 × 20.6 cm)
2006.52.8

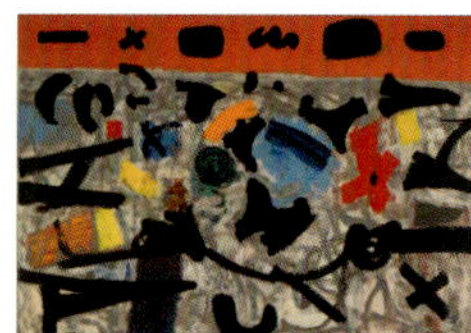

Cat. 20
Adolph Gottlieb
American, 1903–1974
Hot Horizon, 1956
Oil on canvas, 49 ¾ × 71 ⅞ in.
(126.4 × 182.6 cm)
2006.52.6

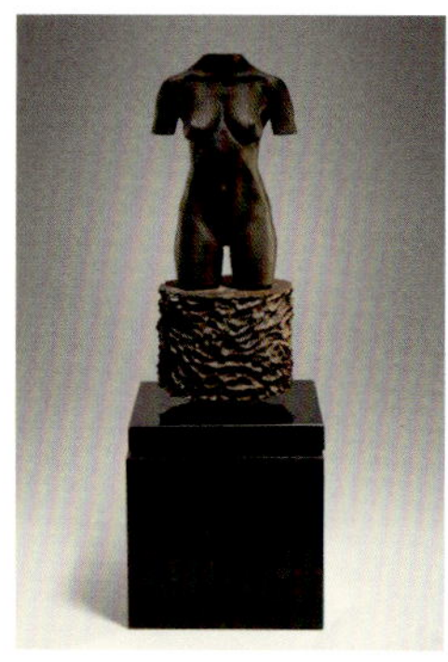

Robert Graham
American, 1938–2008
MOCA Torso, 1992–95
Bronze, unnumbered work from an
edition of 3,500, 11 ¼ × 4 ⅝ × 4 ½ in.
(28.6 × 11.8 × 11.4 cm)
2006.52.38

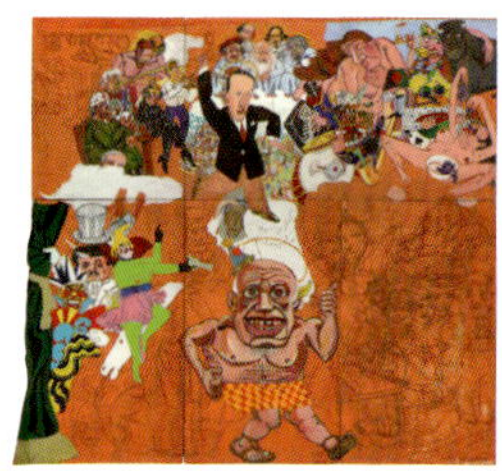

Cat. 52
Red Grooms
American, born 1937
Picasso Goes to Heaven, 1973
Acrylic and charcoal on paper laid
down on canvas; six panels, overall 15 ft. 2 ½ in. × 16 ft. 4 in. (463.6 ×
497.8 cm)
2006.52.42

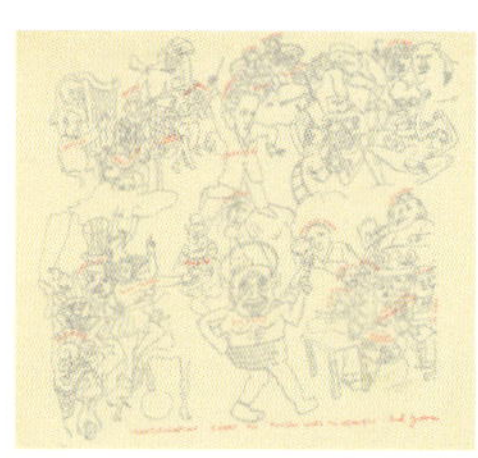

Red Grooms
American, born 1937
Identification chart for *Picasso Goes
to Heaven*, 1973
Pen and blue ink with colored pencil,
15 × 16 in. (38.1 × 40.6 cm)
2006.52.43

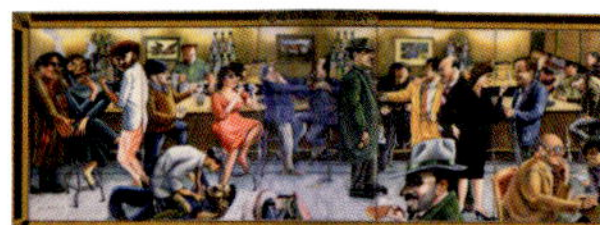

Cat. 54
Red Grooms
American, born 1937
Cedar Bar, 1986
Colored pencil and crayon on paper
mounted to board; five panels, in artist's frame, 9 ft. 11 ½ in. × 27 ft. × 3 in.
(303.5 × 823 × 7.6 cm)
2006.52.56

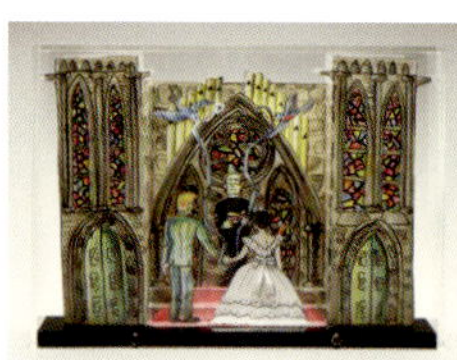

Red Grooms
American, born 1937
Lysiane and Red's Wedding Invitation, 1987
Three-dimensional lithograph in five
colors, in a Plexiglas case, 9 ¼ × 12 ¼ ×
2 ¼ in. (23.5 × 31.1 × 5.7 cm)
2006.52.28

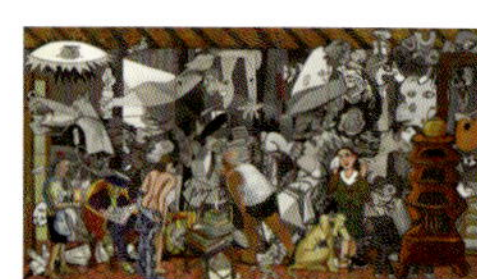

Cat. 53
Red Grooms
American, born 1937
Studio at the Rue des Grands-Augustins,
1990–96
Acrylic on canvas; six panels, overall
10 ft. 3 in. × 18 ft. 3 in. (312.4 × 556.3 cm)
2006.52.3

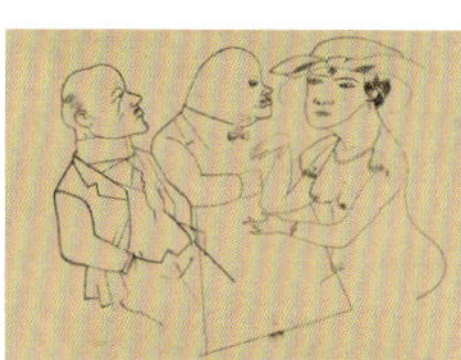

Cat. 5
George Grosz
American, born Germany, 1893–1959
Haifische (Sharks), 1920–21
Transfer lithograph, 14 ⅞ × 20 in.
(37.8 × 50.8 cm)
2006.52.75

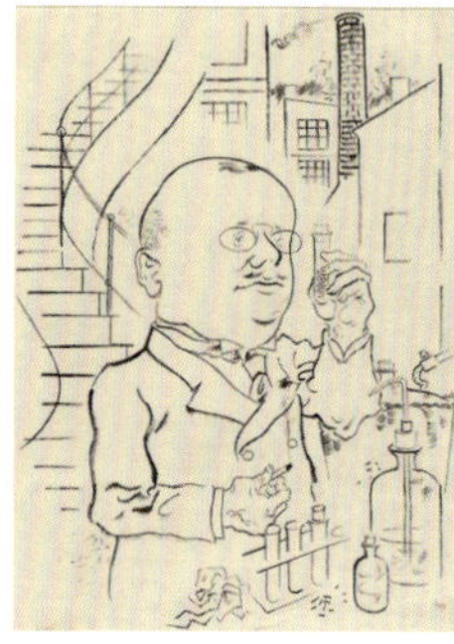

Cat. 6
George Grosz
American, born Germany, 1893–1959
Chemist, ca. 1925
Black ink, 25 ½ × 19 ¾ in. (64.8 × 50.2 cm)
2006.52.34

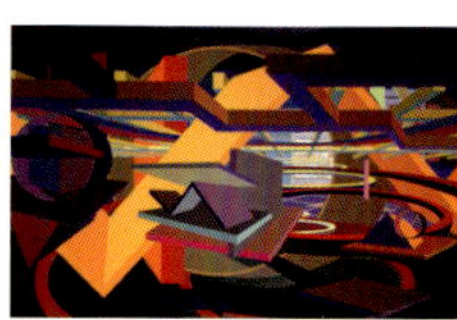

Cat. 71
Al Held
American, 1928–2005
Pan North XI, 1987
Acrylic on canvas, 9 × 14 ft.
(274.3 × 426.7 cm)
2006.52.57

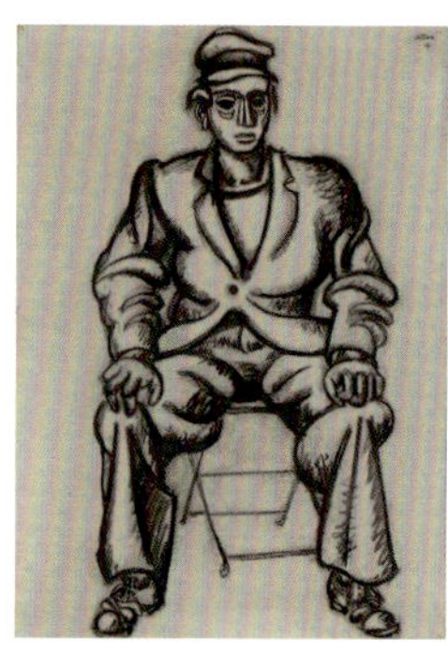

Jean Hélion
French, 1904–1987
Homme assis (Seated Man), 1947
Charcoal on primed canvas, 45 ½ ×
31 ½ in. (115.57 × 80.01 cm)
2006.52.44

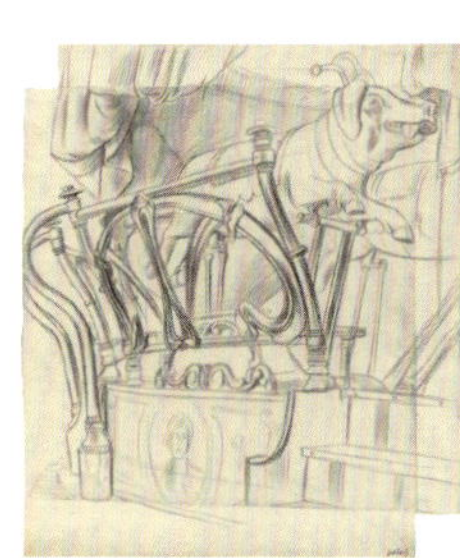

Karl Hubbuch
German, 1891–1979
Karussell (Carousel), 1926
Graphite and crayon on two sheets,
overall 20 ¼ × 17 ¹¹⁄₁₆ in. (51.5 × 44.9 cm)
(irreg.)
2006.52.35

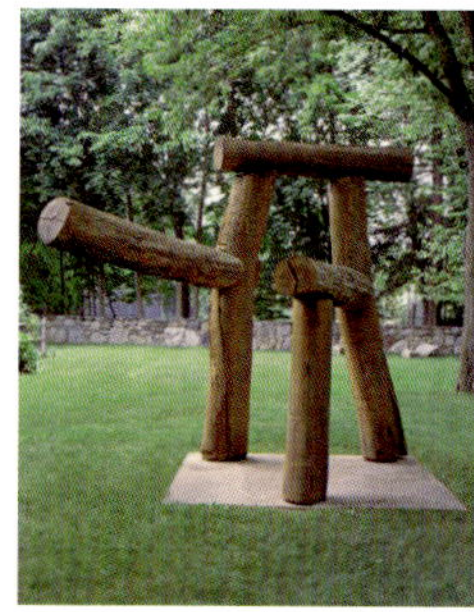

Cat. 70
Magdalena Jetelová
Czech, born 1946
Boban, 1986
Oak, 11 ft. × 11 ft. 2 in. × 10 ft. 10 in.
(335.3 × 340.4 × 330.2 cm)
2006.52.74

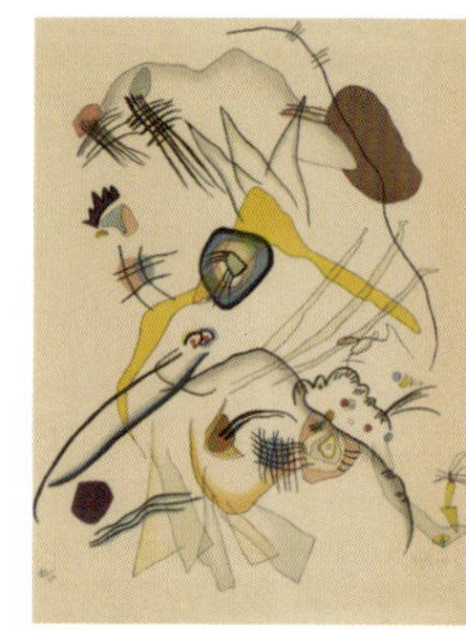

Wassily Kandinsky
Russian, 1866–1944
Abstract Composition, 1920
Color lithograph, edition 4/300,
15 ³⁄₁₆ × 11 ⅛ in. (38.5 × 28.3 cm)
2006.52.83

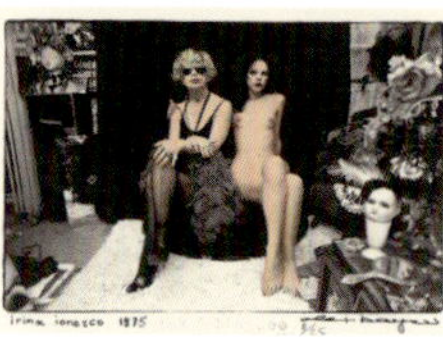

Alex Kayser
Swiss, born 1949
Irina Ionesco, 1975
Offset photograph with hand coloring,
edition 8/25, image 4 ⅛ × 6 ⅛ in.
(10.5 × 15.5 cm)
2006.52.114

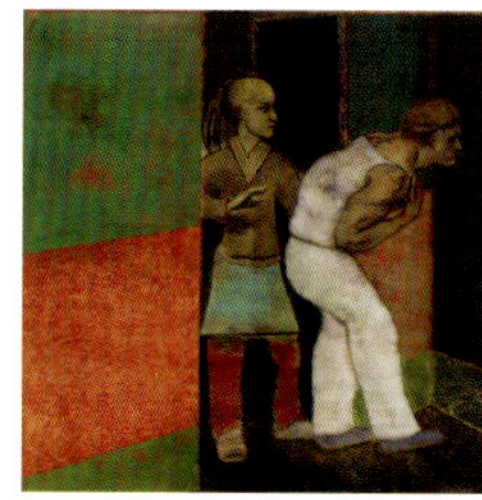

Cat. 69
R. B. Kitaj
American, 1932–2007
China and Russia, 1980
Pastel and charcoal, 30 ³⁄₁₆ × 28 ½ in.
(76.6 × 72.4 cm)
2006.52.100

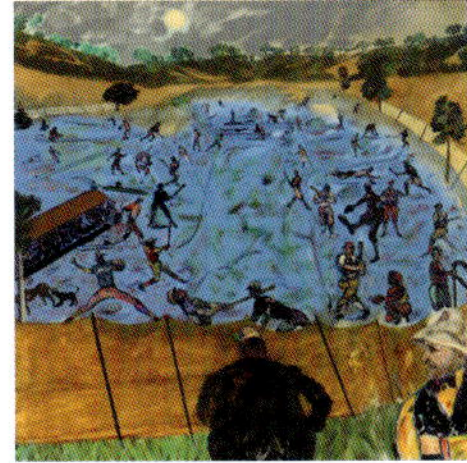

Cat. 68
R. B. Kitaj
American, 1932–2007
Amerika (Baseball), 1983–84
Oil on canvas, 58 × 58 in.
(147.3 × 147.3 cm)
2006.52.14

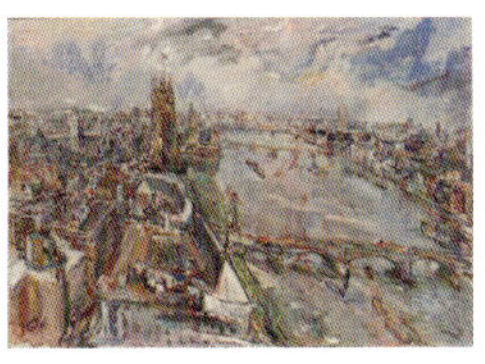

Cat. 32
Oskar Kokoschka
Austrian, 1886–1980
View of the Thames from the Vicker's Building, Millbank, 1962
Oil on canvas, 35 ⅝ × 49 ½ in.
(90.5 × 125.7 cm)
2006.52.15

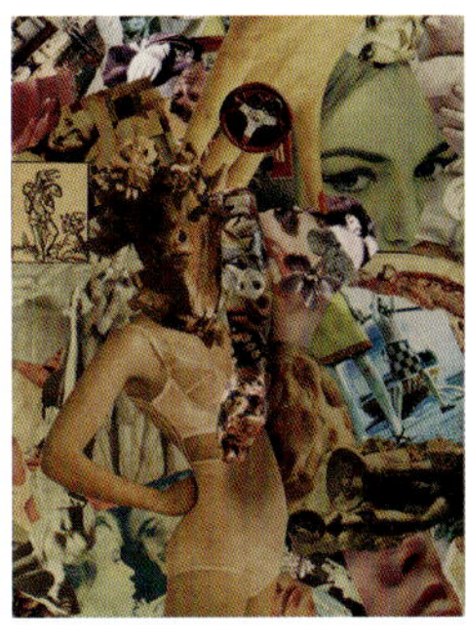

Cat. 38
Jiří Kolář
Czech, 1914–2002
Untitled, 1965
Mixed media on board, 15 ¹⁵⁄₁₆ × 11 ⅞ in.
(40.4 × 30.1 cm)
2006.52.39

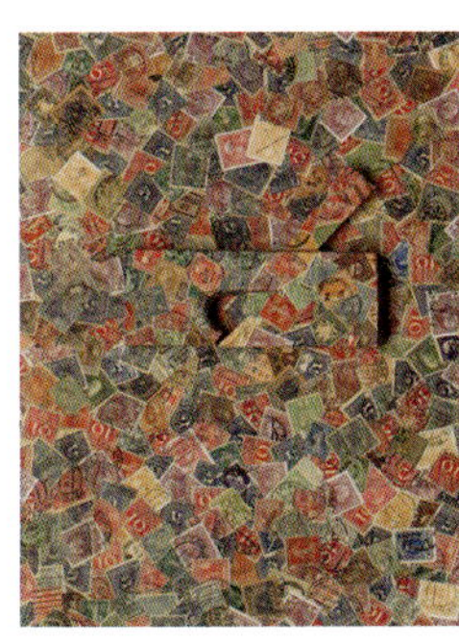

Cat. 39
Jiří Kolář
Czech, 1914–2002
Untitled, 1965
Mixed media on board, 15 ¹⁵⁄₁₆ × 11 ¾ × 1 ³⁄₁₆ in. (40.5 x 29.9 × 3 cm)
2006.52.76

Cat. 40
Jiří Kolář
Czech, 1914–2002
Untitled, 1965
Mixed media on board, 15 ¾ × 11 ¾ in.
(40 × 29.8 cm)
2006.52.77

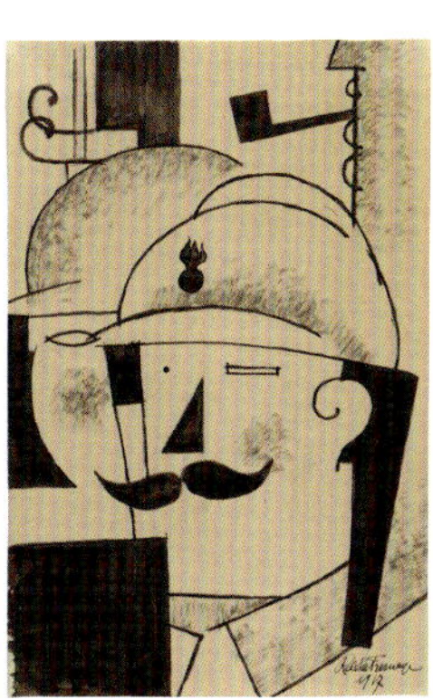

Cat. 2
Roger de La Fresnaye
French, 1885–1925
Deux fantassins casqués (Two Helmeted Infantrymen), 1917
Pen and black ink with wash,
12 ⅛ × 7 ⅝ in. (30.8 × 19.4 cm)
2006.52.7

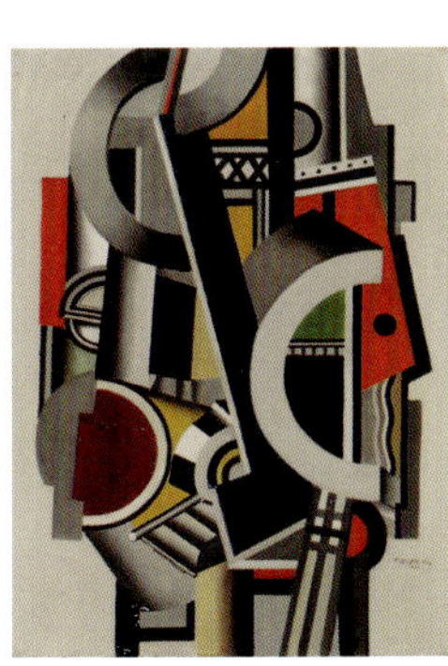

Cat. 7
Fernand Léger
French, 1881–1955
Éléments mécaniques (Mechanical Elements), 1924
Oil on canvas, 36 × 26 in. (91.4 × 66 cm)
2006.52.16

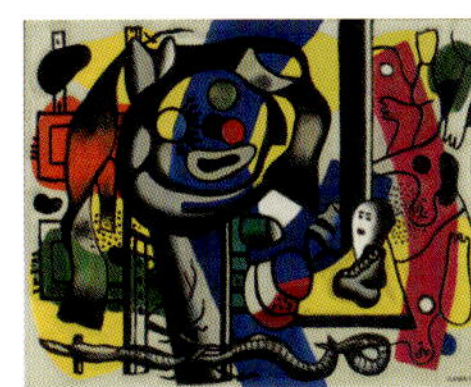

Cat. 8
Fernand Léger
French, 1881–1955
Masque nègre (Negro Mask), 1942
Oil on canvas, 29 × 36 ½ in.
(73.7 × 92.7 cm)
2006.52.25

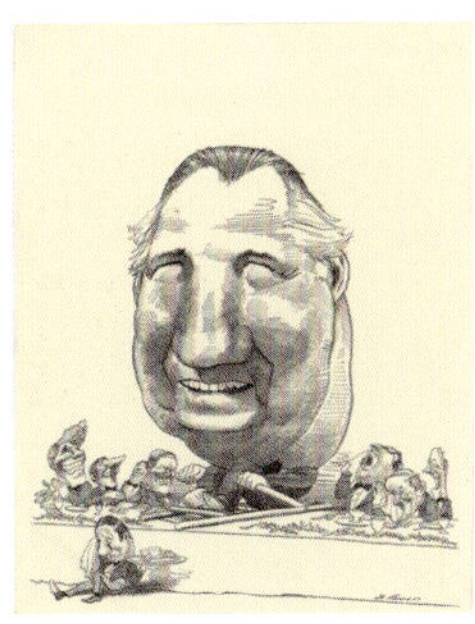

David Levine
American, 1926–2009
Spiro Agnew, 1969
Black ink with traces of pencil,
13 ¹¹⁄₁₆ × 11 in. (34.7 × 27.9 cm)
2006.52.95

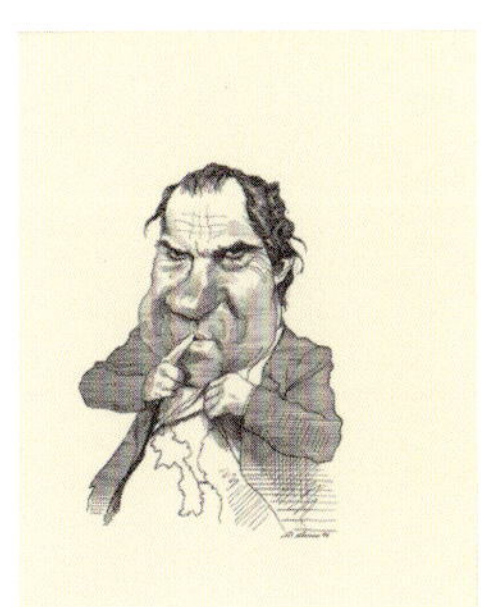

David Levine
American, 1926–2009
Richard Nixon, 1970
Black ink with traces of pencil,
13 ¾ × 11 ¹⁄₁₆ in. (34.9 × 28 cm)
2006.52.94

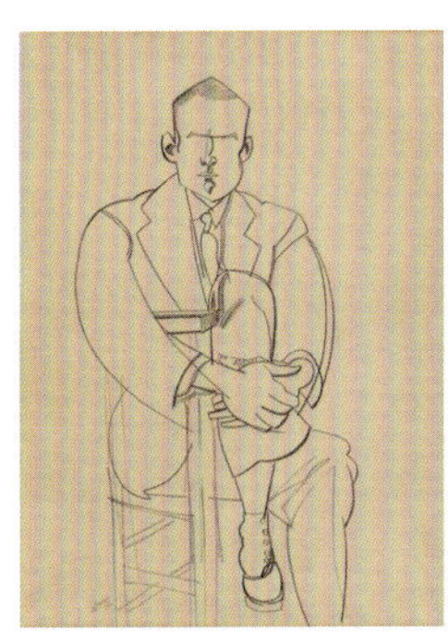

Cat. 4
Wyndham Lewis
British, born Canada, 1882–1957
Seated Man, 1920
Black crayon, 20 ⁵⁄₁₆ × 14 ¹⁵⁄₁₆ in.
(51.5 × 37.9 cm)
2006.52.17

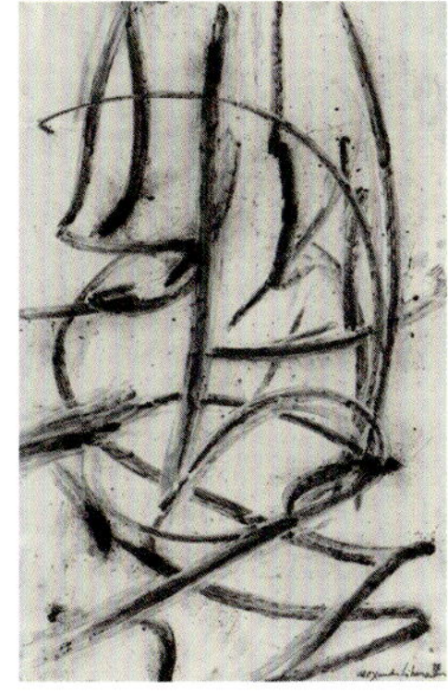

Alexander Liberman
American, 1912–1999
Untitled White V, 1978
Acrylic and charcoal, 40 × 25 ⁵⁄₁₆ in.
(101.5 × 64.2 cm)
2006.52.119

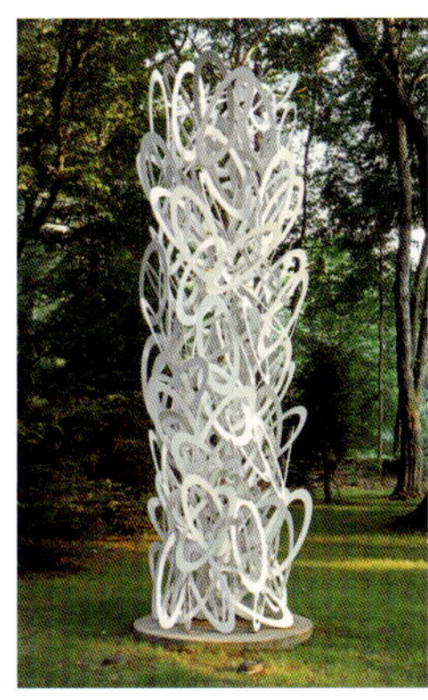

Cat. 78
Alexander Liberman
American, born Russia, 1912–1999
Lightweb, 1991
Welded steel with paint, 15 ft. × 52 in. × 52 in. (457.2 × 132.1 × 132.1 cm)
2006.52.66

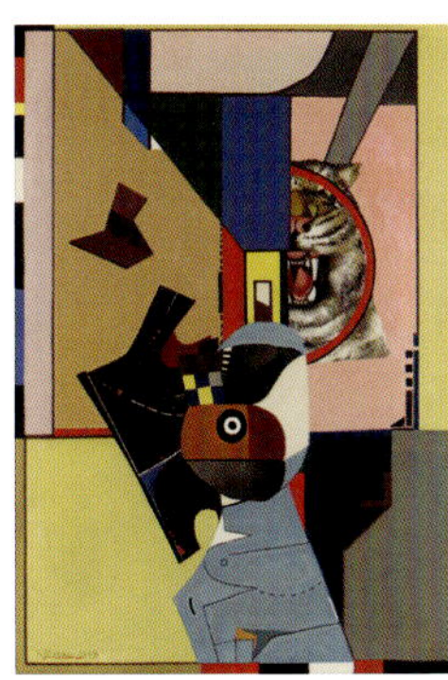

Cat. 21
Richard Lindner
American, born Germany, 1901–1978
The Scream, 1958
Oil on canvas, 60 × 40 in.
(152.4 × 101.6 cm)
2006.52.9

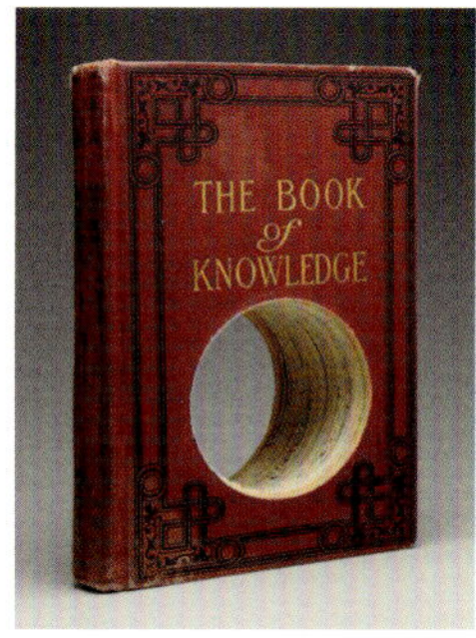

Donald Lipski
American, born 1947
Building Steam #386, 1985
Book, 9 ¾ × 6 ¾ × 1 ¼ in.
(24.8 × 17.1 × 3.2 cm)
2006.52.116

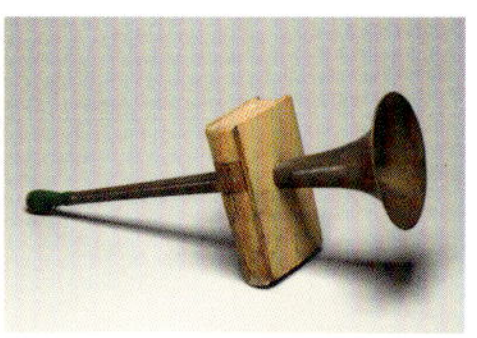

Donald Lipski
American, born 1947
Building Steam #397 (For Mozart), 1985
Book and brass horn, 9 ½ × 24 ½ × 7 ⅛ in.
(24.1 × 62.2 × 18.1 cm)
2006.52.115

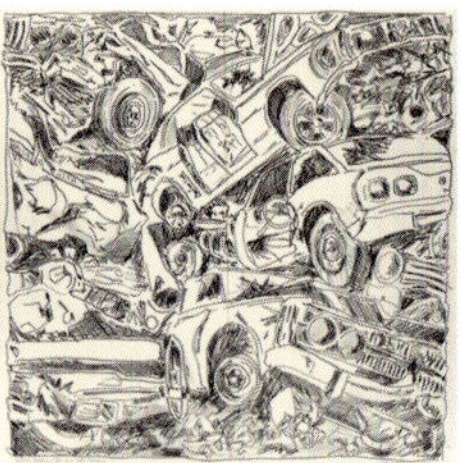

Robert Longo
American, born 1953
Natural History (Doors for Hell), 1983
Charcoal and black felt-tip pen,
27 ½ × 27 ⁷⁄₁₆ in. (69.8 × 69.7 cm)
2006.52.118

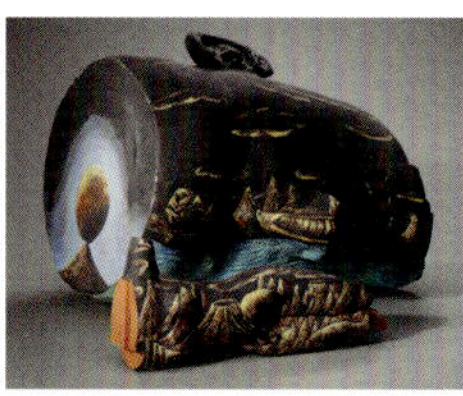

Michael Lucero
American, born 1953
Head and Torso (Dreamer), 1984
Ceramic with paint, head 21 × 24 ¼ ×
17 ⅝ in. (53.3 × 61.6 × 44.8 cm); torso 8 ½ ×
4 ⅜ × 17 ½ in. (21.6 × 11.1 × 44.5 cm)
2006.52.78

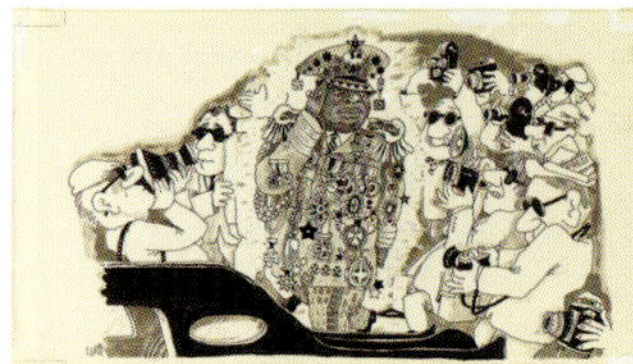

Ranan Raymond Lurie
American, born 1932
Untitled (Idi Amin with Paparazzi), 1971
Black ink and body color with traces of
Wite-Out, 9 ⅝ × 17 ⁹⁄₁₆ in. (24.4 × 44.6 cm)
2006.52.79

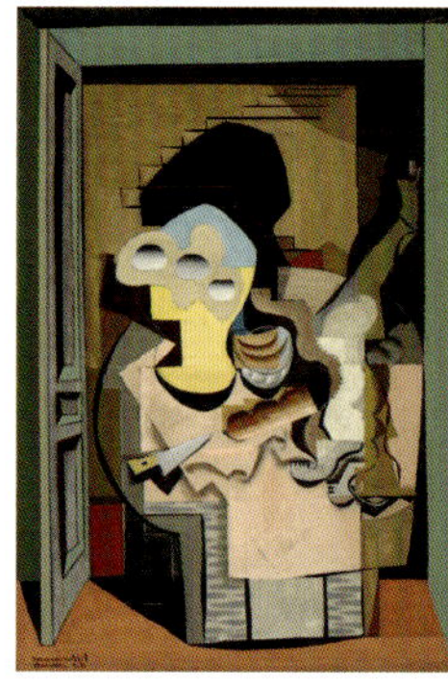

Cat. 9
Louis Marcoussis
French, born Poland, 1878–1941
Anvers (Antwerp), 1928
Oil on canvas, 58 × 39 in.
(147.3 × 99.1 cm)
2006.52.93

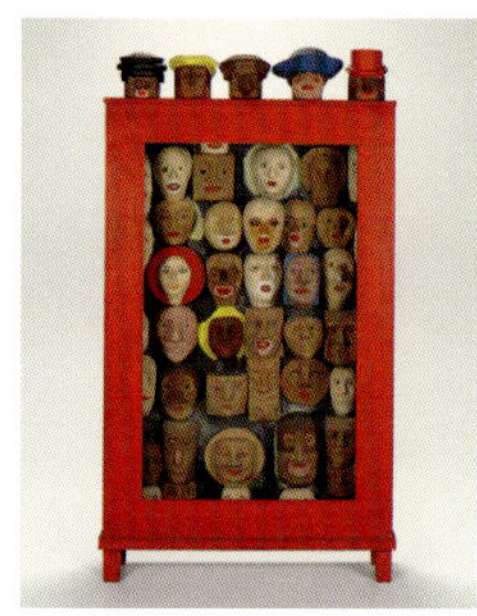

Cat. 31
Marisol (Escobar)
American, born France 1930
Mayflower, 1961–62
Wood with paint and glass, 75 ×
41 ¼ × 11 ¼ in. (190.5 × 104.8 × 28.6 cm)
2006.52.71

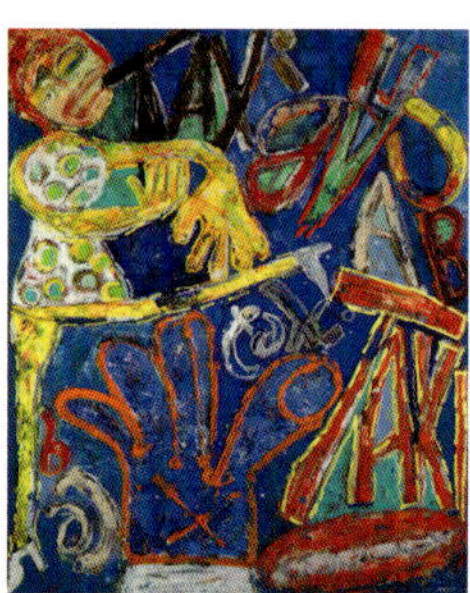

George J. McNeil
American, 1908–1995
Park Avenue: 5 PM, 1982
Oil on canvas, 78 × 64 in.
(198.1 × 162.6 cm)
2006.52.18

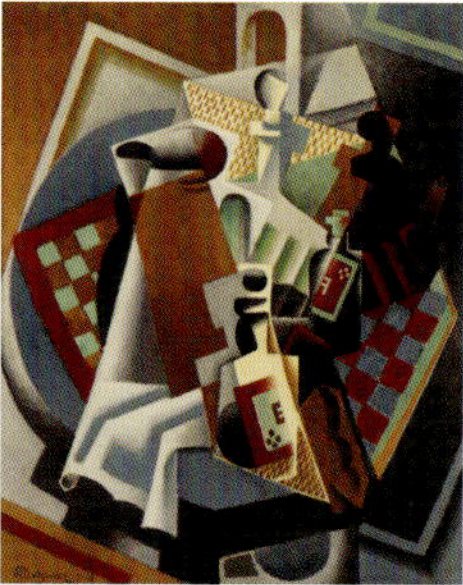

Cat. 3
Jean Metzinger
French, 1883–1956
Nature morte (Still Life), 1918
Oil on canvas, 31 ¾ × 25 ¾ in.
(80.6 × 65.4 cm)
2006.52.19

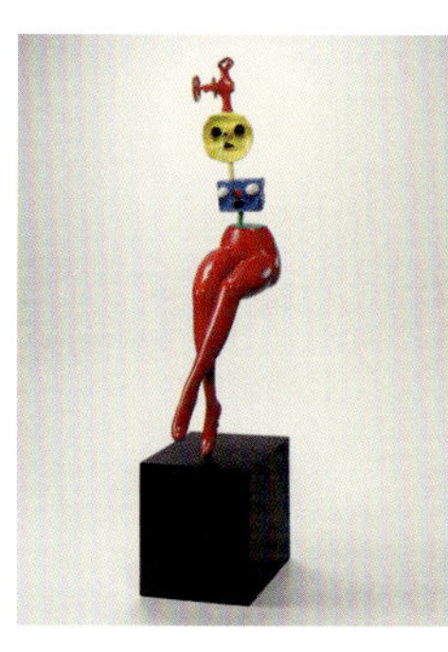

Cat. 42
Joan Miró
Spanish, 1893–1983
Jeune fille s'évadant (Girl Escaping), 1968
Bronze with paint, edition 2/4, 80 ⁷⁄₁₆ ×
16 ⅝ × 28 ¼ in. (204.3 × 42.2 × 71.8 cm)
2006.52.20

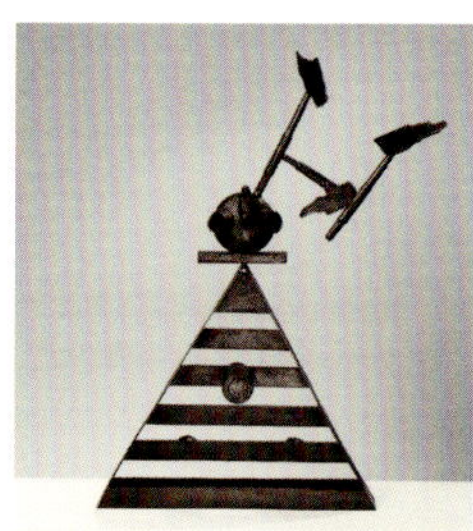

Cat. 43
Joan Miró
Spanish, 1893–1983
Personnage et oiseau (Figure and Bird),
1970
Bronze with brown and green patina,
edition 2/4, 63 × 48 ⅛ × 11 ⅛ in.
(160 × 122 × 28 cm)
2006.52.67

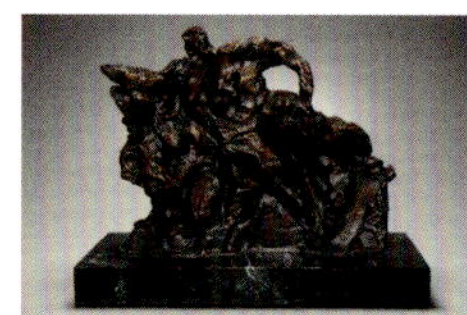

Reuben Nakian
American, 1897–1986
Europa and the Bull, 1986
Bronze and marble, edition 4/7,
15 × 18 ¾ × 8 ¼ in. (38.1 × 47.6 × 21 cm)
2006.52.51

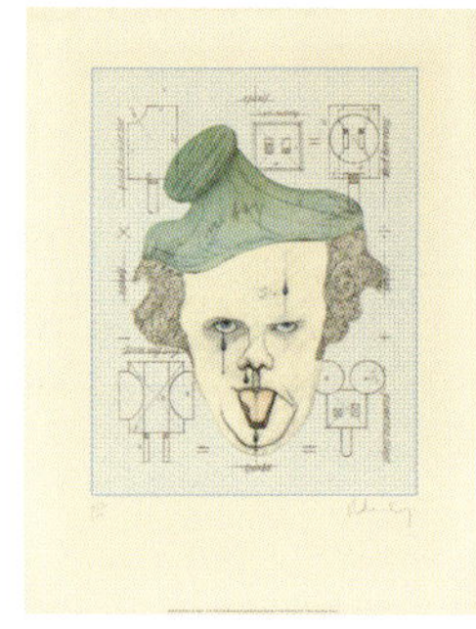

Claes Oldenburg
American, born Sweden, 1929
Symbolic Self-Portrait with "Equals," 1969
Offset lithograph, edition 222/300,
28 ¼ × 21 in. (71.8 × 53.3 cm)
2006.52.80

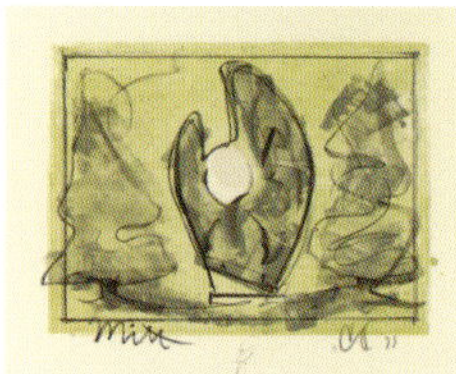

Claes Oldenburg
American, born Sweden, 1929
Standing Mitt with Ball, 1973
Lithograph in four colors, edition 6/75,
19 ⁹⁄₁₆ × 21 ⅝ in. (49.6 × 54.9 cm)
2006.52.90

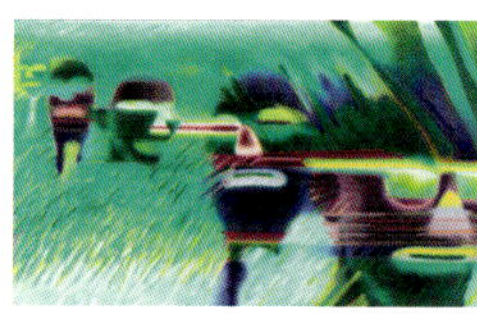

Cat. 67
Ed Paschke
American, 1939–2004
La Bomba (The Bomb), 1983
Acrylic on canvas, 50 × 85 in.
(127 × 215.9 cm)
2006.52.60

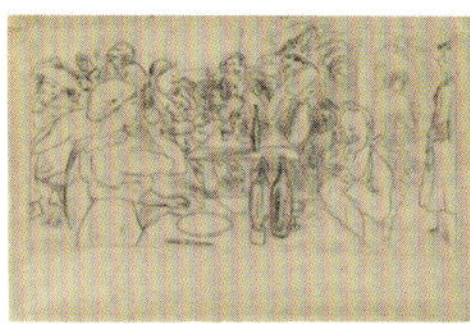

Cat. 1
Jules Pascin
American, born Bulgaria, 1885–1930
Café Scene, 1906–7
Black ink and graphite, 8 ³⁄₁₆ × 12 ¼ in.
(20.8 × 31.1 cm)
2006.52.36

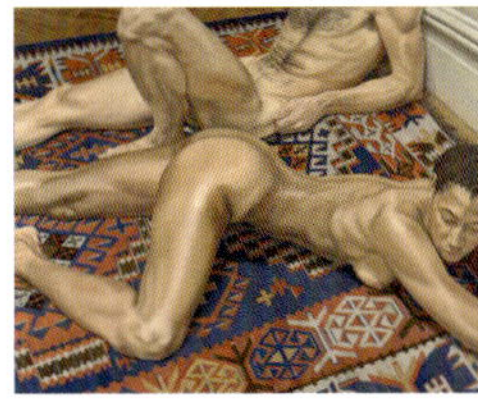

Cat. 61
Philip Pearlstein
American, born 1924
Male and Female Models on a Kilim Rug, 1978
Acrylic on canvas, 60 × 72 in.
(152.4 × 182.9 cm)
2006.52.45

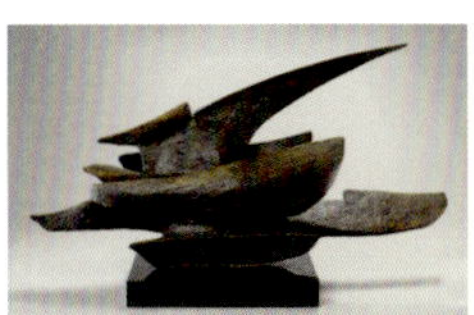

Cat. 23
Alicia Penalba
French, born Argentina, 1913–1982
Faune des mers (Sea Fauna), 1959
Bronze, edition 5/6, 17 ½ × 33 ⅛ × 10 ¼ in.
(44.5 × 84.1 × 26 cm)
2006.52.120

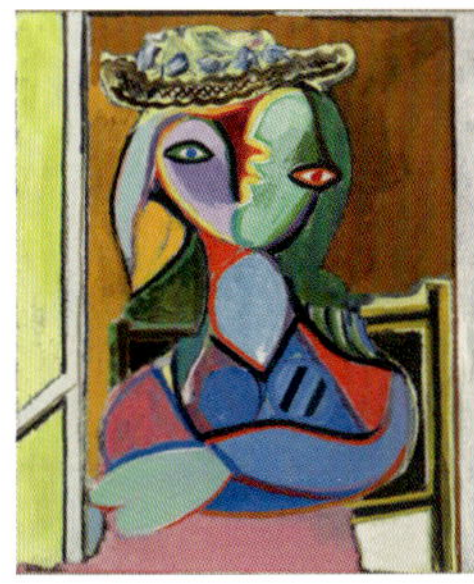

Cat. 15
Pablo Picasso
Spanish, active in France, 1881–1973
Femme assise (Seated Woman), 1936
Oil on canvas, 28 ¾ × 23 ½ in.
(73 × 59.7 cm)
2006.52.22

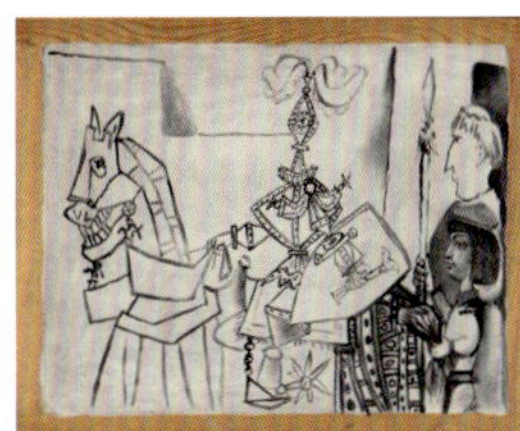

Cat. 16
Pablo Picasso
Spanish, active in France, 1881–1973
Chevalier, page et moine (Horseman, Page, and Monk), 1951
Gesso and oil on panel, 17 × 21 ¾ in.
(43.2 × 55.2 cm)
2006.52.21

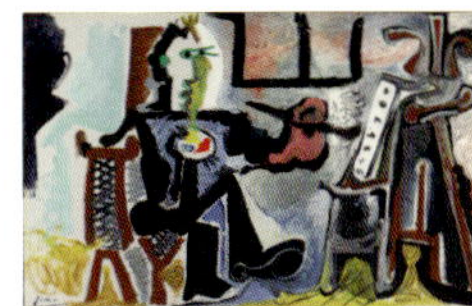

Cat. 17
Pablo Picasso
Spanish, active in France, 1881–1973
Le peintre dans son atelier (The Painter in His Studio), 1963
Oil on canvas, 23 ⅜ × 35 ⅞ in.
(59.4 × 91.1 cm)
2006.52.23

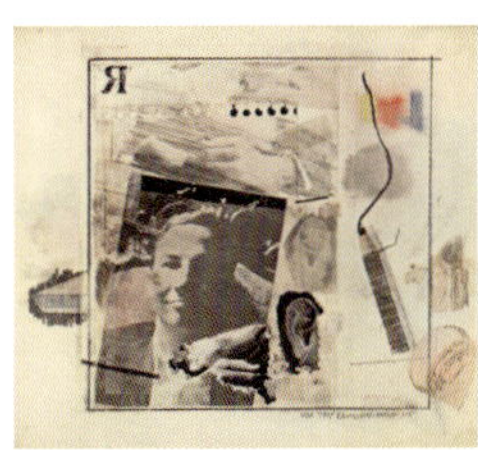

Robert Rauschenberg
American, 1925–2008
Dwan Gallery Poster, 1965
Offset lithograph, 23 ⅛₆ × 24 ¹⁵⁄₁₆ in.
(58.5 × 63.3 cm)
2006.52.81

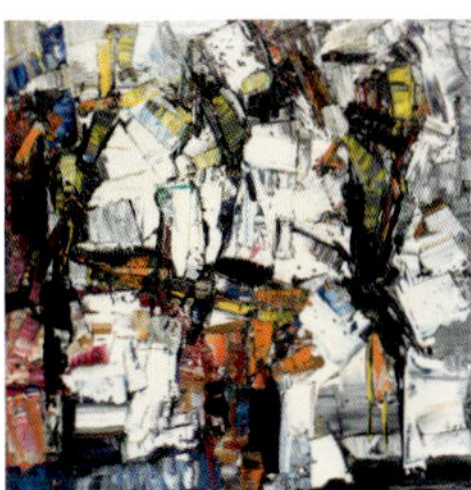

Cat. 30
Jean Paul Riopelle
Canadian, 1923–2002
Plage (Beach), 1960
Oil on canvas, 39 × 38 in. (99.1 × 96.5 cm)
2006.52.96

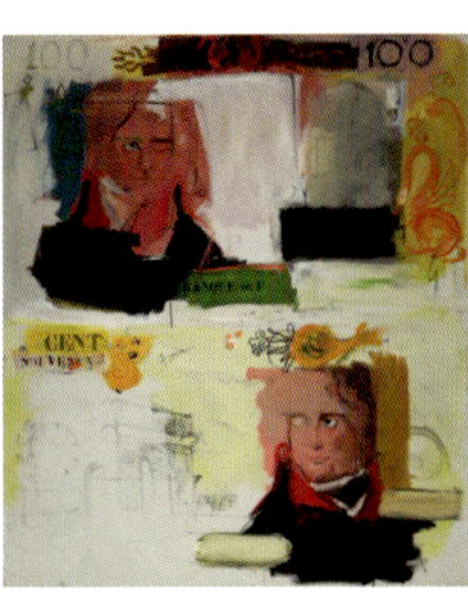

Cat. 33
Larry Rivers
American, 1923–2002
Double French Money, 1962
Oil on canvas, 72 × 60 in.
(182.9 × 152.4 cm)
2006.52.52

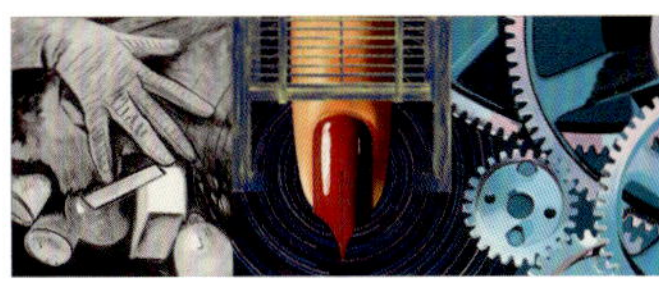

Cat. 64
James Rosenquist
American, born 1933
While the Earth Revolves at Night, 1982
Acrylic on canvas; three panels, overall 78 in. × 16 ft. 6 in. (198.1 × 502.9 cm)
2006.52.53

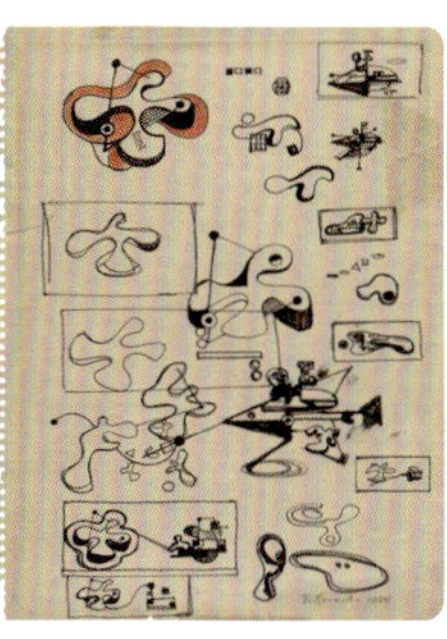

Cat. 10
Theodore Roszak
American, 1907–1981
Untitled, 1934
Black ink and red colored pencil on lined paper, 10 ½ × 7 ¹⁵⁄₁₆ in. (26.6 × 20.1 cm)
2006.52.37.1

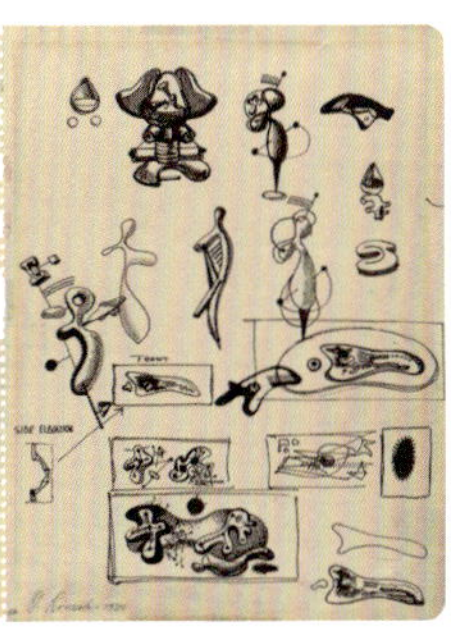

Cat. 11
Theodore Roszak
American, 1907–1981
Untitled, 1934
Black ink on lined paper,
10 ½ × 7 ¹⁵⁄₁₆ in. (26.6 × 20.1 cm)
2006.52.37.2

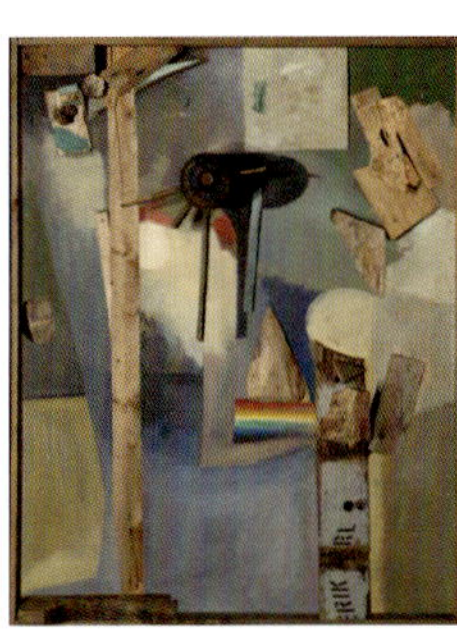

Cat. 13
Kurt Schwitters
German, 1887–1948
Merzbild mit Regenbogen (Merz Picture with Rainbow), 1920–39
Mixed media on plywood, 61 ⅝ × 47 ¾ × 10 ½ in. (156.5 × 121.3 × 26.7 cm)
2006.52.4

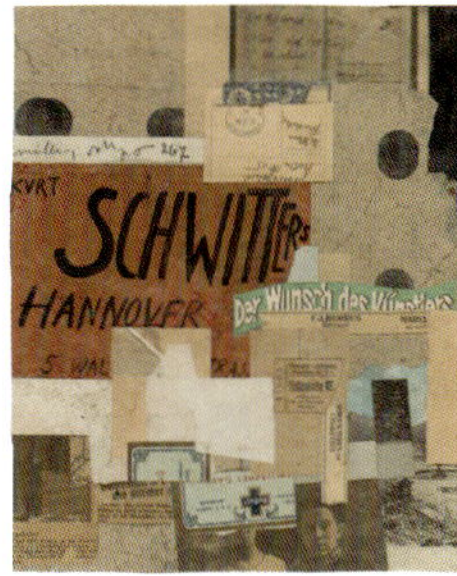

Cat. 12
Kurt Schwitters
German, 1887–1948
Untitled (Der Wunsch des Künstlers) (The Artist's Wish), 1934
Collage on paper, 12 ¾ × 10 ¼ in.
(32.4 × 26 cm)
2006.52.5

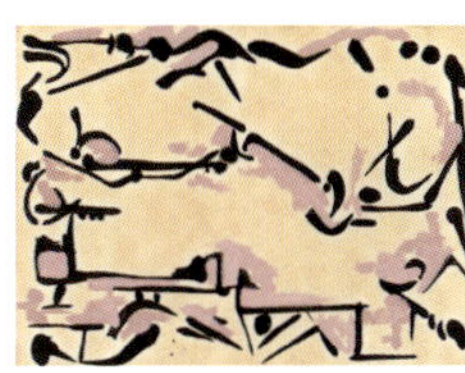

Cat. 35
David Smith
American, 1906–1965
Untitled, 1953
Black ink and tempera, 17 ¹¹⁄₁₆ × 24 ⅛₆ in.
(45 × 61.1 cm)
2006.52.87

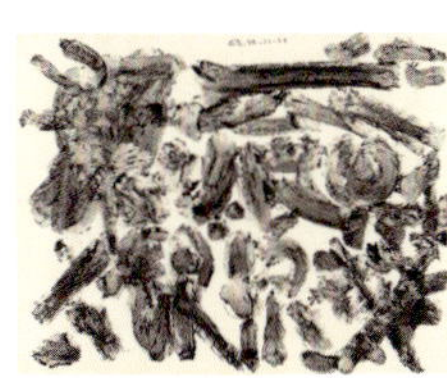

Cat. 36
David Smith
American, 1906–1965
Untitled, 1954
Black ink and wash with tempera,
17 ⁹⁄₁₆ × 22 ⅝ in. (44.6 × 57.4 cm)
2006.52.89

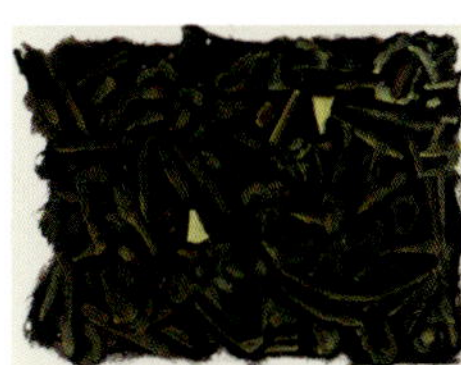

David Smith
American, 1906–1965
Untitled, 1957
Egg tempera, 15 ⁹⁄₁₆ × 20 ¼ in.
(39.5 × 51.4 cm)
2006.52.24

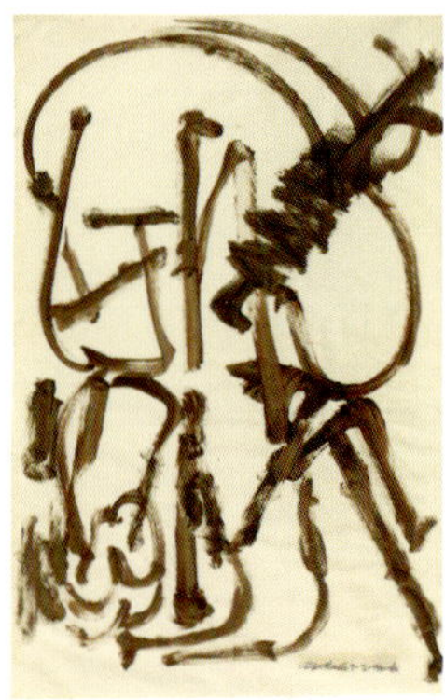

Cat. 37
David Smith
American, 1906–1965
Untitled, 1960
Brown ink, 41 ⅛ × 26 ⅛ in.
(104.4 × 66.4 cm)
2006.52.88

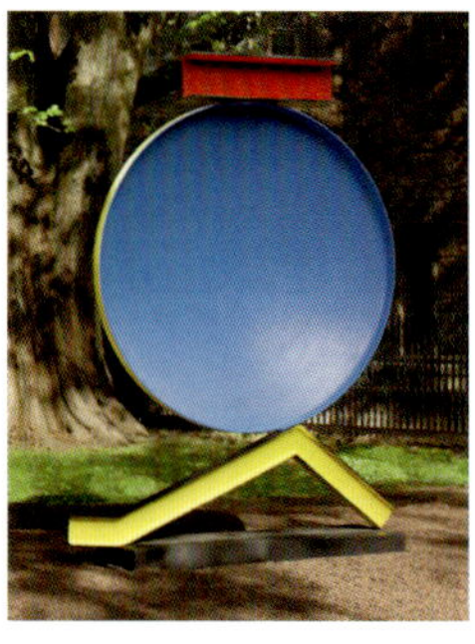

Cat. 34
David Smith
American, 1906–1965
Bec-Dida Day, 1963
Steel with paint, 89 × 65 × 18 in.
(226.1 × 165.1 × 45.7 cm)
2006.52.68

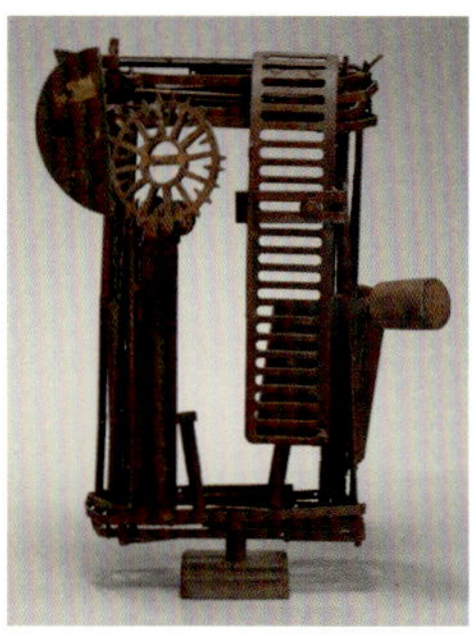

Cat. 24
Richard Stankiewicz
American, 1922–1983
Astrological Surprise, 1959
Rusted steel, 26 ½ × 22 × 33 in.
(67.3 × 55.9 × 83.8 cm)
2006.52.113

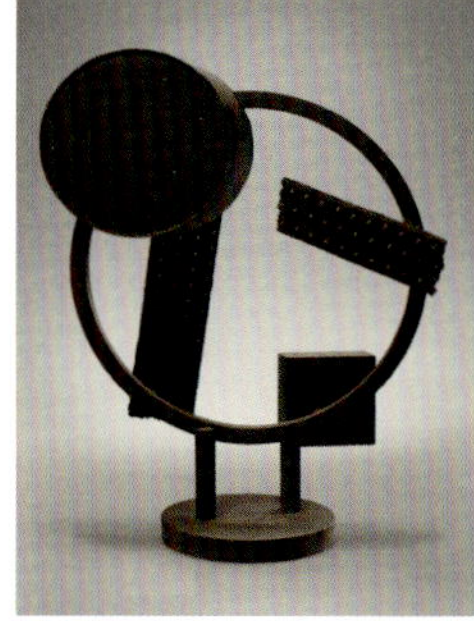

Cat. 26
Richard Stankiewicz
American, 1922–1983
Untitled, ca. 1980
Rusted steel, 70 × 44 × 36 in.
(177.8 × 111.8 × 91.4 cm)
2006.52.69

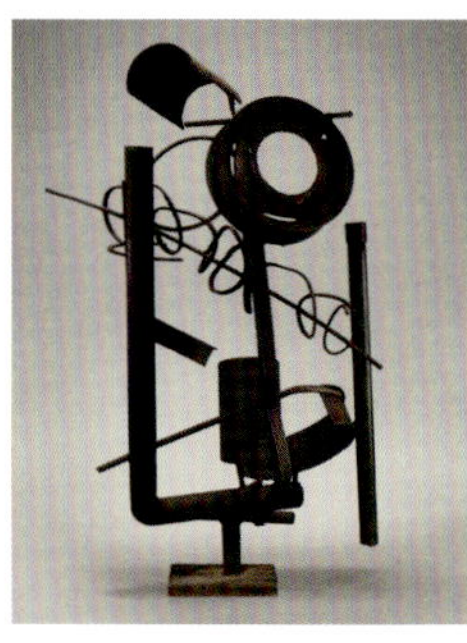

Cat. 25
Richard Stankiewicz
American, 1922–1983
Untitled, ca. 1980
Rusted steel, 72 × 42 × 30 in.
(182.9 × 106.7 × 76.2 cm)
2006.52.70

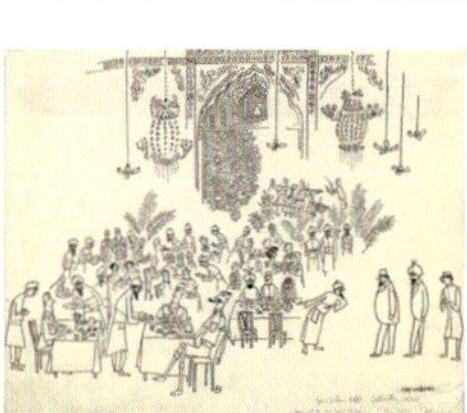

Saul Steinberg
American, born Romania, 1914–1999
Great Eastern Hotel, Calcutta, 1943
Originally published in the *New Yorker*,
February 24, 1945
Black pen and ink, with graphite
inscription and underdrawing (erased),
11 ⁹⁄₁₆ × 14 ⅞ in. (29.3 × 37.7 cm)
2006.52.103

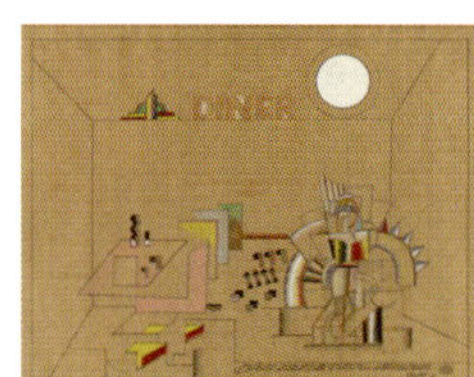

Saul Steinberg
American, born Romania, 1914–1999
Jukebox, 1965
Pen and black and red ink, colored
crayon, and white watercolor, with
graphite underdrawing,
22 ¹⁵⁄₁₆ × 29 in. (58.3 × 73.7 cm)
2006.52.109

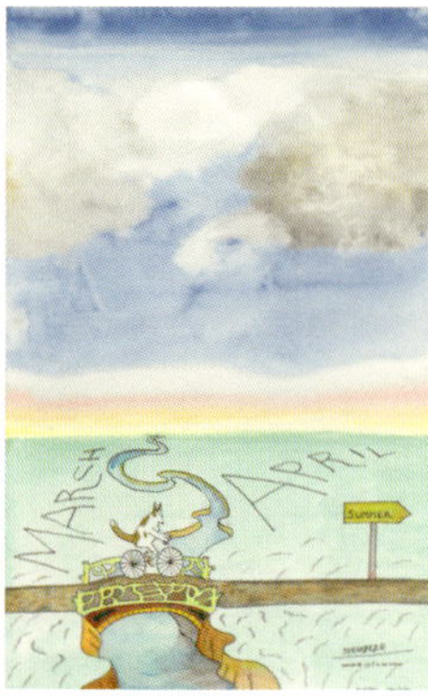

Saul Steinberg
American, born Romania, 1914–1999
March to April, 1965
Watercolor, black ink, and crayon,
23 × 14 ½ in. (58.4 × 36.8 cm)
2006.52.31

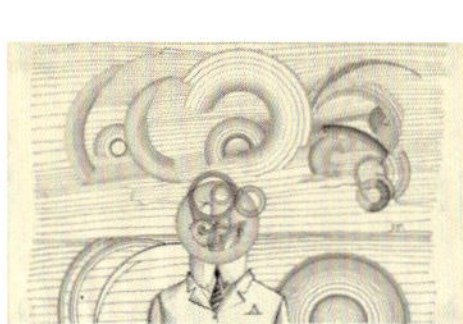

Saul Steinberg
American, born Romania, 1914–1999
Untitled, 1965
Pen and black ink, 14 ½ × 24 ¼ in.
(36.8 × 61.5 cm)
2006.52.110

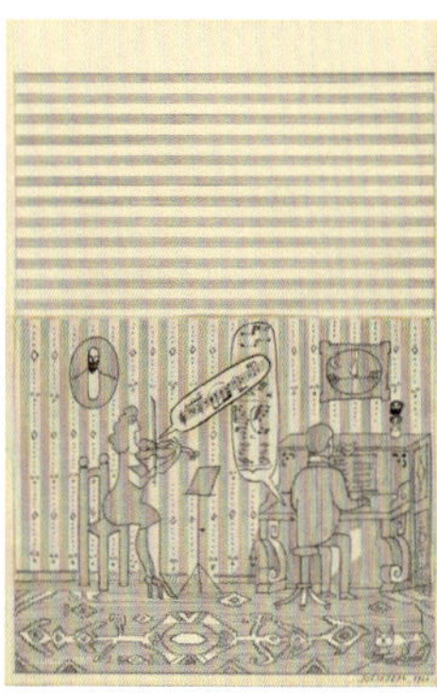

Cat. 50
Saul Steinberg
American, born Romania, 1914–1999
Untitled, 1966
Originally published in the *New Yorker*,
May 6, 1967
Pen and black ink and graphite on
printed paper, 19 ¹⁄₁₆ × 12 ⁹⁄₁₆ in.
(48.4 × 31.9 cm)
2006.52.107

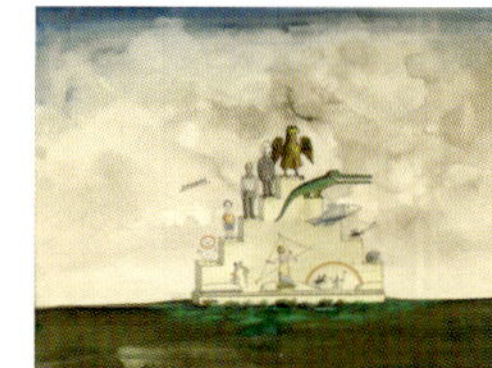

Cat. 48
Saul Steinberg
American, born Romania, 1914–1999
Evolution, 1967
Drawing for the *New Yorker* cover,
November 11, 1967
Graphite, watercolor wash, pen and
colored ink, colored crayon, white
watercolor, and oil pastel, 23 ¹⁄₁₆ × 28 ¾ in.
(58.5 × 73 cm)
2006.52.102

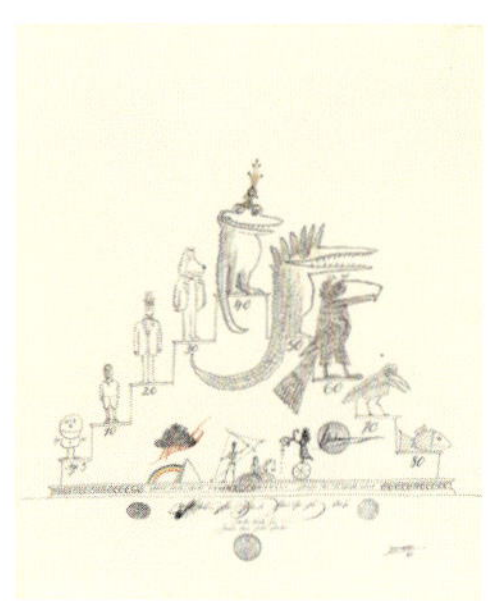

Saul Steinberg
American, born Romania, 1914–1999
Evolution, 1967
Pen and black, red, and yellow ink,
and rubber stamping, 28 ¼₆ × 22 ⁵⁄₁₆ in.
(71.2 × 56.7 cm)
2006.52.112

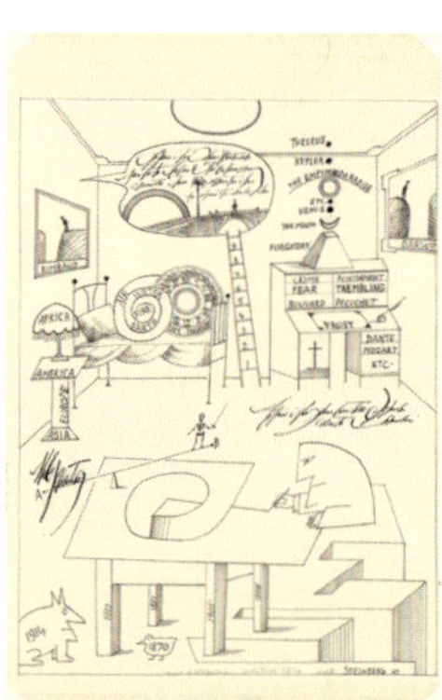

Saul Steinberg
American, born Romania, 1914–1999
Untitled, 1967
Pen and black ink with graphite
underdrawing, 19 ¹¹⁄₁₆ × 12 ½ in.
(50 × 31.8 cm)
2006.52.108

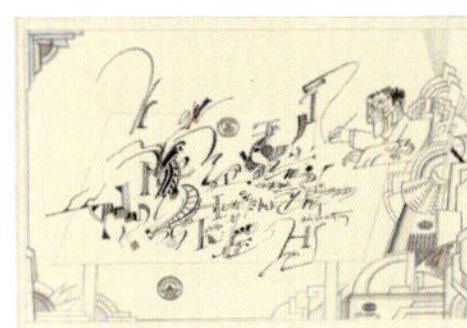

Cat. 51
Saul Steinberg
American, born Romania, 1914–1999
Cacographer, 1968
Graphite, pen and blue, red, and black ink, and gray, blue, and brown colored pencil, with blind stamp and rubber stamping, 20 1/16 × 29 7/16 in.
(51 × 74.8 cm)
2006.52.106

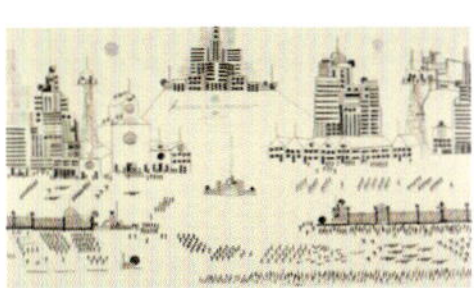

Cat. 49
Saul Steinberg
American, born Romania, 1914–1999
The Administration Building, 1969
Rubber stamping and graphite, 41 1/4 × 71 13/16 in. (104.7 × 182.4 cm)
2006.52.46

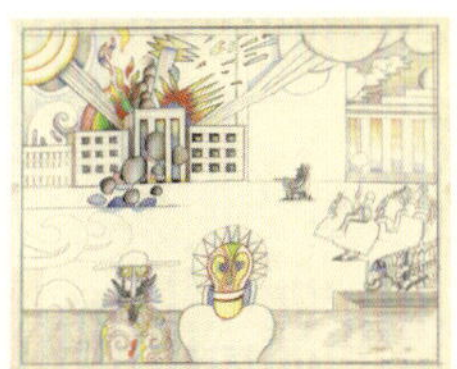

Cat. 47
Saul Steinberg
American, born Romania, 1914–1999
Civil War (High School), 1970
Graphite and colored pencil, 22 3/16 × 27 in. (56.3 × 68.5 cm)
2006.52.30

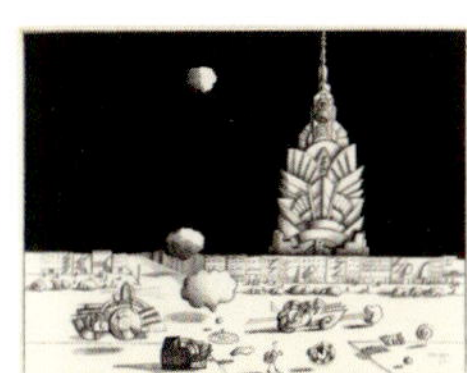

Cat. 46
Saul Steinberg
American, born Romania, 1914–1999
Empire State Building, 1970
Pen and black ink, brush and black ink, waxy black crayon, black pencil, and graphite, 23 3/16 × 29 1/8 in. (58.8 × 74 cm)
2006.52.32

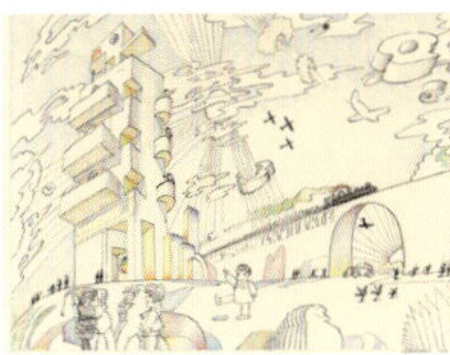

Cat. 45
Saul Steinberg
American, born Romania, 1914–1999
Lambrate, 1971
Pen and black ink, colored crayon, and graphite, 19 3/4 × 25 5/8 in. (50.1 × 65.1 cm)
2006.52.104

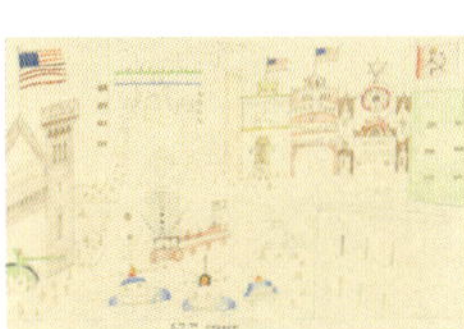

Saul Steinberg
American, born Romania, 1914–1999
67th Street, 1983
Originally published in the *New Yorker*, July 4, 1983
Crayon, graphite, and pen and brown ink, 23 1/16 × 27 1/16 in. (58.5 × 68.7 cm)
2006.52.105

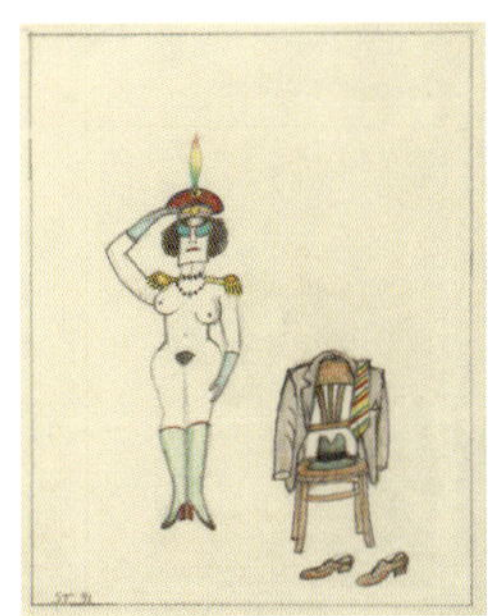

Saul Steinberg
American, born Romania, 1914–1999
Untitled, 1991
Originally published in the *New Yorker*, March 14, 1994
Graphite, crayon, and oil pastel, 14 1/16 × 10 3/4 in. (35.7 × 27.3 cm)
2006.52.111

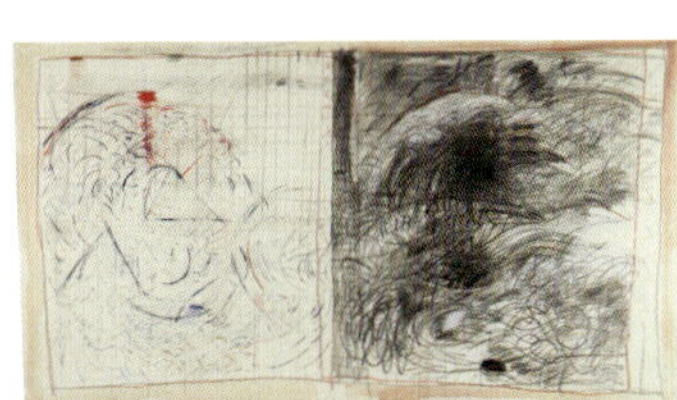

Cat. 76
Pat Steir
American, born 1940
At Sea after Gombrich, 1989
Charcoal and colored chalk, 60 7/16 in. × 9 ft. (153.5 × 273 cm)
2006.52.84

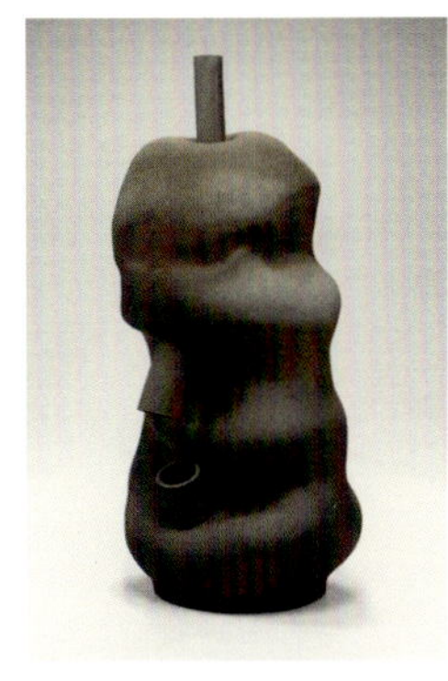

Hiroshi Teshigahara
Japanese, 1927–2001
Kaiyū ōgata kaki (Big Ash Glaze Pottery for Flowers), 1980
Ceramic, 50 3/4 × 23 1/4 × 22 1/8 in.
(128.9 × 59.1 × 56.2 cm)
2006.52.72

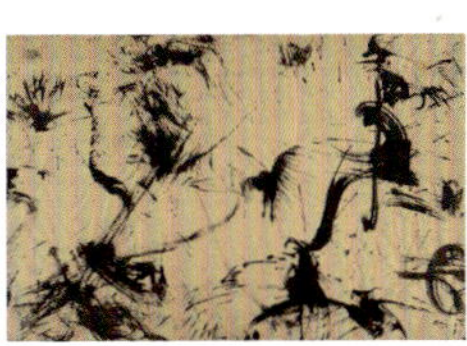

Mark Tobey
American, 1890–1976
Flight, 1957
Sumi ink, 23 3/8 × 34 13/16 in.
(59.3 × 88.4 cm)
2006.52.117

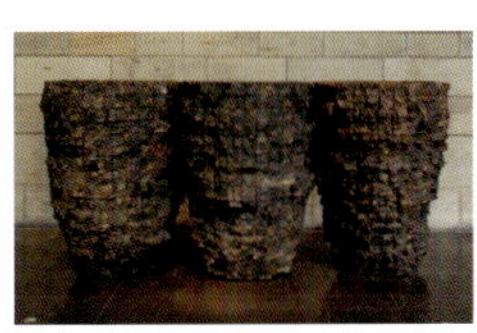

Cat. 77
Ursula von Rydingsvard
American, born Germany 1942
Three Bowls, 1989
Cedar and graphite, 56 3/4 in. × 9 ft. 8 in. × 60 in. (144.1 × 294.6 × 152.4 cm)
2006.52.58

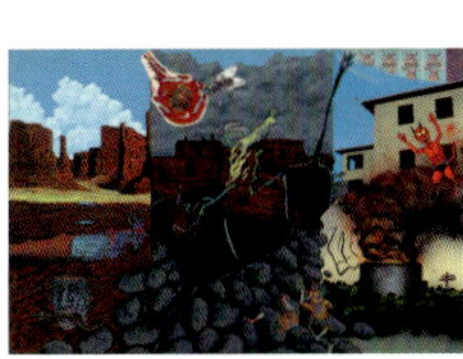

Cat. 72
David Wojnarowicz
American, 1954–1992
When You the Invisible Cowboy, 1987
Mixed media on Masonite, 48 × 72 in.
(121.9 × 182.9 cm)
2006.52.82

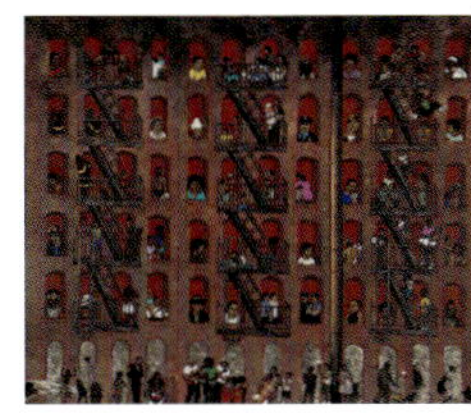

Cat. 74
Martin Wong
American, 1946–1999
La Vida (The Life), 1988
Oil on canvas, 96 in. × 9 ft. 6 in.
(243.8 × 289.6 cm)
2006.52.47

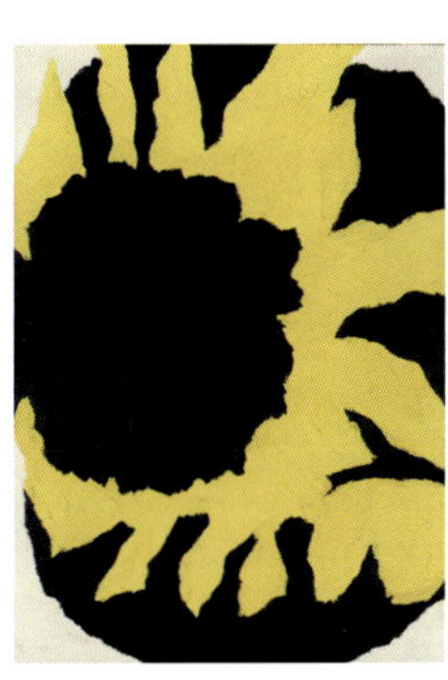

Jack Youngerman
American, born 1926
Aquitane, 1958
Oil on canvas, 69 3/4 × 49 in.
(177.2 × 124.5 cm)
2006.52.48

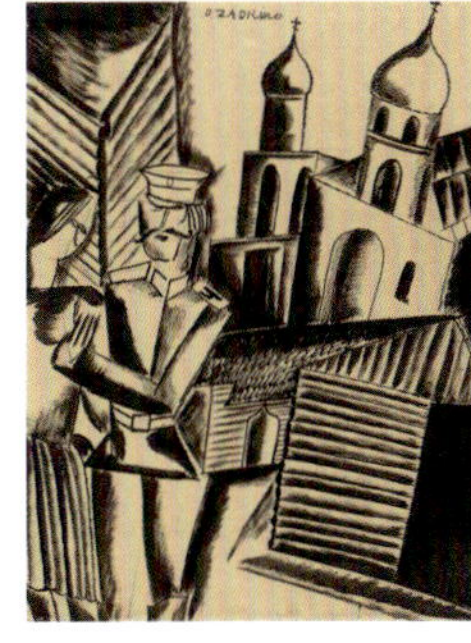

Ossip Zadkine
Russian, active in France, 1890–1967
Le couple russe (The Russian Couple), ca. 1922
Black ink with wash, 18 1/4 × 13 5/8 in.
(46.4 × 34.6 cm)
2006.52.10

Index

Credits

Every effort has been made to credit the artists and the sources; if there are errors or omissions, please contact the Yale University Art Gallery so that corrections can be made in any subsequent editions. Unless otherwise noted, all photographs © Visual Resources Department at the Yale University Art Gallery.

Jean (Hans) Arp: © 2012 Artists Rights Society (ARS), New York/VG Bild-Kunst, Bonn: pp. 67, 170

Collection Banque de France: p. 84

Photo: Richard Barnes: pp. 16, 18–19, 21

Jean-Michel Basquiat: © 2012 Artists Rights Society (ARS), New York/ADAGP, Paris: pp. 133, 170

© Jack Beal: pp. 130, 170

Photo: Lawrence B. Benenson: pp. 2, 12, 23

© Jonathan Borofsky: pp. 154–55, 170; Courtesy Paula Cooper Gallery, New York. Photo: James Dee: pp. 155, 170; Photo: Tom Jenkins: p. 154

© Louise Bourgeois Trust/Licensed by VAGA, New York, NY: pp. 140–41, 170; Photo: Mark Markheim: p. 140

© Antanas Brazdys: p. 170

© Elizabeth Butterworth by courtesy of The Redfern Gallery, London: p. 170

© 2012 Calder Foundation, New York/Artists Rights Society (ARS), New York: pp. 16, 97, 170

© Peter Campus: pp. 129, 170

Anthony Caro: © Barford Sculptures Ltd., Photo: John Goldblatt: pp. 139, 170

© 2012 John Chamberlain/Artists Rights Society (ARS), New York: pp. 167, 170

© Salvador Dalí, Fundació Gala-Salvador Dalí, Artists Rights Society (ARS), New York 2012: p. 170

© Estate of Stuart Davis/Licensed by VAGA, New York, NY: pp. 16, 59–61, 170–71

© L&M Services B.V. The Hague 20120603 for the reproduction of the work by Sonia Delaunay.: p. 16

Paul Delvaux: © 2012 Artists Rights Society (ARS), New York/SABAM, Brussels: pp. 51, 171

© 2012 Jim Dine/Artists Rights Society (ARS), New York: pp. 119–25, 171

© Mark di Suvero: pp. 127, 171

Jean Dubuffet: © 2012 Artists Rights Society (ARS), New York/ADAGP, Paris: pp. 75–77, 171

Mary Frank: Courtesy of the artist and DC Moore Gallery, New York: pp. 101, 171

Viola Frey: © Artists' Legacy Foundation/Licensed by VAGA, New York, NY. Photo: Chris Watson. Courtesy of Nancy Hoffman Gallery, New York: pp. 159, 171

Gilbert & George: © The artist. Courtesy White Cube, London: pp. 135, 171

© Fritz Glarner: p. 171

Albert Gleizes: © 2012 Artists Rights Society (ARS), New York/ADAGP, Paris: p. 171

© The Adolph and Esther Gottlieb Foundation/Licensed by VAGA, New York, NY: pp. 63, 172

© 2012 Robert Graham Studio/Artists Rights Society (ARS), New York: p. 172

© 2012 Red Grooms/Artists Rights Society (ARS), New York: pp. 2, 21, 113–17, 172

© Estate of George Grosz/Licensed by VAGA, New York, NY: pp. 36–37, 172

© Al Held Foundation/Licensed by VAGA, New York, NY: pp. 12, 150–51, 172

Jean Hélion: © 2012 Artists Rights Society (ARS), New York/ADAGP, Paris: p. 172

© Karl Hubbuch: p. 172

© Jean Ipoustéguy: p. 23

© Magdalena Jetelová: pp. 149, 172

Wassily Kandinsky: © 2012 Artists Rights Society (ARS), New York/ADAGP, Paris: p. 172

© Alex Kayser: p. 172

© The Estate of R. B. Kitaj, courtesy Marlborough Gallery, New York: pp. 19, 145, 147, 172–73

Oskar Kokoschka: © 2012 Fondation Oskar Kokoschka/Artists Rights Society (ARS), New York/ProLitteris, Zürich: pp. 83, 173

Jiří Kolář: © 2012 Artists Rights Society (ARS), New York/ProLitteris, Zürich. Courtesy Galerie Lelong: pp. 93–95, 173

Roger de La Fresnaye: Photo: Philip Bernard: p. 30

Fernand Léger: © 2012 Artists Rights Society (ARS), New York/ADAGP, Paris: pp. 39–41, 173

© David Levine: p. 173

© By kind permission of the Wyndham Lewis Memorial Trust (a registered charity): pp. 34–35, 173

© The Alexander Liberman Trust 2012: pp. 164–65, 173

Richard Lindner: © 2012 Artists Rights Society (ARS), New York/ADAGP, Paris: pp. 64, fig. 2, 65, 173; Photo: Banque d'Images ADAGP/Art Resource, NY: p. 64, fig. 2

© Donald Lipski: p. 174

© 2012 Robert Longo/Artists Rights Society (ARS), New York: p. 174

© Michael Lucero: p. 174

© Ranan Raymond Lurie: p. 174

Louis Marcoussis: © 2012 Artists Rights Society (ARS), New York/ADAGP, Paris: pp. 43, 174

© Marisol/Licensed by VAGA, New York, NY: pp. 81, 174

© 2012 Succession H. Matisse/Artists Rights Society (ARS), New York: p. 52; National Gallery of Denmark, Copenhagen © SMK Photo: p. 52, fig. 2

© George J. McNeil: p. 174

Jean Metzinger: © 2012 Artists Rights Society (ARS), New York/ADAGP, Paris: pp. 33, 174

© 2012 Successió Miró/Artists Rights Society (ARS), New York/ADAGP, Paris: pp. 14, 98–99, 174; Photo: Erik M. Stolz. © Courtesy Successió Miró, 2012: p. 98

© 2012 The Munch Museum/The Munch-Ellingsen Group/Artists Rights Society (ARS), NY. Erich Lessing/Art Resource, NY: p. 64, fig. 1

© Atelier Nakian, LLC: p. 174

© Claes Oldenburg: p. 174

© Ed Paschke: pp. 143, 174

© Philip Pearlstein: pp. 131, 175

Max Pechstein: © 2012 Artists Rights Society (ARS), New York/Pechstein Hamburg/Toekendorf/VG Bild-Kunst, Bonn: p. 15

© Alicia Penalba: pp. 69, 175

© 2012 Estate of Pablo Picasso/Artists Rights Society (ARS), New York: pp. 53, 55–57, 175

© Estate of Robert Rauschenberg/Licensed by VAGA, New York, NY: p. 175

Jean Paul Riopelle: © 2012 Artists Rights Society (ARS), New York/SODRAC, Montreal: pp. 79, 175

© Estate of Larry Rivers/Licensed by VAGA, New York, NY: pp. 21, 85, 175

© James Rosenquist/Licensed by VAGA, New York, NY: pp. 18, 136–37, 175

© Estate of Theodore J. Roszak/Licensed by VAGA, New York, NY: pp. 45, 175

Kurt Schwitters: © 2012 Artists Rights Society (ARS), New York/VG Bild-Kunst, Bonn: pp. 47, 49, 175

© Estate of David Smith/Licensed by VAGA, New York, NY: pp. 12, 87–91, 175–76

Courtesy of the estate of Richard Stankiewicz and Zabriskie Gallery: pp. 71–73, 176